THE EMERGENCE OF CHRISTIAN SCIENCE
IN AMERICAN RELIGIOUS LIFE

THE
EMERGENCE OF
CHRISTIAN SCIENCE
IN AMERICAN
RELIGIOUS
LIFE

by
STEPHEN
GOTTSCHALK

UNIVERSITY OF CALIFORNIA PRESS
BERKELEY, LOS ANGELES, LONDON

Grateful acknowledgment is made to The Christian Science Board of Directors for permission to quote from the writings of Mary Baker Eddy.

University of California Press
Berkeley and Los Angeles, California
University of California Press, Ltd.
London, England
Copyright © 1973, by
The Regents of the University of California

ISBN: 0-520-02308-0
Library of Congress Catalog Card Number: 72-85530
Printed in the United States of America

To my parents

Contents

127989

This study was begun a century to the month after the event which Mary Baker Eddy cited as the discovery of Christian Science. As a result of a healing which occurred in February 1866, she claimed to have discovered the full practical meaning of Biblical revelation. Her teaching, which she denominated Christian Science, was first given full statement in her book *Science and Health,* published in 1875. Four years later, Mrs. Eddy founded the Church of Christ, Scientist. And by the time she died in 1910, Christian Science had become an established and growing American denomination. From the perspective of a century, it should be possible to write a balanced assessment of the emergence of Christian Science in American religious life.

Despite the importance of Christian Science as one of the two major indigenous religions of the United States — the other being Mormonism — no such assessment has yet been written. To a large extent, the scholarly literature on Christian Science has been sociological in approach. This study, however, assumes that as a religious teaching Christian Science must be taken seriously in religious terms if its emergence in the American experience is to be understood. To emerge means to stand forth distinctly. And this book contends that, when examined in relation to the currents of American religious life and the Christian tradition as a whole, Christian Science does stand forth as a distinctive religious teaching.

The scope of subjects taken up has been delimited so as to examine Christian Science in these terms. The background and earliest development of Mrs. Eddy's teaching have already received more adequate scholarly treatment than any other phase of the movement's history, and discussion of these subjects will be only incidental to the main purpose of understanding the meaning of Christian Science in its mature formulation. It is, of course, tempting to dwell at length on the personality of the controversial founder of Christian Science, Mary Baker Eddy. But I am concerned in these pages with Mrs. Eddy only in relation to the religion which she taught and her work as leader of the Christian Science movement. Similarly, many details of church history have been subordinated to the larger ideological questions basic to my purpose.

The time frame established for this study is by no means rigid, and at a number of points I have gone outside of it to include material which is vital to an understanding of the issues under discussion. However, the study focuses on the quarter century between 1885 and 1910, the formative years in which the Christian Science movement sprang from relative obscurity to become a familiar, if controversial, phenomenon in American religious life. The prologue centers on an event which dramatizes this emergence: Mrs. Eddy's defense of her teaching against a clerical attack in Boston's Tremont Temple. At the time of this incident, Christian Science was just gaining public attention within New England as one more of Boston's odd assortment of cults. By 1910, it had a well-defined, virtually unalterable doctrine. Membership in the tightly organized institution, The Mother Church, stood at 85,000 and "branch churches" proliferated in the United States and abroad. Identified with the movement and lending it considerable prestige was a newspaper of generally acknowledged excellence, *The Christian Science Monitor*.

Rather than a chronological narrative of the development of the Christian Science movement, this study is an analysis of five major aspects of its emergence in American religious life. While broadly successsive chronologically, these phases overlap and cannot be confined to any single period. To begin with, Christian Science, like many other religious movements, addressed itself to an age of spiritual crisis and claimed to offer new and vital truths to that age. The character of the religious situation in the Gilded Age, together with the claims of Christian Science to constitute a new discovery of religious truth, is the subject of the first chapter, "Sunrise of a Scientific Christianity." The second chapter, "The New Departure," deals with the central teachings of Christian Science, analyzing them in relation to the other major alternatives for religious belief in our period. Chapter Three, entitled "The Tares and The Wheat," takes up a major crisis faced by the Christian Science movement at the point of its emergence in American religious life during the 1880s — its encounter with rival movements, known as "mind-cure," which were in the main its own offshoots, and with various forms of occultism akin to mind-cure. That the Christian Science movement was eventually successful in surmounting this crisis was due in part to the founding of The Mother Church and the whole institutional structure of Christian Science in the 1890s. This development, together with a consideration of the role of Mary Baker Eddy in Christian Science and of the reaction of orthodox Protestantism to the growth of the movement during this period, is the subject of Chapter Four, "Into the Mainstream." The impact of Christian Science on individual lives is taken up in Chapter Five, "Promise and Fulfillment." Through an analysis of the motives that lay behind the practice of Christian Science, the phenomenon of healing, and the social attitudes which Mrs. Eddy's teaching engendered, this chapter discusses what the Christian Science movement meant in terms of the religious situation into which it was projected. The concluding chapter, entitled "Christian Science and the American Pragmatic Orientation," explores the broader question of the relation between Christian Science and the patterns of American culture.

A Note on Textual Usages

Mrs. Eddy's punctuation in some cases does not follow conventional contemporary usage. This study adopts the practice of reproducing her texts exactly, without the use of the designation *sic*.

Christian Scientists generally refer to Mrs. Eddy's teaching as a "discovery." It is hard to avoid the repeated use of this term in an extended discussion of Christian Science. Yet it would also be awkward to surround it with quotation marks in order to indicate a wholly neutral attitude toward its use. Therefore, it is used here without quotation marks, with no intent to signify belief or disbelief in the validity of what Mrs. Eddy claimed to have discovered.

Abbreviations Used in Footnotes

CSJ.   *Christian Science Journal,* Monthly, Boston: Christian Science Publishing Society, 1883 — .

CSS.   *Christian Science Sentinel.* Weekly, Boston: Christian Science Publishing Society, 1898 — .

PUBLISHED WRITINGS OF MARY BAKER EDDY

S&H.   *Science and Health with Key to the Scriptures* (Boston, 1910).

Man.   *Manual of The Mother Church* (Boston, 1919).

Mess. '01. "Message to The Mother Church June 1901 by Mary Baker Eddy" (Boston, 1901).

Mis.   *Miscellaneous Writings, 1883–1896* (Boston, 1896).

My.   *The First Church of Christ, Scientist, and Miscellany* (Boston, 1913).

No.   *No and Yes* (Boston, 1887). First published as *Christian Science: No and Yes.*

Ret.   *Retrospection and Introspection* (Boston, 1892).

Un.   *Unity of Good* (Boston, 1887).

MANUSCRIPT COLLECTIONS

Archives. Archives of The Mother Church, Boston, Mass.

Longyear. The Longyear Foundation, Brookline, Mass.

Prologue:
"Christian Science in Tremont Temple"

On March 16, 1885, Mary Baker Eddy defended Christian Science before an audience of nearly three thousand in Boston's famed Tremont Temple. Though her subject was religious and the place of the address a church, Mrs. Eddy was not delivering a sermon, nor was the day a Sunday. The occasion was one of the Reverend Joseph Cook's popular Monday Noon Lectures. Three weeks before, Cook had read an open letter from the Boston Baptist clergyman Adoniram J. Gordon attacking the new teaching, and had added some hostile corroborative comments of his own. The Christian Scientists were predictably dismayed; some even talked of a lawsuit. But what Mrs. Eddy demanded was the right to reply. She was granted just ten minutes.

The address which she delivered on this occasion occupies little more than three pages in her volume *Miscellaneous Writings, 1883–1896* under the heading "Christian Science in Tremont Temple."[1] Yet it is one of the most significant documents in the development of the Christian Science movement. For Mrs. Eddy's appearance in Tremont Temple marked more conspicuously than any other event the emergence of Christian Science into American religious life.

For the small groups of Christian Scientists assembled in the balcony in support of their teacher, as for Mrs. Eddy herself, this was a momentous occasion. She was answering the attack of two of Boston's most prestigious ministers, in one of its greatest halls, before a distinguished audience including large numbers of clergymen, business figures, and

1. *Mis.*, pp. 95–98.

assorted New England notables. If one recalled that scarcely twenty years earlier Mrs. Eddy had been glad to get a hearing from anyone, that her first pupil had been an uneducated worker in a shoe factory in nearby Lynn — then the occasion, difficult as it was, might have assumed a happier aspect. And if the assembled orthodox in Tremont Temple did not like what they knew of Christian Science, at least they knew of it. A year before the new century dawned, Mrs. Eddy would deliver another address in Tremont Temple, but to a very different audience: a gathering of her followers for the annual meeting of The Mother Church, the membership of which was then 17,000 and soaring rapidly. But in 1885 it was a sufficient sign of the prosperity of "the Cause" for Mrs. Eddy's followers that their leader and the movement she represented could no longer be ignored.

During the previous decade the future of the Christian Science movement had been a subject open to speculation. In 1878 it had almost perished in the wake of a series of lawsuits and internal dissensions. The next year twenty-six of Mrs. Eddy's students — or to put it more exactly, Mrs. Eddy's twenty-six students — formed a church organization, the Church of Christ, Scientist. But the church had no home; and for the first year and a half of its existence services were held at students' quarters in Lynn, where Mrs. Eddy lived, occasionally in Salem, and in Boston. In 1879 Mrs. Eddy intrepidly hired Hawthorne Hall in Boston for the church services. But its two hundred and fifty seats were many times the number of regular churchgoers. At that time the membership of the church was virtually the same as that of the association of Mrs. Eddy's students. But this group was so torn by dissension that nearly a third of its — and the church's — membership withdrew in 1881, leaving the movement in Lynn in ruins.

At this juncture Mrs. Eddy made one of her wisest moves — to Boston. She had lectured and preached there irregularly since 1878 and had come to realize that it was a far more fertile field for the propagation of Christian Science than the factory town of Lynn. Boston was an intellectual center in which ideas traveled fast. And certainly the Christian Science movement did not lack for public attention, nor, more importantly, for new recruits. Christian Science was to have its vicissitudes in Boston; but by the time Mrs. Eddy replied to Gordon and to Cook, Hawthorne Hall, once embarrassingly large, had been outgrown, and the Scientists had found it necessary to search for larger quarters.

In several respects the period of several years just preceding Mrs. Eddy's appearance in Tremont Temple was the take-off point in the growth of the Christian Science movement. By 1885 she had taught more than one hundred and forty students in her Massachusetts Metaphysical College, charterer by the state in 1881. In 1883 she began to publish *The Journal of Christian Science,* the official organ of the movement.[2] The next year she went to Chicago to teach a class that included some of its leading future workers. And by 1885 Christian Science was spreading farther West: to Denver, where many tubercular patients were attracted to its teachings, then to California, which was to prove a fertile field for the propagation of the new faith.

By 1885, it had become clear to observers on the Boston scene, especially the clergy, that Christian Science had caught on. And the clergy in particular was worried. Cook and Gordon's attack on Mrs. Eddy's teachings was but the most conspicuous expression of a mounting clerical attack on Christian Science. In the several years prior to Mrs. Eddy's appearance in Tremont Temple, her teaching had been the subject of hot debate at ministers' associations in the Boston area; a number of ministers had taken it upon themselves to warn their flock against it and several well-known clergymen had denounced it in print.[3] "Clergymen of all denominations," reported a correspondent for the *London Times* in 1885, "are seriously considering how to deal with what they regard as the most dangerous innovation that has threatened the Christian Church in this region for years." He went on to identify the source of their anxiety: "Scores of the most valued church members are joining the Christian Science branch of the metaphysical organization, and it has thus far been impossible to check the defection." [4]

The early and mid-1880s particularly were prolific of converts to Christian Science from strong Christian backgrounds, mostly Congregational and Methodist. Many of those who were to assume prominent roles in the movement during Mrs. Eddy's lifetime were of this group. Julia Bartlett, for example, who accompanied her to Tremont Temple in 1885, had been a Congregationalist; so had Calvin Frye, who became Mrs. Eddy's secretary in 1881 and remained so until her death in 1910. Ira O. Knapp, another convert of the early 1880s who would figure prominently in the movement, had been a Methodist. The list of Christian converts was

2. In April 1885, the title of this periodical was changed to *The Christian Science Journal.*

3. A brief review of early clerical responses to Christian Science can be found in Raymond J. Cunningham, "The Impact of Christian Science on the American Churches, 1880–1910," *American Historical Review,* LXXII (April 1967), 887–892.

4. *London Times,* May 26, 1885.

long — long enough to be deeply disturbing to ministers who saw some of their best sheep wandering away from the fold and devotedly serving what seemed to them a most questionable cause and a controversial leader. Indeed, many of these converts felt they owed Mrs. Eddy their lives and the meaning they found in living. And as the clerical attack on Christian Science mounted in the mid-1880s, their devotion only increased.

At this point Mrs. Eddy was not for most of her followers the remote and revered leader she became after her retirement from the Boston scene in 1889. In 1885 she was still very much in the midst of things: teaching, preaching, writing, corresponding with Christian Scientists in various parts of the country, and attending to the innumerable problems of a burgeoning movement. When she spoke in Tremont Temple, Mrs. Eddy was sixty-four years old but very vigorous indeed; a quarter of a century of work in establishing the Christian Science movement still lay ahead of her. Slim, erect of carriage, with direct unflinching gaze, Mrs. Eddy had the bearing of one who knows she has a mission to perform. The day before she spoke in Tremont Temple, and with obvious reference to the impending address, Mrs. Eddy had delivered a ringing sermon in her church on the text from Matthew, "Thou art Peter, and upon this rock I will build my church; and the gates of hell shall not prevail against it." [5] Once she told an ex-student who had tried to dissuade her from continuing her work that if he could empty the ocean with a bucket, he might expect Christian Science to fail. [6] It was in this spirit that she rode to Tremont Temple to deliver her reply to Gordon and to Cook.

"It was a hard ordeal for her, to encounter this hatred and antagonism against the Truth," Miss Bartlett later recalled, "and when the time came I rode in the carriage with her to the Temple. When we reached there, we were met by Joseph Cook, who was very abusive and insulting in his remarks to her, but she made no reply and took her place on the platform." [7] Cook's hostility to Christian Science, as he expressed it to its discoverer, was no more than symptomatic of the response of orthodox Protestants generally. A small minority of disaffected Protestants might embrace it and a scattering of liberals might look upon it with varying degrees of interest; [8] but as the avid response to his philippics in Tremont Temple indicated, Cook spoke for the majority.

Indeed, it would be hard to find a better index to the most pressing

5. *CSJ*, III (April 1885), 14.
6. Robert Peel, *Mary Baker Eddy: The Years of Discovery* (New York, 1966), p. 261.
7. Julia Bartlett Reminiscences, Archives.
8. See Chap. Five, "Into the Mainstream," pp. 207–215.

concerns of popular Protestant thought in the 1880s than the lectures of Joseph Cook. Consistently well-attended, they also reached an audience of about a million readers in internationally distributed newspaper reprints and were collected yearly in book form. Cook's Monday Lectures had begun as a series of prayer meetings for businessmen in a Y.M.C.A. in 1875, but within two years had grown so popular that they were moved to the enormous Tremont Temple. There Cook's lectureship became virtually a Boston institution. Newspaper accounts documented the "applause" and "laughter" which greeted Cook's orations. Cook was far from being a profound thinker and hardly merits serious attention as an original mind today. But the fact that the *Literary Digest* eulogized him in 1901 as the leading apologist for orthodox Christianity in the United States bears testimony to Cook's importance in his own time.[9]

Actually, Cook's greatest distinction lay in the fact that he was probably the most socially conscious of the prominent conservative Protestant ministers of his time.[10] Though certainly no radical, he was genuinely concerned with the welfare of the working classes, and he usually preceded his lectures with "Preludes on Current Events." Yet Cook was much better known in his time as a defender of Christianity against scientific materialism than as a social critic. He somewhat pretentiously described the main purpose of his Monday Lectures as a presentation of "the results of the freshest German, English, and American scholarship on the more important and difficult topics concerning the relation of religion and science."[11] Theologically, Cook, who was a graduate of Andover Seminary, may have been competent, if not profound. But his scientific training hardly qualified him to treat with such confidence the complex issues he took up; and John Fiske, for one, found his claims to competence so specious and his arguments so misleading that he referred to him as a "theological charlatan" deserving neither serious attention nor respect.[12]

Yet Cook's popularity is understandable. For he spoke to the fears of the faithful at a time when the faithful had much to fear. His lecture audiences badly needed to be assured of the truth of axioms of faith in which they already professed to believe. Cook's great success lay in his skill at taking up the scientific arguments that seemed so inimical to orthodoxy,

9. "Joseph Cook," *Literary Digest,* XVII (May 1901), 430.

10. See the discussion of Cook's social opinions in Henry F. May, *Protestant Churches and Industrial America* (New York, 1949), pp. 164–166.

11. Joseph Cook, *Biology, with Preludes on Current Events* (Boston, 1877), p. i.

12. John Fiske, "Theological Charlatanism," *North American Review,* XXVI (July 1882), 78.

and, with a fine flourish of erudition, apparently dispelling whatever threat to faith they presented. Thus he could convince his audience (and possibly himself as well) that there could be no serious threat to Protestant orthodoxy if only its adherents were sufficiently informed. Few of his partisans searched deeply enough into his arguments to realize how shaky was the scholarship on which they rested; but his audience went to Tremont Temple not to be educated but to be convinced.

Superficially Cook was very reassuring. The tone of his lectures was invariably one of exultant confidence. The year after his encounter with Mrs. Eddy, for instance, he expatiated on the "modern novel opportunity" for religion in almost every area of life.[13] But Cook's constant vigilance against threats to orthodoxy, as well as his generally defensive tone, betray the fact that the degree of his confidence in the future of orthodoxy was in inverse proportion to the reality of the conditions that could justify it. Thus Mrs. Eddy may not have been far wrong when she attributed the hostility of such orthodox opponents of her teaching as Cook to "fear and weakness." [14] Her students, most of whom had defected from the orthodox churches, had long foreseen, as one of them put it, "the speedy passing of the orthodox faith." [15] In 1885 this was a reasonable prediction.

Indeed, the curious element in Mrs. Eddy's encounter with Cook is that in all probability he felt more threatened than she. Mrs. Eddy was the leader of a small but very aggressive religious minority, whereas Cook was an influential spokesman for what was still the majority point of view. But the whole religious situation was such that though he had attacked her position, Cook was on the defensive. Not that he for one moment considered Mrs. Eddy to be anything more than a deluded heretic. But the very successes Christian Science was scoring, the fact that it was necessary to warn his audiences against its appeal — indeed Mrs. Eddy's very presence on the same platform with him — could only have brought home to Cook the lesson that so much else in his time had to teach: that the walls surrounding the citadel of orthodoxy were crumbling.

Certainly the Christian Scientists were aggressive in their support of Mrs. Eddy's teaching. To them, it represented the second coming of Christ promised in the Gospel of John. They were very far, however,

---

13. Joseph Cook, *Current Religious Perils, with Preludes and other addresses on Leading Reforms* (Boston, 1888), p. ii.

14. *Mis.*, p. 245.

15. Mary Beecher Longyear, *Asa Gilbert Eddy* (Brookline, Mass., 1934), p. 47.

from any literal interpretation of the meaning of the second advent. To Reverend Dr. Gordon, a major spokesman for premillenarian fundamentalism, it meant the actual descent of Christ on clouds of glory. When Mrs. Eddy spoke of the Second Coming, however, she had nothing so spectacular in mind. For she meant that Christian Science as the Comforter brought to men the true understanding of Jesus' life and pointed out how all men might follow in his way. In a sermon on the Second Coming delivered the year before she spoke in Tremont Temple, Mrs. Eddy declared that men could claim their inheritance as sons of God now; "and when this attitude of Christ shall once again be in the hearts of his followers, then indeed and in truth has the Second Coming of Christ been fulfilled." [16] Certainly neither Mrs. Eddy nor her followers saw her own role as that of a second Christ. Rather, she regarded herself, in the words of an article from the *Journal* in 1885, as "the faithful messenger of the Second Coming." [17]

In her address in Tremont Temple, Mrs. Eddy did not disguise her ultimate claim for Christian Science. She declared that "to such as are 'waiting for the adoption, to wit, the redemption of our body,' Christian Science reveals the infinitude of divinity and the way of man's salvation from sickness and death." [18] Her citation of the words of St. Paul was but one of a half dozen Biblical quotations which she used in this address of ten minutes. That she should relate her teaching to the Bible in this way was characteristic of her thought. For Mrs. Eddy definitely considered Christian Science to be Christian. She had been raised in a strict form of Calvinist Congregationalism and remained a member of the Congregational church until well *after* her discovery of Christian Science in 1866. She did believe that Christian Science represented an advance beyond orthodoxy in the sense that it provided the "scientific interpretation" or full statement of the practical meaning of Scripture. Yet she always saw her teaching as within the mainstream of Christianity. Indeed, Christian Scientists looked upon their religion as Christianity extended into the present age.

Hence, it is not surprising that a major effort of Mrs. Eddy's address was to disassociate Christian Science from what can be called the Boston spiritual underground — a loose collection of occultists, faddists, and reformists of whom spiritualists constituted perhaps the preponderant number and representative type. Gordon, in his open letter to Cook, had in

---

16. Mary Baker Eddy, "The Second Coming," *CSJ*, II (November 1884), 7.
17. *CSJ*, III (April 1885), 14.
18. *Mis.*, pp. 95–96.

fact made such an association. In the first issue of the *Journal* in April 1883, Mrs. Eddy had written that she did not wish to be classed with "mediums and mesmerists"; though she regretfully noted there remained "much error to be overcome in this direction."[19] If anything, this "error" only increased as Christian Science won mounting public notice. In her address in Tremont Temple, Mrs. Eddy tried to impress upon her audience that, far from being a form of faddist occultism, Christian Science was a thoroughly Christian teaching that could commend itself to Christians in terms they could understand.

This point was implicit in her treatment of two theological questions central to Christian doctrine: the personality of God and the atonement of Christ. Though Mrs. Eddy could only touch upon these problems at Tremont Temple, her comments give a good indication of her general approach to orthodox theological doctrines. Gordon, in his letter to Cook, had declared that Christian Science denied both the personality of God and the atonement. Actually, her view was not so simple. It can best be understood with reference to a work which issued from the incident under discussion here. The month after she spoke in Tremont Temple, Mrs. Eddy expanded her address into an article, later published as a pamphlet entitled "Defense of Christian Science against Rev. Cook and Gordon's Religious Ban";[20] and this text formed the basis for the short book, *Christian Science: No and Yes,* published two years later.[21] In that work Mrs. Eddy took up one by one the main issues Gordon had presented. In response to one of the questions she framed out of the items in his attack, "Is Christian Science of the Same Lineage as Spiritualism or Theosophy," her answer was a firm and decisive "No." But in regard to other doctrinal questions it was more ambiguous, both "No" and "Yes" — "No" in the sense that she could not accept orthodox teaching in its own terms, "Yes" in the sense that she saw some degree of validity in almost every orthodox doctrine.

Hence in Tremont Temple Mrs. Eddy did not wholly repudiate the orthodox idea of a personal God, but indicated that Christian Science offered a fuller understanding of Him. She declared that " 'after the manner of my fathers, so worship I God,' " even while referring to the God that she worshipped in thoroughly unorthodox terms as "divine Princi-

19. Mary Baker Eddy, "Note" *CSJ*, I (April 1883), 6.

20. Mary Baker Eddy, "Defense of Christian Science Against Rev. Cook and Gordon's Religious BAN," (Boston, 1885).

21. Mary Baker Eddy, *Christian Science: No and Yes* (Boston, 1887), later republished under the title *No and Yes.*

ple." [22] Responding to the question "Do I believe in the atonement of Christ," Mrs. Eddy similarly reaffirmed an orthodox doctrine while giving it her own peculiar slant. She declared that she did believe in the atonement, but went on to say that it "becomes more to me since it includes man's redemption from sickness as well as from sin. I reverence and adore Christ as never before." [23]

For Mrs. Eddy true faith in the atonement required following in Jesus' way, which she understood to be overcoming every phase of evil — sin, sickness, eventually even death. Physical healing was and remains the most striking aspect of Christian Science; and Mrs. Eddy took special pains to ensure that her audience understood that the motive behind Christian Science healing was Christian. She referred to healing as "redemption from sickness," a phase of "a *whole* salvation." [24] Given the limited time allotted her, however, she did not feel that she could explain how healing work was accomplished. But she could, she said, indicate how it was *not* accomplished.

The choice had a clear purpose besides meeting the requirements of time; for by defining Christian Science healing in terms of what it was *not*, Mrs. Eddy availed herself of an opportunity to clear up what she regarded as the central confusion in the public mind concerning her teaching. In her address she reiterated a constant theme in her writings during the 1880s: that true spiritual healing did not result from the action of one human mind on another, but from the operation of divine power alone. This power, she said, "is Christ come to destroy the power of the flesh . . . it is not one mortal thought transmitted to another's thought from the human mind that holds within itself all evil." [25] Mrs. Eddy urgently wished to be understood on this point and devoted nearly a third of her address to its elaboration. Her reason for so doing was to distinguish Christian Science as clearly as possible from the mushrooming "mind-cure" movements in Boston, with which it had become to a large extent identified in the press and public mind. Little more than a month before she spoke, the *Boston Post* had noted that there were at least four schools of mental healing in Boston.[26] Within a few years there would be several more, not to speak of the many mind-curers who, riding the crest of the wave, set up shop on their own. Most of the identifiable mind-cure groups in the mid 1880s were led either by defectors from the Christian Science movement or by practitioners of modes of faith healing and mes-

22. *Mis.*, pp. 95–96.
24. *Ibid.*
26. *Boston Post*, February 4, 1885.

23. *Ibid.*, p. 96.
25. *Ibid.*, p. 97.

merism that antedated Christian Science and that Mrs. Eddy felt were antithetical to her teaching.

These groups, the progenitors of the New Thought movement, were split among themselves over many issues. But they did share a common emphasis on the constructive power of human thought and a common dislike for Mrs. Eddy as a "petticoat Pope" who insisted dogmatically upon the sole legitimacy of her teaching. To Mrs. Eddy, the mind-curers' repudiation of her leadership was in reality a rejection of her doctrine. They healed, she felt, not through what she called in her address "the eternal energies of Truth," but through human mind power. "All human control," she declared in her address, " is animal magnetism, more despicable than all other methods of treating disease." Christian Science healed not through thought control, nor through faith alone. Rather, it "combines faith with understanding, through which we may touch the hem of His garment; and know that omnipotence has all power." [27]

Up to this point in her address Mrs. Eddy had for the most part stressed the continuity of Christian Science with Christian tradition, though certainly without compromising the distinctiveness of her teaching. Her treatment of the next subject, however, revealed more clearly than anything she had yet said how far Christian Science was from orthodoxy. In responding to the question "Is there a personal man?" Mrs. Eddy again drew upon Scripture, but interpreted it in a way that wholly separated her teaching from the theology of Cook:

The Scriptures inform us that man was made in the image and likeness of God. . . . To my sense, we have not seen all of man; he is more than personal sense can cognize, who is the image and likeness of the infinite. I have not seen a perfect man in mind or body, — and such must be the personality of him who is the true likeness; the lost image is not this personality, and corporeal man is this lost image; hence, it doth not yet appear what is the real personality of man.[28]

By drawing her text from the first chapter of the book of Genesis, Mrs. Eddy was touching upon issues in the forefront of Christian thought. The Darwinian theory of evolution, most specifically the concept of natural selection, was a direct challenge to the Biblical account of creation and the Protestant view of God, nature, and man. Conservative Protestants, of whom Cook is a good example, faced a hard battle in trying to defend

27. *Mis.,* pp. 96–97.
28. *Ibid.,* p. 97.

Christianity and Scriptural authority against the onslaughts of scientific materialism. What made the fight so difficult was the fact that both antagonists shared a most important but often unnoticed area of agreement: namely, the belief that the workings of a material creation, existing independent of perception, could be known and investigated by men. This conviction was essential to the whole Protestant cosmology and underlay the development of modern science in the seventeenth century.

Assuming the authority of the Biblical record of creation, Protestants generally before Darwin were never fully aware that, taken at their face value, the creation accounts in Genesis were empirical statements about the natural world. When physical science developed to the point of concerning itself with the origin of life forms, as it did in Darwinism, it arrived at conclusions different from those of Protestant faith, and the battle was joined. Ultimately, it was religion that sounded the retreat; for on the empirical grounds that both camps implicitly accepted, the new science more than held its own.

The dilemma of Cook and other orthodox Protestants was this: how could theology take account of the sort of evidence that evolutionists were gathering and still hold to the idea of a living God? One could, of course, simply ignore the evidence of evolution and declare with the venerable Presbyterian theologian Charles Hodge that "Darwinism was atheism." [29] Most Protestants, however, adopted a refurbished version of the old doctrine of design and held, in the words of the popular slogan, that "evolution is God's way of doing things." [30] This view, which John Dewey aptly called "the argument from design on the installment plan," [31] was not acceptable to Darwin himself, who saw too much waste and horror in the evolutionary process to credit it.[32] But for most of the Protestant world it seemed to reconcile evolution with theism quite neatly.

What Cook and others recognized, however, was that this argument could render theism meaningless much as deism had done by separating the Creator from His creation. To avoid this trap, Cook adopted a strongly

29. Charles Hodge, *What is Darwinism* (New York, 1874), p. 177.

30. This statement was popularized by Lyman Abbott, who derived it originally from John Fiske.

31. John Dewey, *The Influence of Darwinism on Philosophy And Other Essays in Contemporary Thought* (New York, 1910), p. 12.

32. Darwin wrote to Asa Gray, "I cannot persuade myself that a beneficent and omnipotent God would have designedly created the Ichneumonidae with the express intention of their feeding within the living bodies of caterpillars, or that a cat should play with mice." Quoted in John C. Greene, *Darwin and the Modern World View* (Baton Rouge, La., 1961), p. 45.

immanentist view of Deity that brought him a good deal closer to many religious liberals than he may have liked to admit. "As science progresses," he declared, "it draws nearer . . . to the proof of the Spiritual Origin of Force; that is, of the Divine Immanence in natural law." [33] Thus with near-mystic rapture he could inform an audience in Tremont Temple of his experience in looking at a living bioplasm through a high-powered microscope; "I felt myself in the presence of an entirely new revelation of the inadequacy of materialism . . . to account for the workings of the humblest and simplest living fibre that ever a bioplast spun." [34] For Cook the personal God of Christians still transcended natural laws; though they were "through his immanence, literally God." And even matter itself "is an effluence of the Divine Nature, and so is all infinite mind, and thus the universe is one in its present ground of existence and in the First Cause." [35]

Here, then, is the point of absolute disjuncture between Cook's Protestant orthodoxy and Christian Science: the impact of evolutionary biology had forced Cook along with other Protestants into an ultimate glorification of animate matter. But Mrs. Eddy's central contention, expressed in "The Scientific Statement of Being," which she termed her "first plank in the platform of Christian Science," was:

There is no life, truth, intelligence, nor substance in matter. All is infinite Mind and its infinite manifestation, for God is All-in-all. Spirit is immortal Truth; matter is mortal error. Spirit is the real and eternal; matter is the unreal and temporal. Spirit is God, and man is His image and likeness. Therefore man is not material; he is spiritual.[36]

By affirming here, as in her address in Tremont Temple, that man as the "image and likeness" of Spirit must be spiritual, Mrs. Eddy was obviously interpreting the Genesis text in a completely different sense than was Cook. For he felt that the material body and finite mind were direct productions of Deity.

Her departure from Protestant orthodoxy on this essential point can better be understood with reference to her comments on the first chapters of Genesis. After the discovery of Christian Science in 1866, Mrs. Eddy's first sustained project was a lengthy exegesis of this the first book of the Bible. She had begun at the beginning in the fullest sense of the term; though it was not any concern with Darwinism that prompted her to do so, but simply the book's place in Scripture, which she intended to

33. Cook, *Biology*, p. 32.   34. *Ibid.*, p. 47.
35. *Ibid.*, p. 120.   36. *S&H.*, p. 468.

analyze book by book. Much revised, her treatment of the book of Genesis found a place in the first edition of *Science and Health* in 1875 and was expanded into a full chapter in a subsequent edition.

For Mrs. Eddy, the Genesis account of creation was spiritually authoritative as revelation, although she did not accept it as a literal record. Rather, she discussed it in terms of what she called its "scientific signification," the inspired reading that Christian Science made possible. On this basis she stated that the two accounts of creation in the first chapters of Genesis represented respectively true and false views of the Creator and His work. In the first record, God creates all things, including man "in His image and likeness," and pronounces all that He has made good. In the second, the "Lord God" supposedly recreates man, Adam, out of the dust of the ground, and woman from him. It was in the *first* account that Mrs. Eddy located the true or divinely normative account of creation.

The second account, Mrs. Eddy noted, begins with the text: "But there went up a mist from the earth and watered the whole face of the ground." For her, the mist symbolizes the obscuring of the reality of the Creator and His creation as presented in the first chapter of *Genesis* and the opening verses of the second. It was *after* the mist arose that the "God" of the first account becomes the "Lord God" of the second. This Lord God then infused life into matter; whereas, for Mrs. Eddy, God is Life and cannot be infused into form. It is not in Adam's fall but in the root error of a material sense of creation that Mrs. Eddy located the source of mortal iniquity and suffering.[37]

What men need to be saved from, in her view, is not an actual mortal or fallen condition, but a false sense of God and man. Jesus' life, Mrs. Eddy taught, furnished the practical model for divinely natural manhood, since Jesus proved himself superior to all conditions of mortality. And Christian Science pointed out the full meaning of what Jesus did and provided the method whereby men might follow in his way. Expunging sin, sickness, and death from their experience, men would then demonstrate what man truly is. Human personality betokened only a very limited concept of perfect manhood. Hence Mrs. Eddy said in Tremont Temple that "it doth not yet appear what is the real personality of man." The practical reason for making this whole question of such importance, she concluded, "is that man's perfect model should be held in mind, whereby to improve his present condition; that his contemplation regarding himself should turn away from inharmony, sickness, and sin,

37. Mrs. Eddy's interpretation of the two accounts of creation in the book of Gensesis is developed in *S&H.*, pp. 502–529.

to that which is the perfect image of his Maker." [38] For Mrs. Eddy, then, mortal man is not truly man; and sense testimony bears false witness as to man's true nature and capacities. She believed that this testimony could be challenged on the basis of revelation. And she taught that, once awakened to the power of the Word, men have the spiritual capacity to turn to the divine model of manhood and thus correct the errors of sense.

There could be no reconciliation between this position and that of Cook. For along with almost all other Protestants, Cook completely credited the reliability of common sense testimony. The philosophy of Scottish realism, which articulated this position, was virtually the official epistemology of nineteenth century Protestantism. It was taught in the seminaries and academies and subscribed to almost universally by orthodox clergymen. Approvingly, Cook once quoted the words of the leading advocate of this philosophy in America, James McCosh:

Aristotle was the first to establish the grand truth that the senses do not deceive, and that the errors arise from the wrong interpretation given by the sense . . . we may follow our natural convictions implicitly, and regard the mind as perceiving things immediately, and run no risks of deceptions or contradictions.[39]

Crediting sense testimony, Cook firmly held that matter was actual, God-created, and imbued with the Creator's living presence, and that man was an animate material being with an indwelling soul. For Mrs. Eddy, however, God, or Life, was not in matter; matter had no independent positive existence; and man's true being was not that of a material organism. The belief of life in matter was, for her, an error which Science must correct. Darwinism was, of course, not the threat to her that it was to Cook. For though she could say that it was more consistent than most other theories about human development,[40] no hypothesis based upon sense evidence could have any ultimate truth for her. To Mrs. Eddy there could be no real contest between religion and science; for her teachings, she believed, undercut the whole perceptual base of physical science and constituted in themselves the true science of creation.

Her thesis, therefore, was that Christian Science represented both the most genuine Christianity and the most comprehensive science. Both of these implications were clear enough in her address; and they were clear affronts to a man like Cook, who claimed to have the last word on

38. *Mis.,* pp. 97–98.
39. Cook, *Current Religious Perils,* p. 122.
40. *S&H.,* p. 547.

both Christianity and science. Just how galling Mrs. Eddy's claims struck him was demonstrated a few minutes after she took her seat. Cook chatted with her for a few minutes, then rose suddenly and demanded of her, "Do you mean to tell me that I have ears and hear not, and eyes and see not, when I have preached the gospel all these years?" [41] This was, of course, just what she meant. And it is little wonder that Cook's cordiality in introducing the next, less controversial speaker, was just opposite to the disrelish with which he had introduced Mrs. Eddy.

Upon leaving Tremont Temple, she rode home with Miss Bartlett and spent the rest of the day alone in her room. The encounter with Cook had been one of the most difficult ordeals Mrs. Eddy had yet endured as leader of the Christian Science movement. Years later, addressing her followers from the same platform that she had shared with Cook, Mrs. Eddy said that "The Christian Scientist knows that spiritual faith and understanding pass through the waters of Meribah here—bitter waters; but he also knows they embark for infinity and anchor in omnipotence." [42] Possibly she had reference here in part to the "bitter waters" through which she had passed in Tremont Temple fourteen years before. Yet in that experience her faith had not been shaken; and the progress of the Cause by 1899 seemed to her to have fully justified it.

41. Bartlett Reminiscences.
42. "Address at Annual Meeting, June 6, 1899," *My.,* p. 132.

"Sunrise of a Scientific Christianity"

Curiously, the heading of this chapter is derived from the title of a sermon delivered in 1871 by none other than Joseph Cook. It is somewhat ironical, too, that Cook appears to have picked up the phrase "scientific Christianity" from a newspaper article by Mrs. Eddy commending his stand on a social issue.[1] Though Cook certainly did not have her teaching in mind when he used the phrase, it is a happy one for our purpose; for it epitomizes perhaps as well as any words can Mrs. Eddy's own sense of the meaning of her teaching in relation to the Christian tradition. Indeed, she often employed some version of the traditional Christian metaphor of the breaking of the light into darkness in reference to the emergence of Christian Science. Through her discovery of the scientific or practical import of Christian revelation, Mrs. Eddy felt that the light of divine Truth had dawned upon an age of spiritual darkness, heralding a new day for mankind. What, specifically, was the meaning of this claim in terms of the religious situation in which it was made? Our answer to this question begins with an analysis of the religious situation in the Gilded Age.

THE RELIGIOUS SITUATION IN THE GILDED AGE

After a prolonged visit to the United States, Lord Bryce predicted in 1893 that in spiritual matters "America seems as unlikely to drift from her

1. See Peel, *Discovery*, p. 245.

ancient mooring as any country of the old world." [2] In many ways an acute observer, Bryce proved in this instance at least a poor prophet. That America *has* drifted from her "ancient mooring" is perhaps the most obvious fact of her spiritual history in the twentieth century. Moreover, it now seems clear that by the time Bryce made his visit this drift had already begun.

In the early 1870s, at the beginning of what Mark Twain called "The Gilded Age," Protestantism was still the overwhelmingly dominant religious and cultural force in American life. Despite denominational diversity and regional variations, American Protestantism was still a fairly unified phenomenon. For the most part the evangelical churches shared a common orientation: a loose Calvinism combined with a tame revivalism. And though their theologies were fortified by a rather hidebound Protestant scholasticism, the religious practice of the denominations tended toward a warm pietism with humanitarian overtones. By the end of the Gilded Age — that is, by the late 1890s — not only had the interior unity of American Protestantism been largely shattered, but the forces leading to the creation of what has been called a post-Protestant America had been set in motion. It is clear, then, that in religious as well as socio-economic life, the Gilded Age was the matrix of modern America. And the religious upheavals of the period were in their own way as wrenching as the more obviously disruptive consequences of the nation's industrial growth — if not more so. That Christian Science emerged into prominence during a period in which such fundamental shifts were taking place is the first fact necessary for an understanding of its meaning in American religious life.

To some extent it is possible to assess the religious situation in the Gilded Age as a function of socio-economic transition. The industrial expansion of America, the enlargement of old cities and the creation of new ones, the staggering influx of European immigrants — in short, the great travail the nation was experiencing in these years — was creating a plural civilization far different from the relatively provincial society in which American Protestantism had matured and flourished. In part, the effect of social change on the religious situation was a matter of the movement of population. The great migration from the farms into the cities disrupted the stability of hundreds of rural congregations, particularly in New England, while the shifting of population within the cities themselves had the same effect on many urban churches. Even more important,

2. Lord Bryce, *The American Commonwealth,* II (New York, 1891), 591.

the "new immigration" of the late nineteenth and early twentieth centuries increased the non-Protestant population of America. In 1870, Roman Catholics in the United States numbered around four million. By 1906 they numbered nearly eleven million, four million *more* than the largest Protestant denomination. In addition, the Jewish population of the United States swelled in the quarter century after 1880 from 250,000 to 1,750,000, while Eastern Orthodoxy became a significant though much smaller, minority. Furthermore, industrialization and its social consequences confronted the American churches with challenges they were ill-prepared to face. So firmly wedded was the Protestant clergy to the ideology of laissez-faire that it inevitably lost touch with a social situation in process of drastic change. More specifically, the tacit alliance of the clergy with the middle class blinded it to the necessity of appealing to the working class until it was too late. Antagonized by the conservatism of the church and far removed from the routine simplicities of rural life, it was easy for the urban worker to drift into religious indifference.

But these factors, important as they were, give us only a partial understanding of the Protestant predicament in the Gilded Age. That Protestantism faced great challenges in a fast industrializing America is clear enough. But that these challenges were insurmountable is far less certain. There was, in fact, nothing in the socio-economic scene that conclusively determined the nature of the Protestant response to it. Socio-economic conditions really explain very little about the *inner* history of American Protestantism in this period. They certainly do not account for what must be regarded as the most crucial factor in the whole religious situation: the devitalization of Protestant doctrines and symbols. For it was in the Gilded Age that Protestant doctrines and symbols discernibly began to lose their hold on the American population and their dominance in the culture in general.

This development was not, of course, unique to America. For it was a phase of that larger process of the devitalization of supernatural Christianity in the Western world which has been called the death of God. It was in 1882, at the beginning of our period, that Friedrich Nietzsche published his *Joyful Wisdom,* in which a madman announced to a crowd in a market place that God is dead, and that they had killed him.[3] By declaring that God is dead, Nietzsche was not so much making a theological pronouncement as performing a cultural analysis. Albert Camus observed that "Nietzsche did not form a project to kill God. He

3. Friedrich Nietzsche, *Joyful Wisdom* (1882), translated by Thomas Common (New York, 1960), pp. 167–168.

found him dead in the souls of his contemporaries." [4] Nietzsche saw that the supernaturalistic and dualistic orientation of Western Christianity, epitomized by the term God, was no longer real to men in his age. To a large extent the devitalization of Christian symbols had already occurred in Europe when Nietzsche wrote. But at this time it was only beginning to become apparent in American popular religious culture.

What makes the decline of Protestantism in the American situation so difficult to understand is that it was not apparent on the surface. Taking the term *gilded* to signify a deceptively bright surface appearance, one can well see why the age deserves the epithet in religious as well as other concerns. Superficially, Protestantism in this period gave the impression of being in a remarkably healthy state. Of course, the religious world was rocked by disputes over Darwinism and the new Biblical studies. Many churchmen, also, were well aware of the difficulties faced by religion in coping with social change. Yet on the whole the outlook at the time seemed quite cheering.

Indeed, there were many gauges by which the prosperity of Protestantism could be measured and found reassuring. Yet if the apparent evidences of religious vitality in this period are examined, they can be seen as indices of religious decline. Church membership was increasing rapidly — from sixteen percent of the population in 1850 to thirty-six percent in 1900. Yet at the same time standards for church admission declined. Churches became more impressive in hundreds of communities where handsome stone or brick buildings replaced the simpler frame structures of the pre-War period. But if appearances gained, devoutness declined; and the Wednesday evening prayer meeting, once a staple feature of denominational life, languished for lack of interest. Religious observance was common in public life, yet fewer and fewer Protestant families carried on private devotions in their homes. The great figures of the Protestant pulpit, men such as Brooklyn's Henry Ward Beecher and Boston's Phillips Brooks, commanded national prestige as leaders of public opinion. Yet after the Gilded Age clerical figures would in general exert far less influence on American public life. The churches were deeply concerned with the private morals of Americans; but with rare exceptions their influence on the political and economic morality of the country was small. The institutional church flourished, but only a small proportion of those who enjoyed its advantages were drawn into a permanent relation with the church. The Young Men's Christian Association had been

4. Albert Camus, *The Rebel* (New York, 1956), p. 68.

founded as a rescue mission to evangelize American youth pouring into the cities, but by the turn of the century it had become mainly a social service institution. Moody's revival meetings were popular, impressive affairs; yet even he had to acknowledge that he was not reaching the great unchurched masses, and that most of those who responded to his preaching were church members already.[5]

Probably the clearest indication of the debility of faith in the Gilded Age was the general social emphasis in the denominations. With their bazaars, church suppers and socials, sewing classes, open forums, moral crusades, city missions, and philanthropic enterprises, among other activities, American Protestants in large numbers had increasingly become somewhat complacent doers of good. What they seriously thought about God and their own ultimate spiritual destiny is another question altogether. Considering the insistence of Reformation Protestantism upon the superiority of faith over works, it does seem that late nineteenth century Protestants were reversing their priorities. Of course there probably remained in this as in any other period of American religious life a substantial number of people who lived lives rich in faith. Yet the general tendency was in quite a different direction.

Exalting action, most Protestants tended to denigrate doctrine. Theology and actual religious faith are, of course, very different things. Still, most people for whom faith is real take seriously the doctrines that articulate that faith. In this period, however, there is every indication that doing good mattered far more than doctrine to the average American Protestant churchgoer. Though he would be hesitant to repudiate belief in orthodox doctrine, he was probably assenting intellectually to beliefs which he had ceased to entertain emotionally. Lord Bryce was a keen observer of this tendency, even if he did not see its full implications. Noting that Americans generally recoiled from "blank negation," he characterized a popular attitude by quoting the remark of one citizen: "We don't mind going a good way along the plank, but we like to stop short of the jump-off." Most sermons except in the conservative South, he noted, tended to be more practical and hortatory than doctrinal.[6] And while he observed that no country surpassed the United States in active beneficence, Bryce also pointed out that popular interest in theological matters here was suffering a decline. As early as 1880, J. B. Harrison, a Unitarian minister, had noted that "There is yet . . . a large amount of moral force and health-

---

5. Winthrop S. Hudson, *Religion in America* (New York, 1965), p. 233.
6. Bryce, *American Commonwealth*, II, 590-599.

ful life in the church. Religion is not extinct. But the really significant fact here is that it is constantly losing ground." [7]

There was yet another symptom of an underlying malaise. The shortage of ministers to fill the pulpits in the land, an old problem in American Protestantism, was becoming much more severe. In desperation, the denominations often granted seminary scholarships to induce young men to go into the ministry. Since many who took advantage of the opportunity had not really heard the call but only sought security, the device tended to lower the quality of the ministry as a whole. Also, many ministers restive under lay control in their churches or disenchanted with the work for other reasons abandoned the ministry for other professions. In view of unattractive conditions in the ministry and the allurements of commercial life, it is not surprising that fewer men felt called to the work. [8]

One novel written in this period about the life of a minister in a small American town helps to explain the religious tendencies under discussion. Harold Frederic's *The Damnation of Theron Ware,* first published in England in 1896 under the title *Illumination,* was a pioneering work of American literary realism. Drawing upon youthful memories of life in the Mohawk Valley of upper New York, Frederic created a study not so much of a single religion as of the spiritual life of the nation as a whole. His protagonist Ware is a somewhat naïve and callow young Methodist minister called to a pulpit in the town of Octavius. Ware's congregation is composed mainly of primitive Methodists who want their religion preached in the most rudimentary terms. As a trustee of the church tells him, "We are a plain sort o' folks up in these parts. . . . What we want here, sir, is straight-out, flatfooted hell — and the burnin' lake of fire and brimstone. Pour it into 'em hot an' strong." [9]

But during the course of his ministry Ware becomes disenchanted with the provinciality of his narrow Protestant world. Through various encounters, he is exposed to the influence of Darwinism and the higher criticism, falls under the spell of aestheticism, and feels the lure of the flesh. Gradually Ware drifts from his spiritual moorings until, in a crucial scene in the book, his break with orthodoxy becomes explicit. Feign-

7. Quoted in Winthrop S. Hudson, *The Great Tradition of the American Churches* (New York, 1953), p. 201.

8. See the discussion of the decline in the ministry during this period in Aron I. Abell, *The Urban Impact on American Protestantism* (Cambridge, Mass., 1943), pp. 255–256.

9. Harold Frederic, *The Damnation of Theron Ware* (New York, 1896), pp. 43–44.

ing illness, he stays home during a mid-week prayer meeting. The droning of the Doxology from the church next door awakens him from the reverie into which he has lapsed. "It had grown quite dark," Frederic writes,

and he rose and lit the gas. "Blest be the Tie that Binds," they were singing. He paused, with hand still in air, to listen. That well-worn phrase arrested his attention, and gave itself a new meaning. He was bound to those people, it was true, but he could never again harbor the delusion that the tie between them was blessed. There was vaguely present in his mind the consciousness that other ties were loosening as well. Be that as it might, one thing was certain. He was passed definitely beyond pretending to himself that there was anything spiritually in common between him and the Methodist Church of Octavious.[10]

Ware finds himself at a stroke uninvolved with the life of the church of which he was the pastor. He is damned not because he leaves the ministry, as he eventually does, but because he has lost all his old spiritual supports and has nothing with which to replace them. Trying to shed his provincialism and impress sophisticated friends, Ware ridicules his congregation, his religious heritage, and even his wife to such an extent that his friends find him odious. His tragedy is his loss of innocence and moral vision. In this portrayal of Ware's spiritual disintegration, Frederic was writing as a profound analyst of American religious life in his time as well as a prophet of the American future.

One significant factor in Ware's spiritual collapse is that it was precipitated only in part by the influence of Darwinism and the higher criticism. So too, the fact that Protestantism was losing ground generally in the Gilded Age is only partially explicable in terms of the impact of these influences on popular religious thought. Undeniably, the debate over Darwinism, which began in earnest in America during the early 1870s, did undermine the authority of the Bible literally construed and challenged the whole Protestant view of God, creation, and man. The higher criticism, which began to arouse popular interest in the early 1880s, was akin to Darwinism both in principle and effect. For it represented the application in Biblical studies of the same evolutionary principle that Darwinism had applied so convincingly in biology. The higher criticism, in assessing the formation of Scripture in terms of cultural evolution, posed an even greater challenge than biological science to Biblical literalism.

10. *Ibid.*, p. 275.

Still, it is doubtful that more than a small proportion of Protestants once convinced of the truth of their faith were likely to be disabused of it by intellectual arguments of any sort. Conviction often builds its own imperviousness to criticism. The extent to which the Protestant laity adopted or rejected religious belief according to rational persuasion can be easily exaggerated. If Darwinism or the higher criticism seemed to strike a telling blow against orthodoxy, it was because its structure was already weak.

In the largest sense, Protestant orthodoxy failed because its implicit dualism between the natural and supernatural became increasingly untenable to the nineteenth century mind. The deepest challenge posed to orthodoxy by Darwinism and the higher criticism lay in the fact that they struck at one vital phase of this dualism: the distinction between natural and supernatural knowledge, between reason and revelation. Those who rejected Darwinism and the higher criticism were usually forced into a radical reaffirmation of this distinction. Those who accepted them and made the necessary theological accommodations generally denied that any such distinction need be made. In either case, the debate over Darwinism and the higher criticism was basically a way of arguing the larger point.

In terms of its impact on practical life-attitudes, Protestant supernaturalism engendered an approach to the meaning of man's experience which the nineteenth century found increasingly difficult to maintain. The idea of Christian resignation, a pervasive concept in popular orthodox Protestantism throughout the eighteenth and nineteenth centuries, provides a good focal point for discussion of the general problem. This attitude encouraged submission to earthly suffering as the will of God, promising a compensating bliss in the beyond for those who endured such disasters as the Almighty might send their way. The death of children particularly — a not uncommon occurrence in American households — was often met by this sort of response. A good example is to be found in this account by the eighteenth century Calvinist theologian Nathaniel Emmons of his reaction to the death of his two small sons shortly after the death of their mother:

It is impossible to describe what I felt. I stood a few moments, and viewed the remains of my two darlings, who had gone to their mother and to their long home, never to return. But I soon found the scene too distressing and retired to my chamber, to meditate in silence upon my forlorn condition. I thought there was no sorrow like unto my sorrow. I thought my burden was greater than I could bear. I felt as though I could not submit to such a complicated affliction. My heart rose in all its strength against the government of God, and then suddenly sunk under its distress, which greatly alarmed me. I sprang up, and said to myself, I am going into immediate distraction; I must submit, or I am undone forever. In a very few minutes my burden was removed, and I felt entirely calm and resigned to the will of God. I soon went down, attended to my family concerns, and gave directions respecting the interment of my children. I never enjoyed greater happiness in the course of my life, than I did all that day and the next. My mind was wholly detached from the world, and altogether employed in pleasing contemplation of God and divine things. I felt as though I could follow my wife and children into eternity, with peculiar satisfaction.[11]

This moving passage clearly displays several dualistic attitudes which had many other ramifications in Protestant thought and which continued to be characteristic of popular Protestantism well into the period with which we are concerned: (1) Duality between this life and a future one. Protestants believed in a future life of a fundamentally different nature from the present one, and pictured it generally in quite literal terms as either blissful heaven or fiery hell. Many of them, to the extent of their devoutness, lived their present existence in terms of their expectations for a future one. (2) Duality between faith and life. The Reformation doctrine of *sola fide* — salvation by faith alone — was an essential element in orthodox Protestantism. To sincerely submit to the will of God, Protestants had to sustain faith as a vital reality, whatever the horror of their outward circumstances. (3) Duality between the ways of God and the desires of men. To reconcile their present sufferings with the idea of God's sovereign power, Protestants had to accept disaster as part of His discipline and plan. Hence they had to adjust their human expectations to what they thought was the divine intention.

Emmon's resignation to the will of God notwithstanding, it is doubtful that Protestants in general succeeded in wholly resolving the psychic tensions induced by these forms of duality. Certainly when they had the means to *avoid* the suffering which they otherwise might have attributed to the divine plan, they did not hesitate to do so. To the degree that men felt increasingly able to take command over their own experiences, their faith in orthodox supernaturalism waned. Just here one can see how popular and pervasive attitudes towards experience engendered by the Enlightenment ran contrary to those projected by supernaturalistic Protestantism. The Enlightened emphasis upon reason tended to preempt the authority of revelation. Possibilities of human progress in the present

11. Quoted in Henry F. May, Introduction to Harriet Beecher Stowe, *Oldtown Folks* (Cambridge, Mass., 1966), pp. 13–14.

order tended to make the idea of heaven more remote. The concrete interest with which these possibilities invested experience tended to lessen the force of symbols and doctrines appealing to faith. And the value placed in human desire and striving tended to discredit belief in a God who demanded that they be subordinated to an arbitrary divine will.

In the late eighteenth century, intellectuals committed to the ideals of the Enlightenment and some segments of the population influenced by Deism had repudiated most of Protestant supernaturalism. Certainly the "village atheist" is not an unfamiliar figure in American life. It should not be forgotten, too, that a sizeable number of people, even when the culture is generally devout, show no signs of religious sensibility anyway. Deists, many Unitarians, and scientific rationalists of various types were among this group. But far more revealing of the general religious situation in the nineteenth century than the abandonment of orthodoxy by the religiously indifferent was its rejection by those who still had a large measure of piety. The major writers of mid-nineteenth century America — Emerson, Thoreau, Hawthorne, Melville, Whitman — were men of acute religious sensibility who nevertheless had no use for Protestant orthodoxy; and in this respect their spiritual situation was prophetic of the American future. Melville turned to primitivism for new symbols to replace the dead symbols of orthodoxy.[12] Similarly, Emerson looked to German and English romanticism, as well as to Indian mysticism, for a new sense of the divine. It could be argued that all these men, despite the various cultural influences to which they were responsive, remained Christian in their basic orientation; and that they were trying to discover the experiential content of that which orthodoxy dealt with in terms of doctrine and symbol.

At the same time that these writers were in their prime, popular religion in the United States was dominated by revivalism. It is not coincidental that just when the most creative individuals in the culture were rejecting the symbols of orthodoxy, revivalists were intensifying their appeal. For when a religion can perpetuate itself only through a series of emotional paroxysms, the time is probably not far distant when it will lose its hold on the culture. In this sense, though revivalism was undoubtedly a powerful force in the culture of pre-Civil War America, its dominance boded ill for the continued vitality of Protestantism. Revivalism itself was one casualty of the new era. For even though revivalism did show some strength in the cities just before the Civil War, it was, on balance, a failure

12. See the discussion of Melville in James Baird, *Ishmael: A Study of the Symbolic Mode in Primitivism* (Baltimore, 1956).

in the post-War decades. Clearly, the primitive simplicities of a rural Protestantism had little staying power in modern life. And the temper of the Gilded Age was not in general responsive to evangelical fervor.

REACTION AND REORIENTATION

What the new religious situation in the Gilded Age demanded was just what revivalism had lacked: real theological creativity. Indeed, the theological simplicity of revivalism — both before and after the Civil War — was a real clue to its bankruptcy. For the emotionalism of the revivalistic style rode roughshod over theological dilemmas that could not permanently be ignored.

Yet even the more traditional representatives of Protestant orthodoxy who were disposed to take up the challenges of the new era in theological terms found themselves, on balance, unequal to the task. Actually, the New England Theology, which had been dominant in almost all Congregational and some Presbyterian seminaries since the days of Jonathan Edwards, was becoming moribund in the last decades of the nineteenth century.[13] At the hands of Edwards' successors, the most prominent of whom was Nathaniel Taylor, it had been modified gradually so as to comport with the tendencies of the nineteenth century mind. The heirs of Edwards more and more allowed for man's initiative in the work of salvation, thereby embracing the very Arminianism he had tried to stem. But there had to be an end to the modification of a system that was obviously outworn. By the mid 1890s the New England Theology was dead. All of its major representatives in the seminaries had been replaced by a new breed more responsive to modern currents of thought. In other denominations at different rates the progress of theological liberalism was turning the older orthodoxies into anachronisms.[14]

Orthodox Protestantism in the late nineteenth century was clearly on the defensive. As far back as 1857, Charles Hodge, the dominant influence at the Princeton Theological Seminary, foresaw the posture that conservatives would assume in the coming decades. Referring to those who were challenging Christianity on scientific grounds, Hodge declared: "We can even afford to acknowledge our incompetence to meet them in

13. Valuable on this topic is Frank Hugh Foster, *A Genetic History of New England Theology* (Chicago, 1907).

14. The development of American liberal Protestantism is best traced in Foster's sequel to the above-named book, *The Modern Movement in American Theology* (New York, 1939).

argument, or to answer their objections; and yet our faith remains unshaken and rational." [15] Though Hodge died in 1872, Princeton remained a bastion of conservative Presbyterians until the 1920s. The Presbyterians, however, were generally more rigid than the other denominational bodies; and most though not all of the heresy trials in the 1890s and 1910s which drew public attention were confined to the Northern Presbyterian Church. But it was not the accused but the accusers in such affairs who were really on the defensive. The little witch hunts of the conservative Protestant denominations were actually symptoms of their theological bankruptcy. Conservative Protestantism from the Gilded Age until the appearance of American neo-orthodoxy neither produced a thinker of real stature nor offered any viable response to the challenge of modernity. In the end, all that conservatives could do in the face of the attack on supernaturalism was to lift the time-worn standard of inerrancy of Scripture. And as a defense of Protestant faith that was not enough.

Another closely related reaction to the religious crisis of the Gilded Age can be found among those Americans who, in the face of the growing secular and modernist drift of the culture, took refuge in a radical reassertion of Protestant supernaturalism. This group, which can be called in general terms the Protestant right wing, was composed of a number of elements: The Seventh-Day Adventists, found in 1860; the Jehovah's Witnesses, formed around twelve years later; and various Pentecostal sects which began to gain strength around the turn of the century. The religious roots of these sects lay in the radical perfectionism of the pre-Civil War era. Yet in the Gilded Age their posture was far less buoyant than the triumphant evangelism of the earlier period. For in their negative response to the currents of modernity that dominated the culture of the Gilded Age and to the compromises that the major denominations had made with the culture, these sects exhibited a decidedly reactionary religious impulse. The key doctrine that united them was premillennialism, which, in its expectation that things would get worse and worse till the second coming of Christ, ran exactly counter to the progressive aspirations of the period. And their temper inclined them more to radical withdrawal from the world than attempts to reform or accommodate to it.

The representatives of the Protestant right wing spoke for a point of view which was to become of increasing significance in the religious life of the twentieth century, for there is a direct link between the premillennialism of the Gilded Age and the fundamentalist movements of the early

15. Quoted in Hudson, *Religion,* p. 277.

twentieth century. Further, the radical supernaturalism of these movements anticipated the amazing growth of the Protestant right wing in
the 1950s and 1960s. The reactionary tendency that these movements
embody never has and probably never will represent a general consensus
among American Protestants. But their mood represents a most significant minority report; and the fact that they first appeared during the
Gilded Age is another indication of the importance of that era as the
matrix of contemporary religious tendencies.[16]

The most creative effort at theological reorientation within Protestantism
during the Gilded Age was the New Theology and its offspring the Social
Gospel. These movements, though strongly influenced by theological
winds blowing from Europe, can best be understood as responses by
thoughtful and concerned Protestants to the urgencies of the religious
situation in America. The New Theology that emerged in the 1880s was
something of a compromise between supernatural Christianity and humanistic secularism. Generally its spokesmen saw it as an effort to restore vitality to Christianity, to reconstruct orthodoxy in terms that the
modern mind could accept. As Harry Emerson Fosdick was to put it some
years later, liberalism made it possible for a man to be "both an intelligent
modern and a serious Christian." [17] One can well understand why many
of the New Theologians characterized their own views as "progressive
orthodoxy" rather than liberalism. Henry Ward Beecher, though certainly
no theologian, was one of the prime movers in the development of the
New Theology. His transition from orthodoxy to liberalism illustrates an
impulse that helped account for the rise of the new outlook.

As he himself acknowledged, Beecher developed his main ideas by
gearing his sermons to what his congregation wanted to hear. His was
the spirit of accommodation.[18] As he told the students at Yale Divinity
School in 1872 in a discussion of Darwinism, "If Ministers do not make
their theological systems conform to the facts as they are; if they do not
recognize what men are studying, the time will not be far distant, when
the pulpit will be like a voice crying in the wilderness." [19] Cheerfully

16. An extended treatment of religious developments in this period can be found
in Paul A. Carter, *The Spiritual Crisis of the Gilded Age* (DeKalb, Ill., 1971).
17. Quoted in Kenneth Cauthen, *The Impact of American Religious Liberalism*
(New York, 1962), p. 4.
18. Hudson, *The Great Tradition*, p. 277.
19. Henry Ward Beecher, *Yale Lectures on Preaching*, I (New York, 1872–1874),
87–89.

Beecher made his peace with Darwinism and styled himself a "cordial Christian evolutionist." And it was Beecher's successor at the Plymouth Congregational Church in Brooklyn, Lyman Abbot, who helped popularize John Fiske's slogan "Evolution is God's way of doing things."

For the New Theologians, God was not distant and unknowable, not an arbitrary being who intervened in human affairs at His pleasure. Rather, He was a spiritual power immanent in and impelling the development of nature and human history. It is thoroughly understandable that the New Theologians, like Horace Bushnell before them, made Christ the center of their theology: for in Christ, they felt, the divine became known to the human. Wrote George Gordon of Boston, one of the most intellectually able of the liberals, "The incarnation is the center of all sane theology," since "man at his best can alone give us God at his best." [20] Liberals like Gordon did not wholly humanize Christ. They accepted, though with their own special emphasis, the Trinity and the Incarnation. And while they generally affirmed the unique divinity of Jesus, the New Theologians spoke of him as a man. They rejected the idea that Jesus' atonement had the purpose of appeasing God's wrath or compensating for man's sin. Rather, they believed its purpose lay in the example of love it provided and its creation of a community of faith among men. For them Jesus was not so much a supernatural saviour as the ideal man after whom all men should model themselves.

The New Theologians shared the belief that human nature being basically good, all men could be educated into ideal manhood. Bushnell's *Christian Nurture,* published in 1847, was a major influence in shaping this point of view, since it argued that children could grow up as good Christians without having experienced a conversion.[21] Phillips Brooks, the most widely revered of the Protestant liberals, once advised a congregation to "Believe in yourselves and reverence your own human nature." [22] Interpreting religion as "the highest reach of our human life," [23] Brooks along with other liberals placed supreme value on the worth and potential of the human personality and saw no limit to man's possible progress on earth.

It was in terms of earthly progress that the New Theologians defined the advancement of the Kingdom of God. The doctrine of the Kingdom was basic in the New Theology. William Adams Brown, author of the

20. Quoted in Hudson, *The Great Tradition,* p. 170.
21. Horace Bushnell, *Christian Nurture* (New York, 1847).
22. Quoted in Hudson, *The Great Tradition,* p. 164.
23. Quoted in *Ibid.*

influential summary of liberal doctrine *Christian Theology in Outline,* wrote of the Kingdom as "a society of redeemed persons," with Christ as its ideal, the union of which is to be "progressively realized in history." This concept of the Kingdom is a key one for an understanding of liberal theology.[24] For liberals saw the salvation of man as inseparable from the evolution of culture and society. Far from opposing Darwinism, liberals converted the evolutionary principle into a sacramental philosophy of progress.

Through these ideas of the immanence of God, the Incarnation and atonement, and the Kingdom on earth, the liberals of the New Theology adjusted Christianity to modernity. They replaced the orthodox view of the discontinuity of the human and the divine with the belief that the divine is immanent in the human. Though they did not abandon supernaturalism entirely, they went far in breaking down the dualism between the spiritual and the secular that was proving fatal to orthodoxy. Yet this was accomplished at no small price. For by reinterpreting the Christian message in terms thoroughly consistent with the highest ideals of secular life, liberalism deprived Christianity of its normative content. It made its peace with modernity at the price of acculturizing Christianity.[25] In terms of practical piety, however, liberalism and orthodoxy in the late nineteenth century were not so far apart as it might seem from the disparity of their theologies. To a large extent liberals made compromises with the culture in theology that conservatives had already made in spirit anyway.

Far more than any group within the Protestant denominations, the preachers of the Social Gospel offered a strong critique of their culture. The Social Gospel neither originated in nor was confined to any particular denomination. It was a movement in the direction of increasing social concern which had significant representation in most of the major denominations. The belief that social action was the essence of Christianity had its basis in the liberalism of the New Theology, which interpreted Christianity largely in ethical terms. Not that the New Theology necessarily implied a radical or even a progressive social position, as the political conservatism of Henry Ward Beecher well shows. Yet the tendency to see the ethical content of Christianity as primary, and its supernaturalistic elements as secondary or even expendable, was common to

24. William Adams Brown, *Christian Theology in Outline* (New York, 1906), pp. 182–183.
25. This point is developed by Sidney Mead in *The Lively Experiment: The Shaping of Christianity in America* (New York, 1963), pp. 134–155.

both the New Theology and the Social Gospel. The difference between liberals and advocates of the Social Gospel was more economic and temperamental than theological. Liberals outside the Social Gospel camp adhered to laissez-faire economics, while those within it, more responsive to the anti-formalist current in their time, rejected it.

Not only did the leaders of the Social Gospel formulate a religious teaching capable of impelling a practical response to the urgent necessities of the social situation: they also provided a means whereby idealistic Americans could go on being Christians even though they had come to disbelieve the more supernaturalistic elements of orthodox Protestantism. Even if the "acids of modernity" had eaten away their faith in the miracles or in an after-life, they could still see ideal value in Christian works and count themselves Christians because they were impelled to perform them.[26] It is interesting in this respect that Frederic's Theron Ware, after leaving the ministry, entered politics to do some practical good for men. Frederic makes no mention of the Social Gospel in his book, but implies that Ware felt he had nowhere else to go. It is at least arguable that many of those who later followed the path pointed out by the Social Gospel felt very much the same way.

In the period we are discussing and for many decades to come, socially concerned Protestants focused their attention upon the massive dislocations resulting from the process of industrialization. But what can be called the Social Gospel *idea* — that the Christian's chief obligation is to better the social order — can find expression in concern for almost any social or international problem. In the 1960s, race and war were to become the twin focal points of a revived and chastened Social Gospel movement that may be said to have spilled outside the churches. In this sense, the Social Gospel idea had proven to be one of the most powerful religious concepts ever to affect the course of American life.

It is easy, though, to mistake the innovative for the normative. Though the Social Gospel was a striking innovation within Protestantism, it was still by the turn of the century just a movement within liberalism. Even liberalism, though it was increasing in influence in the late nineteenth century, was by no means dominant in popular Protestantism until well into the twentieth, if then. Liberalism might make considerable headway in Northern seminaries. But it should not be forgotten that there were still hundreds of thousands of hard-shell Baptists who made no conces-

26. Mead uses this very apt phrase in *Ibid.*, p. 137.

sions to modernity, rejected liberalism and the Social Gospel, and continued to embrace such illiberal doctrines as infant damnation.

Yet there is much evidence that the liberal influence was growing in popular Protestantism by the first decade of the twentieth century. One indication of this tendency was the fact that public sympathy in the heresy trials was usually with the minister who stood accused. This sympathy signified more than the familiar American tendency to support the underdog. For most Protestants except those in certain bastions of orthodoxy, were becoming more and more favorably disposed to liberal religious ideas. Few of them were theologically conscious enough to weigh the merits of liberalism and orthodoxy and to decide between them. In many cases, they might still subscribe to and think they believed an orthodox creed, while having gradually picked up a number of liberal ideas. In this way the complexion of American popular Protestantism was by 1900 becoming more liberal. And many churchgoers were only dimly aware that the process was taking place.

By this time, however, an increasing number of Americans could no longer be located on the liberal-orthodox Protestant spectrum. Immigration, of course, tended to pluralize the American religious scene. Also, indigenous developments opened up a number of other alternatives as serious options for religious belief. One might well say disbelief, as well, for the Gilded Age saw a widespread drift towards secularism and religious indifference in American religious life. Actually, it is difficult to see just where liberal Protestantism ends and secularism begins. One can see some link between the two in the extreme liberalism of the "scientific modernists," a group of theologians who tried to work out a complete accommodation of Christianity to natural science [27] This link can also be discerned in the broad ethical humanism of the Ethical Culture Society founded by Felix Adler in 1876, a group which was attractive to a number of idealistic intellectuals.

While outright unbelief was certainly not unknown in America before the late nineteenth century, it became in that period a much more popular option. Robert Ingersoll, the most vigorous American apostle of free thought, often was denounced by orthodox Christians as a shocking infidel. Yet Ingersoll was heard; and in view of Darwinism and the higher criticism, his agnosticism seemed at least plausible to many Americans —

27. The term "scientific modernism" was coined by Mead in *Ibid.*, p. 173.

perhaps to more than cared to admit it openly. More serious than agnosticism or even atheism, however, was religious indifference. As long as one could be shocked by atheistic or agnostic arguments, he was still to some degree under the hold of supernaturalism. But as the force of supernaturalism waned in American religious life, indifference increased. And it is clear that in many instances it was merely being masked by the persistence of religion as social convention.

Many Americans, too, became absorbed by various forms of belief, some of them occult, that had no relation to the Christian tradition. Spiritualism, which originated in pre-Civil War America, became a popular fad in the Gilded Age. Most of the groups that constituted the New Thought movement were spiritually eclectic and did not consider themselves specifically Christian, and many of them showed deep interest in Oriental religion. The Transcendentalists had helped to introduce the influence of Eastern mysticism into the United States in the pre-War years; but it was only in the last decades of the century that it acquired a vogue, with theosophy, Vedanta, and several forms of Buddhism attracting together thousands of adherents.

And finally, there was one religious teaching which offered quite a different alternative from any of those yet discussed; which attracted many people disenchanted with orthodoxy, but was not liberal; which was in some respects quite conservative, but was not orthodox; which was often identified as non-Christian, yet which insisted that it constituted the revelation of the purest Christianity. This teaching was, of course, Christian Science.

MIRACLES AND THE MEANING OF SCRIPTURE

Christian Scientists saw great significance in the fact that their religion came to prominence and gained a following in a period of profound spiritual upheaval. In 1902, Mrs. Eddy noted that the decrease of students in the seminaries was part of a general "flux and flow" tending to "the final spiritualization of all things." She further remarked that such "signs of the times" had increased since the first publication of *Science and Health* in 1875.[28] That event, she and her followers maintained, had been the harbinger of a new day for mankind. To them, Christian Science was not a product of its age, but spoke to that age with divine authority. They did not regard it as a theology in competition with other theologies,

28. *My.,* p. 266

whether old or new, but as a revelation of spiritual power which provided a wholly new alternative for religious belief and practice. Though differing markedly from traditional Christianity, it was as they saw it thoroughly Christian. Indeed, Mrs. Eddy wrote that "Christian Science and Christianity are one." [29] Through her discovery of Christian Science, she claimed, the vital essence of Biblical Christianity had been grasped, and the Scriptures spoke anew with living meaning to men.

The Bible, Mrs. Eddy felt, was the touchstone of her teachings — her primary point of reference and authority. "The testimony of the material senses," she wrote in *Science and Health*, "is neither absolute nor divine. I therefore plant myself unreservedly on the teachings of Jesus, of his apostles, of the prophets, and on the testimony of the Science of Mind. Other foundations there are none." [30] As we shall see, Mrs. Eddy's theological critics frequently spoke of the teachings of Christian Science as unBiblical. But she was wholly in earnest when she wrote in the first of the "six tenets" of Christian Science, "As adherents of Truth, we take the inspired Word of the Bible as our sufficient guide to eternal Life." [31]

Mrs. Eddy's use of the term *inspired* here can be taken in a qualifying sense. For she did not regard all of the Bible as inspired nor even the inspired portions of it as equally inspired. And though she spoke of the Bible as her authority, she by no means conceived of it as an absolute authority. Though Mrs. Eddy did place much importance on the miracle accounts in the Scriptures, she was by no means a Biblical literalist. Indeed, she felt that the genius of Christian Science lay in the fact that it had penetrated behind the literal interpretation of the Bible and grasped its spiritual signification. The idea that the Scriptures had both a literal and spiritual meaning was not original with her. Mrs. Eddy cites a passage in *Smith's Bible Dictionary* as confirming her interpretation, and she probably encountered it in several forms in the years preceding her discovery of Christian Science.[32] Yet what Mrs. Eddy herself *meant* when she said that Christian Science revealed the spiritual as opposed to the literal signification of Scripture can only be understood in terms of her own teaching.

The spiritual signification of the Scriptures to her meant the living meaning of the Biblical Word — the understanding of the present spiritual power which Biblical events exemplified and which is still potential

29. *S&H.,* p. 372. 30. *Ibid.,* p. 269. 31. *Ibid.,* p. 497.
32. This symbolic interpretation of the Bible is probably traceable to Emmanuel Swedenborg, *Dictionary of Correspondences* (Boston, 1847). See also *S&H.,* pp. 579–599.

in man's experience. Traditional Christianity, she believed, had obscured the living meaning of the Bible and had to a large extent reduced Biblical religion to a formalism devoid of spiritual power. "Christianity as Jesus taught it," she wrote, "was not a creed, nor a system of ceremonies, nor a special gift from a ritualistic Jehovah; but it was the demonstration of divine Love casting out error and healing the sick, not merely in the *name* of Christ, or Truth, but in demonstration of Truth, as must be the case in the cycles of divine light." [33]

The term *demonstration* is central in Mrs. Eddy's vocabulary. It points to her continual emphasis upon the *act*. Some of her best passages — for example, the "Bible Lessons," written in the 1880s — are explications of Scriptural texts.[34] Yet mainly she concerns herself with the *events* portrayed in the Biblical narratives, especially in the Gospel. "Jesus," she wrote, "established what he said by demonstration, thus making his acts of higher importance than his words." [35] For Mrs. Eddy, the Gospel miracle stories could not be explained away psychologically, nor were they mythical encrustations upon the true Gospel message; they constituted an essential element of that message and were historical realities of the greatest import. "Jesus," she flatly states, "walked on the waves, fed the multitude, healed the sick, and raised the dead in direct opposition to material laws. His acts were the demonstration of Science, overcoming the false claims of material sense or law." [36] In this approach to the Gospels, Mrs. Eddy anticipated the general tendency in recent Protestant theology to view revelation as an historical event rather than as the communication of true propositions about God. Her concept of revelation is experiential rather than rationalistic. In Christian Science as in much recent theology the Gospels are not treated as revelations in themselves, but accounts which witness to the revelation which was the life and work of Jesus.[37]

Yet the elements of the Gospel narratives and of the Bible as a whole which Mrs. Eddy finds most momentous — the so-called "miracle" stories — are not those which have been much emphasized in Protestant thought since her time. For in the very period in which she made the works recorded in the Bible the touchstone of her teachings, many Protestants were coming either to doubt their reality or deny their impor-

---

33. *S&H.*, p. 135.
34. These "Bible Lessons" are reprinted in *Mis.*, pp. 180–202.
35. *S&H.*, p. 473.
36. *Ibid.*, p. 273.
37. A helpful overview of recent views of the character of revelation is provided by John Baillie in *The Idea of Revelation in Recent Thought* (New York, 1956).

tance — or both. For some, the prestige of natural science tended to discredit Scriptural miracles. More important, the higher criticism aroused widespread doubt as to the authority of the Bible and so helped to vitiate faith in them. Mrs. Eddy did feel that acquaintance with Biblical scholarship, particularly with varying translations of Scriptural texts, could be of value to the student of Christian Science. Yet she warned her followers against skepticism as to the historicity of the Gospels.[38] Though she felt that Christian Science could stand on its own feet apart from anything written, Mrs. Eddy treated Biblical miracle accounts as precedents for and inspiration of her own teaching.

Most of the New Theologians, by contrast, eagerly embraced the higher criticism and were ready to abandon belief in the validity of Biblical miracles — with the general but important exception of the Resurrection. They tended to see miracles as both incommensurate with liberal theological principles and irrelevant to the essential Gospel message. Stressing the immanence of God in nature, liberals argued that it was not in His character to violate natural process in order to disclose His presence or accomplish His ends. As William Adams Brown wrote, "God is not a transcendent being living in a distant heaven whence from time to time he intervenes in the affairs of earth. He is an everpresent spirit guiding all that happens to a wise and holy end." [39] And since the New Theologians saw Jesus' teaching and example of love as the central element in the Gospels, miracles, even if valid, had no particular meaning to them. George Gordon expressed the general sentiment of liberals when he said that "where miracles have ceased to be regarded as true, Christianity remains in its essence entire." [40]

What Gordon and other liberals rejected here was the orthodox conception of miracles as badges of Jesus' supernatural authority. On this point, the liberalism of the New Theology intersects the earlier and in some other respects quite different Transcendental liberalism of Theodore Parker. While not completely discrediting the Gospel miracle accounts, Parker felt that Jesus' words and life were "more satisfactory evidences of his divine authority than all his miracles, from the transformation of water into wine to the resurrection of Lazarus." [41] To Parker, the moral

38. *My.*, p. 179.

39. Quoted in Shelton H. Smith, Robert T. Handy, and Lefferts A. Loetscher, *American Christianity*, II (New York, 1963), 258.

40. George Gordon, *Religion and Miracles* (Boston, 1909), p. 75.

41. Quoted in Perry Miller, ed., *The Transcendentalists: An Anthology of Their Writings* (Cambridge, Mass., 1950), p. 229.

truths he enunciated were self-authenticating to human intuition; therefore, no miracles were needed to lend authority to the man who proclaimed them. The argument of orthodox Unitarians in opposition to this point of view was the same as that of conservative Protestants facing another form of liberalism later in the century. For Andrews Norton, Parker's most formidable orthodox Unitarian opponent, no proof of Jesus' "divine commission could be afforded, but through miraculous displays of God's power." [42] In 1881, Edwards A. Park, the last prominent representative of the waning New England Theology, defined miracles in much the same supernatural terms. The miracle, he wrote, "is an event which occurs without a cause in created nature, without regularity in the times and places of its occurrence, and in manifest opposition to all those natural laws which have been observed in other events." [43]

Despite the conflict between variant forms of liberalism and orthodoxy on the subject of miracles, they intersect at a point where Christian Science departs from them both. For the orthodox Protestant who believed in divine intervention in nature and for the liberal who believed in divine immanence in nature, physical process and natural law were unquestioned basic realities. The natural world was finite, and as such was ordained by God. Whether or not He was disposed to interrupt the sequence of natural law to effect "special providences," these laws were real and registered His purposes for creation. But it was with just this conception of God and His creation that Christian Science differed. Mrs. Eddy maintained that physical process and material law produce so much destruction and suffering that they cannot be created nor sanctioned by a wholly good God. To her they betokened only a false apprehension of a creation which truly construed is spiritual. What the human mind called a miracle, she maintained, actually represented the demonstration of the reality of creation. "The miracle," she wrote, "introduces no disorder, but unfolds the primal order, establishing the Science of God's unchangeable law." [44] In this sense so-called miracles are not miracles at all, but "natural demonstrations of the divine power." [45] Again, they are "divinely natural, but must be learned humanly." [46]

Traditional Christianity, Mrs. Eddy felt, had been blinded to the full meaning of the Saviour's mission through false belief in the solid reality of matter and material law. Disputing this belief, she held to neither the liberal nor the conservative position regarding miracles. Like the liberals,

42. *Ibid.*, p. 229.　　　　　　　　43. Quoted in Foster, *History*, p. 496
44. *S&H.*, p. 135.　　　　　　　　45. *S&H.*, p. 131.
46. *Ibid.*, p. 59.

she spoke of Jesus as an exemplar. But she differed from them in viewing his example not alone as a matter of moral inspiration, but as the practical demonstration of spiritual power. Like the conservatives, she believed in the miracle accounts in Scripture and felt that they were indispensable to Christianity. But she interpreted them as manifestations of eternal divine law and power, not as unrepeatable evidences of Jesus' supernatural authority.

Indeed, she maintained that to truly follow in Jesus' way *required* the Christian to do the works that he did. Often she and her followers pointed to his words, "He that believeth on me, the works that I do shall he do also; and greater works than these shall he do, because I go unto my Father." Though Mrs. Eddy referred often to Jesus' teachings, her central emphasis was upon his healing works. She asked in *Science and Health,* "Why are the words of Jesus more frequently cited for our instruction than are his remarkable works? Is it not because there are few who have gained a true knowledge of the great import to Christianity of these works?"[47] Mrs. Eddy felt that by emphasizing the *meaning* of Jesus' works, Christian Science had illumined the true significance of the Gospels and of the Bible as a whole.

Mrs. Eddy located the loss of true Biblical Christianity in the abandonment of healing as practiced in the early Christian church. The function of the church which she and her students had founded in 1879 had been "to reinstate primitive Christianity and its lost element of healing."[48] The demonstration of the living power of Spirit, she felt, had been lost "about three centuries after the crucifixion."[49] Specifically, she had reference to that point at which Christianity became the established religion of the Roman Empire. It was then, she felt, that the true impetus of Christianity was submerged in church politics, ritualism, and creed.

That the purity of primitive Christianity had been lost at the point of the inception of the Roman Catholic Church was certainly not an uncommon attitude among Protestants. And whatever the difference between Christian Science and Protestantism, Mrs. Eddy identified herself with the Protestant community in this regard. It was the intention of Reformation Protestantism, particularly of the evangelical groups that settled in America, to undercut the encrustations of dogma and tradition in the Medieval Church in order to return to a faith based solely in the Bible and the practices of the early church. This effort to get back to pure

47. *Ibid.*, p. 358.   48. *Man.*, p. 17.   49. *S&H.*, p. 41.

and normative beginnings is a characteristic of Christian Science as well as other American religious groups.[50] But in the final analysis, Mrs. Eddy claimed far more for her teachings than that they marked a simple return to pristine Christianity.

Mrs. Eddy believed that she had given statement to the science of Christianity which had been grasped as a matter of practical healing power, but had never been consciously articulated before even by Biblical figures. "It is a question today," she wrote in *Science and Health,*

. . . whether the ancient inspired healers understood the Science of Christian healing, or whether they caught its sweet tones, as the natural musician catches the tones of harmony, without being able to explain them. So divinely imbued were they with the spirit of Science, that the lack of the letter could not hinder their work; and that letter, without the spirit, would have made void their practice." [51]

In another passage that her theological critics were to cite often, Mrs. Eddy makes the same point with explicit reference to Jesus: "To those natural Christian Scientists, the ancient worthies, and to Christ Jesus, God certainly revealed the spirit of Christian Science, if not the absolute letter." [52]

As she interpreted Jesus' mission, he accomplished all that could be accomplished as a matter of demonstration. That is, he overcame evil in all its forms and lived out completely the divine ideal of perfect manhood, which in Mrs. Eddy's teaching is the Christ. Thus he fulfilled his individual mission. It was not part of that mission, however, to elucidate fully the basis upon which he demonstrated the power of Spirit. The rule for this demonstration, Mrs. Eddy asserted, "remained to be discovered in Christian Science." [53] She never claimed to go behind Christian revelation in the sense of stating any truth that had not been completely objectified in Jesus' life. But she did see her work as fully explaining the conditions that make following in Jesus' way a present possibility. Further, she felt that Jesus had prophesied the coming of Christian Science. In the Gospel of John he had promised that "the Comforter, which is the Holy Ghost, whom the Father will send in my name, he shall teach you all things, and bring all things to your remembrance, whatsoever I have said unto you." In *Science and Health* Mrs. Eddy declared, "This Comforter I understand to be Divine Science." [54]

---

50. This tendency is discussed in Mead, *The Lively Experiment,* pp. 108–111.
51. *S&H.,* pp. 144–145.   52. *Ibid.,* p. 483.   53. *Ibid.,* p. 147.
54. *Ibid.,* p. 55. The Biblical reference is to John 14: 26.

Mrs. Eddy's identification of the coming of Christian Science with the advent of the Holy Spirit or Comforter clearly relates her teaching to a central concern of contemporary Christianity. For since the late nineteenth century the idea of the Holy Spirit, sometimes termed "the neglected Person of the Trinity," has become a central preoccupation of Christian thought.[55] Josiah Royce pointed out in 1913 that the doctrine of the Holy Spirit must be "understood if the spirit of Christianity in its most human and vital of features is to be understood at all."[56] It is not hard to see why the recapturing of such a "human and vital" aspect of Christianity has assumed this importance. For as orthodoxies and traditional symbols of faith have waned, the revitalization of religious thought has naturally gravitated to concern with the most immediate and experiential aspects of the religious life. Hence in many quarters it has come to center on the idea of Holy Spirit — the activity and power of God in encounter with man. At a very rudimentary level of religious expression, the Pentecostal movement has sought to revivify the immediate sense of Holy Spirit through such practices as "speaking in tongues" and the "laying on of hands." In the mainstream of Protestant theology as well, the growing importance of the concept of Holy Spirit prompted the President of Princeton Theological Seminary to observe in 1966 that "we are on the threshold of a whole new era in theology," in which emphasis shall be on the Third Person of the Trinity, "the God of the present."[57] Even Karl Barth, whose stern neo-orthodoxy emphasized the otherness of God and His judgment, felt it necessary in a late essay on "The Humanity of God" to reaffirm His nearness to man — the essence of the doctrine of Holy Spirit.[58]

In this context one can clearly see the dimensions of Mrs. Eddy's claim for what Christian Science reveals. Explicitly she declared: "This Science of God and man is the Holy Ghost, which reveals and sustains the unbroken and eternal harmony of both God and the universe."[59] For her, Divine Science is the Holy Spirit, God's self-revealing and sustaining power. And Christian Science, she held, makes possible the human apprehension of Holy Spirit by giving full statement to the nature of spiritual power. Mrs. Eddy draws a distinction, though not an absolutely rigid one,

55. For an important representative treatment of this subject in recent theology, see Arnold B. Come, *Human Spirit and Holy Spirit* (Philadelphia, 1959).
56. Josiah Royce, *The Problem of Christianity* (New York, 1913), p. 16.
57. James McCord, *Time* (August 5, 1966), pp. 69–70.
58. Karl Barth, *The Humanity of God* (Richmond, Va., 1960).
59. *Un.,* p. 52.

between "Divine Science" and "Christian Science." Divine Science refers to one office of God. Christian Science refers more to the reduction of Divine Science to humanly comprehensible statement.[60] Just as the Christ, the divine ideal of sonship, had to appear in a form which men could perceive, as the man Jesus, so Divine Science had to be reduced to a form which men could comprehend, Christian Science.

For Mrs. Eddy, Christian Science had a truly scientific character. The word *science* is, of course, one of the broadest in the language and her use of it must be carefully understood. Science had several related meanings for her. In the largest sense, it meant the certain knowledge of universal law. As she wrote: "The term Science, properly understood, refers only to the laws of God and to His government of the universe, inclusive of man." [61] She felt too that Christian Science was scientific because it provided a method or rule for demonstrating universal divine law. In this sense, she advised her readers: "Whoever would demonstrate the healing of Christian Science must abide strictly by its rules, heed every statement, and advance from the rudiments laid down." [62] Closely associated with her use of the term *science* as method was her use of it to imply the certainty with which the method can be applied. Her references to her teaching as a science often imply her view that it is infallible, absolute, and exact. "If the student adheres strictly to the teachings of Christian Science and ventures not to break its rules," Mrs. Eddy stated, "he cannot fail of success in healing." [63] She intended that through the study and practice of Christian Science, men could demonstrate with complete certainty the presence and power of Divine Science.

Mrs. Eddy's use of this term *science* is clearly congruent with its general use in late nineteenth century thought, in which science was a prestige-laden word connoting the ideas of authority, universality and infallibility. Yet this very concept of science has been challenged and strongly modified in the twentieth century through the work of Einstein, Planck, and Heisenberg, among others. Physical scientists on the frontiers of inquiry have become more apt to speak of probabilities than certainties, more conscious of the role of perception in qualifying the conclusions of scientific investigation, and in general more modest in their claims. These changing conceptions of scientific certitude by no means caused Christian Scientists who were aware of them to have misgivings about the scientific character of Mrs. Eddy's teaching. Indeed, they often noted in lectures and articles

60. *S&H.*, p. 471.   61. *Ibid.*, p. 128.   62. *Ibid.*, p. 462.
63. *Ibid.*, p. 448.

that the changed concept of matter in the physical sciences from an objective substance to a structure of energies confirmed Mrs. Eddy's discovery (sometimes, it would appear, with a shaky grasp of just what she and the scientists really meant).[64] Overall, radical changes in the physical sciences only proved to Mrs. Eddy's followers that science on a physical basis *must* be fallible — that, in her words, "All *Science* is *Christian* Science."[65]

REVELATION AS DISCOVERY

Mrs. Eddy claimed that Christian Science was the product of revelation. But this claim could be seriously misconstrued if we fail to grasp the meaning of the idea of revelation in Christian Science. Revelation cannot mean the same thing in Mrs. Eddy's teaching as it does in Christian orthodoxy, that is, the conscious self-disclosure of a personal God in time. Mrs. Eddy did not believe in the reality of a God who had created a race capable of sinning and who was conscious of a sinful human order that needed His revelation to be redeemed. Sometimes she did use language which implies this more anthropomorphic conception of Deity.[66] But in Christian Science it is inconceivable that there could be direct divine initiative in the sense that the ordinary theological concept of revelation involves.

Actually, Mrs. Eddy uses the word revelation in Christian Science to indicate the continuous character of divine action. She maintains that God is continuously self-revealed and self-revealing to His creation, and could not by His very nature be self-concealed or arbitrary in His self-disclosures. Revelation is thus the basic nature of divine activity. Hence, she asks in reference to the account of creation in Genesis: "Was not this a revelation instead of a creation?"[67] Revelation in Christian Science cannot be understood as a conscious communication from the Divine Mind to the human mind. Rather, it must be a divine breakthrough occurring when individuals respond to God's continuous revelatory self-action. To use a term by which Mrs. Eddy described Jesus' life, revelation is "the human and divine coincidence."[68] If, as she wrote, "Christ cannot come to mortal and material sense, which sees not God,"[69] it is only when human thought

---

64. For a brief informed discussion of this subject see Robert Peel, *Mary Baker Eddy: The Years of Trial* (New York, 1971), pp. 309–312.

65. *Mis.*, p. 4.   66. See for example, *Ret.*, p. 37.

67. *S&H.*, p. 504.   68. *Ibid.*, p. 561.

69. *Un.*, p. 60.

is divested of its self-assertiveness and sense of self-sufficiency that this coincidence can take place. She suggested in *Science and Health* that the birth of Jesus came about through such pure receptivity on the part of Mary.[70] And her own experience before 1866, Mrs. Eddy felt, had so divested her of hope in material existence and of faith in material modes of healing that her thought was prepared for the revelation of Christian Science.

In a pivotal passage from *Science and Health* Mrs. Eddy speaks of this revelation as both a revelation *and* a discovery: "In the year 1866, I discovered the Christ Science or divine laws of Life, Truth, and Love, and named my discovery Christian Science. God had been graciously preparing me during many years for the reception of this final revelation of the absolute divine Principle of scientific mental healing." [71] When Mrs. Eddy speaks of revelation in this passage, she is indicating her belief that it was not simply the product of her own human mentality, but that it was divinely inspired and has divine authority. It further implies that the advent of Christian Science marks a major spiritual breakthrough, a breakthrough that was the fulfillment of Scriptural prophecy.

Her use of the term *discovery* in connection with Christian Science indicates her idea of the specific nature of the revelation to which it gives statement. Of course, the discovery of Christian Science, as Mrs. Eddy spoke of it, was vastly greater than a discovery in the natural sciences; for her it was not humanly scientific but *spiritually* scientific. Yet, a meaningful parallel between her idea of the discovery of Christian Science and ordinary scientific discoveries can be drawn. The discovery of a physical process discloses conditions independent of the discoverer. Though previously unrecognized, these conditions have nevertheless been operative. But once discovered and explained, they open up new possibilities for action. So too, Mrs. Eddy felt that she had discovered universal spiritual law absolutely independent of herself. This law had always been in operation; but once discovered by her and given statement in Christian Science, all men could understand and demonstrate it.

Mrs. Eddy did insist that she be acknowledged as the discoverer of Christian Science; this, she felt, was the work that God appointed for her and no one could have taken her place. But she also drew a clear distinction between her role as the discoverer of Christian Science and Jesus' work as the individual who completely demonstrated the truth that she later elucidated. To Mrs. Eddy, Jesus' life was in itself revelation; whereas

70. *S&H.*, pp. 29–30.   71. *Ibid.*, p. 107.

her revelation was not her life but the Science to which she gave statement. "Jesus of Nazareth," she writes in a passage amplifying this concept of her mission,

was a natural and divine Scientist. He was so before the material world saw
him. He who antedated Abraham, and gave the world a new date in the
Christian era, was a Christian Scientist, who needed no discovery of the
Science of being in order to rebuke the evidence. To one "born of the flesh,"
however, divine Science must be a discovery. Woman must give it birth. It
must be begotten of spirituality, since none but the pure in heart can see
God,—the Principle of all things pure; and none but the "poor in spirit"
could first state this Principle, could know yet more of the nothingness of
matter and the allness of Spirit, could utilize Truth, and absolutely reduce
the demonstration of being, in Science, to the apprehension of the age.[72]

Mrs. Eddy felt that Jesus, through the extraordinary conditions of his
birth, was able to live divine manhood, or the Christ completely; but that
she, as "one born of the flesh," came to discover Christian Science only
through long years of preparatory development.

Given her concept of revelation, of course, Mrs. Eddy could hardly have
believed that a God conscious of a race of men that needed saving selected her from among others to help accomplish this purpose. To a student she once said, "It is not because I have been specially chosen to reveal
this Science, but it is as if there were those standing near a window, and
because I was nearest the pane, the light fell upon me."[73] Yet if Mrs.
Eddy did not regard herself as the chosen one in quite the usual sense of
the term, she did see the footsteps that led her to Christian Science as having been divinely directed. Citing Paul's statement that the law was the
schoolmaster to bring him to Christ, she wrote in her autobiography:
"Even so was I led into the mazes of divine metaphysics through the
gospel of suffering, the providence of God, and the cross of Christ."[74]
Even in the verse she wrote in what she later regarded as the years of
preparation for her discovery there is some indication that Mrs. Eddy felt
she had a mission to perform.[75] Later in *Science and Health* she was to
write, "God selects for the highest service one who has grown into such
a fitness for it as renders any abuse of the mission an impossibility."[76]

72. *Ret.*, p. 26.
73. Helen W. Bingham Reminiscences, Archives.
74. *Ret.*, p. 30.
75. See for example her poem entitled "Ode to Adversity" in Peel, *Discovery*,
p. 143.
76. *S&H.*, p. 455.

It is in these terms that she came to see her life history of forty-five years preceding the discovery of Christian Science in 1866 — as a preparation for that which was to be revealed. In her autobiography *Retrospection and Introspection* Mrs. Eddy includes brief accounts of the phases of this preparation: her early years in the Congregational church; her rebellion against her father's stark Calvinist theology; the periods of personal suffering that plagued her life until the discovery of Christian Science; and her experiments with the homeopathic system of medicine.[77] Some of Mrs. Eddy's critics in her own time and since have placed major emphasis in tracing the background of Christian Science on her association with the mental healer Phineas P. Quimby. This question, which is a controversial one, will be taken up later in a discussion of the context in which it arose.[78] Mrs. Eddy herself emphatically denied that Quimby had had anything to do with the discovery of Christian Science, which she insisted occurred after his death. But regardless of one's view of his influence on her development, it is clear that Christian Science as it emerged in American religious life was a different doctrine from anything Quimby originated or would have subscribed to.

Mrs. Eddy identified the discovery of Christian Science with her recovery from the effects of a severe accident in Lynn, Massachusetts, in early February 1866. On the way to a meeting of the Good Templars, she fell on an icy street and was carried into a nearby house with apparently severe injuries. Moved to her own home, Mrs. Eddy showed no improvement for several days. Turning to her Bible, she read an account of one of Jesus' healings and, according to her recollection, was filled with an overpowering sense that her life was in and of God. Instantaneously healed, she rose, dressed, and walked downstairs much to the amazement of her friends. It was in this experience, Mrs. Eddy claimed, that she gained the first clear discernment of the truth that she was later to elaborate in Christian Science.

It is impossible today to determine how seriously she was injured. The physician who attended her gave several conflicting reports, though he did say that he had diagnosed her injuries as a concussion with possible spinal dislocation. Mrs. Eddy felt that her accident had been potentially fatal. But the importance of the event lies not in its spectacularity but in the redirection it effected in her life. At the time it did not seem to her the major turning point that it later became in the annals of Christian

77. *Ret.*, pp. 8–39.
78. See Chapter Three, part three, "The Quimby Contention."

Science; and certainly the "fall at Lynn," in some of its frequent re-tellings in the literature of the movement, has assumed a somewhat mythic character. Careful examination of the incident and of Mrs. Eddy's life in the subsequent months does reveal, however, that it marked the appearance in her thought of the "germ" as she put it, of Christian Science.[79] Quimby had been dead about a month, and she had to work out her own cure. Given what seemed to her the severity of her injuries, it is little wonder that she referred to it a few weeks later as remarkable. More important, she had turned to the Bible in her extremity and thereafter clung to it as her guide in the spiritual investigation she pursued.[80] That the language which she used to describe this experience is so reminiscent of much mystical writing is one evidence that the experience had real depth for her. It was, she wrote, when her need was deepest that "the moment arrived of the heart's bridal to more spiritual existence. When the door opened I was waiting and watching; and, lo, the bridegroom came! The character of the Christ was illuminated by the midnight torches of Spirit. My heart knew its Redeemer." [81]

Mrs. Eddy also referred to this incident as the "falling apple" that prompted her further investigations.[82] Had she left the experience unexplained there would have been no Christian Science, for her final teaching developed as she worked out the implications of what she felt she experienced then and continued to experience of spiritual power. With a distrust of "enthusiasm" characteristic of an essentially Puritan sensibility, Mrs. Eddy at several points in her writings explicitly rejected mysticism. "Science dispels mystery and explains extraordinary phenomena," she wrote, "but Science never removes phenomena from the domain of reason into the domain of mysticism." [83] To be meaningful, ecstatic experiences must generate a "higher experience and a better life." [84] Mrs. Eddy's experience in 1866 seemed to her to perform just this function, for it was the stimulus to the accomplishment of her main work, the full explication of the science of Christianity. "For three years after my discovery," she wrote, "I sought the solution of this problem of Mind-healing, searched the Scriptures and read little else, kept aloof from society, and devoted time and energies to discovering a positive rule." [85]

---

79. See Peel, *Discovery,* Chapter Six, pp. 195–240, for a detailed account of this experience.

80. The Biblical story to which Mrs. Eddy turned in the experience, according to her later recollection, was Matt. 9: 1–8.

81. *Ret.,* p. 23.   82. *Ibid.,* p. 24.   83. *S&H.,* p. 80.

84. *Ibid.,* p. 7.   85. *Ibid.,* p. 109.

Whatever significance Mrs. Eddy's experience in February of 1866 had in her development, she clearly did not feel that she had then received a complete revelation at one stroke. Her discovery, she felt, was revelatory in character; but revelation in the sense of discovery is certainly not an all-at-once affair. Her contention that Christian Science was the product of revelation has therefore quite a different meaning from the similar claim made by Joseph Smith for the religion which he founded, Mormonism. Smith said that he had been divinely led to find the golden plates which he transcribed and published as the *Book of Mormon*. But where he claimed to have simply come upon a completed revelation, Mrs. Eddy maintained that her revelation had the character of a gradual process of unfoldment in which she had played an active part. On several occasions in later years she characterized her part in that process as "research"; and though she felt that the teaching which she worked out was objectively true, she never discounted her own role in its development.

In *Science and Health* Mrs. Eddy described the two major phases of her activity in developing her teaching when she wrote that the revelation of Christian Science "consists of two parts":

1. The discovery of this divine Science of Mind-healing, through a spiritual sense of the Scriptures and through the teachings of the Comforter, as promised by the Master.
2. The proof, by present demonstration, that the so-called miracles of Jesus did not specially belong to a dispensation now ended, but that they illustrated an ever-operative divine Principle. The operation of this Principle indicates the eternality of the scientific order and continuity of being.[86]

It is clear from contemporary testimony about her life during this period that what she described as the two parts of her revelation — whether we accept them as such or not — do point to the major activities in which she was engaged. For Mrs. Eddy spent long hours every day working out her teaching through extended commentary on Biblical texts, mainly the book of Genesis. Moreover, she carried on extensive healing work during this period as a way of confirming the validity of the ideas she was developing. Christian Science — or as she first named it, "Moral Science" — was the product of the interaction of these two pursuits.

The role that reason played in the development of Mrs. Eddy's teaching needs to be carefully understood. In *Science and Health* she writes of her discovery, "I won my way to absolute conclusions through divine revelation, reason, and demonstration."[87] It is no accident that Mrs. Eddy

86. *Ibid.*, p. 123.   87. *Ibid.*, p. 109.

placed revelation first in the series. For her teaching clearly subordinates reason to revelation and she aimed some of her strongest shafts at the concept of the sufficiency of reason based on sense testimony alone. As she put it in the first edition of *Science and Health,* "Reason discounts on revelation when it denies God the things that are his." [88] Mrs. Eddy did refer to reason more positively as "the most active human faculty." [89] But she obviously rejects the possibility of a natural theology: the idea that theological truth is in some degree deducible by human reason from the character of external reality. Her rejection of the sufficiency of human rationality becomes especially significant when we remember that a cardinal element in liberal Protestantism during this period was a strong emphasis upon the autonomy of human reason in religious matters. Indeed, the relation between reason and revelation has been a central topic of debate in modern theology. Mrs. Eddy's position on the subject is clear: revelation, she declares, will "rescue reason from the thrall of error. Revelation must subdue the sophistry of intellect, and spiritualize consciousness with the dictum and the demonstration of Truth and Love." [90]

Certainly Mrs. Eddy had little good to say about the enterprise of human philosophy, which, she wrote, has "ninety-nine parts of error to the one-hundreth part of Truth — an unsafe decoction for the race." In one passage she referred disdainfully to the "circumlocution and cold categories of Kant" and wrote that "Such miscalled metaphysical systems are reeds shaken by the wind. Compared with the inspired wisdom and infinite meaning of the Word of Truth, they are as moonbeams to the sun, or as the Stygian night to the kindling dawn." [91] Mrs. Eddy had read almost no philosophy when she worked out her teaching and certainly never intended to construct a philosophic system as such. Her language is at points borrowed from philosophy, but it is pressed into the service of articulating a religious vision which cannot be reduced to philosophic propositions. She did refer to Christian Science as a "system" at points; but as we shall see in the course of this study, her teaching is far from rigorously systematic in character. The over-all consistency of her teaching is demonstrable. But she can be quoted on both sides of several important issues and does not seek to resolve intellectually some of the paradoxes that appear. These problems do not seem to have affected Christian Science as practiced, but they do make a reduction of it to a closed metaphysical system impossible.

Mrs. Eddy did refer to her teaching as metaphysical; but in this as in

88. *S&H.*, first ed., p. 399. 89. *S&H.*, p. 327.
90. *No.*, p. 11. 91. *Ibid.*, pp. 21–22.

so many other cases she changes the sense in which a term is employed. Metaphysics is usually meant to refer to philosophic inquiry into and proposal about the nature of reality. For Mrs. Eddy, however, metaphysics meant *divine* metaphysics, which she defined as "that which treats of the existence of God, His essence, relations, and attributes." [92] She never thought of her metaphysics as speculative in character, but saw it as a way of working out and communicating the practical significance of Biblical revelation, which she accepted as given in the first place.

The metaphysics of Christian Science, then, signified for Mrs. Eddy the elucidation of the conditions which make the demonstration of divine power an immediate possibility. Since she believed that these conditions had been fully spelled out in her teaching, she held that no further revelation of religious truth was necessary for the salvation of men. It was for this reason that Mrs. Eddy referred to her discovery as "the final revelation of the absolute divine Principle of scientific mental healing." [93] What remained, she felt, is for men to *act* on the truth that she had discovered. In so doing, they would know all that they needed to know in order to follow Jesus' example and demonstrate their spiritual sonship with God completely. Therefore she declared, "Truth is revealed. It needs only to be practised." [94]

"THE EVANGEL OF CHRISTIAN SCIENCE"

The development of the metaphysics of Christian Science occupied Mrs. Eddy wholly during the nine years between her discovery in 1866 and the publication of *Science and Health* in 1875. Since she saw Christian Science as the reduction to statement of Divine Science, she saw the process of its revelation as inseparable from the process of its articulation. And the specific medium of its articulation was the written word. Throughout this period, her progress was registered in her writings — first Scriptural commentaries, then brief summaries of her teaching, finally the textbook *Science and Health*.

It was the writing of this book between 1872 and 1874 that Mrs. Eddy regarded as the culmination of the process of revelation which had been going on since 1866. The inspiration to begin work on it, she later said, came from the Bible. In the midst of a controversy with an ex-student who was publishing misleading comments on her teaching, she opened her Bible, according to her later recollection, to this passage from Isaiah:

92. *Mis.*, p. 69   93. *S&H.*, p. 107.   94. *Ibid.*, p. 174.

"Now go, write it before them in a table, and note it in a book, that it may be for the time to come for ever and ever." [95] Within a short time she had set to work, and her life from then on until the book was finished was wholly dedicated to its composition. One of her friends at the time wrote later of her efforts:

When convinced of the necessity of promulgating that which had been known to her, in book form, Mrs. Eddy secluded herself for over three years for that purpose, depriving herself of all but the bare necessities of life as she wrote. I have known her when nearly crushed with sorrow, but she wrote on. I have known her when friend after friend deserted her, but she wrote on. I have seen student after student bring ridicule and reproach upon her, but she still wrote on.[96]

In retrospect, Mrs. Eddy saw the writing of *Science and Health* as the basic task she had been given to accomplish. She intended it to be the textbook of Christian Science, giving as clear and complete statement to her vision as possible. *Science and Health* was, as she put it, the "evangel" of Christian Science.[97] She wanted there to be no doubt that it alone defined what her teaching was. Indisputably, it is the central document of the Christian Science movement. Mrs. Eddy did write a great deal besides *Science and Health*; indeed, her other published writings total over twice the number of pages in the textbook. But she never regarded any other work as truly definitive. She even saw the purpose of her largest publication other than *Science and Health,* her volume of *Miscellaneous Writings, 1883–1896,* as a preparation of her students' minds for a fuller understanding of the textbook.[98] When in 1893 she was asked to compose an address for the World's Parliament of Religions at Chicago, she commissioned a student to help her select major texts from the book as the most authoritative possible representation of her teaching.

Science and Health, Mrs. Eddy insisted, was not just the product of her own mentality; for she held that its composition had been divinely inspired. She recalled that she had no idea of what to write each day before putting pen to paper; and when she began "the influx of divine interpretation would pour in upon my spiritual sense as gloriously as the sunlight on the material senses." [99] At night when she read over her work for the day, so Mrs. Eddy later told a student, she wondered if she would

95. Peel, *Discovery*, p. 272.   96. Quoted in *Ibid.*, p. 284.
97. "The Christian Science Textbook" in *My.,* p. 113.
98. Mary Baker Eddy, "Notice," *CSJ,* IV (March 1897), 575.
99. *My.,* p. 114.

ever be able to understand it.[100] There is evidence that for the rest of her life Mrs. Eddy regarded *Science and Health* as the product of divine inspiration which she had to study in order to understand. In her later years she declared "I have been learning the higher meaning of this book since writing it." [101] And just before her death she told a student: "I feel I am just beginning to understand *Science and Health*." [102]

To Christian Scientists Mrs. Eddy commended the faithful and assiduous study of the textbook, not only because its statement of Christian Science was authoritative, but because she felt such study in itself tended to spiritualize thought. Referring to her writings, she advised Christian Scientists that "Sometimes she may strengthen the faith by a written text as no one else can." [103] She regarded the actual text of *Science and Health* as inseparable from its meaning: The Word was present in the words. Hence she was reiterating in a different context a point often made in aesthetics: that the substance of a creative idea cannot be divorced from its expression. For this reason Mrs. Eddy was extremely cautious concerning efforts to translate her work into foreign languages or to simplify it into more easily understandable form. She did authorize a translation of *Science and Health* into German, but only with the stipulation that the English text be printed opposite the translation. Mrs. Eddy remained adamant, however, in her opposition to attempts to simplify and condense her book so as to make it more accessible to readers who did not care to expend the effort its study required. The truths therein contained, she felt, could not be separated from their expression and remain as effective as when stated under the original impetus of revelation.

Mrs. Eddy maintained that *Science and Health* registered the revealed Truth uncontaminated by human hypotheses.[104] But for her it was the Truth thus registered and not the register itself that was absolute and divine. For she acknowledged that reducing Divine Science to human apprehension required her to use language that could not wholly express the truths she wanted to impart. "The chief difficulty in conveying the teachings of divine Science accurately to human thought," she found, "lies in this":

100. Martha Bogue Reminiscences, Archives.
101. *My.*, p. 114.
102. Edward Norwood Reminiscences, Archives.
103. *Man.*, p. 43.
104. Prefatory note to the *Christian Science Quarterly*, all editions.

that like all other languages, English is inadequate to the expression of spiritual conceptions and propositions, because one is obliged to use material terms in dealing with spiritual ideas. The elucidation of Christian Science lies in its spiritual sense, and this sense must be gained by its disciples in order to grasp the meaning of this Science.[105]

Mrs. Eddy expended a great deal of effort in formulating a precise vocabulary for her evolving teaching. An early student recalled that she would deliberate for days on the fitness of a word to express her meaning.[106] In later years when revising *Science and Health* she was just as scrupulous, and often pored over dictionaries for hours before changing a single word of her text. These later changes in her vocabulary, however, were more refinements in the expression of her doctrine than basic alterations in her teaching. But in the initial stages of her discovery, Mrs. Eddy's search for an adequate terminology was inseparable from the actual development of her thought. Her main problem was to adapt words already in currency to her own uses, gradually divorcing them from their old freight of associations so as to make them bearers of new but related meanings. This required that she not only find the right words but use them with precision and consistency, for otherwise she could not establish new contexts of association for them. The terms she uses are drawn from a wide variety of sources; and in her writing, one finds the language of traditional theology intermixed with terms and categories drawn from philosophy, physiology, medicine and scientific discourse. Yet the meaning of any of the terms she employs must be understood in terms of its specific use in the language of Christian Science.

Though Mrs. Eddy did use extreme care in formulating a vocabulary for her teaching, she never conducted anything like a systematic search among the disciplines from which her terms were ultimately derived. Rather, her vocabulary grew naturally out of her own experience and was gradually refined and fixed as she found the terms which best suited her needs. A few of her compound phrases — for example the term *mortal mind* — are unique to Christian Science. Most of the words she uses, however, can be traced to various sources in her background: to the Bible and orthodox Protestantism, of course; to the Enlightenment, the spirit of which she imbibed from her culture generally and her brother

---

105. *S&H.*, p. 349.
106. Wallace Wright, "Moral Science Alias Mesmerism," *Lynn Transcript,* Feb. 10, 1872. Wright's statement was not intended as a compliment, but was part of his argument against Mrs. Eddy's claim that her teaching was divinely inspired.

specifically; to Spiritualism and Swedenborgianism; and to the ideas of Quimby, with whom she was intermittently associated during the four years prior to 1866. These various strains of thought in her background have such complex interrelations among themselves that it is impossible to say from just which one of them she might have picked up a given term. The word *error,* for example, which she uses repeatedly, was also conspicuous in Quimby's vocabulary; yet Albert Baker, Mrs. Eddy's brother, had used it years before, and it was not an uncommon term in Enlightenment thought generally.

By the time that the third edition of *Science and Health* was published in 1882, Mrs. Eddy had worked out a language for Christian Science which thereafter remained fixed. The linguistic usages in her mature teaching are for the most part well-defined and invariable, and she tolerated no departure from them in her students. A good example is her insistence upon proper capitalization of words pertaining to God. Without an understanding of this point, she claimed, one cannot grasp Christian Science. In her teaching, Principle is the most comprehensive term that can be used for God. Hence, she insisted that this term cannot be used in the lower case nor in the plural number and still refer to Deity. And what we commonly term the principle of harmonious vibration in numbers or the principle of the inclined plane in mechanics, etc., must be understood as effects or emanations of "the one divine intelligent Principle." [107] Again, since Mrs. Eddy taught that God is Life and cannot be *in* limited forms, she insists that *in* is a term "obsolete in Science if used with reference to Spirit, or Deity." [108]

Actually, full comprehension of the language of *Science and Health* is inseparable from one's grasp of the ideas that the book contains. Not infrequently, new students of Christian Science were stymied by the unfamiliarity of the terms Mrs. Eddy used. "It was indeed 'the new tongue,'" wrote one of them, "for I could not understand it." [109] But gradually most of those who continued to work with *Science and Health* found that its strange terms took on more and more meaning. Mrs. Eddy cited as one consequence of "the inadequacy of material terms for metaphysical statements" the difficulty of "so expressing metaphysical ideas as to make them comprehensible to any reader, who has not personally demonstrated Christian Science as brought forth in my discovery." [110] To

107. *My.,* pp. 225–226.   108. *S&H.,* p. 588.
    109. Gottlieb A. Wizner, "How I Came into Christian Science and What It Has Done for Me," *CSS,* II (Sept. 21, 1899), 43.
    110. *S&H.,* p. 115.

Christian Scientists who did feel that they had demonstrated the truth of Mrs. Eddy's teaching, her language became rich with meaning.

Even after the vocabulary of *Science and Health* had reached the point of stasis, Mrs. Eddy continued to revise the book — until, in fact, the very month before her death. There were seven major revisions: in 1878, 1881, 1883, 1886, 1890, 1902, and 1906. In addition, Mrs. Eddy made numerous smaller changes from edition to edition. The last such alteration was made in November 1910, and involved the change of but one word: the title of the chapter "Christian Science and Spiritualism" was changed to "Christian Science *versus* Spiritualism." Though Mrs. Eddy had called her 1906 revision final, she apparently did not feel that her work with the book was finished; indeed, she told a student "My last changes in *Science and Health* may continue so long as I read the book." [111] By her instructions there have been no changes in *Science and Health* since she ceased reading it.

Mrs. Eddy expended a great deal of time and labor upon her periodic revisions of the textbook. Indeed, part of the reason for her retirement from Boston in 1889 was to devote herself to a thoroughgoing revision of the book for its fiftieth edition, which proved to be a landmark in its history. All the smaller changes in *Science and Health* were made with great scrupulousness. In Mrs. Eddy's later years, she adopted the procedure of first making a change in pencil in her copy, then notifying her publisher of it in a letter, then approving a proof sheet which he sent her, and finally authorizing a change in the plates. These small changes she considered exceedingly important. As she wrote to a student, ". . . sometimes the meaning is flashed forth like lightning by these little touches." [112]

To Mrs. Eddy's critics, the very fact that she continued to revise *Science and Health* seemed a virtual denial of her claim that the book was divinely inspired. As early as 1872 a former student who had turned against her, noting that she had drastically revised a manuscript summary of her teaching, commented sardonically, "So it seems that she has been obliged to correct the dictates (?) of inspiration, and remodel its work." And then he asked, "Does inspiration ever err?" [113] After *Science and Health* was

111. Mary Baker Eddy to Albert F. Conant, n.d., Longyear Foundation. Conant was the compiler of the concordance to *Science and Health*. His concern with Mrs. Eddy's projected changes in the book is understandable.
112. Quoted in Augusta E. Stetson, *Sermons and Other Writings on Christian Science* (New York, 1924), p. 31
113. Wright, "Moral Science Alias Mesmerism."

written, a number of Mrs. Eddy's critics, many of them ministers, took up the same line of attack. "There is an unexpected instability of arrangement," one of them noted, "in a book which its author claims is of the nature of 'final revelation.'"[114] This minister, who had devoted a lengthy book to a minute comparison of Mrs. Eddy's doctrine and Biblical texts, felt that in making her revisions she was deliberately trying to confuse her critics; for the change in the order of chapters and the pagination of *Science and Health* wrought havoc with his page by page analysis. "The whole thing," he concluded, "is subtle."[115]

Certainly Mrs. Eddy's revisions of *Science and Health* did constitute a denial that the book had been literally dictated, though she once said that it had. As she spoke of it, her book was inspired in the sense that through inspiration she clarified and elucidated her vision. The writing of *Science and Health,* she felt, was the culmination of her revelation. But in the years after it was first written she thought herself better able to express the essential vision she had first stated therein. Mrs. Eddy answered her critics, therefore, by saying that she had "revised *Science and Health* only to give a clearer and fuller expression of its original meaning."[116] As she grew in her perception of Christian Science, she became able to "show more minutely the way of Life and Love."[117] She felt that her revisions of *Science and Health* were not violating but fulfilling the vision that had informed the first writing of the work. "Its entire key note has grown steadily clearer and louder, and sweeter," she wrote. "Not a single vibration of its melodious strings has been lost."[118] A study of the major revisions of *Science and Health* does indicate that Mrs. Eddy never altered any important element of the original version, but simply improved the utterance of her message. It should be remembered that she had gone through nine years of intense development before completing the work. As we shall see later in this study, the subsequent development of the book does reflect in some degree the changes going on in the movement; but it can throw little light on her basic vision, the essentials of which had definitely been set forth by 1875.

But it is obvious that in style, not in substance, the edition of *Science and Health* that became standard at Mrs. Eddy's death contrasts strik-

114. H. F. Haldeman, *Christian Science in the Light of Holy Scripture* (New York, 1909), p. 145.
115. *Ibid.,* p. 147.
116. *S&H.,* p. 361.
117. Quoted in Stetson, *Sermons and Other Writings,* p. 31.
118. Mary Baker Eddy, *Footprints Fadeless,* Archives.

ingly with the first edition published thirty-five years before. For one thing, the tone of the book changed considerably. The autobiographical passages, colloquialisms, and references to contemporary events that appear in the first edition were gradually expunged. In addition, Mrs. Eddy considerably amplified her statement of Christian Science. As she continued to expound her teaching, she became better able to state her themes in various forms. In this way she adapted them to the comprehension of different mentalities and the requirements of varying situations. Often she inserted a particularly good phrase, sentence, or even paragraph from a shorter work into *Science and Health.* Also, the numerous controversies over her teaching caused Mrs. Eddy to clarify many points under attack. In the course of adding new materials and recasting what she had written earlier, Mrs. Eddy completely rearranged the contents of the book. Whereas the first edition contained eight chapters, the final edition contained eighteen. The final edition of *Science and Health,* which runs to six hundred pages, is a third again as large as the first.

Important as these differences were, the most obvious change wrought by the revisions of *Science and Health* lay in the character of its prose. Where the prose of the first edition is for the most part convoluted and at points confusing, that of the final version is lucid and coherent. Actually, Mrs. Eddy was far from inexperienced as a writer when she began her work in Christian Science. She had contributed verse, essays, and even one short story (called "Emma Clinton, A Tale of the Frontier") to various New England periodicals for many years prior to 1866. These pieces are all far from distinguished, but what is interesting is that they show Mrs. Eddy to have been more fluent in handling conventional subjects than in struggling to articulate Christian Science. In dealing with it she had to find a new voice; and it was only gradually over the years that she developed real ease and expressiveness in handling her subject.

Never, though, did she master the intricacies of grammar and punctuation. It has been pointed out that the first edition of *Science and Health* began with a dangling participle: "Leaning on the sustaining infinite with loving trust, the trials of today are brief, and tomorrow is big with blessings." The revised version of this statement was not only more grammatical but more direct: "To those leaning on the sustaining infinite, today is big with blessings." [119] Mark Twain made great sport of one unfortunate sentence from Mrs. Eddy's autobiography, in which she

119. Robert Peel, *Christian Science: Its Encounter with American Culture* (New York, 1955), p. 45. The references are to *S&H.,* first ed., p. 3; and *S&H.,* final ed., p. vii.

writes that after one of her sermons, "Many pale cripples went into the Church leaning on their crutches who came out carrying them on their shoulders." He concluded that ". . . none but a seasoned Christian Scientist can examine a literary animal of Mrs. Eddy's creation and tell which end of it the tail is on." [120] Wisely, Mrs. Eddy in her later years made sure that the editors of the Christian Science periodicals carefully corrected the articles she sent them for publication. And a number of her manuscripts bore such requests as "please punctuate."

In preparing the sixteenth edition of *Science and Health* in 1885, Mrs. Eddy engaged as editor a retired Unitarian clergyman named James Henry Wiggin. Just how much he contributed to the book has been one of many controversial questions in the highly polemical literature on Christian Science. That he did manage to bring a good deal of order to Mrs. Eddy's text is unquestionable. His major contribution lay in straightening out Mrs. Eddy's often confusing syntax.[121] And in this respect, as well as in grammatical construction, paragraphing, and punctuation, the sixteenth edition is far superior to any of its predecessors. But there is no evidence that Wiggin rewrote *Science and Health* from start to finish. This claim has been made, but only on the basis of what Wiggin's literary executor, who was most antagonistic to Christian Science, claimed that Wiggin had said to him.[122] In a letter written by Wiggin to Mark Twain in 1899, when Twain was gathering material for his articles on Christian Science, Wiggin referred to Mrs. Eddy in a derogatory manner and said that he had never been a believer in her teachings. But in regard to his services in editing her book, he claimed only to have "polished" it.[123] In a later note to Twain he spoke of the labor he expended in "weeding through and trying to lick into shape" Mrs. Eddy's "extraordinary" work, but not of rewriting it himself.[124] In any event, it is clear that Mrs. Eddy's characteristic expression remained indisputably her own. And whatever Wiggin's role in the revisions of *Science and Health* till 1891, she made many substantial changes in the book thereafter.

The teaching contained in *Science and Health,* as we shall see later, elicited an enormous amount of comment on the part of non-Christian

120. Mark Twain, *Christian Science* (New York, 1907), p. 119. The reference is to *Ret.,* p. 27.

121. See Peel, *Trial,* pp. 186–191 for a fuller account of Wiggin's work on *Science and Health* and association with Mrs. Eddy.

122. Livingston Wright, *New York World,* Nov. 6, 1906.

123. James Henry Wiggin to Mark Twain, Sept. 30, 1899. Mark Twain Papers, University of California at Berkeley.

124. Wiggin to Twain, Nov. 1, 1899.

Scientists — most of it adverse. But they seldom dwelt on the merits of the book as a literary work. The one conspicuous exception to this generalization was Mark Twain. Twain was highly critical of Mrs. Eddy's prose style in her writings other than *Science and Health*. His comment on her passage about the "pale cripples" is a case in point. Even though Twain found *Science and Health* "strange and frantic and uninterpretable," [125] he spoke of it as stylistically admirable. Its English, he wrote, "is clean, compact, dignified, almost perfect." [126] In view of the faults he found with Mrs. Eddy's other writings, Twain suggested that she had not written *Science and Health*. This idea could hardly have been more than playful, for he knew from his correspondence with Wiggin how the book had been polished through heavy revision.

Though Twain is on the whole justified in pointing out that Mrs. Eddy's prose in *Science and Health* is superior to that of her other writings, these other works do contain some of her best passages. One of the most consistent contrasts that emerge from a study of all Mrs. Eddy's writings is the difference between the character of her more personal comments and her treatment of the main theme of Christian Science. Her writing on the main subject is generally marked by directness and simplicity; but when she spoke in a more personal vein, she sometimes lapsed into much less vigorous and more sentimental style.[127] Mrs. Eddy's discussion of her early life in her autobiography *Retrospection and Introspection,* for instance, is quite flat and far from her best prose; but when she begins to deal with her discovery of Christian Science her tone changes almost as markedly as did her life at that point and becomes much more vigorous and compelling.[128]

The most obvious and individual characteristic of Mrs. Eddy's writing is not so much her language as such, but the way in which her ideas are organized. For she did not write in a linear-rational style, with one idea succeeding another in orderly progression. The statements that make up the paragraphs in *Science and Health* have a discernible relationship with each other in that they deal with a common theme, often indicated in a marginal heading. But they do not necessarily have any logical sequence, and in many cases there is no particular reason why one sentence should

125. Twain, *Christian Science,* p. 29.

126. *Ibid.,* p. 114.

127. See, for example, portions of her article "Voices of Spring," *Mis.,* pp. 329–332.

128. This transition becomes apparent at the end of the section "Marriage and Parentage," *Ret.,* p. 21.

be placed just where it is. In the chapter "Christian Science Practice," to take a rather extreme example, we find this paragraph:

> Prayers, in which God is not asked to heal but is besought to take the patient to Himself, do not benefit the sick. An ill-tempered, complaining, or deceitful person should not be a nurse. The nurse should be cheerful, orderly, punctual, patient, full of faith, — receptive to Truth and Love.[129]

It is difficult on first glance to see what Mrs. Eddy's statement on prayer here has to do with the sentences about requirements for a nurse that follow. The marginal heading "Aids in Sickness" indicates that there is an underlying relationship between the two topics; but it is not a relationship which Mrs. Eddy makes *rationally* apparent. She just says what she has to say and trusts the reader to make the necessary connections.

The organization of the individual chapters in *Science and Health* and of the book as a whole partakes of this non-linear quality. For the most part, the chapters of the book are composed of groups of paragraphs all related to some basic subject but most often not clearly related to each other. Mrs. Eddy shifted the chapters of *Science and Health* around from revision to revision, but she never ordered them in such a way as to provide the readers of her book with a systematic exposition of her thought. The apparent design of the arrangement of chapters in the final edition is to lead the reader gradually through the less difficult topics in Christian Science to Mrs. Eddy's treatment of her central metaphysics and its practical application. In two places, the eleven page "Platform" that concludes the chapter "Science of Being" and the full chapter called "Recapitulation," Mrs. Eddy summarized her teaching.[130] Yet these summaries are understandable only with reference to material presented in other parts of the book.

Mrs. Eddy's critics were often annoyed by the lack of organization in *Science and Health*. Roman Catholic commentators, naturally well-schooled in the art of systematic discourse, found her technique of repeatedly amplifying basic themes especially maddening. Yet this open, unstructured quality of *Science and Health* made it workable as a religious textbook. Understanding Christian Science requires that one grasp a few basic points and then see their full ramifications. Since Mrs. Eddy repeats these basic points again and again in varying contexts and terms, one picks them up quite naturally in reading the book. Further, many of her statements, though they have an organic relationship to their contexts,

129. *S&H.*, p. 395.   130. *Ibid.*, pp. 330–340; 465–497.

can easily be lifted out and stand on their own. If one opens *Science and Health* at random, his eyes will very likely fall on just such a statement. This fact makes hundreds of Mrs. Eddy's brief texts suitable for quotation and study. For students of Christian Science, such discrete texts are both propositionally true and inspirationally effective.

Still, Mrs. Eddy meant for *Science and Health* to serve an instrumental and not a sacramental function. She did not intend it to be treated by Christian Scientists as a vehicle of religious experience in itself, mediating between man and God; rather, she expected the fruits of their study of it to be manifest outside the reading of the book itself in healing and changed lives. If, through the study of *Science and Health,* men were awakened to the living meaning of the Scriptures, and translated the spiritual power it illustrated into fact in their own experience, then the textbook had fulfilled its intended function.

2

"The New Departure"

Mrs. Eddy maintained that her teaching was rooted in Christian revelation and that it constituted a discovery of the practical meaning of that revelation. But the ideas that *Science and Health* projected into the religious environment of late nineteenth century America cannot be understood within the framework of Protestant theology. All too often comentators on Christian Science have failed to recognize a point that the following pages should sustain: that Christian Science must be understood in its own terms, and cannot be comprehended merely as a variant upon already familiar theological ideas. In fact, Mrs. Eddy did not look upon her teaching as a theology at all but, in her terms, as a "new departure" — a spiritually empowered discovery of basic religious truth which challenged popular belief and conventional theological wisdom at almost every point. Quite naturally, Christian Science elicited a great deal of comment from the Protestant clergy, most of it negative. But the clerical criticism of Christian Science serve well to bring out the distinctiveness of its teaching, to highlight its differences from orthodoxy, and at points to indicate, if indirectly, its continuity with other forms of Christianity.

Note: Except when indicated otherwise, citations of Mrs. Eddy's works in Chapter Two refer to the final edition of the work cited, for only the final edition is considered by Christian Scientists to constitute standard Christian Science teaching. There is no basic idea expressed in any of these works, however, which was not a part of Christian Science at the beginning of the period we are considering. Further, most of the statements used in this chapter were included in Mrs. Eddy's writings by 1885, though in some cases in slightly different form from their final wording.

THE SOVEREIGNTY OF SPIRIT

In *Science and Health* Mrs. Eddy defined God as "The great I AM; the all-knowing, all-seeing, all-acting, all-wise, all-loving, and eternal; Principle; Mind; Soul; Spirit; Life; Truth; Love; all substance; intelligence." [1] Obviously this definition of God taken as a whole is far from what one might find in orthodox or liberal Protestant theology. It is important in understanding her meaning, however, to take seriously her affirmation in Tremont Temple that "after the manner of my fathers, so worship I God." In a similar vein, she once declared that she had not left the church in heart or in doctrine, but had only begun where the church left off.[2] Perhaps the best way to understand Mrs. Eddy's sense of God, is to view it in terms of her religious background in New England Congregationalism. So doing will make plainer what she rejected and what she retained in her theological heritage.

One characteristic term in Mrs. Eddy's writings establishes a direct link between Christian Science and her Calvinist background. Often she used the word *affections,* as when she wrote in the Daily Prayer from the *Manual,* "And may Thy Word enrich the affections of all mankind, and govern them." [3] This term was central to the thought of Jonathan Edwards, whose *The Nature of True Virtue* Mrs. Eddy read and marked, and it became a commonplace of the New England Theology which dominated her religious background. It points to a deep-seated piety typified by Edwards when he wrote in his "Personal Narrative," "I had vehement longings of soul after God and Christ, and after more holiness, wherewith my heart seemed to be full and ready to break." [4] By her own statement, Mrs. Eddy also felt that impulsion which she calls, in terms reminiscent of St. Augustine, "a hunger and thirst after divine things." It was this impulsion, she goes on to say, that drove her to "seek diligently for the knowledge of God as the one great and ever-present relief from human woe." [5]

1. *S&H.,* p. 587.
2. Mary Baker Eddy, "Message to the Mother Church for 1902" (Boston, 1902) 2.
3. *Man.,* p. 41.
4. Jonathan Edwards, "Personal Narrative," in *Jonathan Edwards: Representative Selections,* ed. and with an introduction by Clarence Faust and Thomas Johnson (New York, 1962), p. 61. See Perry Miller, *The New England Mind: The Seventeenth Century* (Cambridge, Mass., 1939), pp. 3–34, for a discussion of the "Augustinian Strain of Piety" discernible in Mrs. Eddy as well as her Puritan forbearers.
5. *Ret.,* p. 31.

This strain of piety was still very real in the rural New England of Mrs. Eddy's early years. The Puritan embers still glowed in such communities as Bow, New Hampshire, where she was born in 1821 and spent her first fifteen years. Wrote poetess Lucy Larcom of her girlhood in Beverly, Massachusetts, a community quite like Bow, in the 1820s:

> The religion of our fathers overhung us children like the shadow of a mighty tree against the truth of which we rested, while we looked up in wonder through the great boughs that half-hid and half revealed the sky. Some of the boughs were already decaying, so that perhaps we began to see a little more of the sky than our elders; but the tree was sound at its heart. There was life in it that can never be lost to the world.[6]

In a metaphor curiously akin to Miss Larcom's likening of Puritan faith to a mighty tree against which she and the other children of her family rested, Mrs. Eddy referred in her later years to the "falling leaves of old-time faiths." [7] She knew whereof she spoke, for in her youth she like Miss Larcom had seen these leaves just about to fall. During Mrs. Eddy's youth the spirit of New England Puritanism was becoming increasingly a thing of the past and its representatives but a remnant. Yet one cannot understand her character nor appreciate the background of her teaching without seeing how deeply her sensibility had been conditioned by the Puritan piety she imbibed in her early years. Though Mrs. Eddy eventually broke with her father's stern Calvinism, she continued to feel that those responsible for her early religious training possessed the spirit of true religion. In 1902 she recalled that ". . . their piety was the all-important consideration of their being, the original beauty of holiness that today seems to be fading so sensibly from our sight." [8]

Mrs. Eddy believed that through her discovery of Christian Science she was not rejecting the piety that these men possessed, but rather was taking their faith into deeper latitudes. She did, however, emphatically reject what she called her father's "relentless theology," which, she wrote, "emphasized belief in a final judgment-day, in the danger of endless punishment, and in a Jehovah merciless toward unbelievers." [9] The crisis which marked her rejection of this "relentless theology" occurred when she was to be examined for membership in the Congregational Church at the age of seventeen. During the interview she repudiated the doctrine of predestination, declaring her unwillingness to believe in a God so arbitrary that

6. Lucy Larcom, *A New England Girlhood Outlined from Memory* (Boston, 1889), p. 75.
7. *Mis.,* p. 331.   8. *Mess. '01,* pp. 32–33.   9. *Ret.,* p. 13.

He could save her while sending her brothers and sisters, who had not yet professed conversion, to hell. For some time before, as Mrs. Eddy later recalled, she had been deeply distressed by this doctrine. So agitated did she become by her father's efforts to compel her assent to it that she became ill. And it required the prayers and solace of her mother, a gentler soul, to calm and heal her. After this event, she said, "the 'horrible decree' of predestination — as John Calvin rightly called his own tenet — forever lost its power over me." [10]

The rebellion of a sensitive young person against the Calvinist conception of a God of wrath as well as of love was certainly a familiar enough phenomenon in American religious life during this period. Indeed, to a a large extent the theological liberalism that was winning its way when Christian Science came into prominence was traceable to a number of successful rebellions against stark Calvinist orthodoxy. But Protestant liberalism, with its cheerful immanentist view of Deity, dispensed with far more than the doctrine of predestination. For liberalism tended to sacrifice the idea of God's sovereignty in emphasizing the beneficence of His fatherliness.

The concept of the sovereignty of God underlay Puritan piety. It was actually far more essential to Calvinism than the doctrine of predestination, which can best be understood as a logical corollary to the more basic concept. Edwards found it necessary to subdue his natural objection to the doctrine in order to declare unreservedly, "Absolute sovereignty is what I love to ascribe to God." [11] Later, his heir, Samuel Hopkins, carried the Calvinist logic to its extreme by posing and answering affirmatively the question: Would you be willing to be damned for the glory of God? But it was the divine sovereignty, and not the doctrine of predestination, which remained central in both instances. The sense of the divine sovereignty so fundamental to the Calvinist spirit is clearly exemplified in the following passage from the Westminister Confession:

There is but one only living and true God, who is infinite in being and perfection, a most pure spirit, invisible, without body, parts or passions, immutable, immense, eternal, incomprehensible, almighty, most wise, most holy, most free, most absolute, working all things according to the counsel of his own immutable and most righteous will, for his own glory; most living and most gracious, merciful, long-suffering, abundant in goodness and truth, forgiving iniquity, transgression, and sin; and with all most just and terrible in

10. *Ibid.,* pp. 13–14.
11. Edwards, "Personal Narrative," p. 59.

his judgments; hating all sin, and who will by no means clear the guilty.[12]

Mrs. Eddy learned this creed as a child. Later she wrote in *Science and Health* that she could still accept the creed if it were spiritually understood." [13] She felt that through revelation she had grasped the reality of God's sovereignty and supremacy, to which the creed gave but partial statement. "In this new departure of metaphysics," she wrote of her teaching, "God is regarded as more absolute, supreme; . . . God's fatherliness as Life, Truth, and Love, makes His sovereignty glorious." [14]

What is this "new departure" through which God is regarded as "more absolute, supreme"? It is in the first instance a departure from the anthropomorphism so well exemplified in the Calvinist conception of God. Mrs. Eddy defined anthropomorphism as a "mortally mental attempt to reduce Deity to corporeality" [15] and repeatedly expressed her opposition to any conception of God which seemed to humanize, circumscribe, or limit Him. In particular, she found intolerable any view of God which attributed to Him responsibility for imperfection of any sort.[16] The effect of such false views of God on the race, she felt, was incalculable. For a limited sense of God's goodness "limits human thought and action in their goodness, and assigns them mortal fetters in the outset." [17] To Mrs. Eddy, human misconceptions of God were responsible not only for disease and sin in individual lives, but, in the final analysis, for all the historical woes of mankind. "Tyranny, intolerance, and bloodshed, wherever found," she observed, "arise from the belief that the infinite is formed after the pattern of mortal personality, passion, and impulse." [18]

Mrs. Eddy's insistent rejection of anthropomorphic views of Deity is one of the key points that differentiates her theology from Protestant orthodoxy. Not surprisingly, her clerical critics returned to it again and again in their attacks on Christian Science. Regarding Mrs. Eddy's contention that pleading with God as one would with a human being perpetuates the belief that He is humanly circumscribed, a Southern Baptist clergyman said: "I go to the Lord and ask Him to do something for me, he does it. I

12. Williston Walker, *The Creeds and Platforms of Congregationalism* (New York, 1893), p. 370.

13. *S&H.*, p. 351.   14. *Mis.*, p. 234.

15. *S&H.*, p. 517.   16. *Ibid.*, p. 119.

17. Mary Baker Eddy, "The People's Idea of God: Its Effect on Health and Christianity. A Sermon Delivered at Boston" (Boston, 1886), p. 3.

18. *S&H.*, p. 94.

interceded for others and myself, and he proves himself to be a prayer-hearing and prayer-answering God. Because I plead with him, I am circumscribing him according to this doctrine." [19] Indeed he was, and the difference between the two points of view is clear. Little wonder, then, that Mrs. Eddy's Protestant and Catholic critics often found her conception of God unintelligible or at the very least quite abstract. Throughout the critical literature on Christian Science one finds Mrs. Eddy's conception of God referred to in such terms as "an impalpable, impossible, unthinkable thing, which is not even a thing; everywhere and nowhere and nothing at all";[20] "a principle without a personality, love without a lover, and life without a living Being";[21] or "a misty, unconscious abstraction." [22]

One interesting point about Protestant criticisms of Mrs. Eddy's concept of God as too abstract was that they echoed the language of clerical attacks on Transcendentalism a half-century before. In a review of Emerson's *Essays* in 1841, two conservative theologians from Princeton Theological Seminary noted with horror that Emerson's God was "a vague personification of abstract principle . . . which is everything and it might with equal significance be added nothing." [23] It is important to note that Mrs. Eddy had criticized Emerson on the same grounds. In the margin of her copy of *Nature* she observed that he "put so much reason into Mind, and so much philosophy into Science, that he lost the true sense of Spirit, God." [24] In a similar spirit, she urged a congregation in 1885: "Let us have a clearing up of abstractions. Let us come into the presence of Him who removeth all iniquities, and healeth all our diseases." [25]

As the Biblical language of this statement suggests, Mrs. Eddy always felt that hers was the God of Abraham, Isaac, and Jacob, and not the God of the philosophers. Indeed, though Mrs. Eddy did teach that God was not a person in the anthropomorphic sense, she did say that God *could* be understood as Person if the term was carefully used. "If the term personality, as applied to God, means infinite personality," she wrote, "then

19. Ben Cox, "Christian Science Exposed" (Little Rock, Ark., 1909), p. 5.

20. Haldeman, *Christian Science,* p. 133.

21. William H. P. Faunce, "The Philosophy of Christian Science," in *Searchlights on Christian Science* (New York, 1899), p. 108.

22. William R. Huntington, "A Clergyman's Views on Christian Science," *New York Journal,* July 14, 1901.

23. James W. Alexander and Albert Dod, "Emerson's Essays," *Biblical Repetory and Princeton Review,* XIII (Oct. 1841), 72–73.

24. Quoted in Peel, *Christian Science,* p. 102.

25. *Mis.,* p. 174.

God *is* infinite *Person*, — in the sense of infinite personality, but not in the lower sense." [26] In Christian Science, the divine nature is understood to be definite and apprehensible; and in this sense one can speak of His personality. "In divine Science," Mrs. Eddy wrote, "God is 'altogether lovely,' and consistently conceivable as the personality of infinite Love . . ." [27] Though Mrs. Eddy rejected anthropomorphism, she always spoke of man as having an active and felt relationship with his divine source. And in opposing the conception of God as a physical person or a personal Spirit, she by no means dismissed all the conceptions of His nature associated with personality. Hence her qualified but genuine acceptance of the idea of God as Person.

Mrs. Eddy did maintain that much that passed for religious sentiment was ephemeral, the product of excitement and physical sensation. Yet she taught, too, that God and man are completely distinct and that man could know God as God, hold audience with Spirit through prayer, and feel the power of the divine presence. Of the prophets hearing the voice of God she wrote: "Before human knowledge dipped to its depth into a false sense of things, — into belief in material origins which discard the one Mind and true source of being, — it is possible that the impressions from Truth were as distinct as sound, and that they came as sound to the primitive prophets." [28] For men now it is wholly possible to feel that God is present as our helper, that "He pities us. He has mercy on us, and guides every event of our careers." [29] Though Mrs. Eddy condemned pleading with God as with a person, she did not regard petitioning Him for spiritual benefits as necessarily invalid; for she wrote, "When a hungry heart petitions the divine Father-Mother God for bread, it is not given a stone, — but more grace, obedience, and love." [30]

This term "Father-Mother," Mrs. Eddy said, "is the name for Deity, which indicates His tender relationship to His spiritual creation." [31] She was not the first to emphasize the idea of the Motherhood of God. It was held by the Shakers and was a prominent theme in the thought of Theodore Parker. For Mrs. Eddy, however, this idea had a special significance. It was closely associated in her thought with the sustaining presence of Holy Spirit, or the Comforter; and in this sense she saw Christian Science as the revelation of the Motherhood of God. Indeed, in *Science and Health* she wrote, "In divine Science we have not as much authority for considering God masculine, as we have for considering Him feminine, for Love

---

26. *S&H.*, p. 116.
29. *Un.*, p. 3.

27. *Mess. '01*, pp. 6–7.
30. *Mis.*, p. 127.

28. *S&H.*, pp. 213–214.
31. *S&H.*, p. 332.

imparts the clearest idea of Deity." [32] In one chapter of the third edition of the book she had gone even further, speaking of God in the feminine as *She*.[33] This practice was discontinued by the next edition. But it was a temporary way of pointing out what for Mrs. Eddy was a permanent fact: God's loving presence, to which we can respond with the appellation Mother as well as Father.

In one more sense Mrs. Eddy entertained an idea of God usually associated with His personality. For Christian Science has a definite conception of the Trinity. In the orthodox Christian concept of the Trinity, Mrs. Eddy found a glaring instance of the anthropomorphism she opposed. She attacked it on the grounds that the "theory of three persons in one God (that is, a personal Trinity or Tri-Unity) suggests polytheism, rather than the one ever-present I AM." [34] Yet she reappraised rather than rejected the concept of God as triune, holding that God could be known in different *offices* but not as three *persons* in one. In the "Platform" which summarizes her teaching she wrote:

Life, Truth, and Love constitute the triune Person called God,—that is, the triply divine Principle, Love. They represent a trinity in unity, three in one,—the same in essence, though multiform in office: God the Father-Mother; Christ the spiritual idea of sonship; divine Science or the Holy Comforter. These three express in divine Science the threefold, essential nature of the infinite. They also indicate the divine Principle of scientific being, the intelligent relation of God to man and the universe.[35]

Life, Truth, and Love, corresponding to Father, Son, and Holy Ghost, constitute the trinity of Christian Science — as Mrs. Eddy put it, "the individuality of the infinite Person or divine intelligence called God." [36] Mrs. Eddy did not refer to the Trinity as such, except in reference to classical Christian doctrine. Yet the frequency with which she spoke of God by the conjunction of these three words indicates that her conception of Him is, in an important sense, triune. And for Christian Scientists to speak of Life, Truth, and Love in one phrase is as natural as for trinitarian Christians to speak of Father, Son, and Holy Ghost. Of course, Mrs. Eddy's concept of the trinity as representing three offices of one God was not her special property. Edwards had used the term *offices* in the same sense.[37] Horace Bushnell discussed the trinity in terms of God's modes of self-manifestation;[38] and Karl Barth has referred to God's triune

32. *Ibid.,* p. 517.   33. *Ibid.,* 3rd ed.   34. *S&H.,* p. 256.
35. *Ibid.,* pp. 331–332.   36. *Mess. '01,* p. 7.
37. Jonathan Edwards, "An Essay on the Trinity," in Faust, pp. 375–381.
38. Smith, ed., *Horace Bushnell,* pp. 196–219.

nature as His ways of being God.[39] But Mrs. Eddy does depart from any other concept of the trinity through her identification of Father, Son, and Holy Ghost with Life, Truth, and Love, understood as deific synonyms.

Mrs. Eddy's use of the seven deific synonyms — Principle, Mind, Soul, Spirit, in addition to Life, Truth, and Love — is one of the most crucial aspects of her teaching and warrants close examination. In referring to God she most generally makes use of one of these terms. But at several points in her writing she takes pains to prevent misconceptions of her intent in so doing. These synonyms, she insisted, refer to "one absolute God" and were intended to express "the nature, essence, and wholeness of Deity." [40] In no sense did Mrs. Eddy intend her use of these terms to indicate that she held God to be fragmented or divisible. Nor did their use imply that she believed it possible to reduce this "one absolute God" to a precise set of terms, for she maintained that God's nature was "indefinable as a whole." [41] Her synonyms were not, therefore, intended to be fixed definitions, but terms which could best communicate her understanding of the divine nature in all its fullness and multiplicity.

Of all her synonyms, the term *Principle* is perhaps most helpful in understanding Mrs. Eddy's conception of God. She recognized that her characterization of God as Principle might give the false impression that she thought of Him as a blind impersonal abstraction. And it is true that she used this term less frequently than most of her other synonyms. Yet it served well to indicate her rejection of anthropomorphism and to point to the way in which the other synonyms are used. In Christian Science God is not a person who loves, but *is* Love; He is not just the giver of life, but *is* Life; He does not have a mind, He *is* Mind — and so on with the other terms she employed. As deific synonyms they are intended to indicate not His attributes, but His nature as the divine Principle of all.

It must be carefully understood, however, that Mrs. Eddy's characterization of God in terms of these seven synonyms changes the sense in which these words are usually employed. For she attributes to Life, Mind, or Principle, *etc.,* all the infinitude, immutability, and absoluteness that the Westminister Confession ascribes to God. The term *Life* provides a good example; for Mrs. Eddy said that more than any other synonym,

39. For an excellent discussion of Barth's and other recent views of the Trinity see Claude Welch, *In This Name: The Doctrine of the Trinity in Contemporary Theology* (New York, 1959).

40. *S&H.*, p. 465.

41. *Ibid.,* p. 213.

this word conveys the idea of God in Christian Science and that "every other name for the Supreme Being, if properly employed, has the signification of Life." [42] Certainly, by capitalizing this term Mrs. Eddy did not mean to deify that which we commonly call human life — quite the reverse. For she intended to signify that this conception of life as limited, as in or of matter, constitutes a false sense or misconception of what Life really is. "Because Life is God," she wrote, "Life must be eternal, self-existent. Life is the everlasting I AM, the Being who was and is and shall be, whom nothing can erase." [43] In contrast, she noted that "prevalent theories insist that Life, or God, is one and the same with material life so-called. . . . They claim that to be life which is but the objective state of material sense, — such as the structural life of the tree and of material man, — and deem this the manifestation of the one Life, God." [44] These theories, she insisted, though they seem to be supported by the evidence before the senses, must be rejected on the testimony of revelation that God is the only Life.

Mrs. Eddy, then, is not, emphatically not, saying that life is God. She is saying that God is Life. In other words, we do not diminish our conception of God by identifying Him with our present limited concept of life: we bring that concept radically into question in the light of the revealed fact that God is the only Life. And the same point applies to all other deific synonyms that Mrs. Eddy uses. Note in the following definition of God from *Science and Health* how the four adjectives identified with God's nature explicitly modify the synonyms: "God is incorporeal, divine, supreme, infinite Mind, Spirit, Soul, Principle, Life, Truth, Love." [45] Mrs. Eddy understood God to be absolutely one, infinite and indivisible: He cannot be limited nor confined to a form. "This is a leading point in the Science of Soul," she wrote, "that Principle is not in its idea. Spirit, Soul, is not confined in man, and is never in matter." [46] As she more fully elucidated this point:

God is divine Life, and Life is no more confined to the forms which reflect it than substance is in its shadow. If life were in mortal man or material things, it would be subject to their limitations and would end in death. Life is Mind, the creator reflected in His creations. If He dwelt within what He creates, God would not be reflected but absorbed, and the Science of being would be forever lost through a mortal sense, which falsely testifies to a beginning and an end.[47]

42. *Ret.*, p. 59.   43. *S&H.*, pp. 289–290.   44. *Ibid.*, p. 283.
45. *Ibid.*, p. 465.   46. *Ibid.*, p. 467.   47. *Ibid.*, p. 331.

Mrs. Eddy did often speak of God as ever present and of spiritual power as always at hand. But she did not speak of the divine presence *in* anything, and she once took liberal theologian Lyman Abbot to task for stating, characteristically, that "God, Spirit, is ever in universal nature." Quoting this assertion, Mrs. Eddy asked, "How can Spirit be constantly passing out of mankind by death — for the universe includes man?" [48] To her God included the expression of Himself, but in no sense was He included in it. Twentieth century theology was to witness a revolt against the liberal conception of a God immanent in natural as well as historical processes in the form of Neo-orthodoxy. In one sense, Mrs. Eddy may be identified as a precursor of this movement, since she continually insisted upon God's unconfinable otherness (to use a good Neo-orthodox term) to all that He creates. But she did so not on grounds of His transcendence, in the classical sense which Barth and others revived, but on grounds of His sovereignty as one infinite God, unconfinable to finite forms.

Since Mrs. Eddy denied that God is in any sense within finite form, she regarded herself as a strict anti-pantheist — a designation that holds true if we take into account the particular construction which she puts on the term. In the *Institutes,* Calvin referred to the pantheistic doctrine which held the creator to be divided up and infused into his creatures as so many souls as "extreme madness." [49] But with her more impersonal view of God as Life, Soul, and Mind, Mrs. Eddy could claim that the very idea of matter as living, sentient, or intelligent was in itself a form of pantheism. Indeed, she declared, "I am the only anti-pantheist, for I see that God, Spirit, is not in His reflection any more than the sun is in the light that comes to this earth by reflection." [50]

Though Mrs. Eddy was clearly not a material pantheist, she could easily but wrongly be interpreted as a spiritual pantheist — one who believes that God and creation are not only alike spiritually but are not distinct from one another. For she did speak of God as All, writing for example, that "Allness is the measure of the infinite, and nothing less can express God." [51] Were this statement taken as an expression of spiritual

---

48. Mary Baker Eddy, "Christian Science Versus Pantheism" (Boston, 1898), p. 12.
49. Robert T. Kerr, ed., *A Compend of the Institutes of the Christian Religion by John Calvin* (Philadelphia, 1934), p. 32.
50. Quoted in William Lyman Johnson, *The History of the Christian Science Movement,* II (Brookline, Mass., 1926), 70.
51. *S&H.,* p. 336.

pantheism, it would certainly imply that man is either nothing or is himself God. It would also contradict her fundamental assertion that God is not in or identified with that which He creates. Though Mrs. Eddy's clerical critics often attacked her teaching on these grounds, her concept of the allness of God does not really imply a spiritual pantheism, though on the surface it would seem to do so. What it does suggest is that God has absolutely no opposite and that every phase of reality is embraced in the divine infinitude. As she wrote in her short book *Unity of Good:*

God is All-in-all. Hence He is in Himself only, in His own nature and character, and is perfect being, or consciousness. He is all the Life and Mind there is or can be. Within Himself is every embodiment of Life and Mind.

If He is All, He can have no consciousness of anything unlike Himself; because, if He is omnipresent, there can be nothing outside of Himself.[52]

It is obvious that in many ways this whole conception of the nature of God marks a departure from Protestant orthodoxy. Yet Mrs. Eddy felt that her conception of the divine nature honored Deity more than any other and declared in all sincerity that " 'after the manner of my fathers, so worship I God,' "[53] however much objection to such a statement orthodox Protestants might raise. For she felt that Christian Science had advanced beyond limited personal conceptions of God and proclaimed His sovereign allness as Life, Truth, and Love, unconfinable to finite form. Indeed, Mrs. Eddy went so far as to state she believed in God "more than do most Christians, for I have no faith in any other thing or being."[54]

THE ORDER OF SPIRIT

In a note on Christian Science in his massive *Church Dogmatics,* the eminent Protestant theologian Karl Barth conceded that Mrs. Eddy's teaching does have several features reminiscent of the New Testament. But he argued that its basic view of God and His relation to reality invalidates it as a Christian teaching. "God is indeed the basis of all reality," Barth wrote,

but He is not the only reality. As creator and Redeemer He loves a reality which is different from Himself, which depends upon Him, but which is not merely a reflection nor the sum of His powers and thoughts, but which has in face of Him an independent and distinctive nature and is the subject

52. *Un.,* p. 3.   53. *Mis.,* p. 96.   54. *Un.,* p. 48.

of its own history, participating in its own perfection and subjected to its own weakness.[55]

Exploring the implications of this statement brings us to a — one might say *the* — basic distinction between Christian Science and Protestantism. In both, God as Creator is understood to be distinct from His creation; God is God, and cannot be identified with man or the universe. But past this point there is decided disagreement as to the nature of God's creation and His relation to it. Protestantism in almost all of its forms regards man and the universe as not only separate in existence but different in nature from the Creator. Creation, including man, is viewed as finite and imperfect, and as corresponding in actual existence to common sense testimony. Christian Science, however, maintains that since God is the Principle of all real being, the true nature of man and the universe can be known only in the light of the divine nature as revealed. Therefore, it challenges common sense testimony and holds that "in Science" man and the universe are, like God, perfect, spiritual, and eternal.

Mrs. Eddy's major difference with Protestant and Roman Catholic theology as well lies in the radicalism of this ontological claim, and one can best understand the distinctive character of her teaching in ontological terms. In *Science and Health* she quoted a good short definition of ontology as " 'the science of the necessary constituents and relations of all beings' " and says that it "underlies all metaphysical practice." [56] "We must abandon pharmaceutics," Mrs. Eddy declared, "and take up ontology, — the science of real being." [57] Significantly, the lengthy chapter in *Science and Health* in which her central metaphysics is most fully explored is titled "Science of Being." And the most pithy statement of her teaching, her "first plank in the platform of Christian Science," [58] she called "The Scientific Statement of Being."

Indeed, Mrs. Eddy's whole conception of God may be understood as ontological. Unlike Paul Tillich, for whom God *is* Being, Mrs. Eddy did not use the term *being* for God. Yet she did write that God is "the source and condition of all existence" [59] and that "being and Deity are inseparable." [60] And she employed her synonyms for God with what can be called ontological comprehensiveness. That is, they include everything basic to being. In her usage, every real quality of experience is derived from and is an expression of one of them. Mind, Mrs. Eddy maintained,

55. Karl Barth, *Church Dogmatics,* III (Edinborough, 1936–1961), 344–345.
56. *S&H.,* p. 460.   57. *Ibid.,* p. 129.   58. *Mis.,* p. 21.
59. *S&H.,* p. 181.   60. *Ibid.,* p. 554.

is the source of all true intelligence; order has its origin in Principle; beauty is the reflection of Soul. Summarizing this important aspect of her conception of God in *Science and Health,* she wrote:

To grasp the reality and order of being in its Science, you must begin by reckoning God as the divine Principle of all that really is. Spirit, Life, Truth, Love, combine as one,—and are the Scriptural names for God. All substance, intelligence, wisdom, being, immortality, cause, and effect belong to God. These are His attributes, the eternal manifestations of the infinite divine Principle, Love. No wisdom is wise but His wisdom; no truth is true, no love is lovely, no life is Life but the divine; no good is, but the good God bestows.[61]

This conception of God as the animating and sustaining Principle of all reality differs markedly from the understanding of Him as the Creator of an objectively existent physical universe. Though creation is separate from the Creator in the sense of being distinct from Him, it is inseparable in *nature* from the divine. Mrs. Eddy repeatedly insists upon the point that God's expression must be like Him — that there is an unbreakable continuity between the nature of the divine Principle and of its manifestations. Acknowledging the absoluteness and allness of God as Spirit, Mrs. Eddy insists, requires us to challenge our common sense conception of reality as material on the basis of testimony derived from revelation. For according to the theology of Christian Science, the nature of man and the universe, like that of God, must be known through revelation, since they can be understood only as His expression.

Mrs. Eddy's use of the term *Christ* becomes of special importance here. For Christ, she wrote, "illustrates the coincidence, or spiritual agreement, between God and man in His image." [62] Christ in Christian Science is the divine pattern or ideal of perfect manhood — that which all men have in common as sons of God. As such, it is one office of God, the divine nature understood as the actuality of man's being; and at points Mrs. Eddy uses the term *Christ* interchangeably with the deific synonym Truth. And it is the power of Truth, Mrs. Eddy constantly emphasized, which alone redeems and heals mortals from the ills of the flesh. Jesus, she claimed, fully lived and demonstrated the Christ, embodying it so completely that his name is uniquely coupled with the Christ. But the spiritual possibilities that he lived are open to every man in proportion as he understands his genuine selfhood, which is inseparable from the Christ ideal. Mrs. Eddy's understanding of Christ, therefore, underscores the point in Chris-

61. *Ibid.,* p. 275.   62. *Ibid.,* pp. 332–333.

tian Science that man's nature is inseparable from the divine — that he is not a finite creature estranged from his divine source, but the spiritual son of God.

To indicate that "in Science" man and the universe partake of the divine nature alone, Mrs. Eddy speaks of them as the reflection, manifestation, and expression of God. Strictly speaking, one cannot say in Christian Science that man reflects, manifests, or expresses God, for this would imply that he has independent entity as an acting subject who may or may not reflect, manifest, or express his Maker. But for Mrs. Eddy, man's being is *substantively* reflection, manifestation, and expression — without the possibility of being anything else. And as such, man, as well as all the facts of creation, is absolutely necessary to God. As Mrs. Eddy wrote, "God, without the image and likeness of Himself, would be a nonentity, or Mind unexpressed. He would be without a witness or proof of His own nature." [63] God, then, *requires* man and the universe to objectify His nature as God. And if they have no being apart from Him, so too, He has no being apart from them.

This conception of the relation of God to man and creation cannot be understood in terms of the traditional theological categories of either immanence or transcendence. God is other than man and the universe, but He is certainly not transcendent to them, in the sense of being remote, apart, or of a different nature; for they are His expression. At the same time, He is not immanent in man or nature; for if God is man's Life, Soul, and Mind, He is not reducible to a plurality of lives, minds, spirits. Were this the case, God would be both divisible and limited, therefore less than God. "The term *souls* or *spirits*," writes Mrs. Eddy, "is as improper as the term *gods*. Soul or Spirit signifies Deity and nothing else. There is no finite soul nor spirit. Soul or Spirit means only one Mind, and cannot be rendered in the plural." [64]

On this basis, Christian Science breaks radically with the Protestant picture of man. In Protestant theology, both orthodox and liberal, man is considered to be in part a material creature, in part a spiritual one. Hence Protestantism looks upon man in terms of a duality between spirit and flesh, mind and matter, soul and body. Man's soul or spirit is thought of as his animating essence, the divine spark within him which continues after death. This theological view underlies and is congruent with the

63. *Ibid.*, p. 303.   64. *Ibid.*, p. 466.

Cartesian concept that mind indwells the material organism and directs its movements. But Mrs. Eddy insists that man is not matter and mind united, not a body with a soul inside, but one thing alone — and that one thing wholly spiritual.

In clear contradistinction to this view, the Protestant critics of Christian Science, accepting the view of God as the creator of the physical world, affirmed that man's fleshy nature, his creatureliness, is a real aspect of his being. Though Protestants placed ultimate value on man's soul, they marveled at the design of his body created from dust. This body of flesh and bones, declared the Reverend H. F. Haldeman in his book *Christian Science in the Light of Holy Scriptures,* is the "most perfect piece of architecture in which life ever dwelt, the most perfect piece of machinery which ever responded to the human will." [65] Another critic of Christian Science, the Reverend Henry Varley, cited the very passage from the book of *Genesis* that Mrs. Eddy felt portrayed the *false* concept of man as Scriptural evidence against her teaching. Commenting on the text, "The Lord God formed man out of the dust of the ground," he wrote: "Man is declared, so far as his body is concerned, to be formed of matter; he indwells a material house, a body." [66]

For Mrs. Eddy, the revealed understanding of man's nature and relationship to God stands in glaring contrast with the mortal sense of him. The view of man based on the material senses pictures him as having been born into matter and destined to die out of it; but "Divine Science," Mrs. Eddy wrote, "rolls back the clouds of error with the light of Truth, and lifts the curtain on man as never born and as never dying, but as co-existent with his creator." [67] The mortal view of man declares that he is a material organism; but Christian Science holds that "Man is not matter; he is not made up of brain, blood, bones, and other material elements . . . Man is idea, the image of Love; he is not physique." [68] The mortal view of man claims that he is limited in his capacities; but Mrs. Eddy insists that "Man is God's image and likeness; whatever is possible to God, is possible to man *as God's reflection.*" [69] The mortal view of man pictures him as tending toward evil-doing; but Christian Science maintains that "The real man cannot depart from holiness, nor can God, by whom man is evolved, engender the capacity or freedom to sin." [70] In short, the mortal

65. Haldeman, *Christian Science,* pp. 25–26.
66. Henry Varley, *Christian Science Examined* (New York, 1898), p. 37.
67. *S&H.,* p. 557.   68. *Ibid.,* p. 475.   69. *Mis.,* p. 183.
70. *S&H.,* p. 475.

view of man holds him to be imperfect, while Christian Science holds him to be the perfect son of a perfect God. Mrs. Eddy summarized her position in these terms:

> God is the creator of man, and, the divine Principle of man remaining perfect, the divine idea or reflection, man, remains perfect. Man is the expression of God's being. If there ever was a moment when man did not express the divine perfection, then there was a moment when man did not express God, and consequently a time when Deity was unexpressed—that is, without entity. If man has lost his perfection, then he has lost his perfect Principle, the divine Mind. If man ever existed without this perfect Principle or Mind, then man's existence was a myth.
>
> The relations of God and man, divine Principle and idea, are indestructible in Science; and Science knows no lapse from nor return to harmony, but holds the divine order or spiritual law, in which God and all that He creates are perfect and eternal, to have remained unchanged in its eternal history.[71]

The perfection of which Mrs. Eddy speaks in this passage is not to be understood as a static condition of abstract bliss in which development has forever ceased. Perfecion for her was the *standpoint* from which man acted, not the cessation of action. Man's spiritual perfection in Christian Science consists in his unimpairable capacity to manifest ever more of what God has made spiritually possible to him. Mrs. Eddy writes that "God expresses in man the infinite idea forever developing itself, broadening and rising higher and higher from a boundless basis." [72] In answering the question, "Is there infinite progression with man after the destruction of mortal mind," she wrote that, ". . . man is forever unfolding the endless beatitudes of Being." [73] This unfolding is not, of course, identified with the mortal sense of progression through cycles of birth, maturity, and decay. For it points to man's uninterruptible spiritual capacity to manifest ever more of his spiritual identity.

Similarly, the real character of that which men call nature in Christian Science can be known only through revelation. "The universe, like man," Mrs. Eddy insisted, "is to be interpreted by Science from its divine Principle, God, and then it can be understood." [74] Thus understood, the universe is not a static physical creation, but the unfolding of the varying expressions and manifestations of God. Mrs. Eddy did not believe that there was a once-and-for-all creation in time, but rather that "Creation is ever appearing and must ever continue to appear from the nature of its

71. *Ibid.*, pp. 470–471.   72. *Ibid.*, p. 258.   73. *Mis.*, p. 82.
74. *S&H.*, p. 124.

inexhaustible source." [75] Commenting on the text from *Genesis:* "In the beginning God created the heaven and the earth," she wrote: "There is but one creator and one creation. This creation consists of the unfolding of spiritual ideas and their identities, which are embraced in the infinite Mind and forever reflected. These ideas range from the infinitesimal to infinity, and the highest ideas are the sons and daughters of God." [76] She excludes no phase of life from her concept of that which is spiritually natural. Beasts, she asserted, are part of the spiritual order of creation, though they are lesser reflections of God than man.[77] "All is Mind and its manifestation," she wrote, "from the rolling of worlds, in the most subtle ether, to a potato patch." [78]

But these formations of Mind, she insisted, are not material. Then what is their nature, and how can they be considered to have any discernible existence at all? Mrs. Eddy referred to them as *ideas.* "Mind creates His own likeness in ideas," she wrote, "and the substance of an idea is very far from being the supposed substance of non-intelligent matter." [79] The ideas of which she speaks cannot be interpreted as universal Platonic essences, for they refer to specific formations which truly understood are spiritual. Mrs. Eddy asserted that "Metaphysics resolves things into thoughts, and exchanges the objects of sense for the ideas of Soul." But she went on to explain that "These ideas are perfectly real and tangible to spiritual consciousness." [80] In no sense did she believe that anything but material limitation was lost by this resolution of the "objects of sense" into the "ideas of Soul." For she declared that "Thought will finally be understood and seen in all form, substance, and color, but without material accompaniments." [81] This, then, is one of the fundamental assertions of Christian Science: that all the elements of creation of being are real, concrete, and apprehensible, yet not in any sense dependent upon material structure for their manifestation.

FACT AND FALSITY

Thus far in this chapter we have discussed what Mrs. Eddy calls the spiritual facts of creation — perfect God, man, and creation. This term *the spiritual fact* is pivotal in the lexicon of Christian Science. Mrs. Eddy wrote of Christian Science as that "with which can be discerned the

75. *Ibid.,* p. 507.   76. *Ibid.,* pp. 502–503.   77. *Mis.,* p. 36.
78. *Ibid.,* p. 26.   79. *S&H.,* p. 257.   80. *Ibid.,* p. 269.
81. *Ibid.,* p. 310.

spiritual fact of whatever the material senses behold." [82] She sometimes used the term *fact* in a propositional sense. [83] But in many other instances she used it as a reference to that which *is*. In this sense she wrote, for instance, "In the vast forever, in the Science and truth of being, the only facts are Spirit and its innumerable creations." [84]

To human belief, of course, these spiritual facts are clearly not factual at all, and are precisely contrary to the character of reality as commonly understood. What, then, is the material condition that men commonly identify as reality, whence does it originate, and what is its relation to the real facts of being? In dealing with this question, Mrs. Eddy always emphasized that there is and can be but one real order of being, which is spiritual. Then what appears as a self-constituted material order is not such at all, for it can have no legitimacy nor source. It can only be a mortal misapprehension of the one real order of being. And if one accepts this misapprehension as true, he is in error; for he is accepting a faulty view of reality as reality itself, confusing percept with fact. This error is very costly to those who entertain it. From it proceed all the inharmonies of mortal existence. "Sin, sickness, and death," declared Mrs. Eddy, "are to be classified as effects of error." [85]

This term *error* is one of the most important in the vocabulary of Christian Science. [86] In Mrs. Eddy's teaching, error is not a self-existent power or a permanent feature of experience. It is a mistake about being — pure failure, falsity, negation. When challenged by divine Truth, Mrs. Eddy asserted, error simply vanishes. Its only possible claim to power is to be accepted as fact. If men so accept it, they will suffer from the effects of error. But men always have recourse, Mrs. Eddy taught, to the spiritual Truth that dissolves material error and acts as healing power in the life situation.

Mrs. Eddy saw as wholly erroneous any form of belief that holds that there is a reality or a power apart from God. Hence, the category of error in her teaching *includes* the concept of evil. For she held that the belief in the actuality of evil is in itself an error. Evil is therefore utterly baseless in being. "Evil," Mrs. Eddy wrote, "is neither quality nor quantity; it is not intelligence, a person or a principle, a man or a woman, a place or a thing, and God never made it." [87]

Mrs. Eddy's assertion in this statement that God never made evil is the

---

82. *Ibid.*, p. 585.   83. See, for example, *Ibid.*, p. 116.
84. *Ibid.*, p. 479.   85. *Ibid.*, p. 473.
86. See the discussion of the background of Mrs. Eddy's use of this term on p. 38.
87. *Mess. '01*, pp. 12–13.

basis for her claim as to its unreality. She categorically denied that an infinite and good God could possibly create, sanction, or know the existence of evil.[88] On this ground she obviously was opposed to any theology that made room for its reality. She denied that there was a personal devil any more than a personal God and referred to Satan as only an "illusive personification" [89] of mortal belief. Of course, liberal theologies that rejected the idea of a personal devil often made room for evil as a necessary element in existence which in some way works for good if only we understand the divine scheme. But this belief Mrs. Eddy termed a "frail hypothesis" which Science reverses.[90] She also dismissed that classic Christian explanation for the existence of evil: that had God made man incapable of sin, his moral perfection would have no meaning. To her it was inconceivable that God could have made man capable of sin, then punished him for sinning. Whatever the apparent reality of sin and evil, Mrs. Eddy insisted, they must be seen to be "without actual origin or rightful existence," [91] if God is to be honored as All-in-all.[92]

Yet it is of central importance to recognize that even though Mrs. Eddy denied the existence of evil as an entity, she was careful to state that it does *seem* a terrible reality to human consciousness. She therefore responded to the question "Do Christian Scientists believe that evil exists?" both affirmatively and negatively: "Yes, inasmuch as we do know that evil, as a false claim, false entity, and utter falsity, does exist in thought; and No, as something that enjoys, suffers, or is real." She went on to say that "our only departure from ecclesiasticism on this subject is, that our faith takes hold of the fact that evil cannot be made so real as to frighten us and so master us, or to make us love it and so hinder our way of holiness." [93]

Even with this important qualification, however, the theological problem raised by Mrs. Eddy's denial of the entity of evil seemed insurmountable, both to her critics and to a number of sincere students of Christian Science. The problem was this: she said that evil has no real existence as a power, person, or principle opposed to God; that its supposed existence was entirely due to mortal belief in its power and failure to grasp the infinite might of Spirit. But then, is not the mind that believes in and

---

88. Mrs. Eddy explores this point at length in *Un.*, pp. 1–7.
89. *S&H.*, p. 187.   90. *Mis.*, p. 13.   91. *S&H.*, p. 281.
92. An able general treatment of the problem of evil in Christian thought can be found in John Hick, *Evil and the God of Love* (New York, 1966), though its discussion of the position of Christian Science on the subject is quite inadequate.
93. *Mess. '01*, p. 14.

experiences evil real? In other words, even if evil is an illusion, is not the illusion real as an illusion? Many of Mrs. Eddy's critics delighted in pushing this problem as it appeared in Christian Science to its furthest extreme. The Reverend J. W. Conley cited Mrs. Eddy's failure to account for the origin of evil as the most glaring deficiency in the logic of Christian Science. "While Mrs. Eddy smuggles in the fact of the fall," he wrote, "she gives no rational account of it." The dream of evil is real in Christian Science; it is in itself a fact, "a horrible protracted nightmare." [94] Similarly, the most thorough early Roman Catholic critic of Christian Science, L. A. Lambert, wrote in a series of articles entitled "Christian Science Before the Bar of Reason":

You may call it a false claim, an entire fallacy, a false entity, as Mrs. Eddy does; but a false claim is still a claim, a false entity must be an entity before it can be false; just as a counterfeit note must be a note before it can be a counterfeit, so sin must be a thing, an act, or quality of some real being before it can be an evil thing, act, or quality.

A false claim must have an origin—a cause.[95]

A clever summary of this whole line of argument was offered years later by one who definitely was not a clergyman: H. L. Mencken. Christian Science, he wrote, "is the theory that since the sky-rockets seen following a wallop on the eye are an illusion, the eye is one illusion and the wallop another." [96]

Mrs. Eddy took up this problem at many points in her writings. One of her central statements on the subject is found in the chapter "Recapitulation," from *Science and Health,* wherein she answers a self-put question which is in substance the same as that raised by her theological opponents: "You speak of belief. Who or what is it that believes?" Her answer to this question reads in part as follows:

Spirit is all-knowing; this precludes the need of believing. Matter cannot believe, and Mind understands. The body cannot believe. The believer and the belief are one and are mortal. Christian evidence is founded on Science or demonstrable Truth, flowing from immortal Mind, and there is in reality no such thing as *mortal* mind.[97]

94. J. W. Conley, "The Inherent Difficulties of Christian Science," in *Searchlights,* p. 56.

95. L. A. Lambert, *Christian Science Before the Bar of Reason* (New York, 1908), p. 154.

96. H. L. Mencken, in *Bulletin of the Freethinkers of America* (n.d.).

97. *S&H.,* p. 487.

The very use of this term *mortal mind,* Mrs. Eddy realized, tended to make a reality of it. And she said that if a better term could have been suggested she would have used it.[98] For she wanted it to be understood that mortal mind did not refer to an actually existing intelligence, but to a faulty grasp of reality. And like a mathematical error, it disappears into nothingness once the true fact is seen. Since man's true individuality is not mortal or limited, mortal mind is to be totally dispelled. *Mortal mind alone believes that evil is real and seeks an explanation of its origin.* From the standpoint of the divine Mind alone is evil seen to be unreal. Hence the unreality of evil can be known to us only as we put on the Mind of Christ. As one follows in Jesus' way, actually dissolving all forms of evil in his experience, he knows and understands the unreality of evil. Without the attainment of this Christly vision, evil is as real to one man as to another. For this reason Mrs. Eddy counseled her students to defer discussion of the unreality of evil to the divine Mind until "they draw nearer to the divine character, and are practically able to testify, by their lives, that as they come closer to the true understanding of God they lose all sense of error." [99]

The understanding of the unreality of evil in Christian Science, therefore, is inseparable from its demonstration; indeed, this understanding confronts us as a possibility for demonstration. Those who believe in its reality can never explain it, and those who have demonstrated its unreality need no explanation of it. Mrs. Eddy felt that it was futile to speculate on the origins of evil, for so doing only confirms the lie that it is real. The better way is to seek to demonstrate that which has been revealed as possible to man: freedom from all forms of evil, including sin, sickness, and death. Those who do not actually break with mortal mind, she indicated, can never find any satisfactory solution to the problem of evil. For mortal mind by its very nature accepts as true the testimony of the corporeal senses, which Mrs. Eddy declared, are "the only source of evil or error." [100] Hence, she wrote, "when we put off the false sense for the true, and see that sin and mortality have neither Principle nor permanency, we shall learn that sin and mortality are without actual origin or rightful existence." [101] Until corporeal sense is destroyed, it will appear to mortal mind as bearing valid testimony to the reality of evil. "Mortal mind," Mrs. Eddy wrote, "judges by the testimony of the material senses, until Science obliterates this false testimony." [102] Once this testimony is obliterated,

98. *Ibid.,* p. 114.   99. *Un.,* p. 1.   100. *S&H.,* p. 489.
101. *Ibid.,* p. 281.   102. *Ibid.,* p. 296.

there remains nothing of evil to explain. The problem of evil is solved when evil is destroyed.

In Christian Science the unreality of evil is virtually synonymous with the unreality of matter. Matter, Mrs. Eddy said, was the "substratum of evil,"[103] that through which evil obtains. What she called the "mists of matter"[104] — sin, sickness, and death — were to her also the modes of evil. The sinner thinks he finds pleasure in matter, the sick man pain, and the dying that it is destroying his life. Matter, then, claims to rule the lives of men, limit their capacities, determine the conditions of their experience, and condemn them to suffering and eventual death. To Mrs. Eddy, its claim to power usurps the divine authority, and those who fear and obey material law are actually acknowledging a power apart from God. "We bow down to matter," she wrote, "and entertain finite thoughts of God like the pagan idolater. Mortals are inclined to fear and to obey what they consider a material body more than they do a spiritual God."[105]

Again and again Mrs. Eddy stresses the absolutely antithetical natures of matter and Spirit. Matter, she wrote, "is substance in error; Spirit is substance in Truth."[106] And she asserted that "When the substance of Spirit appears in Christian Science, the nothingness of matter is recognized."[107] She is emphatic that there cannot be two independent bases of being, two universal yet contradictory principles of existence. "The theories I combat are these," Mrs. Eddy explained:

(1) that all is matter; (2) that matter originates in Mind, and is as real as Mind, possessing intelligence and Life. The first theory, that matter is everything is quite as reasonable as the second, that Mind and matter coexist and cooperate. Only one of the following statements can be true: (1) that everything is matter; (2) that everything is Mind. Which one is it?[108]

To mortal mind judging by the testimony of the senses, matter does, of course, appear as an objective solid reality. Yet *only* to this false mentality, Mrs. Eddy maintained, does matter appear real. She wrote that "The physical senses (matter having really no sense) give the only pretended testimony there can be as to the existence of a substance called *matter*. Now these senses, being material, can only testify from their own evidence, and concerning themselves. . . ."[109] So then, what appears to the limited senses as an actual substance only objectifies the limits of material percep-

103. *No.*, p. 16.   104. *Ibid.*   105. *S&H.*, p. 214.
106. *Ret.*, p. 57.   107. *S&H.*, p. 480.   108. *Ibid.*, pp. 269–270.
109. *Un.*, p. 33.

tion. In Christian Science matter is not a substance, but the hypothesis of a substance devised to explain man's present sense of limitation. Mrs. Eddy defined matter in various places in her writings as "an image in mortal mind";[110] "the objective supposition of Spirit's opposite";[111] "an error of statement";[112] "a misstatement of Mind";[113] and "a frail conception of mortal mind." [114] That which seems so real to mortal mind is but the appearance of thought to thought, and as thought changes appearance alters too. "The elements and functions of the physical body and of the physical world," Mrs. Eddy explained, "will change as mortal mind changes its beliefs." [115]

Yet so mesmerized are men by the belief that matter is something in itself that they endow it with power it does not really possess. In other words, men treat as causative that which is only phenomenal, fearing as a reality that which has no basis in being. To Mrs. Eddy the mesmerism of the belief of life in matter is all that blocks the spiritual progress of mankind. "What is it that seems a stone between us and the resurrection morning?" she asked. "It is the belief of mind in matter." [116]

It is important to understand that in Christian Science matter objectifies a false sense *of* something — of Spirit and its formations. Hence Mrs. Eddy does not posit the existence of a material universe of illusion set against a spiritual universe already complete. In Christian Science, what mortals call the material universe actually represents their faulty perception of the one order of Spirit. It would not, however, be correct in Christian Science to say that the material universe *is* the spiritual universe dimly seen; one would have to say, rather, that material forms objectify the faulty human grasp of this one spiritual order.

Take, for example, Mrs. Eddy's comments on the nature of body. Mrs. Eddy denies that man lives in a material body and that Life is either structural or organic. "Life is inorganic, infinite Spirit," she wrote; "if Life, or Spirit, were organic, disorganization would destroy Spirit and annihilate man." [117] Man's capacities are not, therefore, mediated through matter, and he does not in actuality depend upon a material structure to exercise them. Men believe that they think *through* a brain, for instance; but Mrs. Eddy claims that the brain simply manifests the limited belief that life can be material. "The belief that a pulpy substance under the skull is mind," she wrote, "is a mockery of intelligence, a mimicry of

---

110. *S&H.*, p. 116.   111. *Ibid.*, p. 287.   112. *Ibid.*, p. 277.
113. *Mis.*, p. 174.   114. *Mis.*, p. 87   115. *S&H.*, pp. 124–125.
116. *Mis.*, p. 179.   117. *Ibid.*, p. 56.

Mind." [118] Elsewhere she said that "The mind supposed to exist in matter or beneath a skull bone is a myth, a misconceived sense and false conception as to man and Mind." [119] So too, one would say in Christian Science that men do not actually hear or see through material organs, even temporarily; but rather, that the ear and eye simply manifest the limited sense of true spiritual hearing and sight that they are entertaining. These capacities, for Mrs. Eddy, reside in Mind, God, not in matter; hence their unimpaired perfection can be demonstrated as men discern this fact.

On this basis, body is not without significance and one cannot in Christian Science consider it an unreality to be ignored. For though man does not have a private material body, he does have, according to Christian Science, imperishable spiritual entity, with individual and recognizable characteristics and capacities. Therefore, when answering the question, "What are body and Soul?" in the chapter "Recapitulation," Mrs. Eddy did not begin by referring to body at all. Rather, she wrote that "Identity is the reflection of Spirit, the reflection in multifarious forms of the living Principle, Love." [120] Though the physical body represents a false way of identifying man, true spiritual man does have identity and, in a sense, embodiment. "Rightly understood," Mrs. Eddy wrote, "instead of possessing a sentient material form, man has a sensationless body." [121] At the point of the ascension, she taught, Jesus demonstrated this spiritual body. He did not really go anywhere; rather, he rose above the beliefs of the flesh and was therefore no longer perceptible to physical sense.[122] When he demonstrated his true identity, or body, the false physical sense of him simply disappeared.

The same point pertains to all so-called physical phenomena. Again, in discussing nature in *Science and Health,* Mrs. Eddy explained:

Spirit is the life, substance, and continuity of all things. We tread on forces. Withdraw them, and creation must collapse. Human knowledge calls them forces of matter; but divine Science declares that they belong wholly to divine Mind, are inherent in this Mind, and so restores them to their rightful home and classification.[123]

Right where physical sense says that man and creation are physical, then, Christian Science says that they are spiritual. Where Protestant liberalism made its peace with physical science by abstracting religion from the realm of scientific verification, Mrs. Eddy challenged the validity of physical sci-

118. *S&H.,* p. 192.   119. *Ibid.,* p. 281.   120. *Ibid.,* p. 477.
121. *Ibid.,* p. 280.   122. *Ibid.,* p. 46.   123. *Ibid.,* p. 124.

ence where it claims to operate and declared that "All *Science* is *Christian* Science." [124]

If this is the true science of creation, what of material science? *"Natural science,* as it is commonly called," Mrs. Eddy declared, "is not really natural nor scientific, because it deduces from the evidence of the material senses." [125] To the extent that any knowledge rests upon such evidence, it is in her view fallacious. And human thought, she maintained, must eventually be educated out of its false conceptions. "The education of the future," she declared, "will be instruction, in spiritual Science, against the material symbolic counterfeit sciences." [126] To some extent, the physical sciences as she described them do point to the government of the universe by divine Principle. But for her, physical science can reach only as far as its limited perceptual base will permit. Mrs. Eddy observed that Newton named the force that made the apple fall gravitation, "having learned so much." But his was only a limited sense of "The primal cause or Mind-force." [127] The physical sciences, then, do not investigate a world of physical phenomena separate from the order of Spirit. They only report on a limited mortal apprehension of this one order.

Taken in its own terms, therefore, Christian Science cannot be considered a form of metaphysical dualism. Mrs. Eddy's metaphysics is incompatible with a dualistic ontology which posits two separate realms of being opposed to one another, even though she continually contrasts matter with Spirit, unreality with reality, and mortality with immortality. For what appears as a material man in a material creation only objectifies a misconception of true manhood and the one true creation. A basic question, then, is: does this misconception result in what amounts to an inverted image of man and creation as something in itself? From the standpoint of strict Christian Science, Mrs. Eddy would answer no. But from the standpoint of what seems to be the case to mortal belief, she would answer yes. She felt that since men believe themselves to be mortal and to be living in a material world, they must be addressed in terms appropriate to their level of belief. Hence, she spoke in places as if to all intents and purposes those whom she was addressing were mortals in a material world. After stating one important point, for example, she wrote, "Learn this, O mortal, and earnestly seek the spiritual status of man which is outside of all material selfhood." [128] Mrs. Eddy also felt that while still

124. *Mis.*, p. 4. 125. *Ibid.*, p. 274. 126. *Ibid.*, p. 61.
127. *Ibid.*, pp. 22–23. 128. *S&H.*, p. 476.

entertaining a material sense of life, men should not claim too much for what they have demonstrated of their spiritual perfection. Hence she wrote, "Our highest sense of infinite good in this mortal sphere is but the sign and symbol, not the substance of good." [129] On the other hand, she also said that the terms she had to use were sometimes concessions to the requirements of communication. She did refer to mortals, mortal mind, the material world, and the physical body, *etc;* but she wanted these terms to be construed as indicating shifting misconceptions of the actual, rather than specific integral entities.

Even though Christian Science cannot validly be interpreted as a form of ontological dualism, it has so been understood by some of Mrs. Eddy's followers as well as her critics. Take, for example, the use of the terms *absolute* and *relative* in connection with Christian Science. Mrs. Eddy employed the term *absolute* often, writing of the "absolute demonstration of Science," [130] of "one absolute God," [131] of the "absolute unreality of sin," [132] etc. But she always used the term as an adjective, never as a noun. She never referred to God in the philosophic sense as the Absolute, nor did she speak of *the* absolute as an ontological realm of essence. Moreover, she never counterposed *the* absolute and *the* relative as two metaphysical realms. This usage, however, became quite common among her followers, but it gives a wholly misleading idea of the direction of her teaching. Here is the crucial difference. The distinction which she made between spiritually scientific or unscientific apprehensions of what is real posits only one basic reality to be understood. But the conception of the absolute and the relative implies the existence of two ontological realms. Even if one of these realms — the relative — is understood as illusory, the elements that comprise it have their own reality relative to the framework of that realm. For Mrs. Eddy, however, material appearance is in no sense a self-constituted realm which may ultimately be labeled unreal. For it is only the objectified misapprehension of the spiritual order of being which alone is real, and will change as mortal belief yields to spiritual understanding.

Whatever common ground Mrs. Eddy shared with orthodoxy, Catholic and Protestant, it is just here that her teaching and orthodox doctrine collide. For her denial of the veracity of common sense testimony is for-

129. *Un.,* p. 61.   130. *Mis.,* p. 355.   131. *S&H.,* p. 465.
132. *Un.,* p. 58.

eign to orthodox teaching as is her assertion that the spiritual fact of being is alone "perfect God and perfect man." [133]

Indeed, predominant clerical opinion in the latter nineteenth century was especially adamant in support of the veracity of the senses. The acceptance of the materiality of man and the universe, which for both Protestants and Catholics was sanctioned by Biblical teaching, was also reinforced by the philosophy of Scottish common sense realism. This philosophy, which undergirded Protestant orthodoxy throughout the nineteenth century, had taken root in America at the end of the eighteenth century as a means of combating both idealism and materialism. It served to give orthodoxy a plausibility apart from the authority of revelation and to defend it from the attacks of rationalism. For it posited an innate moral sense by which one could be assured of the self-evident truth of basic moral principles. Scottish philosophy also had an epistemological side useful to the orthodox in combating idealism. Its realistic epistemology held to the absolute disjunction of mind and matter as the dual elements in the knowing process. The existence of objects perceived by the senses in this philosophy is in no sense contingent upon consciousness.[134]

It is true, of course, that the claims of Christian Science seemed preposterous to many people who knew nothing of theology or philosophy. But given the fact that the mass of orthodox Protestant clergymen were steeped in common sense realism, one can better understand their readiness to attack Christian Science for its obvious departure from it. For Mrs. Eddy, common sense perception must be challenged for the spiritual fact to be discerned. For Protestants, however, what she saw as mere percept *was* the fact. In an article called "The Absurd Paradox of Christian Science," written for the *North American Review* in 1901, the Reverend James Monroe Buckley championed common sense metaphysics as against Mrs. Eddy's teaching in explicit terms. The universe seems so alike to all of us, he argued, that "can I not say to my neighbor or all mankind, as Shylock said to Salarino: 'Have I not eyes, hands, organs, sense, affections.' " [135] As if to detail Buckley's argument, the Reverend A. L. Moore listed a series of statements from the then current edition of *Science and*

133. *S&H.*, p. 259.

134. For a good brief discussion of Scottish common sense philosophy in general and its influence on American theology in particular, see Sydney F. Ahlstrom, "The Scottish Philosophy and American Theology," *Church History*, XXIV (Sept. 1955), pp. 257–272.

135. James Monroe Buckley, "The Absurd Paradox of Christian Science," *North American Review* (July 1901), pp. 22–23.

Health which ran contrary to common sense perception. He quoted Mrs. Eddy as saying, for example, that "Bones have no substantiality. They are only an appearance, a subjective state of mortal mind." [136] This idea that matter was but the "subjective state of mortal mind" denied the dualism of mind and matter which was so fundamental to common sense metaphysics, and some of Mrs. Eddy's critics attacked her on this point specifically. The Reverend C. F. Winbigler, a Presbyterian, insisted, "In philosophy all consciousness involves duality." He went on to cite the story of a missionary who told a cannibal that he had to give up his second wife. Returning later to baptize the cannibal and finding the wife gone, the missionary asked him what he had done with her. "Me eat her," came the reply. Just so, said Winbigler, in Mrs. Eddy's teaching "mind or spirit has eaten up matter." [137]

Roman Catholic critics of Christian Science had reason to find Mrs. Eddy's denial of the validity of physical perception even more grating than did her Protestant opponents. And though the tone of their comments was generally cooler and more rational, their opposition was no less uncompromising. For Thomistic philosophy, which is heavily indebted to Aristotle, is firmly wedded to perceptual realism. The Protestant liaison with common sense realism, though it endured for more than a century in America, was temporary; and Protestant theology was compatible with other philosophies as well. Indeed, the temporary triumph of common sense philosophy in Protestantism was to some degree made possible by the influence of Aquinas and Aristotle in Scottish thought. However, the perceptual realism which found expression in common sense philosophy is basic to the supernaturalism of Roman Catholic theology. For Thomistic thought holds that human reason based upon sense testimony can accurately inform us of earthly realities, but must leave to supernatural revelation the disclosure of ultimate matters of faith. Thus Aquinas wrote of the "ascent, by the natural light of reason, through created things to the knowledge of God," and the "descent, by the modes of revelation, of divine truth which exceeds human intellect." [138]

In this light one can better understand the total opposition of Roman Catholics to the metaphysics of Christian Science. The Reverend F. S. Jewell of Milwaukee tried to refute the "peculiar philosophy" of Christian

---

136. A. Lincoln Moore, *Christian Science: Its Manifold Attractions* (New York, 1906), pp. 44–45.

137. Charles F. Winbigler, *Christian Science and Kindred Subjects: Their Facts and Fallacies* (Washington, D.C., 1906), p. 42.

138. Quoted in Baillie, *The Idea of Revelation,* p. 2.

Science by arguing that God must have made human reason "approximate to the truth of beings and things." Therefore "it is the duty of the philosopher reverently to accept the voice of the race as the voice of God. The common consciousness of all mankind may fall short of the full truth, but it cannot grossly falsify it." [139] The Reverend Lambert, quoted earlier, took up the same line of attack. Defining common sense testimony as the united report of two or more of the five senses, he wrote:

the common sense of mankind has not erred. . . . It is one of the best authorities in its own field that the individual man can rest his convictions on; it is next to divine positive revelation and the divinely commissioned teacher of it. And this common sense condemns the idealism of Christian Science.[140]

The description of Christian Science as a form of idealism in the preceding passage was standard in theological attacks upon it. Another Roman Catholic critic of Mrs. Eddy's teaching, Thomas J. Campbell, remarked in an article on "The Delusion of Christian Science" in 1900 that "Berkeley's fun is repeated by the Massachusetts Metaphysical College." And he went on to describe Berkeley as "the old Irish Protestant prelate of the eighteenth century." [141] Orthodox Protestants, however, were just as opposed to idealism as was Campbell. They had done battle not only with Berkeleyian idealism, against which the fortification of common sense philosophy had been erected, but with Transcendentalism as well. And in the late nineteenth century, orthodox Protestants were confronted with the idealism of Eastern religions and with the Hegelian idealism that was winning its way into American academic philosophy. One major difference between orthodox and liberal Protestantism in this period lay in the fact that liberals showed strong interest in Hegelian idealism as an evolutionary philosophy of history, whereas the orthodox consistently opposed it. Only a few orthodox critics of Christian Science associated it with Hegelianism; the charge that Mrs. Eddy had borrowed directly from Hegel was of a later origin and is wholly unfounded.[142]

139. F. S. Jewell, "The Claims of 'Christian Science' as so Styled and Its Peculiar Philosophy," pamphlet (Milwaukee, 1897), p. 13.

140. Lambert, *Christian Science Before the Bar of Reason,* pp. 135–136.

141. Thomas J. Campbell, "The Delusion of Christian Science," *The Catholic Mind* (Dec. 22, 1906), p. 492.

142. Walter M. Haushalter claimed in his book *Mrs. Eddy Purloins from Hegel* (Boston, 1936), that she had heavily plagiarized Hegel's works in writing *Science and Health.* Haushalter based his charge on a purported manuscript digest of Hegel's thought prepared by Francis Lieber which Mrs. Eddy was supposed to have marked and used. However, subsequent investigation disclosed that this docu-

Many more of her critics identified Christian Science with Eastern religion; yet when they did so they were generally trying to prove that it was a form of pantheism, rather than a form of epistemological idealism as such. Most Protestants who tried to trace the origins of Christian Science to some form of idealism had Berkeleyian or Emersonian idealism in mind.

Mrs. Eddy, as we have said, had little use for philosophy. She was not well read in it and certainly did not feel that any philosopher had been the source of her teaching. In the most general sense, of course, that teaching can be understood as a form of idealism. For broadly speaking, one can call any system which construes experience in terms of mind or spirit idealistic. Yet there is no evidence that in her discovery and statement of Christian Science, Mrs. Eddy was directly influenced by any form of philosophic idealism. Some of her followers spoke of Christian Science as the fulfillment of idealism.[143] But she appears to have felt no impulse to reconcile her teachings, which she believed to have been derived from revelation, with the more intellectually prestigious modes of human thought. And whatever one thinks of Christian Science, it is clear that what it claims to make possible in experience far exceeds anything claimed by philosophy, idealistic or otherwise.

A number of Mrs. Eddy's critics recognized that her teaching was far more radical than the idealism to which they attributed its central ideas. Often one finds ministers drawing a distinction between Christian Science and what seemed to them more sensible forms of idealism which made no factual claims about the nature of things. Berkeley, wrote one of them, "never reduces idealism to absurdity attempting to apply it to the affairs of every day life, and the conclusions of universal experience."[144] Another critic arguing this point quoted the Bishop himself to the same effect:

I do not argue against the existence of any one thing that we can comprehend either of sensation or reflection; that the things I see with my eyes

---

ment was a forgery. See Conrad Moelman, *Ordeal by Concordance* (New York, 1955), and Peel, *Discovery,* pp. 305–307.

143. The earliest coherent attempt to link Christian Science with idealism is the article by Joel Rufus Mosley, "Christian Science and Idealism," *Cosmopolitan* (July 1907) XLIII, 330–334. For a fuller and more recent attempt to relate Christian Science to idealistic philosophy, see Henry Steiger, *Christian Science and Philosophy* (New York, 1946).

144. P. F. Wolcott, "What is Christian Science," pamphlet (New York, 1896), p. 15.

and touch with my hands do exist, really exist, I make not the slightest question. The only thing whose existence I do deny is that which philosophers call matter or corporeal substance.[145]

Clearly Berkeley never intended, as Mrs. Eddy did intend, to say anything of a factual nature about experience. He was an Anglican Bishop defending Christianity against the materialistic conclusions that many were drawing from Newtonian physics. As such, he was concerned with offering a metaphysical interpretation of matter to refute the materialistic premise that matter in motion constitutes reality. Material forms for him were perfectly real as perceived. But he interpreted them as being a sort of divine language, an infusion of divine ideas into human consciousness. Practically speaking, the Bishop would have had no real quarrel with the sensible Dr. Johnson who, as the story goes, vigorously kicked a post in refutation of Berkeleyian subtleties about the non-existence of matter. More than one Protestant clergyman repeated this tale in trying to discredit Christian Science. What is even more significant is that the *Journal* once printed a version of it with the intent to lampoon Berkeleyian metaphysics precisely because it had no practical consequence. Mrs. Eddy's critique of Berkeley, written in answer to the clerical charge that she had stolen her main idea from him, makes the same point: that whatever his interpretation of the metaphysical status of matter, he continued to think of it and treat it as a God-ordained reality. The passage is of sufficient relevance and interest to be quoted in full:

Bishop Berkeley published a book in 1710 entitled "Treatise Concerning the Principle of Human Knowledge." Its object was to deny on received principles of philosophy, the reality of an external material world. In later publications he declared physical substance to be "only the constant relation between phenomena connected by association and conjoined by the operations of the universal mind, nature being nothing more than conscious experience. Matter apart from conscious mind is an impossible and unreal concept." He denies the existence of matter, and argues that matter is not *without* the mind but within it, and that that which is generally called matter is an impression produced by divine power on the mind by means of invariable rules styled the laws of nature. Here he makes God the cause of all the ills of mortals and the casualties of earth.

Again, while descanting on the virtues of tar-water he writes: "I esteem my having taken this medicine the greatest of all temporary blessings, and am

145. Quoted in Buckley, "The Absurd Paradox of Christian Science," p. 23.

convinced that under Providence I owe my life to it," making matter more potent than Mind. When the storms of disease beat against Bishop Berkeley's metaphysics and personality he fell, and great was the fall — from divine metaphysics to tar-water.[146]

Protestant critics of Christian Science sometimes associated it with the vagaries of Transcendentalism. Yet it is interesting to note how suspicious at least two major representatives of that movement were of Mrs. Eddy's claims. After the publication of the first edition of *Science and Health,* Bronson Alcott visited its author in appreciation of her protest against materialism. But he soon became disquieted by the radicalism of her teaching, and after his final meeting with her in 1878 wrote that there "is perhaps a touch of fanaticism, though of genial quality, interposed into her faith, which a deeper insight into the mysteries of life may ultimately remove." [147] The failing Emerson seems to have echoed the same sentiments. Alcott had informed him and his circle of Mrs. Eddy's ideas, which they considered with some interest. Yet according to her own account of a visit to him a few months before his death in 1882, he rejected the essence of her message. He had long since moved away from the confidence of *Nature* to a darker view of the necessity for man's submission to fate. In the grip of senility, his capitulation to the determinism of physical process was complete. Mrs. Eddy wrote that when

I got into the deep recesses of his thought I saw his case was hopeless. . . . So when I said, in reply to his remark, "I am old and my brains are wearing out from hard-labor," — and then chattered like a babe, — "But you believe in the powers of God above all other causation, do you not?" He answered: "Yes," and this followed in substance: but it would be profane for me to believe a man does not wear out. I don't believe God can or wants to prevent this result of old age.[148]

For all practical purposes, then, the idealism of Berkeley, Alcott, and Emerson did no violence to common sense perception. So too, the philosophic idealists who flourished in America during the last decades of the nineteenth century never really argued that physical percepts are not what they seem. "Bowne and Royce," observed one of Mrs. Eddy's Protestant critics, "are idealists, and construe what we call matter in terms of mind; but they would never dream of calling that system of things, that estab-

146. *Mess. '01,* pp. 23–24.
147. Odell Shepherd, ed., *The Journals of Bronson Alcott* (Boston, 1938), 489–490
148. Quoted in Peel, *Christian Science,* p. 90.

lished and permanent order, to which we give the name of matter, an illusion." [149] Borden Parker Bowne, whose personalism was one of the chief monuments of post-Civil War American philosophy, confirmed this conclusion in a small pamphlet which he devoted to distinguishing his own idealism from Christian Science. Here he stated explicitly that idealistic metaphysics never claimed to offer anything more than an interpretation of experience. "The experience," he wrote, "remains the same under one system of metaphysics as under another. If the philosopher can do anything, it must be in the way of interpreting experience, not in the way of producing or verifying it." [150]

This assertion is thoroughly compatible with Mrs. Eddy's statement of the "cardinal point" that distinguished her metaphysical system from others: ". . . that *by knowing the unreality of disease, sin, and death,* you demonstrate the allness of God." [151] This affirmation is clearly not within the circumference of philosophic idealism, even though Mrs. Eddy uses the language of metaphysics; for it asserts that the true understanding of reality makes a *difference in experience* and is not merely an interpretation of it. Further, Mrs. Eddy maintained that her claim as to the demonstrability of the allness of God and the nothingness of evil was based, not on philosophic supposition, but on divine revelation. Her implicit claim is that as men awaken to the revealed spiritual facts of being in Science, they can progressively demonstrate their spiritual status as sons of God and overcome all the phases of material sense. In a statement from *Science and Health* which expresses this point and epitomizes the central contention of her teaching, Mrs. Eddy wrote: "As human thought changes from one stage to another of conscious pain and painlessness, sorrow and joy, — from fear to hope and from faith to understanding, — the visible manifestation will at last be man governed by Soul, not by material sense.[152]

REDEMPTION AND THE NEED OF A MEDIATOR

For Christian Scientists, one of the central texts in the Bible is the following passage from I John, Third Chapter:

---

149. Franklin Johnson, "The Precursors of Christian Science," in *Searchlights,* p. 101.

150. Quoted in Charles Reynolds Brown, *Faith and Health* (New York, 1910), pp. 102–103.

151. *Un.,* p. 9.

152. *S&H.,* p. 125.

Behold, what manner of love the Father hath bestowed upon us, that we should be called the sons of God: therefore, the world knoweth us not, because it knew him not.

Beloved, now are we the sons of God, and it doth not yet appear what we shall be: but we know that, when he shall appear, we shall be like him; for we shall see him as he is.

And every man that hath this hope in him purifieth himself, even as he is pure.

This text is read every Sunday at the close of Christian Science church services as the correlative Scripture to Mrs. Eddy's "Scientific Statement of Being." [153] In her teaching, both passages point to the present perfection of man — a perfection which, though yet to be fully demonstrated, is nevertheless the reality of his being.

This assertion of man's *present* perfection markedly differentiates Christian Science from the current of Christian perfectionism that was so vital a part of mid-nineteenth century American religious life. This perfectionism did assert, like Christian Science, that the attainment of the Christian goal of holiness is a possibility in man's present life. Yet it predicated the possibility of sanctification on the reception of Christ's saving love by inherently sinful men. In Christian Science, however, men are awakened through the power of the Christ to an understanding of the perfection which is already theirs as sons of God. The practical difference between the two doctrines lies in the conviction entertained by the Christian Scientist that he is demonstrating a perfection which is spiritually natural to him, rather than struggling for holiness against the current of his own inherent disposition to sin.

Indeed, this idea that man's perfection is real now but needs to be discerned and demonstrated points to a vital difference between the concept of salvation in Christian Science and in Protestant orthodoxy. In orthodoxy salvation implies a process of transformation: a finite creature estranged from God is brought into living relation with Him and vouchsafed eternal bliss. In Christian Science, however, salvation understood as demonstration indicates a *showing forth of that which is spiritually established in Science*. As Mrs. Eddy wrote, "The great spiritual fact must be brought out that man *is,* not *shall be,* perfect and immortal." She went on to say, "The evidence of man's immortality will become more apparent, as material beliefs are given up and the immortal facts of being are admitted.[154]

153. *Ibid.,* p. 468.   154. *Ibid.,* p. 428.

Note that in this passage Mrs. Eddy says that the spiritual fact must be *brought out* and that the evidence of man's immortality will become more *apparent*. The spiritual fact, in other words, must be objectified, or as she often put it, demonstrated. Without this demonstration, Mrs. Eddy insisted, the assertion of the spiritual fact remains an abstraction.[155] Indeed, to assert a spiritual fact in Christian Science is to assert the possibility of its demonstration. But at the same time, were not the spiritual fact *established in Science,* it could not be demonstrated. Mrs. Eddy's reply to an inquiry from a student on this point is illuminating. The student said that she had been reprimanded by a Christian Science practitioner for having referred to herself as an "immortal idea of the one Mind," the practitioner maintaining that the student was wrong, since she still lived in the flesh. Asked to give the truth of the matter, Mrs. Eddy wrote:

You are scientifically correct in your statement about yourself. You can never demonstrate spirituality until you declare yourself to be immortal and understand that you are so. Christian Science is absolute; it is neither behind the point of perfection nor advancing towards it; it is at this point and must be practiced therefrom. Unless you fully perceive that you are the child of God, hence perfect, you have no Principle to demonstrate and no rule for its demonstration. By this I do not mean that mortals are the children of God, — far from it. In practicing Christian Science you must state its Principle correctly or you forfeit your ability to demonstrate it.[156]

Mrs. Eddy's qualification toward the close of this statement that she did not mean that mortals are the children of God is important to bear in mind, for she always drew a clear distinction between the mortal picture of man and the spiritual fact, man. "Mortal man," she wrote, "is the antipode of immortal man in origin, in existence, and in his relation to God." [157] Not that there are two men; but the mortal sense of man being false, those who entertain it are temporarily under the mesmerism of the belief of life in matter. As indicated earlier, Mrs. Eddy does not try to explain why men are faced with the necessity of challenging the beliefs of mortality. She is concerned, rather, with urging them to do so and thus to demonstrate their true spiritual sonship.

Mrs. Eddy predicates the possibility of man's awakening to and demonstration of his spiritual sonship with God entirely on revelation. To her, those under the illusion of life in matter could not possibly break

---

155. On this point, see, for example, *Ibid.,* pp. 323, 448.
156. *My.,* pp. 241–242. 157. *S&H.,* p. 215.

that illusion and discern the spiritual fact through unaided efforts of their own. In Mrs. Eddy's words, ". . . erring, finite, human mind has an absolute need of something beyond itself for its redemption and healing." [158] Though nothing in her teaching mediates between God and man as His reflection, she does maintain that men under the belief of life in matter need a mediator to awaken them from this belief. And in *Science and Health* she quotes approvingly these words from Paul: "There is one God, and one mediator between God and men, the man Christ Jesus." [159]

Jesus, Mrs. Eddy wrote, "was the mediator between Spirit and the flesh, between Truth and error. Explaining and demonstrating the way of divine Science, he became the way of salvation to all who accepted his word. From him mortals may learn how to escape from evil." [160] She referred to him also as the "incarnate Jesus, — that life-link forming the connection through which the real reaches the unreal, Soul rebukes sense, and Truth destroys error." [161] As the mediator between Spirit and flesh, Jesus had to differ in nature from mortals. "Sin, sickness, appetites, and passions, constitute no part of man, but obscure man," Mrs. Eddy explained. "Therefore it required the divinity of our Master to perceive the real man, and to cast out the unreal or counterfeit." [162]

Mrs. Eddy spoke of Jesus' birth as the "incarnation of Truth, that amplification of wonder and glory which angels could only whisper" [163] and referred to this event as the Word made flesh. She fully accepts the Virgin Birth as the means through which divinity became apprehensible to humanity. These key passages from *Science and Health* make her position plain:

> The illumination of Mary's spiritual sense put to silence material law and its order of generation, and brought forth her child by the revelation of Truth, demonstrating God as the Father of men. The Holy Ghost, or divine Spirit, over-shadowed the pure sense of the Virgin-mother with the full recognition that being is Spirit.
>
> . . . Jesus was the offspring of Mary's self-conscious communion with God. Hence he could give a more spiritual idea of life than other men, and could demonstrate the Science of Love — his Father or divine Principle.[164]

158. *Ibid.,* p. 151.
159. I Timothy 2:5, quoted in *S&H.,* pp. 332.
160. *S&H.,* pp. 315–316.　　161. *Ibid.,* p. 350.　　　　162. *Pan.,* pp. 10–11.
163. *S&H.,* p. 501.　　　164. *Ibid.,* pp. 29–30.

It was, therefore, the Virgin Birth of Jesus which enabled him to be the wayshower of mankind. For this reason, the role of the Virgin Mary in Christian Science teaching, though not often emphasized, is of considerable importance.

Yet Mary's child, according to Mrs. Eddy, was not God taking the form of man, but a man. She wholly rejects the belief that Jesus was God and distinguished between Jesus as a man and Christ as one office of God. In Christian Science, Christ is the divine ideal of manhood, the model of perfect spiritual sonship; while Jesus was a human being who through the extraordinary conditions of his birth completely demonstrated this Christ ideal. In *Science and Health* Mrs. Eddy defined Christ as "The divine manifestation of God, which comes to the flesh to destroy incarnate error" [165] and Jesus as "The highest human corporeal concept of the divine idea." [166] In no sense, therefore, was the Christ confined to Jesus. Indeed, Mrs. Eddy wrote: "Throughout all generations both before and after the Christian era, the Christ, as the spiritual idea, — the reflection of God, — has come with some measure of power and grace to all prepared to receive Christ, Truth." [167] Yet at the same time, Jesus was uniquely inseparable from the Christ; for he represented the individualization of the Christ to human consciousness. He had, therefore, a dual nature:

Born of a woman, Jesus' advent in the flesh partook partly of Mary's earthly condition, although he was endowed with the Christ, the divine Spirit, without measure. This accounts for his struggles in Gethsemane and on Calvary, and this enabled him to be the mediator, or *way-shower* between God and men. Had his origin and birth been wholly apart from mortal usage, Jesus would not have been appreciable to mortal mind as "the way." [168]

The very contention that Jesus had a fleshly element was unacceptable to many of Mrs. Eddy's theological critics. One minister who believed him "to be perfect God and perfect Man, all-wise and all-holy," spoke of her as an "audacious blasphemer" because of her differing conception of Jesus' nature.[169] Yet it should be obvious, too, that since Mrs. Eddy taught that Jesus uniquely among men embodied the Christ, she shared more

---

165. *Ibid.,* p. 583.   166. *Ibid.,* p. 589.   167. *Ibid.,* p. 333.
168. *S&H.,* p. 30.
169. William Harmon Van Allen, "The Falsity of Christian Science, So-Called," pamphlet (Boston, 1908), p. 7.

common ground with her orthodox opponents than they generally understood.

Interestingly enough, it was a Jewish critic of Christian Science who most clearly grasped this point. Converts from Judaism to Christian Science were numerous enough to cause Jewish leaders grave concern. Many of these converts cherished the convenient belief that they could practice Christian Science while remaining good Jews. In an address read before the Central Conference of American Rabbis at Baltimore in April 1912, Rabbi Maurice Lefkovitz devoted himself to refuting this notion. His main point was that since Christian Science was essentially Christian, a Jew could not practice it without breaking faith with Judaism. Lefkovitz placed special emphasis upon the place of Jesus in Christian Science:

Christian Science does not believe in the deity of Jesus, but it does believe that he was the off-spring of Mary's self-conscious communion with God; and it supplements this belief with the statement that thus far only he, and no one else, has had such consciously divine descent. The creed of Christian Science thus assigns to Jesus a position in human thought and belief that is absolutely unique and distinct. . . . The man who subscribes to the creed of Christian Science affirms his belief in this unique unmatched, and unmatchable position of Christ Jesus.[170]

The correctness of Lefkovitz's argument can be seen by examining Mrs. Eddy's conception of the atonement. In the most general sense, atonement refers to the restoration of man's right relationship with God through the life and sacrificial death of Jesus. Beyond this general statement, there has been profound theological disagreement as to its precise nature. Most forms of orthodoxy have regarded it as a propitiary sacrifice, a vicarious appeasement of God's justice through the shedding of the blood of His son. Liberal theology since the mid-nineteenth century has tended to reject this view, claiming instead that Jesus' suffering and death exerted a sublime moral influence on mankind.

The idea of the atonement in Christian Science, however, fits into neither of these categories. Mrs. Eddy spoke of Jesus' atonement not as an act of restoration but of exemplification. "Atonement," she wrote, "is the exemplification of man's unity with God, whereby man reflects divine Truth, Life, and Love." [171] Just as she rejected the view of salvation as transformation, so she opposed the idea of atonement as restoration. To

170. Rabbi Maurice Lefkovitz, "The Attitude of Judaism toward Christian Science," pamphlet (Baltimore, 1912), p. 4.

171. *S&H.*, p. 18.

her it meant a showing forth of that which is true of man in Science — his inseparability from God and freedom from all forms of evil. Jesus' atonement in Christian Science is understood as literally his "at-one-ment" with God — his example of divine manhood which points the way of salvation to mortals. Jesus, Mrs. Eddy observed, did not have to go through the experience of the crucifixion; his willingness to do so was a sacrifice, the crowning proof of his love for mankind. "The efficacy of the crucifixion," Mrs. Eddy explained, "lay in the practical affection and goodness it demonstrated for mankind"; and she related the importance of the crucifixion directly to that of the resurrection by writing that Jesus "allowed men to attempt the destruction of the mortal body in order that he might furnish the proof of immortal life." [172] Jesus knew that he could not be separated from his true Life, God. His resurrection, which Mrs. Eddy unreservedly accepted as an actual historical event, provided full proof of this fact. It afforded mortals vital evidence of the triumph of Spirit over the most extreme claims of the flesh.

Christian theology, Mrs. Eddy felt, had largely missed the importance of Jesus' work by clinging to his person rather than by understanding the divine Principle of his acts. To her it seemed clear that though mankind needed Jesus' mediatory mission to show the way out of material sense, all men must walk in this way in order to make his work effective. In many passages Mrs. Eddy emphasized a point that she perhaps best expressed when she wrote:

While we adore Jesus, and the heart overflows with gratitude for what he did for mortals, — treading alone his loving pathway up to the throne of glory, in speechless agony exploring the way for us, — yet Jesus spares us not one individual experience, if we follow his commands faithfully; and all have the cup of sorrowful effort to drink in proportion to their demonstration of his love, till all are redeemed through divine Love.[173]

This attitude drew heavy fire from her conservative theological critics. One of them, referring to her characteristic statement that "The atonement requires constant self-immolation on the sinner's part," expressed himself in these terms: "I thank my God tonight that I preach the Gospel of the Lord Jesus Christ, who did a finished work on Calvary, who made a complete atonement. . . . Christ died once for all. . . . I thank God that my hope for eternal life does not depend on the little good I have done, or what I shall do in the future." [174] Mrs. Eddy did not wholly

172. *Ibid.,* pp. 24, 51.   173. *Ibid.,* p. 26.
174. Cox, "Christian Science Exposed," p. 7.

reject the doctrine of the vicarious atonement, as many of her critics suggested. The atonement, as she understood it, was not substitutionary, but it was in a very real sense sacrificial. For she maintained that Jesus' sacrifice and suffering "purchased the means of mortals' redemption from sin." [175] And it was with much feeling that she wrote in reply to criticism on this issue:

> The real blood or Life of Spirit is not yet discerned. Love bruised and bleeding, yet mounting to the throne of glory in purity and peace, over the steps of uplifted humanity, — this is the deep significance of the blood of Christ. Nameless woe, everlasting victories, are the blood, the vital currents of Christ Jesus' life, purchasing the freedom of mortals from sin and death.
>
> This blood of Jesus is everything to human hope and faith. Without it, how poor the precedents of Christianity! What manner of Science were Christian Science without the power to demonstrate the Principle of such Life; and what hope have mortals but through deep humility and adoration to reach the understanding of this Principle! [176]

"NOW IS THE DAY OF SALVATION"

Every man, Mrs. Eddy taught, must eventually make Jesus' atonement effective in his own experience by awakening to the truth of being and demonstrating his actual spiritual selfhood. In the article "The New Birth" she wrote that "Nothing aside from the spiritualization — yea, the highest Christianization — of thought and desire, can give the true perception of God and divine Science, that results in health, happiness, and holiness." This new birth for Mrs. Eddy meant the awakening out of the belief of life in matter into the apprehension of God as the only Life and man as the reflection of that Life. Where human birth marks the appearance of a mortal, the spiritual birth is the dawning of "man's primitive, sinless, spiritual existence" upon human thought.[177]

The New Birth, therefore, marks the awakening of what Mrs. Eddy called *spiritual sense* in human consciousness. For only through this faculty can man begin to understand the spiritual facts of being which are not yet objectified in experience, but which are nevertheless real in Science. For her, the accession of spiritual sense is the awakening from the sleep of matter to the life of Spirit. It is that which makes demonstration possible, for without it men would continue to treat the false material picture of existence as basic reality itself. With the awakening of spiritual sense,

175. *Mis.*, p. 165.   176. *No.*, pp. 34–35.   177. *Mis.*, pp. 15–17.

Mrs. Eddy indicates, men gain an inward or subjective sense of that which
is real in Science but is not real to material sense. Though spiritual sense
is subjective, in that it is consciousness of that which is not yet objectified
in experience, it is for that reason no less *sense*. For in speaking of spiritual sense, Mrs. Eddy often uses the terms to *apprehend, behold,* or *discern* — thus indicating an immediate or unmediated grasp of the spiritual
fact. "Jesus," she wrote, for example, "beheld in Science the perfect man,
who appeared to him where sinning mortal man appears to mortals. In
this perfect man the Saviour saw God's own likeness, and this correct
view of man healed the sick." [178]

This conception of spiritual sense relates Mrs. Eddy's teaching to the
theology of the towering figure in her religious background, Jonathan
Edwards. The differences between Christian Science and Edwardsian
theology are, of course, in many respects very great indeed. But they are
united in linking man's whole spiritual condition with his perceptual
faculties. For Edwards, the man who is newly born gains a spiritual sense
that endows him with new perceptual capacities, through which he becomes able to discern the "excellency" of the Creator and His created
works in nature as never before.[179] "A new kind of perception or sensation," according to Edwards, is instilled in the mind of the man under
grace. "And here is, as it were," he continues,

a new spiritual sense that the mind has, or a principle of a new kind of perception or spiritual sensation, which is in its whole nature different from any
former kinds of sensation of the mind, as tasting is diverse from any of the
other senses; and something is perceived by a true saint, in the exercise of
this new sense of mind, in spiritual and divine things, as entirely diverse
from anything that is perceived in them, by natural men, as the sweet taste
of honey is diverse from the ideas men have on honey only by looking at it.[180]

In Edwards' theology, man's whole sense of existence cannot be separated
from his sense of the divine. As he put it in his early *Notes on the Mind,*
"God and Real existence are the same." [181] The man under grace beholds
the real being of the things of nature which God has made. Taken as
physical objects, the things of nature have no spiritual significance. But

178. *S&H.,* pp. 476–477.
179. See the discussion of this central aspect of Edwards' thought in Conrad
Cherry, *The Theology of Jonathan Edwards: A Reappraisal* (New York, 1966), pp.
25–43.
180. Jonathan Edwards, "A Divine and Supernatural Light," in Faust, p. 107.
181. Jonathan Edwards, "Notes on the Mind," in Faust, p. 31.

through spiritual sense one can see them in their true meaning as "images and shadows of divine things." [182]

Mrs. Eddy's early religious teachers were representative of the New England Theology which drew its inspiration from Edwards. The meaning of the term *spiritual sense* in Christian Science relates to its use in the Edwardsian tradition. For in both, spiritual sense indicates the new vision of reality itself entertained by the newly born. It points to the effect of spiritual vision in reshaping man's sense of what is real through the enlargement of his faculties for perception. For Mrs. Eddy, however, this effect is much more drastic than for Edwards. In his theology, the change brought by the accession of spiritual sense is the poetic illumination of nature. But Mrs. Eddy insists that spiritual sense awakens one to the utter falsity of *all* material sense testimony and to the reality of the spiritual fact which is not perceptible to the physical senses. Her use of this idea of spiritual sense, then, is to some degree a reflection of her close ties with the New England Theology which stems back to Edwards. But her departure from Edwards in regard to the meaning of spiritual sense is also a measure of the radicalism of her concept of what regeneration must include.

"The new birth," wrote Mrs. Eddy, "is not the work of a moment. It begins with moments, and goes on with years; moments of surrender to God, of childlike trust and joyful adoption of good; moments of self-abnegation, self-consecration, heaven-born hope, and spiritual love." [183] As this passage indicates, regeneration in Christian Science is understood as a step-by-step growth into spiritual manhood which demands nothing short of total dedication. Though the spiritual fact of "perfect God and perfect man" remains eternally true, the human perception and demonstration of this fact requires continued struggle and growth. In *Science and Health* Mrs. Eddy wrote of this process as a progression through three degrees of development. The first degree, which she termed physical and is characterized by depravity, includes the worst elements of mortal mind and is wholly unreal. The second degree is transitional. Mrs. Eddy referred to it as the moral degree in which evil beliefs are disappearing and such good qualities as compassion, affection, honesty, and hope are appearing. In the third or spiritual degree, which Mrs. Eddy refers to as under-

182. See Perry Miller's introduction to Jonathan Edwards, *Images and Shadows of Divine Things* (New Haven, 1948), pp. 1–41.
183. *Mis.*, p. 15.

standing, "mortal mind disappears, and man as God's image appears." [184]

Until the "final degree of regeneration" is attained, Mrs. Eddy wrote, "the Christian Scientist must continue to strive with sickness, sin and death — though in lessening degrees — and manifest growth at every experience." [185] All men, she taught, face the necessity of working out their salvation in this way; and they had better begin right now in their present circumstances to do it. This is not an easy way, but it must be trod. "Be watchful, sober, and vigilant," she counseled her readers in *Science and Health.* "The way is straight and narrow, which leads to the understanding that God is the only Life. It is a warfare with the flesh, in which we must conquer sin, sickness, and death, either here or hereafter, — certainly before we can reach the goal of Spirit, or life in God." [186]

Mrs. Eddy departed from Protestant orthodoxy by including in this warfare with the flesh the overcoming of sickness and death, as well as sin. All three to her were simply forms of the belief of life in matter. By overcoming disease, and eventually death as well, one proves in the most tangible way the power of Spirit to destroy the false beliefs of mortal mind; and this practical working out of material sense is, Mrs. Eddy held, most essential to the full demonstration of man's spiritual perfection. Even so, she subordinated the cure of disease to the redemption of mortals from sin, writing that "Healing physical sickness is the smallest part of Christian Science. It is only the bugle-call to thought and action, in the higher range of infinite goodness. The emphatic purpose of Christian Science is the healing of sin." This task, she observed, is sometimes the harder of the two, for "while mortals love to sin, they do not love to be sick." [187] One simple gauge of the importance of the regeneration of mortals from sin in Christian Science is the fact that in Mrs. Eddy's 1700 pages of published writings the word sin and its derivatives appear well over 1000 times.

In Christian Science, sin indicates the basic belief of mortal mind— that is, the claim of a selfhood apart from God. Frequently Mrs. Eddy speaks of sin in terms of self, as when she wrote: "In patient obedience to a patient God, let us labor to dissolve with the universal solvent of Love the adamant of error, — self-will, self-justification, and self-love, — which wars against spirituality and is the law of sin and death." [188] The indulgence of sin seemed to Mrs. Eddy by its very nature to be destruc-

184. *S&H.,* 115–116.   185. *Mis.,* p. 86.   186. *S&H.,* p. 324.
187. *Rud.,* pp. 2–3.   188. *S&H.,* p. 242.

tive, for it is contrary to the law of God and is punished by that law. Mrs. Eddy wrote that the "law of Life and Truth . . . does more than forgive the false sense named sin, for it pursues and punishes it, and will not let sin go until it is destroyed, — until nothing is left to be forgiven, to suffer, or to be punished." [189] The agony which sin brings to the sinner can be ended only when he ceases to be a sinner. "The way to escape the misery of sin," Mrs. Eddy declared, "is to cease sinning. There is no other way." [190]

To her, the working out of mankind's salvation from sin required a mighty struggle; for she saw mortal mind, in which sin inheres, as capable of all evil. In one place she spoke of "the inner vile affections of mortals," [191] and in another of the "total depravity of . . . mortal mind." [192] Mrs. Eddy once wrote that she could conceive of "little short of the old orthodox hell" to awaken some sinners from their "deluded sense." "Some mortals," she went on, "may even need to hear the following thunderbolt of Jonathan Edwards:" — and then she quoted the passage from his Enfield Sermon beginning, "It is nothing but God's mere pleasure that keeps you from being this moment swallowed up in everlasting destruction." [193]

Had Mrs. Eddy's theological opponents taken this and other comparable statements of hers more seriously, they might have spared themselves a good deal of energy in denouncing her teaching. For nothing galled them more about Christian Science than their belief that since Mrs. Eddy proclaimed the ultimate unreality of evil, she had undermined the Christian requirement of regeneration. "That underlying principle of the 'unreality of evil,'" wrote one minister in 1898, "plunges a dagger through the Bible doctrine of a man's individual accountability and lets out the very heart-blood of Christ's distinctive teaching." [194] The Reverend Robert A. Edwards of Philadelphia warned his congregation against Christian Science with specific reference to a local incident:

. . . what a shocking statement to make, to call *sin* — SIN — nothingness! Sin is the most dreadful fact in this world of ours. The young mulatto who the other week over in Jersey killed the good old clergyman and his wife who had been his lifelong benefactors, apparently considered sin as nothingness.[195]

189. *No,* p. 30.   190. *S&H.,* p. 327.
191. Mary Baker Eddy, "Questions Answered," *CSJ,* VI (Nov. 1886), 161.
192. *Mis.,* p. 2.   193. *Mess.* '01, p 15.
194. Faunce, "The Philosophy of Christian Science," in *Searchlights,* p. 46.
195. Robert A. Edwards, "Eddyism: A Review," pamphlet (Philadelphia, n.d.), p. 3.

To a minister well-schooled in the art of detecting heresy, a doctrine that denied the reality of evil and so opened wide the door to wrongdoing could suggest only one thing: a revivification of the Gnostic heresy which had plagued the early Christian era. The early Church Father Irenaeus had written that since according to Gnosticism men are to be saved "through the mere fact of their being by nature 'spiritual,' . . . then nothing can injure them, even if their deeds immerse them in matter, and nothing can change their spiritual essence." [196] The same fear was expressed in very similar language by many Protestant critics of Christian Science. "If sin is only an error of mortal mind," wrote one of Mrs. Eddy's Baptist critics, "then the practical outcome of this theory will surely be that man being spiritual, his nature cannot be corrupted by anything his mortal mind can do." [197] Roman Catholic critics of Christian Science were if anything even more sensitive than Protestants to a recrudescence of Gnosticism. To the Jesuit Henry Woods, Christian Science seemed to revive the error of the most extreme of Gnostics, the Manicheans of the third century. Repeating their errors, he maintained, Mrs. Eddy and her followers "may come to fall into the horrible uncleanliness of their predecessors." [198]

Mrs. Eddy's denial of the reality of evil is, of course, basic to Christian Science, and she never modified it in the slightest. But she did realize, too, that Christian Science could be dangerously distorted in practice. Therefore she took special pains to disabuse her critics, and her followers as well, of the notion that her assertion of the unreality of evil could be used as a justification for its indulgence. "To assume that there are no claims of evil and yet to indulge them," she wrote, "is a moral offense." [199] Sin and evil, she frequently emphasized, were unreal *only* in the sense that they were unreal to God and hence had no spiritual legitimacy. Once men grasped this fact through spiritual awakening, she maintained, they could demonstrate the unreality of evil. They could make nothing of evil only by literally making nothing of it — reducing it in practice to what she called its "native nothingness."

Indeed, Mrs. Eddy felt that Christian Science revealed as did no other

196. Quoted in Hans Jonas, *The Gnostic Religion: The Message of the Alien God and the Beginnings of Christianity* (Boston, 1958), pp. 270–271.

197. Moore, *Christian Science: Its Manifold Attractions*, p. 75. Moore also quotes A. J. Gordon to the same effect.

198. Henry Woods, "Christian Science," *The Catholic Mind* (May 22, 1918), p. 231.

199. *S&H.*, pp. 447–448.

religious teaching the full nature of sin and the character of its operation. In its ultimate character, sin in her teaching is identical with what she called *animal magnetism*. Though Mrs. Eddy does not discuss the subject of animal magnetism at length in her writings, it is one of the central reference points in the teaching and practice of Christian Science.[200] And what she does have to say about it is central to an understanding of her teaching as a whole and most necessary to its practice. As Mrs. Eddy describes it, animal magnetism is not a power, but a claim to power which if credited would deny all that divine Science declares is true of God and man. Animal magnetism operates hypnotically, she explains; for it holds men spellbound in error, mesmerically attracted to the very beliefs which would blast their harmony and peace. "As named in Christian Science," Mrs. Eddy wrote, "animal magnetism or hypnotism is the specific term for error, or mortal mind. It is the false belief that mind is in matter, and is both evil and good; that evil is as real as good and more powerful." [201] This term "animal magnetism" is "the specific term for error or mortal mind" in that it suggests the *operation* of error, the mesmeric hold of the belief that mind is mortal. In this sense, it is in Mrs. Eddy's words, "the human antipode of divine Science." [202] For if divine Science means the sustaining operation of Spirit, animal magnetism refers to the destructive operation of error. And the discovery of animal magnetism, Mrs. Eddy felt, was the necessary complement to the revelation of Divine Science.

One of the most controversial aspects of Mrs. Eddy's teaching was her insistence that the generalized error animal magnetism operated through persons as what she called "mental malpractice." This malpractice could be ignorant, but it could also be malicious. In either case, it was the injurious influence of one mind upon another. Mrs. Eddy identified the "giant sin" of intentional malpractice as the sin against the Holy Ghost spoken of by Jesus.[203] And as we shall see, she was convinced that it was the operation of animal magnetism that impeded the progress of the Christian Science movement. She pictured animal magnetism symbolically as the great red dragon of the Apocalypse, "full of lust and hate, loathing the brightness of divine glory." [204] And she felt compelled to warn mankind against it. In *Science and Health,* for example, she wrote:

200. Her major statement on the subject is the chapter "Animal Magnetism Unmasked," in *S&H.*, pp. 100–106.

201. *S&H.*, p. 103.   202. *Ibid.*, p. 484.   203. *Mis.*, p. 55.
204. *S&H.*, p. 565.

The mild forms of animal magnetism are disappearing, and its aggressive features are coming to the front. The looms of crime, hidden in the dark recesses of mortal thought, are every hour weaving webs more complicated and subtle. So secret are the present methods of animal magnetism that they ensnare the age into indolence, and produce the very apathy on the subject which the criminal desires.[205]

How does one, then, master sin in himself and prevent himself from being subject to the adverse mental influences of others? Mrs. Eddy said that this can be done only by demonstrating that one has no Mind but God. "There can be but one Mind," Mrs. Eddy asserted, "because there is but one God; and if mortals claimed no other Mind and accepted no other, sin would be unknown." [206] In this sense, the overcoming of sin as a phase of salvation from the flesh must be understood as the positive demonstration of the spiritual fact in Science.

The phenomenon of physical healing, though the best known aspect of Christian Science, is at the same time perhaps the least understood. For the intent behind Christian Science healing is not in the first instance therapeutic. Its purpose is not the correction of material disorders for the sake of human comfort, but the progressive demonstration of the spiritual status of man. That is, healing can be understood only in the context of Mrs. Eddy's insistence upon the need for the total regeneration of mortals from all phases of the flesh. If all disease proceeds, as Mrs. Eddy claimed that it did, from the belief of life in matter, then the healing of disease through spiritual power is an essential phase of the destruction of this belief. Mrs. Eddy is most insistent upon this point. "Admit the existence of matter," she wrote, "and you admit that mortality (and therefore disease) has a foundation in fact. Deny the existence of matter, and you can destroy the belief in material conditions." [207]

The material conditions of which she spoke included *any* sort of physical disorder. Mrs. Eddy taught that thought determines every bodily function and formation. The mortal body, she said, is really but the objectified state of mortal mind; in actuality, the two are one. Obviously, Mrs. Eddy's position goes well beyond the assertion that mind *influences* body — a claim that has been made with increasing frequency since her day. Even before *Science and Health* was published, a pioneering medical work had already appeared tracing *The Influence of the Mind Upon the*

205. *Ibid.,* p. 102.   206. *Ibid.,* p. 469.   207. *Ibid.,* p. 368.

Body;[208] since that time, both psychology and psychosomatic medicine have investigated this influence extensively. But Mrs. Eddy maintained that in any disease of whatever severity, "the remote, exciting, and the predisposing cause" is mental.[209] She claimed that there is no involuntary action, for "the valves of the heart, opening and closing for the passage of blood, obey the mandate of mortal mind as directly as does the hand, admittedly moved by the will." [210] And she also stated that "bones have only the substance of thought which forms them." [211] The immediate cause of disease in most instances, Mrs. Eddy indicated, is fear, terrifying images of thought impressed upon the body. But the basic cause of disease is the belief of life in matter.

Since this belief can be corrected through prayer, all disease can be healed. Christian Science claims to heal any disorder that medicine can cure. Indeed, it claims to go much further than medicine by destroying the fundamental cause of disease. Where medicine, for example, claims in some instances to control the effects of hereditary predisposition to some degree, Christian Science claims to wipe out the predisposition itself on the basis that Life is and proceeds only from God.[212] Mrs. Eddy required that step by step her followers prove their superiority over the belief in material conditions through the healing of disease. She explains the motivation behind Christian Science healing by writing that Jesus

restored the diseased body to its normal action, functions, and organization, and in explanation of his deeds he said, "Suffer it to be so now: for thus it becometh us to fulfill all righteousness." Job said, "In my flesh shall I see God." Neither the Old nor the New Testament furnishes reasons or examples for the destruction of the human body, but for its restoration to life and health as the scientific proof of "God with us." The power and prerogative of Truth are to destroy all disease and to raise the dead — even the self-same Lazarus. The *spiritual* body, the incorporeal idea, came with the *ascension*.[213]

Mrs. Eddy did not expect that men could achieve the final victory over mortality in the present age before death; for she felt that mankind had not yet attained sufficient spiritual growth for this demonstration to be made. Yet she did mantain that "Resurrection from the dead (that is, from the belief in death) must come to all sooner or later." [214] All men, that is, must triumph over death, as well as sickness and sin. What seems

---

208. Hack Tuke, *The Influence of the Mind on the Body* (London, 1872).
209. *S&H.*, p. 230.   210. *Ibid.*, p. 187.   211. *Ibid.*, p. 423.
212. See *S&H.*, pp. 178, 228, for Mrs. Eddy's discussion of heredity.
213. *My.*, p. 218.   214. *Un.*, p. 41.

to be human death is therefore not death at all. For she taught that men continue at the same point of spiritual development after what is called death as before the transition. They awaken after death with conscious identity and with the same sense of body as they had before. Those who bury the body, Mrs. Eddy asserted, are merely burying their own false sense of man.[215] She did not believe that those who had already died could communicate with those who had not. Yet she did maintain that they could recognize and commune with others who had also died. And all men, she taught, would go on dying until they mastered the belief of life in matter and demonstrated that God is the only Life of man. "Universal salvation," wrote Mrs. Eddy, "rests on progression and probation, and is unattainable without them."[216]

By referring to man's condition beyond the grave as a period of probation, Mrs. Eddy was touching upon a theological issue that was the subject of hot debate in the late nineteenth century. Many of the New Theologians believed that those who had not been converted in this life might have an opportunity to know Christ hereafter. This idea was anathema to conservatives, who held that in this life alone would the issues of salvation be decided for each man. This controversy over the question of the "second probation" was the focal point of conflict between the liberal vanguard and its orthodox opponents at Andover Theological Seminary in the 1880s. Clearly, Mrs. Eddy falls on the liberal side of the question. Yet she does not stop with just the *second* probation, for she maintained that men would go on dying until they awakened to the reality of Life.

In Christian Science, judgment stands for a continuing and not just a final process. "No final judgment awaits mortals," Mrs. Eddy wrote, "for the judgment day of wisdom comes hourly and continually, even the judgment by which mortal man is divested of all material error."[217] Hence, she does not view heaven and hell as places to which one goes or states which one enters after death. Both stand in her teachings for conditions of consciousness possible to man now. Mrs. Eddy wrote of heaven not as "a locality, but a divine state of Mind in which all the manifestations of Mind are harmonious and immortal, because sin is not there and man is found having no righteousness of his own, but in possession of the 'mind of the Lord,' as the Scripture says."[218] Similarly, she wrote that

---

215. Mrs. Eddy's discussion of death can be found in *S&H.*, pp. 426–430.
216. *S&H.*, p. 291.   217. *Ibid.*   218. *Ibid.*

"The evil beliefs which originate in mortals are hell" [219] and spoke of "hidden unpunished sin" as an "internal fire" which tortures the sinner until his sinfulness is destroyed.[220]

In an important passage from *Science and Health,* Mrs. Eddy spoke in apocalyptic accents of a consummation in which error will end and Truth will be demonstrated forever and for all men. "Love will finally mark the hour of harmony," she declared, "and spiritualization will follow, for Love is Spirit." This consummation, Mrs. Eddy said, will be preceded by interruptions in the general material routine, by an intensification of evil, and a clear division between the forces of "discord and dismay" and of "Science and peace." Even so, we can still rejoice in "the certainty of ultimate perfection." [221] And Mrs. Eddy also taught that men need not wait for this final consummation to achieve a state of spiritual blessedness, for the perfection which must ultimately be demonstrated is discernible by spiritual sense now. Mrs. Eddy dwells on John's vision of a "new heaven and a new earth" in the Book of Revelation:

The Revelator was on our plane of existence, while yet beholding what the eye cannot see, — that which is invisible to the uninspired thought. This testimony of Holy Writ sustains the fact in Science, that the heavens and earth to one human consciousness, that consciousness which God bestows, are spiritual, while to another, the unillumined human mind, the vision is material. . . . This is Scriptural authority for concluding that such a recognition of being is, and has been, possible to men in this present state of existence, — that we can become conscious, here and now, of a cessation of death, sorrow, and pain. This is indeed a foretaste of absolute Christian Science. Take heart, dear sufferer, for this reality of being will surely appear sometime and in some way. There will be no more pain, and all tears will be wiped away. When you read this, remember Jesus' words, "The Kingdom of God is within you." This spiritual consciousness is therefore a present possibility.[222]

Mrs. Eddy's eschatology, as represented in this passage, differs in revealing ways from that to be found in both orthodox and liberal Protestantism. It is neither the apocalyptic return of Christ in Judgment prophesied in orthodoxy nor the gradual amelioration of human affairs through spiritually-empowered evolution preached in liberalism. To Mrs. Eddy, God's kingdom was not of the future. It was not a kingdom to come, but a kingdom already come — established as the reality of being. Man's great need, Mrs. Eddy declared, is to become conscious of this

219. *Ibid.*, p. 266. 220. *My.*, p. 160. 221. *S&H.*, pp. 96–97.
222. *Ibid.*, pp. 573–574.

kingdom through the awakening of spiritual sense and to demonstrate the reality of this one order of being. There is no divine timetable for this demonstration. The appearing of the kingdom, which Mrs. Eddy holds is certain, awaits men's efforts, and no objective power impedes this achievement. The way, Mrs. Eddy asserts, is clear. It has been demonstrated by Jesus and explained in Christian Science. Her message to the world was that all who seek true Christianity may walk in it and realize that in truth, "Now is the day of Salvation."

Mrs. Eddy interpreted this statement of St. Paul as meaning "not that now men must prepare for a future-world salvation, or safety, but that now is the time in which to experience that salvation in spirit and in life." [222] This concept of salvation as the presently-possible demonstration of man's freedom from all forms of evil clearly differentiates Christian Science from Christian orthodoxy, whether Roman Catholic or Protestant. For Mrs. Eddy is asserting that the spiritual fact of "perfect God and perfect man" is established in Science and through revelation can be comprehended and demonstrated by men—a claim that no form of Christian orthodoxy would grant. But it must also be emphasized that in departing from orthodoxy meaning specifically the Protestant orthodoxy that constituted the immediate religious background of Christian Science — Mrs. Eddy by no means embraced Protestant liberalism. When in 1902 she obsrved that in the previous decade religion in the United States had passed "from stern Protestantism to doubtful liberalism," [223] she was obviously identifying her teaching with neither. And it should be no surprise that her one published comment on the New Theology was definitely in the negative.[224]

The conclusion is warranted, therefore, that Christian Science emerged into American religious life, not as a variant form of Protestantism, but as a genuinely distinct alternative for religious thought and practice. Yet Mrs. Eddy contended also that her teaching was based upon Christian revelation, constituted the purest Christianity, and could be fathomed only by a Christian.[225] The meaning of these assertions is perhaps best understood in terms of the relationship between Christian Science and the essentially non-Christian movements that arose to challenge it in the 1880's — a relationship which forms the subject of our next chapter.

---

222. *S&H.*, p. 39.
223. Eddy, "Message for 1902," p. 13.
224. Mary Baker Eddy, "The Creed of the New Theology" *CSJ*, VI (April 1888), 48–49.
225. *S&H.*, p. 556.

"The Tares and the Wheat"

It is often the fate of a religious movement to find itself gravely threatened by the rise of rival movements which seem in some respects doctrinally close to it, but which are in essential points different. Instances of this rivalry in the Christian tradition alone include the conflicts of the early Christian fathers with the Gnostics, of Lutherans with Anabaptists, and of American Puritans with Quakers and Antinomians. The fledgling Christian Science movement faced a similar crisis at the point of its emergence in American religious life — that is, when it first began to attract public notice and to gain a sizeable following in Boston in the mid 1880s — in its encounter with various "mind-cure" groups, which were in the main its own offshoots, and with various forms of occultism akin to "mind-cure." The rise of these movements forced Mrs. Eddy and her followers in this crucial period to struggle, with eventual success, for the preservation of the very identity of her teaching and the continuity of the movement.

BABEL IN BOSTON — AND BEYOND

In his book, *A History of the New Thought Movement,* published in 1919, Horatio Dresser observed that many erstwhile sympathizers had broken away from Mrs. Eddy "to set up for themselves, meanwhile keeping such ideas as had proved of value." His bias in the matter becomes clear when he predicts that "in due time, the last Christian Scientist will probably take leave in the same way. In retrospect, people will wonder why such a reaction did not occur long before." [1]

The bias is understandable: Dresser himself was one of the major theoreticians of the New Thought movement, his father Julius Dresser had been one of its founders, and both were exceedingly hostile to Mrs. Eddy. But he hardly had justification for making this prediction in 1919. For at that date the Christian Science movement was at the threshold of a period of tremendous growth. Thirty years before the picture had not been so encouraging for the Christian Scientists. For in the late 1880s, many people unable to accept Mrs. Eddy's authority and the radicalism of her teaching gravitated into the emerging New Thought movement, then known as mind-cure;[2] while in their militancy and dogmatism, as Dresser saw it, the Christian Scientists remained faithful to the spirit of their leader.

Certainly no one could accuse the New Thought movement of either militancy or dogmatism. For the movement had no organization cohesive enough to be militant and no dogma fixed enough to be militant about. The only organization that embraced most of the New Thought groups was the International New Thought Alliance, formed in London in 1914. The I.N.T.A., as it was generally known, was a loose federation of genuinely autonomous groups and had no real powers of its own. Its Declaration of Principles, adopted in 1917, was so broad as to include most of the New Thought groups; and in later years it was broadened even further by amendment to include others.[3] These groups did differ widely in the metaphysical emphasis of their teachings, though they shared the common attitudes enshrined in the Declaration. The only item of faith which could be called a dogma for them was antidogmatism itself, a liberal eclecticism that stood firmly opposed to all religious authority. The very term New Thought, wrote Dresser, was adopted in 1895 as the name for the "liberal wing of the therapeutic movement." [4]

1. Horatio Dresser, *A History of the New Thought Movement* (New York, 1919), p. 17.

2. It is difficult to find an adequate term for this movement as it existed in the 1880s. Only in the mid-1890s did the term "New Thought" come into general use as the name of the metaphysical groups opposed to Christian Science. Not all of those referred to here as "mind-curers" would have accepted this label. Some of them preferred to be known as "mental scientists." But "mind-cure" is the single term which was most often used for their movements and which seems most satisfactory.

3. For further information on the I.N.T.A., see Charles Braden, *Spirits in Rebellion* (Dallas, 1963), pp. 170–232.

4. Dresser, *History*, p. 187.

It was this liberalism, this anti-dogmatism, that defined the character of the emerging New Thought movement during the period of its encounter with Christian Science in the late 1880s. For the mind-curers, the progenitors of New Thought, Christian Science was a negative reference in contrast to which they defined their own character. They viewed themselves as the true liberals in the field of mental healing, arrayed against the arch-conservatives of Mrs. Eddy's camp. Where she held that metaphysics was an exact science rooted in a universal Principle, they looked upon it as an open invitation to the most far-flung of speculative flights. And where she insisted that her teaching was based upon Christian revelation, they saw Christianity as just one among a number of viable religious traditions from which inspiration could be drawn.

Those apostates from Christian Science who helped to launch the mind-cure and New Thought movement invariably championed this sort of spiritual eclecticism. But in many, if not most, cases there is good evidence, as we shall see, that their rejection of Mrs. Eddy and her teaching sprang more from personal rivalry and desire for power than from any ideological considerations as such. As these apostates rebelled against Mrs. Eddy's authority and set off on their own, they found allies in Boston in representatives of older systems of mental healing. These older systems, Dresser acknowledged, would not have gained any real notoriety had it not been for the interest in mental healing aroused by Christian Science.[5] The New Thought movement began to take shape (though very amorphous shape) as apostates from Christian Science found common ground with older advocates of mind-healing both in doctrine and common hostility to Christian Science.

Dissension in and apostasy from the Christian Science movement did not always have ideological ramifications. Those of Mrs. Eddy's students who rebelled against her leadership in Lynn in 1881 proposed no variant form of Christian Science to rival hers. Similarly, the first prominent student to break away from Mrs. Eddy in Boston, Clara M. Choate, never drifted as far away from her teaching as did later rebels. Before the end of the century, Mrs. Choate had found her way back into the movement. But her "Institute of Christian Science," founded in 1884 after her break with Mrs. Eddy, was the first of many institutions set up in rivalry to the Massachusetts Metaphysical College.

Far more representative of the apostates of the 1880s was Luther Mar-

5. *Ibid.,* p. 187.

ston, who had studied with Mrs. Eddy in 1884. A former physician, Marston felt that Christian Scientists should be trained in medicine so as to be able to recognize the diseases they were asked to treat. He further advocated that the teaching of Christian Science embrace any form of metaphysics or mental practice whatever — hypnotism, mesmerism, spiritualism, anything in which its students showed an interest. Mrs. Eddy had no use for this sort of catholicity. With reference to Marston, she said in the *Journal* during 1885 when he had already turned against her, "The hypocrite alone wishes to be known as antagonistic to no one, for he has no truth to defend." [6] Before long, Marston had a publication of his own in which to defend, if no particular truth, then at least himself; for in 1886 he founded the *Mental Healing Monthly,* which soon attained a circulation of over one thousand. In that year, too, he published his own book, *Essentials of Mental Healing,* and in 1888 he organized the "Church of the Divine Unity," a haven for many ex-Christian Scientists.

Besides Mrs. Choate and Marston, there were a number of other apostates from Christian Science active in Boston by the mid-1880s. Though Marston was the most vigorous of them, his name like most of the others has faded into obscurity as an organizer of New Thought. A far more important link between Christian Science and the New Thought movement, and certainly the most impressive apostate of these years, was Mrs. Emma Hopkins who took instruction from Mrs. Eddy in 1883 and became editor of the *Journal* the following year. Even before her appointment as editor, Mrs. Hopkins had given evidence of an eclecticism that clearly indicated her disinclination to preach and practice strict Christian Science. In April 1884, she wrote an article for the *Journal* on "God's Omnipresence," in which she implied that the study of metaphysical literature outside of Christian Science could deepen one's grasp of the essentially similar mystical principles common to them all.[7]

Mrs. Hopkins' tendency toward spiritual free-wheeling was encouraged by another of the more extraordinary women of this period, Mary H. Plunkett. Mrs. Plunkett, who had been asked to leave one of Mrs. Eddy's classes in 1883, taught her own version of Christian Science in New York, where she became known as its "High Priestess." Power-seeking and in need of an ally, she had sought out Mrs. Hopkins, then editor of the *Journal,* and encouraged her in rebellion against Mrs. Eddy. In 1886, Mrs. Hopkins, having left the *Journal* the preceding year, threw in her lot with

6. Mary Baker Eddy, "Definition of Purpose," *CSJ*, III (Nov. 1885), 140.
7. Emma Curtis Hopkins, "God's Omnipresence," *CSJ*, II (April 1884), 17.

Mrs. Plunkett. Five years later, with Mrs. Hopkins safely in tow, Mrs. Plunkett raptly informed an audience of Mrs. Hopkins' students of her efforts to wean their teacher away from Mrs. Eddy: "It would be sacrilege were I to attempt to tell you of the heart throbs and tears with which this already great teacher . . . was finally induced to enter upon the work . . . this little woman, so modest in her personality yet so mighty in her powers to teach the great Truth that the rays of Divine Light seem to radiate directly through her." [8]

As this quotation illustrates, Mrs. Plunkett played the role of promoter in their partnership, while Mrs. Hopkins took on that of a charismatic leader. Together they established yet another periodical, called *Truth: A Magazine of Christian Science,* later changed to the *International Magazine of Christian Science.* "Beautiful things lie waiting in the silence for you, dear reader," Mrs. Plunkett wrote in the first issue in November 1887. Then, defending herself in advance from accusations of false teaching from the Christian Scientists, she treated her reader to this magnificent *non-sequitur:* "Great hue and cry are raised about false teaching and false doctrine. Now if this is really an exact Science, there can be no false teaching." [9] The two women also built up an extensive system of metaphysical instruction based partly on plans Mrs. Hopkins had taken from Mrs. Eddy. They established schools, colleges, and seminaries of Christian Science — as they still called their teaching — in St. Paul, Louisville, Milwaukee, New York, and Chicago. The most successful of these institutions was the one under Mrs. Hopkins' direction in Chicago, the graduates of which she sent forth into the fertile fields of the midwest.

By this time, however, Mrs. Plunkett was no longer in the picture; for in 1889 she had committed a rather monumental indiscretion that insured her downfall in the eyes of the devotees of metaphysics. Falling in love with a clerk in her employ by the name of A. Bently Worthington, she announced through her periodical that she had taken him as her spiritual husband — all this without the formality of a legal divorce from Mr. Plunkett, who had long since ceased to count. A series of articles from her pen defending the action persuaded nobody, and the Christian Scientists made much of the affair in the *Journal.* [10] When it was learned that

8. Mary H. Plunkett, "Annual Address," *Truth: A Magazine of Christian Science,* I (Nov. 1887), 5.

9. Plunkett, "Our Mission," *Truth,* I (Nov. 1887), 3.

10. See, for example, Mary Baker Eddy, "Conjugal Rights," *CSJ,* VII (June 1889), 109–113.

A. Bently Worthington was a bigamist and thief, and was wanted in two states, Mrs. Plunkett was completely discredited.

At the beginning of the affair, Mrs. Hopkins very sensibly bowed out. Disassociating herself from Mrs. Plunkett, she began an independent career as a teacher of metaphysics. It was in this work that she made her greatest contribution to the development of the New Thought movement. Among its leaders whom she taught were Charles and Myrtle Filmore, founders of the Unity School of Christianity; H. Emile Cady, author of the widely read *Lessons in Truth;* Francis Lord, who helped to establish New Thought in Great Britain; Malinda E. Cramer, co-founder of Divine Science; and Ernest Holmes, founder of the Church of Religious Science. Thousands learned from her lips or from her pen how "to shiver and thrill," as she put it, "with the consciousness of the immortal in us." [11]

Next to Mrs. Hopkins, the most celebrated apostate from Christian Science in the 1880s was Ursula N. Gestefeld of Chicago. A member of the class that Mrs. Eddy taught in Chicago in 1884, Mrs. Gestefeld soon became a popular practitioner and writer in that city. In 1888 she published a book entitled *Ursula N. Gestefeld's Statement of Christian Science, Comprised in Eighteen Lessons and Twelve Sections.*[12] Mrs. Gestefeld claimed that her book was not intended to supplant *Science and Health,* but only to make it more accessible by simplifying and systematizing its message. Actually, her version of Christian Science was far from correct in its statement of Mrs. Eddy's teaching. For she had interlaced her explanation of it with terms and ideas borrowed from quite different sources, most conspicuously Buddhism and Theosophy.

When her book was rejected by the movement, Mrs. Gestefeld issued a violent attack on Mrs. Eddy in the form of a pamphlet called "Jesuitism in Christian Science." Therein she vigorously attacked Mrs. Eddy's leadership of the movement, declaring that Christian Science was being adulterated through the inability of Mrs. Eddy and her followers to "separate person from principle." "Making Mrs. Eddy a necessity to Christian Science," wrote Mrs. Gestefeld, "is following in the footsteps of the Roman Catholic Church, and creating a pope who is a necessity to God; and who is, in consequence, declared to be infallible." [13] Mrs. Eddy retorted through the *Journal* that the loyalty of Christian Scientists was not to herself per-

11. Emma Curtis Hopkins, "Sixth Lesson in Truth," (Chicago, 1891), p. 7.
12. Ursula N. Gestefeld, *Ursula N. Gestefeld's Statement of Christian Science, Comprised in Eighteen Lessons and Twelve Sections* (New York, 1888).
13. Gestefeld, "Jesuitism in Christian Science" (Chicago, 1888), p. 12.

sonally but to God, and that she was united with those students who stood by her only by bonds of common motive and aim. She further pointed to what she felt was Mrs. Gestefeld's complete incompetence to explain *Science and Health* and her impudence in attacking the discoverer of Christian Science. "She attempts to villify my life and to criticize my works, in the face of twenty-two years of unstained labor in Christian Science Mind-healing," wrote Mrs. Eddy, "while she, a suckling, is drawing her nutriment from them. This is at least, silly." [14]

Though this episode completely alienated Mrs. Gestefeld from the Christian Science movement, she was not thereby discouraged from practicing and teaching her own version of Christian Science. Mrs. Eddy's "proprietorship," she claimed, did not extend to the substance of her work, which was no more than mystics and metaphysicians from Buddha to Emerson had always known anyway. Unhampered by Mrs. Eddy's supervision, she proceeded, like Marston and Mrs. Hopkins before her, to found a periodical and publish further works on metaphysics. Her book purporting to explain *Science and Health,* which had sold few copies among Christian Scientists, reached a far larger audience outside the movement than it ever could have reached within it. Its author became a well-respected figure in New Thought, and when the I.N.T.A. was formed in London in 1914, she was present.

The tradition of mind-cure that predates the apostates just discussed owes its existence to two individuals: Phineas P. Quimby and Warren Felt Evans. Of the two, Evans was probably the more important figure in the actual development of New Thought. But Quimby has been given much greater notoriety, chiefly because of the controversy that arose in the 1880s concerning his influence upon Mrs. Eddy.

In his own right, Quimby was a most interesting figure. Part humanitarian, part crank, he can best be understood as a backwoods medical reformer who labored long and faithfully to develop a method for the cure of the sick. Beginning as a mesmerist, he developed in the 1840s and 1850s a technique of healing through the constructive power of thought alone, without the use of the induced trance state which was the hallmark of magnetic practice. As Quimby, somewhat ungrammatically, explained it, he took on the feeling of his patients and

discovered that ideas took form and the patient was affected just according to

14. Mary Baker Eddy, "Jesuitism in Christian Science," *CSJ*, VI (Nov. 1888), 427.

the impression contained in the idea. For example, if a person lost a friend at sea, the shock upon their system would disturb the fluids of their body and create around them a vapor, and in that are all their ideas, right or wrong. This vapor or fluid contains the identity of the person.[15]

Note here that Quimby refers to mind as a "vapor" or "fluid." Though he used the term *mind* often, he did not use it to indicate anything purely mental, as might a philosophical idealist. Rather, he used the term *mind,* and *spirit* as well, as did mesmerists generally, in a materialist sense to mean an etherialized form of matter. It was mind in this sense which Quimby felt was disturbed by false opinions or emotional shock, and so produced disease. And disease, he felt, could be cured by explaining to patients the real source of their ailments and imparting to them confidence in their own recuperative powers. In a circular which he used for many years Quimby wrote of his own method: ". . . he gives no medicines and makes no outward applications, but simply sits down by the patients, tells them their feelings, and what they think is their disease. If the patients admit that he tells them their feelings . . . then his explanation is the cure." [16]

Quimby's treatments, however, were not always so mild as this circular might suggest. One of the methods he seems to have used most frequently might be described as emotional shock tactics. A short but vital and commanding figure, he conveyed in the words of one patient "that indescribable sense of conviction, of clear-sightedness, of energetic action." In many instances, according to one observer, he would stride over to an invalid patient saying "in a quick, sharp voice: 'Get up, walk away! you can walk!' the patient almost always doing as he bid." [17] That many of his patients suffered relapses when away from Quimby's personal influence suggests that a large number of his cures were effected through hypnoidal suggestion.

The element of Quimby's practice which many people remembered best seems to have been not vocal but physical. Accounts of Quimby's later practice refer to his use of varying forms of physical manipulation, often involving the application of water to the face, neck and head. This technique was a familiar element of magnetic practice. But according to Julius Dresser, he did not consider physical manipulation as efficacious in itself, as would a mesmerist who employed it. Rather, he claimed, Quimby thought it "so hard for the patient to believe that his mere talk with him

15. Horatio W. Dresser, ed., *The Quimby Manuscripts* (New York, 1921), p. 72.
16. Dresser, *Manuscripts,* p. 144.   17. Quoted in Peel, *Discovery,* p. 165.

produced the cure, that he did this rubbing simply so that the patient would have more confidence in him." [18] No words of Quimby's support this view, however; and since he continued to hold to the fluidic theory of mind, he may well have regarded physical manipulation as a means of exciting the action of the fluids. Regardless, it is clear that Quimby was still under the shadow of mesmerism, which he had claimed to have left behind. In the final analysis, it is impossible to say exactly where mesmerism leaves off and Quimbyism begins.

But Quimby's theory in some points differed from his practice. And though his healing practice always remained central to him, he did devote considerable effort to arriving at some coherent notion of the principles that underlay the healing work. Endowed with a rough but genuine speculative capacity, he wrote over the period 1860–1866 a series of articles giving wholly unsystematic statement to his ideas. Quimby's writings contained a great deal that was not original; and one can trace in them the influence of Swedenborg, the mesmerist theoretician John Bovie Dodds, and the American spiritualist seer Andrew Jackson Davis. But in the extent to which he pushed their ideas and mixed them with his own observations, Quimby showed himself to be a vigorous and crudely original thinker.

Quimby's main interest, however, was in practice and not in theory. Thousands of patients crowded his offices in Portland, Maine, from the late 1850s till shortly before his death in 1866. Around him gathered a small band of devotees, among whom were Julius Dresser, the father of Horatio, and Mrs. Patterson, who later became Mrs. Eddy. For some years she had been ill with that classic nineteenth century nervous complaint "chronic dyspepsia," complicated by a mysterious ailment that she referred to as "spinal inflammation." Whatever the origin of her illness, there can be no doubt of the severity of her sufferings; and by 1862, when she first appealed to Quimby for aid, she was almost an invalid.

Mrs. Eddy already had come to believe that disease was the effect of thought, for in the early 1850s she had conducted extensive experiments as an amateur practitioner of the medical system called homeopathy. In contrast to regular practitioners, who dosed patients mercilessly with powerful drugs, homeopaths diluted the drug under the conviction that so doing would more effectively diffuse it throughout the system. But Mrs. Eddy came to believe that it was not the diluted drug but the faith of the

18. Julius Dresser, "Doctor Phineas P. Quimby, The Founder of Mental Science," *Mental Healing Monthly,* II (April 1887), 169.

patient in its power that actually effected recovery. Hence the expectant confidence of her appeal to Quimby for aid.

She did improve rapidly after two treatments at his hands — quite literally at his hands, for the treatment consisted of a psychological pep talk accompanied by vigorous rubbings of the head. Overcome with gratitude, she wrote to a newspaper less than a month later that Quimby "speaks as never man before spake, and heals as never man healed since Christ." [19] But her recovery was not to be as complete as she thought and she soon relapsed intermittently into her old ailments. Still she had a great new purpose in life — to understand Quimby's method of healing. And over the next several years she devoted much energy to this pursuit, conversing at length with Quimby, reading and revising his notes, defending him publicly, writing on the subject of healing and doing healing work herself.

The distinction between her own developing teaching and Quimby's ideas, though real by 1866, was by no means clear to Mrs. Eddy until some years later. In a classbook she used around 1868 or 1869 she declared that the principle of her teaching "has never been taught in science by any written or published MSS [manuscripts] but me . . ." and she also claimed that "it cannot have been understood, except by Elijah, Jesus, his disciples, and Paul." [20] In her commentary on Genesis, Mrs. Eddy also insisted that the Bible had been her only textbook. Yet for several years after 1866 she continued to speak of Quimby with reverence and to associate her teaching with his name. It was not until 1872 that Mrs. Eddy came to explicitly differentiate Christian Science (or Moral Science, as she then called it) from Quimby's thought. The reasons for her so doing will be analyzed at a later point. Here it is enough to note that the disassociation of her own teaching from Quimby's ideas was central to Mrs. Eddy's development in the important period 1872–1874 during which *Science and Health* was being written, and in that book she maintained that Quimby had never studied the science she taught.

Yet Quimby cast a long shadow. In 1883, Julius Dresser, who had been a member of Quimby's circle in Portland, was living in California. Learning of the growth of the Christian Science movement and realizing that its leader was the same Mrs. Patterson he had known years before, Dresser

19. Mary Baker Eddy (then Mrs. Patterson) *Letter to the Portland Currier,* Nov. 7, 1862.
20. Quoted in Peel, *Discovery,* p. 233.

came to Boston. It is impossible to know whether he simply wanted to cash in on the rising interest in mental healing, which he had practiced only sporadically since Quimby's death, or whether he was genuinely motivated to protect the Quimby legacy. Once in Boston, Dresser set up as the self-appointed heir and defender of Quimby. In February of 1883 he initiated a newspaper controversy with Mrs. Eddy in which he charged and she denied that Quimby was the source of the system she was teaching as Christian Science.

Dresser knew nothing of Mrs. Eddy's development after 1866 when he arrived in Boston sixteen years later. He had had no contact with her at all since two weeks after her fall in February. Fearing a relapse, she had written him for help and urged him to take up Quimby's mantle. In reply, Dresser had declared himself unwilling and unready to do so. He was not even able, he said, to help his wife or newborn son; how then could he cure people he hardly knew at all? [21] This brief exchange assumed much importance in the controversy that arose years later between Dresser and Mrs. Eddy over her debt to Quimby. Dresser cited her letter to him as evidence that she was still a disciple of Quimby even after the healing which she said marked the discovery of Christian Science.[22] She, in turn, made use of his letter to prove that he had had neither the capacity nor the intention of taking up mental healing before her own activities were underway. Had Dresser known that for nearly six years after 1866 Mrs. Eddy continued to link, though not identify, her teaching with Quimby's name, he would have had that much more ammunition to use. But perhaps, too, he might have understood that she had her own independent development after Quimby's death — a possibility that never seems to have occurred to him. As Quimby's self-proclaimed heir, Dresser began to teach; and within a few years his followers constituted yet another school of mental healing in Boston. It was Dresser's son Horatio who in 1921 finally edited and published the large body of writings in which Quimby in his own rough fashion had developed his ideas. Almost none of Quimby's writings had been before the public before that time.

By contrast, Warren Felt Evans had published six sizeable books on mental healing before his death in 1889 — two of them before the publication of *Science and Health* in 1875. And it was Evans, much more than Dresser, who fulfilled the role of a successor to Quimby, whom he first

---

21. Julius Dresser to Mary Baker Eddy (then Mrs. Patterson), March 2, 1866, in *Ibid.*, p. 199.

22. Julius Dresser, letter to *The Boston Post*, Feb. 8, 1883.

met in 1863. Even before that time he had already ventured into the field of mental healing. Encouraged by Quimby, who was already working along similar lines, Evans began to devote himself more seriously to the study and practice of mental healing the next year. How much of Evans' thought derives from Quimby is a moot point. Dresser states that Evans said what Quimby would have wished to say had he had the education and skill to do so.[23] Besides his extensive writing, Evans established a sanitorium for the sick in Salisbury, Massachusetts, and practiced healing in and around Boston during the 1870s and 1880s. His ideas aroused interest among a small group of people before Christian Science began making headway there; but it was the advent of Mrs. Eddy in Boston in 1882 that effectively crystallized "the Evans school." [24]

It was natural that the two streams of mind-cure represented by apostates from the Christian Science movement and by Quimby *via* Dresser and Evans should merge. Bit by bit informal links were established. Dresser allied himself with Marston; Mrs. Gestefeld and Mrs. Choate joined the International Christian Scientist Association founded in 1866 by Mrs. Plunkett and Mrs. Hopkins; and mind-curers wrote for each other's periodicals and advertised each other's books. But establishing any formal unity among them proved to be impossible. The International Association was no more than a loose promotional organization, and it collapsed with Mrs. Plunkett's fall from grace in 1889. In Boston, Marston did manage to make a going institution of the "Church of the Divine Unity," which became as much as anything a focus of loyalties for the mind-curers. Its Sunday services in a beautifully-appointed hall in Park Street were well-attended; and occasionally so eminent a figure as veteran Transcendentalist Cyrus Bartol preached from its pulpit.

But it was really Marston's ambition to gather up all the mind-curers into a single organization that he could control. To this end he promoted several conventions, none of which realized his hopes. The proceedings at these gatherings appear to have been hopelessly confused. The *Chicago Tribune* reported of one of them that Marston, "a man with an immense amount of black whisker and very little voice . . . managed to make it clear that he didn't know anything about the Committee on Credentials." [25] In Boston, two years later the *Mental Healing Monthly* adver-

23. Horatio W. Dresser, *Health and the Inner Life* (New York, 1906), p. 88.
24. Georgine Milmine, *The Life of Mary Baker G. Eddy and the History of Christian Science* (London, 1909), p. 336.
25. Quoted in *CSJ*, VI (July 1888), 27.

tised yet another convention, declaring that if representatives of any school of mental healing "stand aloof, it is not because they are repelled. No person, or party, or school is considered as having precedence. . . . Let this spirit prevail and the result will be satisfactory." [26] As it turned out, the results were somewhat catastrophic, for the convention was so disrupted by wrangling that the *Journal* gloated over its failure and some of the mind-cure publications admitted that mental healers needed to learn more about fraternity. The character of the I.N.T.A. showed that only the loosest of organizations could contain the varying points of view represented by the different mind-cure groups. By its very nature the movement was so radically pluralized that no single person nor institution could become a focus for the loyalties of the mind-curers.

One personal loyalty that these groups all shared can be negatively defined, for they were united by common hostility to Mrs. Eddy. Seldom did mind-curers refer to her by name in their periodicals. But hostile references to her, though indirect, were nevertheless unmistakable. In an article for Mrs. Plunkett's *International Magazine of Christian Science*, Marston declared that "there is no 'vice-regent of inspiration' needed to interpret truth or to intercede for us." [27] This rhetorical association of Mrs. Eddy with Rome was quite common: Mrs. Gestefeld's "Jesuitism in Christian Science" is another case in point. Still another mind-curer asked, "And what, in the name of all that is broad and high, is the matter with the royal and transcendent word 'truth,' that its limitless sky must be shut away by any dome however vaulted or vast? *The sky is free to all!*" [28]

"The sky is free to all!" This statement might well serve as a motto for the mind-cure groups of this period. As one might expect, the later 1880s were prolific of metaphysics drawn from various sources and compounded in innumerable shadings. One finds periodically in the mind-cure journals the announcement of some new school of thought. Often it had a very impressive name but somehow was never heard of again. In May of 1866, for example, one Bryan J. Butts announced through the *Mental Science Magazine* the formation of "The Highland School of Mental Philosophy";[29] while the next year William Gill, an ex-Christian Scientist, ex-

26. William Gill, "The World's Convention of Mental Healers," *Mental Healing Monthly*, II (Oct. 1887), 326–327.

27. Luther Marston, "Welcome," *International Magazine of Christian Science*, III (July 1888), 1.

28. A. T. Buswell, "Human Leadership and Heavenly Liberty in Christian Science Culture," *Mental Science Magazine*, III (July 1887), 217.

29. Bryan J. Butts, "Position of the 'Highland School of Mental Philosophy,'" *Mental Science Magazine*, II (May 1886), 176–177.

plained to the readers of the *Mental Healing Monthly* a new all-embracing metaphysical concept which he named "Pneumatopathy." [30]

In this heady atmosphere anything was possible. Just how far things could go was perhaps best illustrated by "Doctor" Jean Hazzard of the "New York School of Practical Christian Science." Dr. Hazzard advertised himself in the *Mental Healing Magazine* as a "Professor of Christian Science and Oriental Philosophy: Practitioner of Applied Metaphysics and Mind-Cure. Assisted by competent teachers and healers." [31] Characterizing Jesus as the central individual "for our race and this round in Humanity's cyclic progress," Hazzard went on to say that he was certainly "the holiest, healthiest, handsomest, happiest, man that ever walked upon this planet." [32] In 1887 Hazzard published his own guidebook to mental treatment, *The Mind-Cure Mentor, A Hand-Book of Healing, A Textbook of Treatments, A Compendium of Practical Christian Science.* Among his instructions was a lesson on how to concentrate:

1. Look at an object on the ceiling ten minutes; think of that object alone. 2. Write a proposition on a sheet of paper as, "God is the only reality." Think of it for ten minutes with your eyes fixed upon the paper. 3. Begin to think of a subject, and give a dollar to the poor for every time your mind wanders.[33]

Even more quotable is his memorable "Prayer for a Dyspeptic":

Holy Reality. We BELIEVE in Thee that Thou are EVERYWHERE present. We *really* believe it. Blessed reality we do not pretend to believe. WE BELIEVE. Believing that Thou are everywhere present, we believe that Thou are in the patient's stomach. Help us to stoutly affirm with our hand in Your hand, with our eyes fixed on Thee, that we have no Dyspepsia, that we never had Dyspepsia, that we will never have Dyspepsia, and that there is no such thing, that there will never be any such thing. Amen.[34]

Hazzard had never been a student of Mrs. Eddy; but because he called himself a Christian Scientist and sometimes quoted her, his teaching was mixed with hers in the New York press and public mind.

---

30. William Gill, "Religion and Pneumatopathy," *Mental Healing Monthly,* II (June 1887), 215–217.

31. Regular advertisement in the *Mental Healing Monthly.*

32. Dr. J. B. Hazzard, "Christian Science: The Name and the Thing," *Mental Science Magazine,* III (Jan. 1887), 79.

33. Quoted in James Monroe Buckley, " 'Christian Science' and 'Mind-Cure,' " *The Century Illustrated Monthly Magazine,* XXXIV (July 1887), 474.

34. Quoted in Norman Beasley, *The Cross and the Crown: A History of Christian Science* (New York, 1952), pp. 153–154.

One newspaper linked their names by observing that "Mrs. Eddy had staked her reputation upon the Hazzard of a die." [35] More disturbing to the Scientists, this sort of confusion appeared in the *Century,* a national publication of considerable prestige. In July 1887, Reverend James Monroe Buckley, a well-known Methodist and something of a professional anti-Christian Scientist, wrote an artcle on the mental healing movement. Making little distinction between Christian Science and mind-cure, Buckley casually included Dr. Hazzard's "Prayer for a Dyspeptic" as an example of Christian Science healing method.[36] The Scientists lost no time protesting: the *Journal* for August set the record straight.[37] But this was just the summer of 1887. It was in the three years thereafter that the mind-cure movement attained its greatest strength. Mrs. Eddy's followers were dismayed enough at Buckley's article; but at the time they tried to offset its influence, the public confusion of Christian Science with mind-cure had barely begun.

Mrs. Eddy had enough trouble keeping the confusion between Christian Science and mind-cure out of the movement itself. Many of her students in the 1880s had an insatiable appetite for any literature of a religious or metaphysical character. Along with such items as *Ben Hur* and Sir Edwin Arnold's *The Light of Asia,* they took to reading many of the mind-cure periodicals and works like Evans' *Esoteric Christianity.* Mrs. Eddy felt obliged to strongly rebuke this practice. In the *Journal* for March 1888, she declared:

I wish the students of Christian Science (and many who are not my students who would understand enough of this matter to heed the advice) to keep out of their heads the notion that compound metaphysics (so-called) is, or can be, Christian Science. They should . . . get the cobwebs out of their minds which spurious literature engenders.[38]

Mind-curers were not nearly as scrupulous; indeed, with an almost defiant casualness they sometimes advertised Mrs. Eddy's works right alongside those of her ex-students.

By the last years of the decade the literature of mind-cure was growing to staggering proportions. Thorstein Veblen, commenting on the flood of religious literature in the Gilded Age, marveled at the steady

35. *Ibid.,* 187.
36. Buckley, " 'Christian Science' and 'Mind-Cure,' " p. 425.
37. *CSJ,* V (Aug. 1887), 47.
38. Mary Baker Eddy, "Compound Metaphysics," *CSJ,* V (March 1888), 388.

flow of "vendible imponderables in the nth dimension." [39] The mind-cure and later the New Thought movements helped to swell this flood with more than a dozen periodicals, hundreds of pamphlets, and scores of books. Practically no mind-cure or New Thought leader was unrepresented by at least one title; many of them were prolific. The most popular of the New Thought items, Ralph Waldo Trine's *In Tune with the Infinite,* was translated into several foreign languages and sold well over two million copies. For many readers of metaphysical literature, *Science and Health* became just one among a number of books. One writer for *The International Magazine of Christian Science* observed that it no longer mattered if he abstained from reading the Christian Science textbook, "as there are now plenty of good writings on the same subject. Mrs. Gestefeld's lectures I prefer to any statements of the Science that have yet been made," he went on, "although Mrs. Hopkins' are very fine and helpful. How thankful we should be for all of them." [40]

One point about this literature that disturbed Mrs. Eddy greatly was the frequency with which terms and ideas borrowed from her writings were used without credit. In some instances the alteration of her words in a plagiarized passage can be most revealing. Contrast Mrs. Eddy's statement:

Prayer cannot change the unalterable Truth, nor can prayer alone give us an understanding of Truth; but prayer, coupled with a fervent habitual desire to know and do the will of God, will *bring us into all Truth.**

with the following passage from Charles Townsend's pamphlet "All Things are Yours":

Truth cannot be changed by prayer; but prayer, which is a real desire to know and do the whole will of God, will always bring *the desired result.** [41]

On many occasions Mrs. Eddy expressed her concern about such direct and indirect plagiarisms of her work. These borrowings, she felt, tended to adulterate Christian Science.

The teaching of Christian Science by those who had not been qualified by her or one of her students, she felt, had the same effect. It

39. Quoted in Joseph Dorfman, *Thorstein Veblen and His America* (New York, 1939), p. 480.

40. Hector Vyr, "A Metaphysical Drummer," *International Magazine of Christian Science,* III (Dec. 1888), 206.

41. The original quotation is from *S&H.,* p. 11.

* Italics mine.

was the proliferation of what a Christian Scientist once called "wildcat teaching" [42] that constituted the most direct source for the spread of heterodox Christian Science. Indeed, teaching was confused enough among students loyal to Mrs. Eddy. After studying with her, a student would return home, perhaps far from Massachusetts, and teach a class of five, ten, or fifty pupils, any one of whom might in turn strike out on his own. Though often woefully unprepared to teach Christian Science, such individuals still claimed in many instances to operate under Mrs. Eddy's authority. Mind-curers who had no loyalty to her whatever had no hesitation in spreading variant forms of metaphysics that they were pleased to call Christian Science. Few apostates from Christian Science till around 1890 ceased calling themselves Christian Scientists just because they had broken away from Mrs. Eddy. Further, some who had never studied with her at all made free use of the term. In Edward Eggleston's novel *The Faith Doctor,* for example, the ominous figure of Mrs. Brewer is identified as a Christian Scientist and she refers to herself as one; yet her language is not that of Mrs. Eddy and she recommends the *International Magazine of Christian Science* as reading fare.[43]

The situation was particularly chaotic in the West — which for Bostonians in 1885 meant Chicago and any place west of it. The main stimulus to "wildcat teaching" in the West came from Mrs. Hopkins' Institute in Chicago. The teachers and practitioners trained there did what one Christian Scientist called "a land-office business — their responsibilities began nowhere and ended in the same place";[44] and they provided stiff competition for Christian Scientists loyal to Mrs. Eddy. One woman returning to her home city in Nebraska after a course of study at the Massachusetts Metaphysical College in 1891 wrote to Mrs. Eddy that

the tares of mind-cure have been thickly sown in the city, far and wide, and all under the name of Christian Science. . . . Our main work has seemed to be, in an eminent degree, "to root out, and to pull down, and to destroy, and to throw down" before we could begin to build, and to plant.[45]

In California the situation was especially grave for the Christian Scientists. "Babel is already in California," reported a student of Mrs. Eddy

42. Quoted in Johnson, *History,* I, 423.
43. Edward Eggleston, *The Faith Doctor: A Story of New York* (London, 1891).
44. Johnson, *History,* II, 83.
45. Unsigned, "An Echo from Nebraska," *CSJ,* IX (June 1891), 103.

as early as 1886, "but it will be our privilege to confound it." [46] Later he spelled out the situation in more detail: "Institutes of Metaphysical Science have been started which include the teaching of mind-cure, animal magnetism, mesmerism, spiritualism, clairvoyance, and mediumship; while we, as Christian Scientists, are denounced for having our jacket too straight." [47] (It is worthwhile noting that within three years the individual who made these reports had himself gravitated into mind-cure.) Within a year after Mrs. Eddy received this report, the situation was to grow even worse for Californian Christian Scientists. For in 1887 Mrs. Hopkins traveled West to teach a class of two hundred and fifty in San Francisco. Mrs. Eddy's student Sue Ella Bradshaw, whom she had commissioned to establish the movement in that city, had to report that it was all she could do to keep her head above water. "I have no compromise to make," wrote Miss Bradshaw to her teacher, "nor will I turn hypocrite even if I cannot succeed honestly." [48]

Christian Scientists were just as seriously concerned about the confusion of their religion with mind-cure in the realm of practice as in the realm of teaching. It was a difficult enough problem for the movement to bear the blame in cases where patients were not healed or perhaps had died; to take on the onus of guilt for mind-curers who had failed to effect cures was asking too much. The clearest instance of such a confusion in this period did not involve a serious case, but it was widely publicized enough to give it particular importance. In 1885, Louisa May Alcott, whose father Bronson Alcott had shown sympathy for Mrs. Eddy a decade before, sought healing of one Anna B. Newman in Boston, an apostate Christian Scientist. The treatments proving unsuccessful, Miss Alcott announced in the *Women's Journal* for April that she had tried mind-cure and found it a failure. The only effects of the treatments, she said, had been "mesmeric sensations, sunshine in the head, walking on the air, slight trances, etc." [49] This account, much publicized in the press and pulpit because of Miss Alcott's fame, was generally interpreted as a failure in Christian Science treatment. And in the May *Journal,* Calvin Frye, Mrs. Eddy's secretary, set the record straight.[50]

46. Joseph Adams, letter to Mrs. Eddy, n.d. published in *CSJ*, IV (May 1886), 58.
47. Joseph Adams, "The Christian Scientist Association," *CSJ*, V (Nov. 1887), 236.
48. Sue Ella Bradshaw, letter to Mrs. Eddy, n.d. published in *CSJ*, V (Nov. 1887), 236.
49. Quoted in Beasley, *The Cross and the Crown*, p. 136.
50. Calvin Frye, "Massachusetts Metaphysical College," *CSJ*, III (June 1885), 56.

Actually, the gravest danger faced by the Christian Science movement as a result of its encounter with mind-cure went considerably beyond the confusion of the two. For the very survival of Christian Science as Mrs. Eddy taught it was jeopardized. The mind-cure flood came very near to drowning it out. In Boston, at least six different schools of mind-cure, all friendly with each other but hostile to Mrs. Eddy, confronted her as rivals. According to one estimate, of about 5,000 people in some way connected with Christian Science and mind-cure in Boston around 1887, less than 1,000 were followers of Mrs. Eddy.[51] The situation in the West was even less favorable for the Christian Scientists, due largely but not wholly to the activities of the energetic Mrs. Hopkins. The Christian Scientists at this time had one periodical, the *Journal,* which faced the competition of three major mind-cure periodicals, each ably edited and widely circulated — in addition to at least a dozen lesser ones. And mind-cure practitioners and teachers numbered many times those loyal to Mrs. Eddy.

Moreover, the Christian Science movement itself was torn by dissension in these years. In 1888 a rebellion involving almost a third of Mrs. Eddy's Association left the movement in Boston nearly in shambles. She judged at that time that there were no more than a dozen practitioners still loyal to her in the city. Her followers, who formerly filled Chickering Hall where services were being held, now huddled in the middle of the auditorium. The Church of the Divine Unity, however, was crowded. And mind-curers lost no time in improving the opportunity that schisms among the Christian Scientists afforded them. The *International* issued a call in July 1888, for all who had left Mrs. Eddy to join the International Association; and it promised that the constitution of the Association "will be found simple and broad enough for the most exacting." [52] The defections were many. Truly it seemed in 1888 that Horatio Dresser's later prediction about the exit of the last Christian Scientist from the movement was in process of being fulfilled.

CHRISTIAN SCIENCE *versus* MIND-CURE

By the time Mrs. Eddy compiled her *Miscellaneous Writings, 1883–1896,* The Mother Church had been founded and was flourishing, the old mind-cure groups had largely passed out of existence, and the New Thought movement was developing independently of Christian Science. So it was

51. Johnson, *History,* II, 253.
52. Unsigned, "The Christian Scientists," *International Magazine of Christian Science,* III (July 1888), 31.

with an evident sense of triumph that she wrote in the preface to the book: "In compiling this work I have tried to remove the pioneer signs and ensigns of war, and to retain at this date the privileged armaments of peace." [53] What she meant by "removing the pioneer signs and ensigns of war" can be seen in part with reference to the articles she did not see fit to reprint at all. For the material which she excluded from the book contained a number of surprisingly severe personal references. Mrs. Eddy spoke indirectly of Marston, for example, as "an ass whose ears stick out." [54] She named Mrs. Hopkins as one of the "unprincipled claimants" to her ideas and wrote that "dishonesty — yes, fraud — is conspicuous" in her "verbose" lectures.[55] She also observed that she had found Mrs. Gestefeld's reasoning "intoned with Pagan philosophy, her humanity besprinkled with Buddhism, and her pride and purpose nerved with the spirit of a Judas." [56]

This zeal in battling the foe sprang from Mrs. Eddy's conviction that the cause of Christian Science desperately needed defending against the teachers of false doctrine. It was what the mind-curers *taught* that she objected to. Mrs. Eddy was not primarily concerned about the fact that they did not operate under her personal supervision, for she refused to discourage several publications on Christian Science completely outside the movement in Boston for as long as she felt their presentation of Christian Science was correct.[57]

Though mind-curers in general took doctrine a good deal less seriously than did Mrs. Eddy, her teaching in several respects was as objectionable to them as theirs was to her. To understand the emergence of Christian Science, it is important to clarify just what these differences were. Of course, identifying the position of Christian Science on the major issues in dispute presents no problem, since it is by definition what Mrs. Eddy said it is. But given the diversity of thought in the mind-cure movement, it might seem difficult to find sufficient areas of agreement among mind-curers on which to base a contrast. Despite real and sometimes wide differences, however, they tended to differ from Christian Science on the same points. And since there is virtually no difference in the teaching of mind-curers and New Thought writers in these areas, the contrast may

53. *Mis.*, pp. xi–xii.
54. Eddy, "Definition of Purpose," p. 140.
55. Eddy, "Pro Bono Publico," *CSJ*, III (July 1886), 105.
56. Eddy, "Jesuitism in Christian Science," p. 427.
57. Oliver Sabin's *Washington Newsletter* and Joseph Adams' *Chicago Christian Scientist*.

as well be made in terms of the relation of New Thought to Christian Science.

The values of New Thought — its emphasis upon individual spiritual freedom and the validity of human intuition, and its correlative distaste for doctrine, system, and authority — furnish a good clue as to its root theological differences from Christian Science. These values are strongly reminiscent of Emersonian Transcendentalism; and it should be no surprise that Emerson became a patron saint of New Thought after his compatibility with it was demonstrated by a mind-cure writer in 1887.[58] Mrs. Eddy does use the word *intuition* at several points,[59] but never places as much emphasis upon it as do both Emerson and New Thought writers. Far more characteristic of her writing is the use of the term *spiritual sense.* That which is sensed when man exercises spiritual sense is, for her, nothing that human intuition could ever apprehend on its own: it is that which is known in the first instance only through the revealed Word.

This distinction points to an underlying theological difference between Christian Science and the New Thought on the meaning of revelation. When apostates from Christian Science rejected Mrs. Eddy's claim that Christian Science had the authority of revelation, they rejected far more than her leadership. They showed disinclination, which was essentially ideological rather than personal, to accept the *idea* of revelation implicit in her claim. Usually, New Thought writers did not speak of revelation at all, except to disparage it as a general theological idea. They did talk often about a great new age of spiritual progress for the race. But for them this progress was evolutionary, general, and diffuse. On no point is Mrs. Eddy clearer, however, than in her insistence that revelation is definite, specific, and in the case of Christian Science, final.[60]

In 1905 a prominent spokesman of New Thought, Charles Brodie Patterson, contrasted these two views of revelation. The New Thought, he wrote,

teaches the universality of religion; that God's spirit is more or less active in the minds of all people, and that each individual receives according to his desires and needs; that there is a natural evolutionary process in the life of man, and little by little he is unfolding his latent powers and possibilities. . . .

58. C. M. Barrows. See Braden, *Spirits in Rebellion,* p. 53.
59. See, for example, *S&H.,* p. 298.
60. See Chapter One, section four, "Revelation as Discovery."

I believe there is no religion in the world devoid of truth — that the truth it contains is that which holds it together.

In contrast, Patterson observed, Christian Science says: "Read the Bible, and then take *Science and Health* as its interpreter, and leave all the other sources of knowledge alone." [61] In this he was quite correct. During one of her classes in the late 1880s, when many of her students had begun to read widely in the literature of various religions, Mrs. Eddy said: "If you break a bottle you will be cut by the fragments, never by the vessel. There is a little truth in all creeds, isms, and ologies, but if you try to find the truth in a part of the vessel, you will get cut. Study the Bible and Science and Health and leave the fragments alone." [62]

Mrs. Eddy utterly rejected the essentially antinomian claim of New Thought that any inspired individual could have his (or, more pertinently, her) private revelation of basic divine truth. It was characteristic of the Puritan in her to insist that if Christian Science was revelation, it was *major* revelation, not just her own happy inspiration. For her, there were absolutely no resources within human thought by which it could devise a method for its own salvation or reach out to grasp the spiritual fact. As she wrote, "If mortal mind knew how to be better, it would be better." [63] Human thought needed revelation; and revelation had to come from outside, from above, from the top down; and its coming was definitive.

Hence the role of Christ Jesus in Christian Science is far different from that in New Thought. For New Thought writers, Jesus was but one of a number of revered religious teachers. Most of these writers were agreed that Jesus was a man who differed from other men only in the degree of his spiritual clearsightedness. As one of them wrote, "Jesus was the most simple, sublime, spiritual, and Godlike of all the great religious teachers and healers." [64] But one could as well look to Buddha, Swedenborg, or Emerson for revelations of truth. Seldom, if ever, does one find any reference to Jesus as the Saviour in New Thought. Certainly, any mention of the cross is foreign to its spirit. It is one symbolic indication of the gulf between Mrs. Eddy's teaching and New Thought that the "Cross and the Crown" is the official insignia of Christian Science and adorns every copy of *Science and Health. Only* through Jesus' suffering and triumph which the "Cross and Crown" symbolized, Mrs. Eddy felt, could

61. Charles Brodie Patterson, "What the New Thought Stands For" (Oscawana on Hudson, N.Y., 1905), pp. 5–6.
62. Bogue Reminiscences.   63. *S&H.*, p. 186.
64. Gill, "Religion and Pneumatopathy," p. 215.

mortals be shown the way out of the flesh. For her, Jesus' life was revelation, unique in and central to human history. He was not one of a number of inspired teachers, but the mediator between the Spirit and the flesh, the one and only mediator. For it required the work of one who was not bound by the beliefs of the flesh to awaken mankind out of the belief of life in matter. Hence to Mrs. Eddy, the central Christian revelation was absolutely essential to the salvation of men.

One clear indication of the contrast between Christian Science and New Thought lies in their differing relationships with Calvinism. Clearly, Mrs. Eddy's thought was deeply affected by her Calvinist heritage. She did say that she had gone beyond Calvinism; but she felt as well that Christian Science included all that was of value in it. In Christian Science as in Calvinism, one is clearly confronted with the Pauline antithesis of the Spirit and the flesh. Of course, Christian Science does take a broad definition of the meaning of the flesh. In Mrs. Eddy's teaching, it refers to everything indigenous to mortality — sickness and death as well as sin. Yet salvation from the flesh, in this expanded sense, remains paramount in Christian Science as in Calvinism.

In New Thought, however, one finds a conscious and almost total repudiation of Calvinism — or, better, of what was left of Calvinism in late nineteenth century Protestant orthodoxy. Indeed, New Thought writers often spoke of Calvinism with scorn. To some degree, it was the Calvinism in Mrs. Eddy that apostates from Christian Science rejected — her insistence that the unaided human mentality cannot save itself. No form of New Thought places anything like her emphasis upon redemption, for its leaders did not believe that there was anything that needs to be redeemed. They did feel that there were conditions of sickness and suffering that needed amelioration through the beneficent powers of thought, and they often spoke of the need to improve the moral condition of mankind. But New Thought writers did not in general regard the mortal condition as radically distorted. Indeed, they did not speak of sin, sickness, and death as radical evils at all. They saw them in evolutionary terms as means to something higher — in Patterson's words, "as stepping-stones to greater knowledge, to truer understanding." [65] Henry Wood, a popular New Thought author, echoed Emerson when he wrote in 1889 that "when fully interpreted, evil ceases to be evil and becomes educational experi-

65. Patterson, "What the New Thought Stands For," p. 8.

ence." [66] But for Mrs. Eddy, evil, though it was no ultimate principle of existence, *was* evil and must be totally destroyed. Men had to be radically saved from the flesh, from the belief of life in matter.

This question of the reality of matter constitutes a metaphysical dividing line between Mrs. Eddy's teaching and that of almost all New Thought writers. Where she declared that matter was completely unreal, the erroneous sense of true substance, they maintained that it was real but susceptible to thought control. As one of them put it, ". . . matter has its own relative reality and validity, and is not to be ignored as illusion." [67] Another wrote that the New Thought holds that the "great material universe is the visible word of God — God's word becoming manifest in material form." [68] Regarding the body specifically, one critic of Christian Science noted in 1887 that she "could not quite accept Mrs. Eddy's statement that a bone is no more substance than a thought. Granted that the thought is the 'power behind the throne,' still the bone is an actual something that can be touched and handled, can be broken or cause suffering." [69]

Mrs. Eddy's position on this point was clear: "Man is not matter; he is not made up of brain, blood, bones, and other material elements." [70] The physical senses, she taught, could not discern the reality of man; for the spiritual fact of man's being could be known only through revelation and discerned only through spiritual sense. Hence, in Christian Science treatment, denial of material sense evidence plays an important part as a preparation for the discernment of what man really is. What is denied, however, is not the body but its corporeality. In Christian Science, bone or any part of the body may hint some spiritual actuality, some real aspect of man's true functioning and formation. But considered as a *material* substance, even one expressive of thought, bone is definitely unreal. That the condition of bone or any part of the body can affect man's absolute Life in Science is just what the Christian Scientist denies. The proof of healing is not the destruction of the bone, but its restoration to normal formation and functioning.

In New Thought, however, this denial of sense appearance has little

66. Henry Wood, *The New Thought Simplified: How to Gain Harmony and Health* (Boston, 1889), p. 323.

67. Wood, *New Thought*, p. 326.

68. Patterson, "What the New Thought Stands For," p. 4.

69. M. B. Gage, "Is Christian Science Practical?" *Mental Healing Monthy*, II (Sept. 1887), 323.

70. *S&H.*, p. 475.

or no meaning. What the Christian Scientist saw as a manifestation of a *false belief* that must be dissolved, the mind-curer saw as an *actual* condition that could be overcome by the power of thought. Patterson wrote that whereas Christian Science "denies away" sin, sickness, and death, "the New Thought claims that all three have an existence, but an existence that is overcome, not through any process of denial, but through the introduction of the true thought into the mind of man." [71] New Thought writers spoke of healing as the result of the influence of purely affirmative thought on the body susceptible to mental molding. In New Thought, the power of beneficent human thought projects a more healthy image upon the mind of the sick person, whose body then externalizes this more healthy picture. Julius Dresser, for example, asked to explain the workings of mind-cure, cited the case of a man hurled toward a circular saw in motion. Fear of being killed by the saw actually did kill him, though he landed a few feet away from it. "Now if mind can kill, why can it not cure?" asked Dresser. "The mind can be educated to realize this truth of its superiority, and the more thoroughly it realizes this truth the stronger its powers." [72]

New Thought writers generally conceived of the human mind as the medium of Deity. Marston believed that "the power that heals is Divine Spirit working through mind or thought." [73] Often these higher powers of the human mind in New Thought literature become indistinguishable from the deific Mind or Spirit. "Thought is the spirit in motion," reads one article in the *Mental Healing Monthly*; "it is the mind power, or force, in activity. Spirit goes in and with the thought. They cannot be separated." [74] Charles Fillmore, founder of Unity, explicitly differentiated his thought from Mrs. Eddy's by declaring that God, Spirit, dwells *in* man, and is not just reflected by him.[75] Often New Thought authors spoke of the subconscious mind as the divinity within man — as one of them put it, "the hidden partner which acts automatically upon the physical organism." [76] Others, like Mrs. Hopkins, were more apt to use mys-

71. Patterson, "What the New Thought Stands For," p. 7.
72. *Boston Morning Journal*, May 10, 1884.
73. Luther Marston, "What Is It That Heals?" *Mental Healing Monthly*, II (March 1887), 150.
74. Unsigned, untitled, *Mental Healing Monthly*, II (Feb. 1887), 113.
75. Charles Fillmore, "Practical Christianity: An Explanation of the Teaching of the Unity School of Christianity and its Relation to some Modern Cults" (Kansas: Unity School of Christianity; n.d.), pamphlet, p. 5.
76. Wood, *The New Thought Simplified*, p. 44.

tical language in referring to the "vivific Life-principle within us." [77] At points the language of mind-cure becomes overtly pantheistic. A writer for the *International Magazine of Christian Science* stated that she was "denying the arrogant, foolish personality, and affirming with an abiding faith that God is my personality, that I am nothing in and of myself, that God is myself." [78] But however the idea was expressed, all representatives of mind-cure and New Thought spoke in some sense of "the God within," of divinity indwelling the mind of man. It was this principle, for them, which validated human intuition and legitimized the exercise of the mind's beneficent powers.

To Christian Scientists this principle virtually deified mortal mind, which, said Mrs. Eddy, "holds within itself all evil." [79] Reflecting upon struggle with mind-cure, one of her followers defined the Christian Scientists' attitude toward this central idea of the "God within" in the *Sentinel*. "The human mind," she wrote, "is flattered by being told that 'Mind is God,' and it gradually arrives at the false conclusion 'I am God!' So it clothes the old error with a semblance of Truth, which merely illumines its filthiness and gives it seeming power and self-respect." [80] That which in New Thought was the *subject* of the healing is in Christian Science the *object* of the healing. Mrs. Eddy found it necessary to make a radical distinction between mortal mind and the divine Mind. She explained healing in Christian Science as the action of divine Mind alone. In *Science and Health* she spoke of the "fact that the human mind alone suffers, is sick, and that the divine Mind alone heals." [81] Understandably, New Thought writers found this distinction one of the most objectionable elements in Mrs. Eddy's teaching. One of them observed that the use of the term *mortal mind* is inappropriate "if the mind be the thinking principle of spirit," for then "it must necessarily be *immortal* and the term is not only a misnomer but is self-contradictory." [82]

Actually, Mrs. Eddy had made a similar point. For she wrote in *Science and Health*:

Mortal mind is a solecism in language, and involves an improper use of the word *mind*. As Mind is immortal, the phrase *mortal mind* implies something

77. Hopkins, "Third Lesson in Truth," p. 44.
78. Quoted in Johnson, *History*, I, 203.   79. *Mis.*, p. 97.
80. Andrea H. Proudefoot, "Spurious Literature," *CSS*, II (Oct. 5, 1899), 75–76.
81. *S&H.*, p. 270.
82. S.H.A., "Employ Simply Words," *Mental Healing Monthly*, II (March 1887), 146.

untrue and therefore unreal; and as the phrase is used in teaching Christian Science, it is meant to designate that which has no real existence.[83]

Here again was the problem of language. She did not wish to treat mortal mind as an entity. But until its claim was destroyed it could not be ignored, much less glorified. The very act of naming it tended to create a false impression; yet as Mrs. Eddy saw it, unless this were done her teaching was open to gross abuse. For radical evil, which for her had no ultimate reality but was wholly real to mortal sense, would thereby be unnamed and go unchecked. To her, a religious teaching which failed to make the basic distinction between the mortal and the divine could not be truly redemptive. Mortal mind, she felt, was the source of all human suffering; *but what it caused it could not cure.* "The theology of Christian Science," she wrote, in differentiating her teaching from mind-cure, "is based on the action of the divine Mind over the human mind and body; whereas, 'mind-cure' rests on the notion that the human mind can cure its own disease, or that which it causes, and the *sickness of matter,* — which is infidel in the one case, and anomalous in the other." [84]

One reason for the difficulty in distinguishing clearly between Christian Science and New Thought is that similarities in language often obscure differences in thought. In New Thought, for example, one often finds God spoken of in Mrs. Eddy's terms as Life or Soul; yet these terms are used in New Thought in a radically immanentist sense exactly opposite to the way she employs them. Yet there is one term of great importance in Christian Science which is never employed in New Thought and which mind-curers used only in derision: *animal magnetism.* In *Science and Health,* it will be remembered, Mrs. Eddy spoke of animal magnetism as the "human antipode of divine Science," and as "the specific term for error, or mortal mind." To her, the most conspicuous but not the only form of animal magnetism was mental malpractice, the ignorant or intentional effect of one mind upon another. It was through what she believed to be her experience with mental malpractice that Mrs. Eddy came to her conclusions as to the nature of the ultimate evil of which it was a phase. These experiences predate the period we are considering and need no lengthy examination here. It is enough to indicate briefly what they were in order to set her later evaluation of mind-cure and New Thought in perspective.

In 1872, in the process of refining her teaching, Mrs. Eddy alienated a

---

83. *S&H.,* p. 114.   84. *Mis.,* pp. 62–63.

young man named Richard Kennedy who had been her closest student. Gradually a series of episodes over the next few years convinced her that Kennedy was trying to see how far he could go in the use of mental control. She felt that he was consciously trying by mental means to cause her personal suffering and to subvert her students' practice. Believing that this malpractice depended for its success upon the victim's ignorance of the process, she sought to warn the public of the possibility of the despotic use of mental power. In her autobiography, Mrs. Eddy wrote that at first she was reluctant to include a brief discussion of the subject in the first edition of *Science and Health*. But she found that the publication of the book was delayed, providentially, she believed, until she "inserted . . . a partial history" of what she had "already observed of mental malpractice." [85] In the book Mrs. Eddy commented:

> In coming years the person or mind that hates his neighbor will have no need to traverse his fields to destroy his flocks and herds and spoil his vines; or to enter his house to demoralize his household; for the evil mind will do this enough through mesmerism; and not *in propria persona* to be seen admitting the deed. Unless this terrible hour be met and restrained by *Science*, mesmerism, the scourge of man, will leave nothing sacred when mind begins to act under the direction of conscious power.[86]

To Mrs. Eddy developments in the movement in the seven years following the publication of *Science and Health* in 1875 seemed amply to confirm this conviction. The whole mood of the movement reflected her growing horror and dismay at the evil she felt she was uncovering. In this period two other individuals once close to her became estranged and, she felt, began to impede the progress of the movement by mental means as Kennedy had done and was doing. "The peril of Salem witchcraft is not passed," she had written in *Science and Health*.[87] And the year 1878 found her embroiled in a court case tried in Salem in which one of the ex-students whom she came to feel was a malpractitioner stood accused of trying to damage another's health by mental means. In the next edition of *Science and Health*, published in 1881, Mrs. Eddy discussed the operations of mental malpractice at greater length than ever before, including a forty-seven page chapter on the subject of "Demonology." The climax of this phase of the movement's history came in 1882 with the death of Mrs. Eddy's husband of five years, Asa Gilbert Eddy. According to the autopsy, his death was the result of heart disease. But she claimed that it had actually been the result of mental assassination. The guilty party, she

85. *Ret.*, p. 38. 86. *S&H.*, first ed., p. 123. 87. *Ibid.*

said, was one Edward J. Arens, an ex-student who had already given abundant proof of his hostility toward the Eddys.[88]

Asa Gilbert Eddy died in the summer of 1882, two years before Mrs. Choate's defection, three years before that of Mrs. Hopkins, and seven years before the mind-cure movement reached the peak of its success in Boston. With the background just sketched, one can see why Mrs. Eddy felt the theology of mind-cure was erroneous and its practice dangerous. For it virtually deified and relied upon in healing that very mentality which she named mortal and had come to see as capable of the most insidious evil. To her, the mind-curers relied upon the action of mortal mind, or the erroneous sense of mind. In this sense they relied upon animal magnetism, which she called the "voluntary or involuntary action of error in all of its forms." [89] And to her, mind-cure, even when practiced with beneficent intent, could work only ill. It expunged no error, for it was based on error. And the apparent healings that it sometimes achieved were but one belief taking the place of another. This "mortal 'mind-cure' " Mrs. Eddy wrote, "produces the effect of mesmerism. It is using the power of human will, instead of the divine power understood, as in Christian Science; and without this Science there had better be no 'mind-cure,' — in which the last state of patients is worse than the first." [90]

Mrs. Eddy saw the development of the mind-cure movement as the appearing of animal magnetism, aping the revelation of Truth. In *Science and Health* she wrote, "The higher Truth lifts her voice, the louder will error scream, until its inarticulate sound is forever silenced in oblivion." [91] With specific reference to the mushrooming mind-cure groups, she wrote in the *Journal* in 1886 that "the growth of human inquiry and the increasing popularity of Christian Science, I regret to say have called out of their hiding places and set upon us the poisonous reptiles and devouring beasts of mortal mind." [92] Mrs. Eddy did not feel that the factionalization which produced the mind-cure movements and contributed so greatly to the growth of New Thought was the product of honest disagreement. Rather, she saw it as the effect of the worst tendencies of mortal mind. In one of her strongest statements on the subject she wrote in late 1886:

Just now, the darkest spot on the horizon of mortal mind that Christian Science can illumine is envy, and the strife for "who shall be greatest." It

88. Mrs. Eddy made a public statement to this effect in an interview published in the *Boston Post*, June 5, 1882. See the discussion of Mr. Eddy's death in Peel, *Trial.*, pp. 112–116.
89. *S&H.*, p. 484.   90. *Mis.*, p. 59.   91. *S&H.*, p. 97.
92. "The Massachusetts Metaphysical College," *My.*, p. 245.

pushes Christianity aside to elbow in a crowd of robbers, that enter not in by the door, Truth, but would climb up some other way. Obscure, unlettered, unprincipled people are filling the field as mind-healers, who are mind-killers, building their only superstructure on false foundations — the power of evil and substance of matter. They are working out, through mortal mind, the claim of total depravity, in all its forms of animal magnetism. They rise on the merits of the true healer, to at length fall from their own demerits.[93]

Mind-curers not only denied that their principle was animal magnetism and their practice malpractice; they consistently asserted that neither animal magnetism nor mental malpractice was anything to cope with at all. If mind, the thinking principle, is divine, they asked, how can it consciously do evil? "I do not discriminate between powers for good and evil," wrote Julius Dresser, "because no one will do bad things except through ignorance. The knowledge that our powers and capacities are God in us takes away all desire to act recklessly or for otherwise than with the best of motives and for the best of results."[94] Even if you do become the object of another's hostility, Mrs. Hopkins maintained in answering an inquirer, "your mind's pure quality will simply chase it out of its presence."[95] Mrs. Eddy professed to believe that fear and evil will have no real power, observed one of her mind-cure critics, "yet she suffers untold tortures from the devil she will not banish from her life."[96] If she believes in God at all, asked another, why is she so obsessed with "spooks, voodoos, evil spirits and all else that comes in the class of so-called mesmerism?"[97]

In an article entitled "Ways That Are Vain," Mrs. Eddy, replying specifically to an attack by Marston on this score, took account of the general mind-cure argument on the subject of animal magnetism. "Certain individuals," she wrote, "entertain the notion that Christian Science Mind-healing should be two sided, and only denounce error in general, — saying nothing in particular of error that is damning men." These people she called "sticklers for a false, convenient peace." It was the very method of error to ask to be let alone. "This mistaken way, of hiding sin in order to maintain harmony, has licensed evil, allowing it first to smoulder, and then to break out in devouring flames."[98] In her classes Mrs. Eddy put

93. Eddy, "Questions Answered," p. 160.
94. Julius Dresser, "Man a Medium of God," p. 53.
95. Emma Curtis Hopkins, "Questions and Answers," *Truth,* I (Nov. 1887), 12.
96. Luther Marston, "Animal Magnetism," *Mental Science Magazine,* III (July 1888), 27.
97. Unsigned, *Pomeroy's Advanced Thought,* I (Feb. 1888).
98. *My.,* pp. 210–213. First printed in *CSJ,* V (April 1887), 90–92.

special emphasis upon the necessity to meet and master every form of error. At one meeting she described to her students a beautiful white bridge, underneath which was all manner of slime, mud, venomous reptiles, beasts, and all that was unclean. What path, she asked, would you take? Would you go over the white bridge or under it? Her students responded that they would go over the bridge. But this was just the wrong choice, she explained: they would go over it *only* after they had been underneath — "The whole of mortal mind must be overcome first." [99] Similarly, Mrs. Eddy continually urged upon her household the necessity of "handling" evil specifically in their mental work; and she presented them with terrifying pictures of the result of not so doing — suffering, moral idiocy, the experience of hell. When a student sent her a replica of the proverbial three monkeys — hear no evil, speak no evil, see no evil — she sent it back with a rebuke.

Most mind-curers on principle would have kept the monkeys. They were avowed optimists. In mind-cure and New Thought publications one often finds expressed such sentiments as: "Mirth is heaven's medicine. Everyone ought to bathe in it. Grim care, moroseness, anxiety, all the rust of life, ought to be scoured off by the oil of mirth." [100] Or, "Open your mouth, God will fill it." [101] This optimism was grounded in the principle that if good is really supreme and its triumph assured, men need only affirm its presence to destroy any appearance of evil, for evil is but the lack of good. But it would be incorrect to ascribe to Mrs. Eddy the private view of evil characteristic of mind-cure and New Thought. For she puts this important qualification on her statement of the unreality of evil: though it is nothing to God and has no intrinsic reality, it *is* a terrible reality to mortals; it confronts them with nothingness — "no-thing-ness." If its claims are ignored, if men do not challenge them specifically, they will be overcome by them and will not be able to demonstrate the "some-thingness" of Spirit.

In his *Varieties of Religious Experience,* William James identified the spirit of optimism so characteristic of mind-cure as the hallmark of what he called the religion of healthy-mindedness — "the tendency which looks upon all things and sees they are good." And he found, so he believed, no more systematized form of healthy-minded religion than Christian Science. "For it," James wrote, "evil is simply a *lie,* and any one who

99. Clara Shannon Reminiscences, Archives.
100. Unsigned, *Mental Healing Monthly,* II (Aug. 1887), 278.
101. Margaret Ford Moran, "Eleve," *International Magazine of Christian Science,* III (Oct. 1888), 123.

mentions it is a liar." From the standpoint of Christian Science, he argued, it is our duty not even to pay evil "the compliment of explicit attention." [102] James never professed to comprehend the theology of Christian Science; and by associating it with mind-cure as a form of healthy-mindedness which ignores the question of evil, he proved that he did not. For mind-curers almost universally condemned Christian Science because they felt, in effect, that it was not healthy-minded enough, that Mrs. Eddy had paid far too much "explicit attention" to evil. They deplored her use of the term *mortal mind,* disputed her claims as to the operations of animal magnetism and mental malpractice, and rejected her insistence upon the need for regeneration.

Yet these emphases are basic to the practice of Christian Science. And whatever Mrs. Eddy's differences with orthodox Christianity, her insistence upon the redemption of mortals from evil and sin establishes a basic continuity between Christian Science and the Christian tradition. Little wonder that in a number of her comments on the difference between Christian Science and mind-cure, Mrs. Eddy made a point that she most succinctly stated when she said to a class in 1888 that the Scientist could be a Christian whereas the mind-curer could not.[103]

THE QUIMBY CONTENTION

The distinctions made thus far in this chapter may seem excessively nice unless we take the issues involved, at least provisionally, as seriously as did those originally concerned with them. It is in this spirit that we must examine the much discussed Quimby controversy initiated by Julius Dresser in 1883 and carried on in the polemical literature on Christian Science even after Mrs. Eddy's death. Taking up this question in the context in which it first arose can help to unravel some of the complexities of the dispute, and can also illuminate the basic issues involved in the conflict of Christian Science and mind-cure. For the Quimby contention, though it concerns the origins of Christian Science, was nevertheless in itself distinctly a part of the situation in Boston in the 1880s.

Unfortunately, the Quimby controversy was so charged with partisan passion in Mrs. Eddy's day that the real issues involved were obscured. That she derived Christian Science from Quimby or that he played no part in her development are both misleading assertions, yet both were

102. James, *Varieties of Religious Experience* (New York, 1902), p. 96.
103. Janet Coleman Reminiscences, Archives.

often made. In 1887, for example, we find Julius Dresser discussing Mrs. Eddy's association with Quimby and declaring positively that "it is now easy to see just *when* and *where* she discovered Christian Science." Eleven years later, to take a sample of the opposite viewpoint, we find a devoted follower of Mrs. Eddy writing that "she never was, as some have erroneously asserted, a student of the magnetic doctor, the late Phineas P. Quimby, but on the contrary has disapproved of his methods of practice, as her works show." [104]

Actually the resolution of the Quimby dispute lies with neither of these extreme positions nor even somewhere in between. It lies in a clarification of a fundamental issue which has often been obscured in the course of the debate: the differing religious characters of Christian Science and of Quimby's thought. Christian Science is a religious teaching and only incidentally a healing method. Quimbyism was a healing method and only incidentally a religious teaching. If one examines the religious implications or aspects of Quimby's thought, it is clear that in these terms it has nothing whatever in common with Christian Science.

In 1857, while Quimby's practice was growing in Portland and his reputation spreading through New England, Herman Melville published a novel called *The Confidence Man*. The very title of the book conveys a double meaning: a man who possesses confidence, but also a "con man," a fraud. Its narrative is concerned with the activities of a mysterious character on a steamboat on the Mississippi. In encounters with various members of the ship's company, he tries to inspire in them such confidence in himself as to make them act at variance with their constricted idea of what they could and should be. A miser, for example, under the compelling influence of the Confidence Man, finds himself donating large sums to a charity, of whose very existence he has no proof beyond the stranger's word. What Melville is in part pointing to in this and the series of like incidents that make up much of the book are the latent capacities for good or ill that can be released in individuals when they seriously entertain possibilities that project them past the ordinary structures of their existence.

The most revealing application of the principle of confidence for our purposes occurs when the Confidence Man, under the guise of an herb

---

104. Julius Dresser, "Doctor Phineas P. Quimby, The Founder of Mental Science," p. 171.
Septimus B. Hanna, "Christian Science," *Progress* (June 1898), p. 638.

doctor, offers his aid to a man who is desperately ill with consumption. "Work upon yourself," he tells him; "invoke confidence, though from ashes; rouse it; for your life, rouse it, and invoke it, I say . . . the mind so acts upon the body that if one have no confidence, neither has the other." [105] Phineas Quimby could have made this statement. Indeed, the word *confidence* appears repeatedly in his writings. In *The Confidence Man,* Melville portrayed the increasing confidence of nineteenth century Americans in man's own powers — more specifically, in the possibilities of human power, consciousness, and will. With greater irony and far less savagery than in *Moby Dick,* Melville explores in this book the spiritual bankruptcy of a culture which, even though nominally committed to evangelical Protestantism, has replaced faith in God by faith in man.

This was a faith Quimby shared. And it is only in this sense that he can be regarded as a religious figure at all. Quimby made virtually a religion out of confidence; and in his scattered comments on Christianity, he transmuted virtually every Christian doctrine he touched into an expression of an essentially secular faith. The character of his quasi-religion can best be understood in terms of his reason for developing it. Through years of experience in treating the sick, Quimby found that in a large number of cases, the disturbance was traceable to the patient's religion. In most cases of this sort, the religion was some form of evangelical orthodoxy which he loosely called Calvinism. Of one intensely religious aged invalid he wrote: "She was a Calvinist Baptist and by her belief she had imprisoned her senses in a creed so small and contracted that she could not stand upright or move ahead. Here in the tomb of Calvin her senses were laid, wrapt in her creed." [106] Since Quimby well knew how firm a hold orthodox Christianity had on the minds of such sufferers, he did not try to disabuse them of their religious faith entirely, but to so reinterpret Christian teaching as to make it work for, rather than against, his patients' recovery. Many mesmerists claimed that in their healing work they were employing the method used by Jesus in his work. In some cases this was rhetoric only. But Quimby did come to believe deeply that he had gained an insight into the true interpretation of the Gospel.

In his writings on religion almost every element of traditional faith is transmuted. Quimby's God is indistinguishable from the higher powers of man's own mind. "I will give you the attributes of my God," he wrote

105. Herman Melville, *The Confidence Man: His Masquerade* [1857] (New York, 1961), p. 98.

106. Dresser, *Manuscripts,* p. 351.

one inquirer. "The Wisdom of God is in this letter, and if you understand you will hear his voice saying I understand this. So the understanding is God . . . and to understand is Wisdom . . . and to know wisdom is to know God." [107] Elsewhere he wrote, "Every man is a part of God, just so far as he is wisdom. . . . I worship no God except my own"; again, "To know God is to know ourselves." [108] Quimby's God was what man prayed *with*, not *to*. "In curing the sick," wrote Quimby's son of him, "religion played no part. There were no prayers, there was no asking for assistance from God or any other divinity. He cured by his wisdom." [109]

The cure of the sick was the only salvation that Quimby taught. The only sin from which Jesus had come to save mankind, he taught, was slavery to false opinions which breeds disease. Jesus was a humanitarian healer whose mission, as Quimby saw it, was to break the bands that bound the sick and restore them to health and happiness.[110] The faculty that enabled Jesus to perform these cures was his "clairvoyance," his "higher intelligence" or intuitive sensitivity to the opinions of the sick. This clairvoyance, Quimby taught, was the Christ. Jesus proved that the Christ or the "clairvoyant man could correct the errors of the man of the flesh and blood and keep him in subjection to his wisdom." [111] The heaven to which men thus attained was one of health and happiness on this earth. Quimby did believe in an after-life, but his main concern was the health of men now. "People believe that religion is one thing and health another," he wrote. "This is a false idea, and if you will look at it you will see that to be happy is the chief end of man." [112]

Even during the period of Mrs. Eddy's association with Quimby in the early 1860s, the conflict between his basic secularism and her essentially religious orientation is discernible. Much of her mental energies in the three years after she first met Quimby went into an attempt to reconcile his ideas with her own strongly Christian point of view. In so doing, she inevitably put a construction on them which he had never intended. In her letter to the *Portland Courier* she had written, "Now I can see dimly and only as trees walking the great principle which underlies Dr. Quimby's faith and works." [113] In view of her own unbridgeable religious differences from Quimby and of her later work in Christian Science, it is doubtful that this principle was anything he himself had in mind.

107. *Ibid.*
109. Quoted in *Ibid.*, p. 436.
111. *Ibid.*, p. 341.
113. Quoted in *Ibid.*, p. 161.

108. *Ibid.*, p. 367.
110. See particularly *Ibid.*, pp. 350–361.
112. *Ibid.*, p. 360.

Certainly Mrs. Eddy's continual study of the Bible was quite foreign to Quimby's way of thought. He did originate some novel interpretations of Scripture; yet he never regarded the Bible as a source of inspiration nor encouraged others to do so. But it was to the Bible that Mrs. Eddy turned at the time of her injury in February 1866, less than a month after Quimby's death. In later years she wrote that in her association with him she had lacked the "one thing needed," which came only when she looked to the Bible for aid; and turning "from Quimbyism to the Bible was like turning from Leviticus to St. John." [114]

The underlying issue involved in her differentiation of Christian Science from Quimby's ideas in the early 1870s was, again, mesmerism. Mrs. Eddy had defended Quimby against the charge that he practiced mesmerism soon after their first meeting in 1862, and it is true that Quimby had forsaken the use of the induced trance state, the hallmark of mesmeric practice. Yet by the time of the first publication of *Science and Health* in 1875, Mrs. Eddy was identifying Quimby with mesmerism, even though she said in that book that he was growing out of it. For beginning in 1872, the word had come to assume for her a meaning much larger than the usual practices associated with mesmerism as popularly known. It came to mean the conscious projection of one human mentality upon another. In that year, as a result of controversy with an ex-student, she had come to realize the incompatibility between her idea of God as the only healer and Quimby's approach to healing as the action of mind on mind. Further, as Mrs. Eddy uncovered what she believed to be the workings of mental malpractice through her experience with young Richard Kennedy, she came to see the human mind as capable of all evil.

Through these experiences, Mrs. Eddy came reluctantly to identify Quimbyism as in essence a form of mesmerism and to see mesmerism as a most dangerous evil. In a letter to a friend written at the end of 1872, Mrs. Eddy had said, "I have never since my first perceptions of God in science gained the understanding I have this year past and been able to so sift the tares from the wheat." [115] More than a decade later she would use the same metaphor to apply to the distinction between mind-cure and Christian Science. The tares represented to her mesmerism, the projection of human will. The wheat represented divine Science, the operation of divine power. Mrs. Eddy always retained the greatest personal admiration and affection for Quimby as a man. But ultimately, she felt compelled to place his ideas among the tares. In the first years of research in Christian

114. Quoted in Peel, *Discovery*, p. 205.
115. *Ibid.*, 271–272.

Science, Mrs. Eddy later felt, the tares and the wheat had grown side by side. "Ask any loyal student today," she wrote in 1896, "if he could learn Christian Science as I now teach it, from the manuscripts I wrote for my first student." That the answer to this question must be in the negative she cited as proof that Quimby's teaching was "mental leagues apart from Christian Science." [116] In the final edition of *Science and Health* she summarized her development in these years by writing, "As former beliefs were gradually expelled from her thought, the teaching became clearer, until finally the shadow of old errors was no longer cast upon divine Science." [117]

It is obvious from any consideration of the record of their relationship that Quimby was an enormous stimulus to Mrs. Eddy's development. Traces of his thought do appear in her mature teaching in the use of a number of terms which she employed in common with him — terms like *belief, error,* and *science* — though it should be remembered that she usually changed the sense in which he had employed them. Quimby and Mrs. Eddy also shared a view of bodily conditions as not primarily causative in themselves, but as products of states of mind — though again Quimby took a far more materialist definition of mind than did she. But it should be obvious too, that Mrs. Eddy did not owe what is essential in Christian Science to Quimby. She passed through Portland on her way to Boston, but she ended up in Boston and not in Portland. Her encounter with Quimby was an important stage in her development. But had Mrs. Eddy gone no further, there would have been no Christian Science. From the standpoint of her final teaching, Mrs. Eddy could declare that whatever the importance of Quimby was to her at one time, she could not have learned from him the spiritual actuality of "perfect God and perfect man" she had first begun to understand in 1866.

Perhaps the most effective contrast between Mrs. Eddy and Quimby can be presented by the juxtaposition of two characteristic writings of theirs on the subject of healing. In 1861 Quimby explained his healing method in these terms:

A patient comes to see Dr. Quimby. He renders himself absent to everything but the impression of the person's feelings. These are quickly daguerreotyped on him. They contain no intelligence, but shadow forth a reflection of themselves which he looks at. This contains the disease as it appears to the patient. Being confident that it is the shadow of a false idea, he is not afraid of it. Then

116. Mary Baker Eddy, *Footprints Fadeless.*
117. *S&H.,* p. 460.

his feelings in regard to health and strength, are daguerreotyped on the receptive plate of the patient. . . . The patient sees the disease typed on the doctor again . . . and he sees the change and continues . . . the shadow changes and grows dim, and finally disappears, the light takes its place, and there is nothing left of the disease.[118]

In the preface to *Science and Health,* Mrs. Eddy writes of healing in Christian Science:

Many imagine that the phenomena of physical healing in Christian Science present only a phase of the action of the human mind, which action in some unexplained way results in the cure of the disease. On the contrary, Christian Science rationally explains that all other pathological methods are the fruits of human faith in matter, — faith in the workings, not of Spirit, but of the fleshly mind which must yield to Science.

The physical healing of Christian Science results now, as in Jesus' time, from the operation of divine Principle, before which sin and disease lose their reality in human consciousness and disappear as naturally and as necessarily as darkness gives place to light and sin to reformation.[119]

To understand the confusion between Mrs. Eddy's teaching and Quimby's thought, one must look to the situation at Boston in the 1880s in which this confusion first arose. Specifically, one must understand the role of Julius Dresser in that situation. For initially *the whole Quimby controversy hinges upon Dresser's conception of what Christian Science was.* He saw in Mrs. Eddy's teaching no more than a variant on the idea that disease was the product of mind and that the sick could be healed through the power of mind. His attitude on the subject can be most clearly shown by a fuller quotation from the article on the workings of mind-cure that he wrote in 1887. Quoting Mrs. Eddy's grateful tribute to Quimby in the *Portland Courier* just after her first meeting with him, Dresser went on:

The reader will observe, by reading the foregoing statements closely, that the lady did not understand that disease was an error of mind until this experience took place, and it will be seen how rapidly during the three weeks experience she refers to, she had been taking in that truth, and understanding that the real truth of life is the cure, and was being her cure. It is now easy to see just when and where she discovered Christian Science.[120]

So, according to Dresser, Mrs. Eddy got the essential idea of Christian

118. Dresser, *History,* pp. 57–58.
119. *S&H.,* p. xi.
120. Julius Dresser, "Doctor Phineas P. Quimby," p. 173.

Science when she learned that "disease was an error of mind." As we have seen, she had already begun to entertain this idea as a result of her experiments with homeopathy. And if Christian Science stands essentially for the belief that disease is an error of mind, what are we to say of the theology and metaphysics with which the six hundred pages of *Science and Health* are largely concerned? Quimby's son, who along with Dresser steadfastly proclaimed Mrs. Eddy's indebtedness to Quimby, stated quite openly: "The *religion* which she teaches certainly *is hers,* for which I cannot be too thankful; for I should be loath to go down into my grave feeling that my father was in any way connected with 'Christian Science.'" The controversy becomes clearer when we read on and find George Quimby saying: "That she got her inspiration and idea from father is beyond question. Father claimed to believe, and taught and practiced his belief, that disease was a mental condition and was an invention of man. . . . Don't confuse his method of healing with Mrs. Eddy's Christian Science, so far as her religious teachings go." [121]

By choosing not to heed George Quimby's warning against confusing his father's method of healing with Christian Science, Dresser contributed to the controversy. For not only did Dresser read Mrs. Eddy in terms of Quimby, he also read Quimby in terms of Mrs. Eddy. That is, his teaching of supposedly pure Quimbyism was interlaced with terms and ideas of Mrs. Eddy which were quite foreign to Quimby. For example, Quimby never used the triad of terms "sin, sickness, and death" which was so conspicuous in Mrs. Eddy's vocabulary and also became a part of Dresser's teaching.[122] Dresser's son Horatio (who was born shortly before the date that Mrs. Eddy gives as the discovery of Christian Science) continued, like his father, to read into Quimby theological and metaphysical ideas drawn from other sources, including Christian Science.

To add fuel to the fire, Christian Scientists did not approach the question of Mrs. Eddy's relation with Quimby with any reasoned consideration of the part he had played in her development. They tended to see her revelation more as a lightning flash from the skies than a process of discovery in the initial stages of which Quimby might have played some part. In her own articles on the subject of her relation to Quimby written in the heat of battle during the 1880s, Mrs. Eddy was less than generous in her references to him. It is possible that she had to do a good deal of thinking through the matter before the main lines of her own develop-

121. Quoted in Dresser, *Manuscripts,* p. 436.
122. Harriet S. Hemmenway, notes on a class taught by J. Dresser and Anita Dresser in Jan. 1887. Boston University.

ment through the first edition of *Science and Health* became clear to her. After the passions engendered by the disputes of the 1880s had begun to cool, Mrs. Eddy wrote several quite reasonable estimates of the role Quimby played in her life. In one of them, for example, she stated:

> . . . I tried him, as a healer, and because he seemed to help me for the time, and had a higher ideal than I had heard of up to that time, I praised him to the skies. . . . I was enthusiastic, and couldn't say too much in praise of him; I actually loved him, I mean his high and noble character . . . but when I found that Quimbyism was too short, and would not answer the cry of the human heart for succor, for real aid, I went, being driven thence by my extremity, to the Bible, and there I discovered Christian Science.[123]

If Quimby had a successor, it was not Mrs. Eddy but Warren Felt Evans, who published several books on mind-cure before *Science and Health* was written. Evans may not have gotten his main idea from Quimby — he refers to him in only one place in all his eight books.[124] But Evans' main idea, however expressed, was essentially that which Quimby had expounded in his own cruder way: the action of mind on mind. In Evans' first book he wrote that there are

> a variety of phenomena, passing under the name of Mesmerism, Psychology, Biology, Animal Magnetism, Pantheism, Hypnotism, and even Psychometry, that are reducible to one general principle, — the influence or action of mind upon mind, and the communication of spiritual life from one person to another, who is negatively receptive of it.[125]

Where Quimby had been uneducated, Evans had read widely if not deeply in theology and metaphysics. Something of a metaphysical virtuoso, he elaborated upon this idea of the influence of mind on mind in ways that Quimby might not have even understood. He related it to the idealism of Hegel, of Fichte, and of Edwards, as well as to various forms of Oriental thought. Evans' writings, as much as anyone's, became standard fare for mind-cure and New Thought readers. More than anyone else, he is the link between Quimby and the later movements. And the idea that Quimby, Evans, and later mind-cure and New Thought writers

123. Quoted in Peel, *Discovery*, p. 183.
124. "The late Dr. Quimby of Portland, one of the most successful healers of this or any age, embraced this view of the nature of disease (that it is mental in origin) and by a long succession of the most remarkable cures effected by psychopathic remedies, at the same time proved the truth of the theory of the efficiency of that mode of treatment. He seemed to reproduce the wonders of Gospel history." Warren Felt Evans, *The Mental Cure* (Boston, 1869), p. 210.
125. *Ibid.*, p. 210.

all share, whatever the differences among them, is one that Mrs. Eddy explicitly repudiates: the exaltation of the mind of man as a beneficent influence acting upon other minds.

In essence, the attribution of Mrs. Eddy's basic idea to Quimby is the same as the confusion of this idea with mind-cure. Those who first brought up the Quimby contention differed from Mrs. Eddy in very much the same respect as she differed from Quimby. They were, therefore, closer to Quimby's ideas themselves, and were as much identifying their own differences from her as establishing the supposed origins of her teachings. Furthermore, it was through her experience with the mind-cure movement that Mrs. Eddy came to her final assessment of the role of Quimby in her development. For his position was sufficiently like that of the mind-curers, that distinguishing her teaching from theirs was virtually the same as distinguishing it from his. Assessing Quimby's ideas in 1891 on the basis of her experience with mind-cure, Mrs. Eddy wrote, "Mr. Quimby's practice was the mortal mind-cure, on a material basis, — one belief displacing another. This is the opposite of Christian Science, which rests on the divine Mind as its Principle of healing, and on the understanding of this Mind as the healthiest and holiest influence over the human mind and body." [126]

OCCULTISM AMERICAN STYLE

It is not too much to say that the New England culture of the mid-nineteenth century out of which Phineas Quimby sprang was a mind-centered culture. At one level, this mind-centeredness was apparent in the emphasis upon the possibilities of consciousness and perception to be found in transcendentalism. At another, it is evident in Quimby's exploration of the curative potentials of human thought. At still another level, it is discernible in the vogue of occultism that began to assume significant proportions on the New England scene during the 1840s and '50s. "How slowly, how slowly," wrote Ralph Waldo Emerson in an essay on "Demonology,"

we learn that witchcraft and ghostcraft, palmistry and magic, and all the other superstitions, which, with so much police, boastful skepticism and scientific committees, we had finally dismissed to the moon as nonsense, are really no nonsense at all, but subtle and valid influences, always starting up, moving, muttering in our path, and shading our day.[127]

126. *Ret.,* first ed., p. 45.
127. Quoted in Peel, *Christian Science,* p. 77.

By the time Emerson wrote these words, most New Englanders were familiar with the feats of mesmerizers who traveled from town to town giving exhibitions of their strange skills; the mysterious rappings at the home of the Fox sisters in Rochester, New York, had sparked a widespread flurry of interest in spiritualism; and the Transcendentalists themselves had begun to read widely in the religious literature of the Orient.

Occultism in its various forms has always been highly suspect in Western Christianity. The Medieval Church opposed occult practices as remnants of paganism; and Luther, among other great figures of the Reformation, condemned them as well, singling out astrology for special attention. And Christian opponents of occultism have found no difficulty in finding Scriptural texts to support their views.[128] Yet the fascination with the occult as an alternative to traditional Christianity has been a persistent if subordinate theme in Western intellectual and religious life.

Occultism as it has appeared in the West may be understood as a kind of inverted transcendence — a quest, in William James' phrase, for "the more" in terms of the expanded potentials of the human mind and will.[129] The religious impulse, starved and finding no sustenance in transcendental orthodoxies, may gravitate back to the self and become fascinated with its unexplored powers. As the supernatural was once a refuge, so the self becomes a reservoir. This line of analysis may serve to explain the relation of the rise of occultism to the increasing secular rationalism in Western culture which, by sapping the foundations of religious supernaturalism, has made occultism an alternative for those who find something lacking in a religionless culture of modernity and progress. In America since the mid-nineteenth century, interest in occultism has increased in rough proportion to the waning of Protestantism. A. J. Gordon, commenting in 1885 on one of the more conspicuous late nineteenth century forms of occultism, theosophy, noted that in it the "attenuated unbelief of our times is seeking to find relief from the *ennui* of denial."[130] This was a perceptive estimate, as applicable, perhaps, to the 1960s and 1970s as to the 1880s. And Gordon, along with a number of other ministers, classed Christian Science with theosophy and spiritualism as manifestations of the occult spirit.

Mrs. Eddy, however, emphatically denied that Christian Science was

128. See, for example, *Lev.* 19: 31 and *Isaiah* 8: 19.
129. James was strongly interested in occult phenomena, which he understood as indicating the vast unexplored potentials of the human psyche.
130. A. J. Gordon, "Spiritualism, Ritualism, Theosophy," in *Prophetic Studies of the Southern Prophetic Convention* (Chicago, 1886), p. 68.

occult in character. It is true that she gained much of her following from people who, like the devotees of occultism, had become disenchanted with orthodox Protestantism. Yet she did not conceive of Christian Science as in any sense esoteric; and with very few exceptions, her followers displayed anything but the spirit of select initiates. In writing *Science and Health,* Mrs. Eddy had tried to give as clear and complete statement as possible to her teaching. Asked if there were not some secret, behind the book's contents, she replied: "there is absolutely no additional secret outside of its teachings, or that gives one the power to heal." [131]

The purpose of class instruction, which became an important feature of institutionalized Christian Science, was sometimes misinterpreted as being a means whereby secret lore was passed along in the movement through private channels. Mrs. Eddy's actual intent in providing for it, however, was quite practical; for it proved to be a necessary instrument for the elucidation of her teaching so that students could practice it more effectively. Further, Mrs. Eddy's use of the term *science* is far removed from the use of the term in connection with the "occult sciences" of alchemy or astrology. For her, science did not mean esoteric knowledge, but a clear setting forth of ideas susceptible to rational comprehension and practical demonstration. It was that which dissolved rather than perpetuated mystery.

Actually, few words had a more sinister connotation to Mrs. Eddy than the term *occult.* The Science she taught, Mrs. Eddy maintained, in no sense partook "of the nature of occultism, magic, alchemy, or necromancy. These 'ways that are vain' are the inventions of animal magnetism, which would deceive, if possible, the very elect." [132] Significantly, she placed one of her central statements on occultism in the chapter "The Apocalypse" in *Science and Health.* Commenting on the text from *Revelation*: "And when the dragon saw that he was cast unto the earth, he persecuted the woman which brought forth the man child," she wrote:

The march of mind and of honest investigation will bring the hour when the people will chain, with fetters of some sort, the growing occultism of this period. The present apathy as to the tendency of certain active yet unseen mental agencies will finally be shocked into yet another extreme mortal mood, — into human indignation; for one extreme follows another. [133]

To Mrs. Eddy, all forms of occultism were phases of animal magnetism, phases of the activity of mortal mind, not manifestations of true divine

131. *Mis.,* p. 50.   132. *Ibid.,* p. 78.   133. *S&H.,* p. 570.

power. The problem of differentiating her own teaching from occultism was not, however, new to Mrs. Eddy; for many years she had been laboring to distinguish her teaching from perhaps the most popular occult fad of the nineteenth century, spiritualism. Though spiritualism had first come to public attention in pre-Civil War America, it was only in the post-War years that it gained a widespread popular following. To some extent, the Civil War, with its half million dead, facilitated the development of spiritualism as a popular fad in the post-War decades; for many who had lost relatives and friends in the conflict resorted to seances to contact them. Mainly, though, spiritualism was something of an indoor occult sport. And thousands of Americans could cherish, as did Mrs. Terrant in Henry James' *The Bostonians,* "reminiscences of the darkened room, the waiting circle, the little taps on table and wall, the little touches on cheek and foot, the music in the air, the rain of flowers, the sense of something mysteriously flitting." [134]

No one aspect of Mrs. Eddy's work in Christian Science is more consistent than her opposition to spiritualism. Indeed, she felt that she had done more than any other person to stem its influence. As a young person, Mrs. Eddy had shown some curiosity about the craze; yet by the mid-1850s, a decade before her discovery, she was arguing against it. [135] The first edition of *Science and Health* contained a number of strictures on spiritualism. She wrote, for example, "We ought to know the consequences of launching into new and stronger fellowship with error, when we are already in it up to our necks." [136] And several reviews of the book took note of the strong shafts she aimed at mediumship. It will be remembered, also, that the last change she made in *Science and Health* was the alteration of the chapter title "Christian Science and Spiritualism" to "Christian Science *versus* Spiritualism."

Yet spiritualism did play a curious and significant role in the life of the Christian Science movement. For it was among spiritualists, who had rejected orthodoxy and were open to new ideas that Mrs. Eddy first found a hearing. Her first pupil, Hiram Crafts, who began to study with her in late 1866, had been a spiritualist until Mrs. Eddy's teaching changed his views. For ten months during 1867 and 1868 she found shelter with a spiritualist named Mother Webster; and in August 1868 she first advertised for students in the leading spiritualist organ in the United States, *The Banner of Light.*[137] Not all spiritualists were friendly to her, however;

134. Henry James, *The Bostonians* (New York, 1886), p. 74.
135. Peel, *Discovery,* p. 133.   136. *S&H.,* first edition, p. 321.
137. *The Banner of Light,* July 4, 1868.

and some of them took advantage of the question and answer periods that followed the talks she gave at informal services in 1875 to heckle her. Yet until the early 1880s a significant proportion of her students were gathered from the ranks of spiritualists or had a spiritualist background. Very few students with this background stayed with her, and it was only when Christian Science began to garner converts from the orthodox Protestant denominations that it built a really stable following. It is not hard to see why this should have been the case. For Christian Science, though at first it might have seemed quite bizarre, had none of that titillating supernaturalism that had made spiritualism so attractive to many. "It is mysticism which gives spiritualism its force," wrote Mrs. Eddy.[138] Certainly she did not consider herself a mystic nor her teaching mystical. And neither did Christian Science appeal primarily to those of mystical temperament.

In *Science and Health,* Mrs. Eddy devoted considerable attention to detailing her argument against spiritualism. In the first place, she wrote, spiritualism is dependent upon belief in a plurality of spirits; and this belief in what she called "corporeal communicators"[139] was wholly at variance with her central contention that there is but one Spirit, of whom individual men are the expressions. Further, Mrs. Eddy opposed the idea that there could be communion between those living and those who had died. "The mental states are so unlike," she wrote, "that intercommunion is as impossible as it would be between a mole and a human being."[140] The only possible instance where such communion was possible, she felt, was at the point of transition between the two states. In this vestibule, she maintained, men may become conscious of the presence of those who have gone before.[141] Yet even were spiritualist communications possible, Mrs. Eddy felt that they would have no particular significance. "At the very best and on its own theories," she wrote, "spiritualism can only prove that certain individuals have a continued existence after death and maintain their affiliation with mortal flesh; but that fact affords no certainty of everlasting life."[142] The certainty of man's immortality did not depend upon proof that spirits survive the grave; rather, it could be gained only through growth into the certain consciousness that God is the only Life of man. Knowing God as Life, one is assured of his own continuity. The usual evidences of spiritualism Mrs. Eddy interpreted either as products of imagination or as mental phenomena explicable in Christian Sci-

138. *S&H.*, p. 80.   139. *Ibid.*, p. 72.   140. *Ibid.*, p. 82.
141. *Ibid.*, p. 75.   142. *Ibid.*, p. 81.

ence. "Haunted houses, ghostly voices, unusual noises, and apparitions brought out in dark seances," she explained, "either involve feats by tricksters, or they are images and sounds evolved involuntarily by mortal mind." [143]

Mrs. Eddy felt it was possible for spiritualists sensitive to the currents of human thought to discern in the mind of the living remembrance of the departed, then to describe the dead as though contact had been made. Yet this sort of mind-reading was but the reading of *mortal* mind, and it had no spiritual significance whatever. *Immortal* Mind-reading, Mrs. Eddy felt, was possible to the spiritually-minded. It was "a revelation of the divine purpose through spiritual understanding, by which man gains the divine Principle and explanation of all things." Of man's spiritual prophetic capacities she further wrote:

When sufficiently advanced in Science to be in harmony with the truth of being, men become seers and prophets involuntarily, controlled not by demons, spirits, or demigods, but by the one Spirit. It is the prerogative of the ever-present, divine Mind, and of thought which is in rapport with this Mind, to know the past, the present, and the future.[144]

Mrs. Eddy cites as examples of true spiritual Mind reading the Gospel accounts of Jesus' discernment of the thoughts of others. This sort of intuition, she felt, was the spiritual detection of error in human thought in order to destroy it, and was neither esoteric nor supernatural.

Mrs. Eddy saw the spiritualists' fascination with latent mental powers as anticipating the broader evil of mesmerism and animal magnetism, to which she devoted more sustained attention in her work in Christian Science. Indeed, there is a real historical connection between these two forms of occultism; for the spiritual seance originated with Anton Mesmer as a technique for group mesmerism. The belief that an individual in an entranced state can become capable of curing others or contacting departed spirits owes much, in its modern revivification, to the influence of Mesmer and his followers both in France and in the United States. And it was during the same period in which spiritualism began to arouse interest in the United States that mesmerism first suggested to some thoughtful Americans the dangers of despotic mental control. Mesmeric healing was something of a craze in New England, when, in 1841, Nathaniel Hawthorne's fiancée asked him if she should investigate it for the

143. *Ibid.*, p. 86.   144. *Ibid.*, pp. 83, 84.

cure of headaches. He warned her against so doing, explaining his attitude in these terms: "Supposing that this power arises from the transfusion of one spirit into another, it seems to me that the sacredness of an individual is violated by it; there would be an intrusion into the holy of holies." [145] In his works of fiction as well, Hawthorne expresses his horror at the violation of the sacredness of individuality through demonic control — a theme which, particularly in *The House of the Seven Gables,* resonates with the memories of Salem witchcraft.[146]

Though in later years Mrs. Eddy was to write that "The peril of Salem witchcraft is not passed," there was nothing magical or even esoteric to her in this phenomenon. She saw mesmerism, necromancy, and witchcraft as manifestations of the latent powers of mortal mind, and felt that the reason these powers were not better understood was only a consequence of mortal mind's ignorance of itself. Mrs. Eddy felt, however, that she had thoroughly investigated the character of what she called "erring, mortal, misnamed *mind*" [147] beginning with her experiments with homeopathy and continuing with her association with Quimby. The inquiring spirit in which she pursued this work had more in common with scientific investigations into the character of hypnotism and extra-sensory perception than with popular occult dabblings. And her work along these lines was only preliminary to the discovery of Christian Science. From the standpoint of Mrs. Eddy's mature teaching, the phenomenon of mesmerism in all of its manifestations was only a projection of human thought, subject to rational comprehension, and analogous in Biblical terms to the operation of what Paul called "the carnal mind."

Understandably, Mrs. Eddy and her followers took very seriously the increasing medical interest in hypnotism in the late nineteenth century. The *Journal* made careful note of Charcôt's experiments with hypnotic phenomena in Paris — experiments which, from the Scientists' point of view, constituted only a revivification of an old error in new form.[148] "The necromancy of yesterday," Mrs. Eddy wrote, "foreshadowed the mesmerism and hypnotism of today." [149] She explained the gulf between Christian Science and hypnotic practice by writing that "The Christian Scientist demonstrates that the divine Mind heals, while the hypnotist

145. Quoted in Randall Stewart, ed., *The American Notebooks of Nathaniel Hawthorne* (New Haven, 1932), p. lxxv.

146. It is also worth noting that Chillingworth in *The Scarlet Letter* is a "chilling" figure in part because of his use of the art of necromancy.

147. *S&H.*, p. 108.   148. *CSJ*, VII (May 1889), 470.

149. *S&H.*, p. 322.

dispossesses the patient of his individuality in order to control him. No person is benefited by yielding his mentality to any mental despotism or malpractice." [150]

Not all malpractice, Mrs. Eddy taught, constitutes a conscious attempt to harm another by mental means. For one might ignorantly malpractice upon others by, say, entertaining strong fears for their health or safety, and so perhaps unwittingly do them harm by the projection of this fear into their thought and experience. But malpractice, Mrs. Eddy argued, could be and often was conscious and malicious. And malicious mental malpractice was, for her, occult in the most terrible sense of the term.

She saw the twisting of the spiritual power Christian Science revealed into the destructive ends of "psychological tyranny" as the "greatest evil that ever entered the province of mortal mind." [151] In the first instance, she felt, the factionalization that produced the mind-cure movement had been brought about through the mental efforts of two of the malpractitioners mentioned in the previous chapter: Richard Kennedy and Edward J. Arens. (There may or may not be some significance in the fact that both of them died in mental institutions.) As the mind-cure movement proliferated, she feared that the number of those who knew how to use thought power for destructive ends was multiplying. Mrs. Eddy felt that some of the "mind-quacks," as she called them, had no compunction about mentally creating dissension in the Christian Science movement in order to attract more of her students into their ranks. [152] Certain promising students of hers, she noted, "have first been completely demoralized by this novel class of human mental operators; and then they have been pressed into the service of their masters, to plot and execute almost inconceivable schemes for the injury of myself and the common cause of Christian Science." Of their methods she further wrote, "While turning the screws the malpractitioner offers these conditions: Renounce Christian Science! Slander Mrs. Eddy! Plagiarize her works! Set up an originator! Write a book, to mislead the public, or else you must die." [153]

150. *S&H.*, p. 375.

151. Eddy, *Christian Science: No and Yes*, pp. 34, 38.

152. Mrs. Eddy's most forceful statement of this attitude was in the section on "Animal Magnetism" in *Christian Science: No and Yes*, just referred to. Only a small number of copies of this work as originally published have been preserved, for Mrs. Eddy felt that in it she had been too personal in her references to mind-curers. She refers to her withdrawal of the book from circulation in *Mis.*, pp. 284–285. Yet there is no reason to believe that Mrs. Eddy changed the attitudes that this deleted section of her book contained.

153. Eddy, *Christian Science: No and Yes*, pp. 35–36.

Mrs. Eddy felt that Mrs. Hopkins' defection had been brought about in just this way, and referred to an alleged boast by the individual responsible that it had taken him six months to bend her to his purpose. At one point Mrs. Eddy is reported to have told Mrs. Hopkins, "You are so full of mesmerism that your eyes stick out like a boiled codfish." [154]

It was the *covert* character of the operations of mental malpractice that Mrs. Eddy felt most needed exposing. "The modes of mental malpractice," she wrote, work "so subtly that we mistake its suggestions for the impulses of our own thought." [155] Detailing the effects of animal magnetism, she further explained:

Animal magnetism fosters suspicious distrust where honor is due, fear where courage should be strongest, reliance where there should be avoidance, a belief in safety where there is most danger; and these miserable lies, poured constantly into his mind, fret and confuse it, spoiling that individual's disposition, undermining his health, and sealing his doom, unless the cause of the mischief is found out and destroyed.[156]

If Mrs. Eddy's analysis is correct, then obviously the ordinary understanding of causation in many instances of death, disaster, and suffering is completely erroneous. She held, for example, that the early death of Theodore Parker had been caused not by a physical ailment, but by the "prayers of the unrighteous." [157] To take another case, a well-known practitioner in the movement during the mid-1890s, Mrs. Ira Knapp, fell ill of what appeared to be pneumonia after going out in bitterly cold weather to see a patient. Mrs. Knapp treated herself and was treated by other Christian Scientists for pneumonia, but the treatments proved unsuccessful and she died. Later, when Mrs. Eddy was told how Mrs. Knapp's case was handled, she said that pneumonia was only the decoy — that had the Christian Scientists handled mental assassination, the patient would have recovered.[158]

From 1887 to 1889 the *Journal* ran a regular column on "Animal Magnetism," which included a number of accounts of the effects of malpractice. Various reports from the fields bore witness to the operation of the danger that Mrs. Eddy had pointed out. One woman testified that suddenly, after having been taught by Mrs. Eddy, she was possessed of an irrational

154. Ernest Sutherland Bates and John V. Dittimore, *Mary Baker Eddy: The Truth and the Tradition* (New York, 1932), p. 272.
155. *My.,* p. 213.   156. *Ibid.*
157. Eddy, *Repaid Pages.*
158. Bliss Knapp, *Ira Knapp and Flavia Stickney Knapp* (Norwood, Mass., 1925), p. 135.

fear of her, which finally yielded to Christian Science treatment.[159] Another Christian Scientist who had once been a patient of a mind-cure leader testified that she was haunted by the command to write a book and slander Mrs. Eddy, until she realized the mental influence that was operating on her.[160] Still another worker reported that he was called to the bedside of a young woman stricken with what her friends thought to be food poisoning; but the patient insisted that she had an unaccountable conviction that someone wanted her to suffer. When the case was taken up on this basis, the patient was instantaneously healed.[161] The lengthiest and most compelling of these reports told of the death by mental assassination of F. N. Snider, a pioneer worker for the Christian Science movement in New York. The story of Snider's death was related in chilling detail by his wife in several installments in the *Journal*. The purpose of the narratives was to alert Christian Scientists to the dangers which they faced and the necessity of handling mental malpractice as Mrs. Eddy instructed.[162]

It would be easy, of course, to dismiss these accounts as evidences of gross superstition; and it is true that some of them do have the ring of rather paranoidal fictions. The eminent scholar Barrett Wendell, however, took the subject of adverse mental influence seriously. Indeed, in 1892, he believed he had found enough justification in his delvings into the occult to ask if the Salem witches were really guiltless.[163] And even if one discredits the existence of what Mrs. Eddy called mental malpractice, there is quite convincing evidence that some people in her time did believe in it and actually tried to injure others by mental means as she said. The most conspicuous case was that of a woman who will come into our discussion again at a later point, Mrs. Augusta Stetson. In 1908 Mrs. Stetson, one of the most prominent figures in the movement and the virtual boss of the largest Christian Science church in New York, was brought before the Board of Directors of The Mother Church for interrogation on a number of serious charges. One of the gravest of them was that she and the circle of practitioners close to her consciously attempted to harm their enemies by mental means. A witness against her reported to the press that she had addressed meetings of practitioners as follows:

159. "Malicious Mesmerism," *CSJ*, III (May 1885), 2.
160. "Multifarious Malign Methods," *CSJ*, V (Aug. 1887), 5.
161. *CSJ*, III (July 1885), 72.
162. The account of Snider's case is given in *CSJ*, VI, 616–619; VII, 29–30.
163. Barrett Wendell, *Stelligiere, and Other Essays* (New York, 1893). See also Alan Heimert, introduction to Barrett Wendell, *Cotton Mather: The Puritan Priest* (New York, 1963), p. xxix.

"You all know Mr. So-and-so. You all know that his place is six feet under the ground, that is where he should be. As the words were spoken," the account continued, "the silent circle of practitioners concentrated their minds on one thought." [164] Another of Mrs. Stetson's inner circle testified:

> Relays of practitioners were employed to keep up a continuous mental effort directed toward a certain person who was in disfavor; . . . each practitioner was told the end sought to be attained by the direction of this steady thought on the victim of it, and . . . by replacing the practitioner at intervals of one or two hours, the victim of their thought was under constant and terrible strain.[165]

And one man who by his own account was the victim of this sort of treatment wrote that the "strain of malpractice on me was so great that to get peace of mind I rode in the noisiest parts of the city. I could hug the noise for the relief it gave me." [166]

It should be emphasized, though, that Mrs. Eddy did not believe the victims of mental attack to be powerless. For she taught that the Christian Scientist who is awake to the nature of animal magnetism can defend himself fully from its operation. As she put it in *Science and Health*: "Evil thoughts and aims reach no further and do no more harm than one's belief permits. Evil thoughts, lusts, and malicious purposes cannot go forth, like wandering pollen, from one human mind to another, finding unsuspected lodgement, if virtue and truth build a strong defense." [167] It was to awaken Christian Scientists to the need to defend themselves against mental attack that she wrote extensively on the subject, discussed it in her classes, and instructed that it be given explicit attention in both normal and primary Christian Science class teaching.

The complete opposition of Christian Science to the occult practice of mesmerism is clear enough. But it is also apparent that some of Mrs. Eddy's followers were afflicted with what amounted to a morbid fascination with the subject — a fascination which was in itself almost occult. This became noticeably the case in the late 1880s when, as a result of the proliferation of mind-cure, the discussion of "malicious animal magnetism" — often abbreviated to "M.A.M." — was at a high point in the movement. One Christian Scientist recalled that in this period "M.A.M." was feared by some more than the wrath of God in the old theology. Some Christian Scientists who were extremists in the matter attributed

---

164. Altman K. Swihart, *Since Mrs. Eddy* (New York, 1931), p. 102.
165. *Ibid.*, p. 102. See also pp. 95–96 for a similar and more lengthy account.
166. *Ibid.*, p. 102.   167. *S&H.*, pp. 234–235.

almost anything that went wrong in their lives to its influence. Students easily became suspicious, and the worst of accusations could spring out of any quarrel.[168]

In this situation Mrs. Eddy came to feel that the agitation over animal magnetism and mental malpractice was beginning to get out of hand. Accordingly, she wrote in the August 1890 *Journal,* "The discussion of malicious animal magnetism had better be dropped until Scientists understand clearly how to handle error." In their frantic zeal, some Christian Scientists, she maintained, were in "danger of dwarfing their growth in love"; and only "patient unceasing love for all mankind, — love that cannot mistake Love's aid, — can determine this question on the Principle of Christian Science." [169] Furthermore, in the revised edition of *Science and Health* published late in the same year, Mrs. Eddy cut the chapter on "Animal Magnetism" to seven pages, less than half its former length. In so doing, she disappointed some of her followers who were eagerly anticipating an extended statement from her on the subject. This chapter, revised and retitled "Animal Magnetism Unmasked," occupies the same number of pages in the final edition of the work.

After this point there appeared very few articles on animal magnetism and mental malpractice in the Christian Science periodicals, the regular column was dropped and the whole subject became much less a topic of conversation in the movement. Yet it certainly did not disappear from the teaching of Christian Science, in which it occupies a very fundamental place indeed. From time to time Mrs. Eddy would refer to the need of handling some aspect of mental malpractice in a published statement,[170] and her followers continued to deal with it in their mental work. Hysterics over the subject still did occur in the movement, of course. Yet by her actions in 1890 Mrs. Eddy prevented her protest against occultism from being converted into a form of occultism itself.

THE EASTERN INCURSION

Whether or not the Eastern religions that have attained substantial following in the United States since the Gilded Age can be spoken of as occult in character is problematic. Though it would probably be a mistake to refer to Buddhism and Hinduism as occult in themselves, the spirit

---

168. Johnson, *History,* I, 334.
169. Mary Baker Eddy, "Animal Magnetism," *CSJ,* VIII (Aug. 1890), 168.
170. See, for example, Mary Baker Eddy, "Take Notice," *My.,* p. 367.

in which many Americans have taken up their study often merited this designation. The first substantial indication of Eastern influence on American thought can be seen in the earlier part of the nineteenth century in the Transcendentalist movement. Yet what Hinduism and Buddhism meant to an Emerson or to a Thoreau was in many respects quite different from what they meant to large numbers of Americans who took an interest in them in the later decades of the century. Such publications as James Freeman Clarke's study of comparative religion, *Ten Great Religions,* published in 1871, were widely disseminated among the reading public. And Sir Edwin Arnold's narrative poem on the life of Buddha, *The Light of Asia,* which appeared nine years later, was one of the most popular religious publications of the period.[171] Americans read such works in sufficient number to give point to Edgar Lee Masters' poem spoken by the village mystic Tennessee Clafin Shope in the *Spoon River Anthology*:

> I asserted the sovereignty of my own soul
> Before Mary Baker G. Eddy ever got started
> With what she called science
> I had mastered the "Bhagavad Gita,"
> And cured my soul, before Mary
> Began to cure bodies with souls —
> Peace to all world! [172]

The most conspicuous manifestation of the influence of Eastern religion in the United States before the turn of the century can be seen in its role at the World's Parliament of Religions at Chicago in 1893. Two of the highlights of the Parliament were the presentations on Vedanta by Swami Vivekananda and on Theosophy by Annie Besant. Indeed, Americans showed themselves to be fascinated by the "wisdom of the East"; and when Vivekananda appeared he was swamped with admirers, most of them female, who responded to his handsome presence and persuasive tones with nearly rapturous passion.[173] It is important to note that Christian Science shared the limelight with Vedanta and Theosophy as stellar attractions of the Parliament. Whatever the difference between Christian Science and these other two teachings, all three elicited enormous attention as forms of belief outside the Christian mainstream. In the years after

171. For a good account of the impact of Oriental thought in America see Wendell Thomas, *Hinduism Invades America* (New York, 1930).
172. Edgar Lee Masters, *Spoon River Anthology* (New York, 1914), p. 186.
173. Thomas, *Hinduism Invades America,* p. 132.

the Parliament, many ministers found a way to discredit Christian Science
through associating it with, as one of them put it, "the flotsam and jetsam
of the Orient." [174] Vivekananda himself had written back to India that the
Christian Scientists, who were "spreading by leaps and bounds and causing heartburn to the orthodox," were obviously Vedantans. "I mean," he
explained, "they have picked up a few doctrines of the Advaita and
grafted them upon the Bible. And they cure diseases by proclaiming . . .
'I am He. I am He.' — through strength of mind. They all admire me
highly." [175]

The view that Christian Science bore a strong resemblance to Eastern
religion was further supported by a highcaste Indian woman, the Pundita
Rambai. After her conversion to Christianity, the Pundita embarked
upon a crusade to end the practice of immolating Hindu wives with their
dead husbands. Arriving in America to win support for her cause, she
heard of Christian Science, inquired about it, and discovered to her horror,
she said, that "it was the same doctrine which had enslaved our people
for centuries." The pernicious teaching that the world is unreal, she went
on, "has caused immeasurable suffering in my land, for it is based on
selfishness, and knows no sympathy and compassion." [176] The Pundita's
words, as one might expect, were eagerly seized upon by clergymen intent
upon discrediting Christian Science, and hence the link between it and
Eastern religion was more firmly forged in the public mind.

Christian Scientists were concerned with this confusion and tried to
correct it whenever possible. For they had long since tried to draw clear
lines of distinction between their religion and forms of Eastern faith. At
one time the association between the two had been a problem within the
movement itself. This point brings us back again to the chaotic situation
in the movement at the time of the apostasies of the 1880s. Mind-curers
who once had been Christian Scientists but rejected Mrs. Eddy's leadership faced one very real problem: they appeared to accept much of her
teaching even while denying her credit for her discovery. For those who
accepted Dresser's charge that she had stolen her main idea from Quimby,
this problem did not exist. But most mind-curers could not make use of
this explanation, for they had neither known Quimby nor read his writings. But they did read widely in mystical and metaphysical literatures,
and claimed to find therein principles that Mrs. Eddy had not discovered

174. Faunce, "The Philosophy of Christian Science," in *Searchlights*, p. 38.
175. Vivekananda, *Letters of Swami Vivekananda* (Calcutta, 1940), p. 118.
176. Pundita Rambai, "Fruits of Christian Science and Theosophy in India"
(1886), pp. 5–6.

but had just restated. As one mind-curer who had once been a student of hers wrote, there was no human being "whom we should deify for the great service of *reinforcing* a truth which . . . the race has always been more or less familiar with." [177] Repeatedly, mind-curers stressed the fundamental unity in all great mystical teaching. Mrs. Hopkins, to take a notable example, observed that

the remarkable analogies of the Christian Bible, and Hindu Sacred Books, Egyptian Ancient Teachings, Persian Bible, Chinese Great Learning, Oriental Yohar, Saga, and many others, show that the whole world has had life teachings so wonderfully identical as to make them all subjects for respectful attention and investigation by the thoughtful of our age.[178]

In part, the identification of the central idea of Christian Science with ancient mystical principles was a tactic adopted by those who did not break utterly from Mrs. Eddy's teaching, but who wished to deny her credit for her discovery. In part, too, it represented their departure from Christian Science as Mrs. Eddy taught it. For many people inclined to occultism in the movement found Eastern teachings most attractive. Of these Mrs. Hopkins was easily the most influential. In a series of "Lessons on Christian Science" which she published after breaking with Mrs. Eddy, she quoted from a wide variety of mystic and occult sources, and her writings are studded with such statements as, "I feel the waiting Silence stir. The vivific Life-Principle thrills and shivers through me." [179] Even in an article she had written for the *Journal* Mrs. Hopkins had said that the "Buddhist Nirvana finds a point of contact with Christ's 'I and my father are one.' " [180]

The association of Christian Science with Eastern religion would seem to have had some basis in Mrs. Eddy's own writings. For in some early editions of *Science and Health* she had quoted from and commented favorably upon a few Hindu and Buddhist texts. In the first edition of her textbook she remarked of Buddhism, for example, "The history of the Chinese Empire derives its antiquity and renown from the truer idea the Buddhist entertains of God, contrasted with the tyranny, intolerance, and bloodshed based on the belief that Truth, Life, and Love are in matter." [181] In some later editions, too, one finds at the head of one chapter a

177. Elizabeth Sartwell, "Two Ways of Thinking," *Truth,* II (March 1888), 110.
178. Emma Curtis Hopkins, "First Lesson in Christian Science," (Chicago, 1888), pp. 16–17.
179. Hopkins, "Sixth Lesson in Christian Science," (Chicago, 1891), p. 7.
180. Hopkins, "God's Omnipresence," *CSJ,* II (June 1884), 9.
181. *S&H.,* 1st ed., p. 104.

central passage from Sir Edwin Arnold's translation of the *Bhagavad-Gita*. Yet it is doubtful that at the time these references and quotations were added to *Science and Health* Mrs. Eddy had any serious intent to link Christian Science with Eastern thought. Indeed, the quote just mentioned from the *Bhagavad-Gita* was probably inserted by Wiggin, who sought to increase the appeal of her book by using this and many other quotations at the heads of the chapters.[182] And though Mrs. Eddy had referred to an analogy between her teaching and Hinduism, she never cited it as her source.

None of these references, however, was to remain a part of *Science and Health* as it finally stood. Indeed, the passage in the final edition corresponding to her statement just quoted about the "truer idea the Buddhist entertains of God" reads, "The eastern nations and empires owe their false government to the misconceptions of Deity there prevalent." [183] Increasingly from the mid-1880s on, Mrs. Eddy made a sharp distinction between Christian Science and Eastern religions. The confusion between the two was one aspect of the general confusion of ideas resulting from the development of mind-cure; and as Mrs. Eddy more clearly stated the distinction between her teaching and that of the mind-curers, she also differentiated it from Eastern thought.

Mrs. Eddy did not write at length on the relation between Christian Science and Eastern religion, of which her knowledge was probably quite limited. Yet in a number of direct and indirect references scattered throughout her published writings, one does find a consistent approach to the subject — a differentiation of Christian Science and Eastern religion in terms of certain broad tendencies of thought and practice.

To begin with, Mrs. Eddy rejected the strongly mystical, subjective tendency implicit in both Hinduism and Buddhism. Never did she urge the cultivation of mystical inner consciousness as an end in itself. In the first edition of *Science and Health* she had written, "There is no inner life, for Life is God." [184] She once indicated her rejection of mystical subjectivity by writing that man "is not an iceberg; he is the image and likeness of his Maker." [185] There are passages in her writings which point out the tremendous importance of moments of exalted spiritual consciousness, as when she wrote: "One moment of divine consciousness, or the spiritual understanding of Life and Love, is a foretaste of eternity." [186]

182. Peel, *Trial*, p. 187.   183. *S&H.*, p. 94.   184. *S&H.*, first edition.
185. "Questions Answered," *CSJ*, IV (Oct. 1886), 160–161.
186. *S&H.*, p. 598.

But Mrs. Eddy maintained that for such moments to be meaningful, they must bear fruit in demonstration and in higher lives lived.

True Christianity, she taught, must have a *practical* healing and redemptive effect. She discouraged passivity in the face of suffering of any sort and utterly opposed the belief that man must acknowledge the cycle of fatality, which Hinduism calls the "wheel of fate." Indeed, Christian Science itself stood for her as the means whereby man could rise up and take control over his own destiny. She saw redemption as including the redemption of the body. It is well to remember her statement, quoted earlier, that the Bible furnishes no reasons for the destruction of the body, "but for its restoration to life and health as the scientific proof of 'God with us.'"[187] According to Christian Science, one cannot attain final spiritualized consciousness while submitting to any form of suffering. Mrs. Eddy refused to recognize as legitimate the division between an inner mental state and an outward bodily condition, for to her the latter objectified the former.

That which redeems men, Mrs. Eddy insisted, is divine power absolutely objective to human consciousness. "Christian Science," she wrote, "demands as did Paul's Christianity, that we look outward for divine power, and away from human consciousness. St. Paul argues against introspection whereby to work out the salvation of man."[188] Here as elsewhere she clearly opposed the belief that God indwells man's consciousness — a radical immanentism characteristic of both Buddhism and Hinduism. In other passages, she indicates that Buddhism lacks any real concept of God and should be thought of as a philosophy rather than a religion.[189]

Just as Mrs. Eddy insisted that God does not indwell human consciousness, so she maintained that man is not absorbed in God. "Christian Science," she declared, "absolutely refutes the amalgamation, transmigration, absorption, or annihilation of individuality."[190] It was this cardinal point of the unique identity of every man that Mrs. Eddy emphasized in a reply to a clergyman who had coupled Christian Science with Buddhism. In her teaching, she wrote, "man is not absorbed in the divine nature, but is absolved by it."[191] In *Science and Health* she emphasized that "man cannot lose his individuality,"[192] that his concrete conscious identity is as eternal as his Life, which is God. As Mrs. Eddy defined it, the result of truly spiritualized consciousness was to make men more individually

187. *My.*, p. 218.   188. "Questions Answered," p. 161.
189. Eddy, "Message for 1902," p. 3.   190. *Mis.*, p. 22.
191. *My.*, p. 119.   192. *S&H.*, p. 259.

effective in experience, rather than to wipe out their individuality. The "scientific sense of being, forsaking matter for Spirit," she wrote, "by no means suggests man's absorption into Deity and the loss of his identity, but confers upon man enlarged individuality, a wider sphere of thought and action, a more expansive love, a higher and more permanent peace." [193]

Desire, Mrs. Eddy indicated, is not to be extinguished, but transformed and redeemed. "Desire is prayer," she wrote, "and no loss can occur from trusting God with our desires, that they may be moulded and exalted before they take form in words and in deeds." [194] In common with Buddhism particularly, Mrs. Eddy does emphasize the importance of denying material selfhood. But she does so because, in her words, "The denial of material selfhood aids the discernment of man's spiritual and eternal individuality, and destroys the erroneous knowledge gained from matter or through what are termed the material senses." [195] The "spiritual and eternal individuality" of which Mrs. Eddy speaks in this passage is identical in her teaching with the Christ. Since she accepts the revelation of the Christ, or ideal manhood, through the life of Christ Jesus, Mrs. Eddy asserts that the standard for the positive demonstration of man's sonship with God is known, and is not the mere negation of human striving and desire.

In 1886, Mrs. Eddy received a letter from a most confused woman in Chicago. She had just taken a course in what she supposed to be Christian Science, the woman explained, from a teacher who was a Theosophist and who advised her class to read up on Buddhism as well. "I am now all confusion and mixed," Mrs. Eddy's inquirer went on. "Tell me, dear Mrs. Eddy, can one be a thorough, consistent believer in Theosophy and the occult sciences, and a successful healer?" Mrs. Eddy's reply published along with the letter in the *Journal,* was definitely in the negative. [196] For she believed that Theosophy was the most destructive specific influence then at work in human thought.

Though the Theosophical movement attracts little attention now, it was perhaps the most distilled expression of the occult spirit in the late nineteenth century. It would hardly be possible to give any clear account of so eclectic a teaching as Theosophy, which is a mixture of spiritualism, hypnotism, Eastern and Egyptian myth and mysticism, speculative astronomy, and exotic anthropology. The movement may not have been large

193. *Ibid.,* p. 265. 194. *Ibid.,* p. 1. 195. *Ibid.,* p. 91.
196. Eddy, "Questions Answered," pp. 160–161.

in number, but it was certainly broad in scope. By the time of the death of its founder, Madame Helene Blavatsky, in 1891, it had branches in India, Great Britain, and the United States. In a limited way, there are parallels between the growth of Christian Science and Theosophy. Both movements were led by women — even though there is an almost complete contrast between Mrs. Eddy and the immensely fat, often foul-mouthed Madame Blavatsky. Further, the Theosophical Society was founded in America in 1875, just two weeks after the first publication of *Science and Health*. Both movements began to gain a substantial following in the 1880s and had gained sufficient notoriety to be the subjects of much interest at the World's Parliament of Religions at Chicago in 1893.

Yet in spirit and teaching Christian Science and Theosophy were wholly irreconcilable, as their respective founders both noted. In a message to the Theosophical Convention in America in 1885, Madame Blavatsky said that Christian Science, along with other forms of mental healing, represented distorted appearances of the latent occult and psychic powers germinating in man. "Understand once and for all," she declared, "that there is nothing 'spiritual' or 'divine' in ANY of these manifestations." [197] The next year Mrs. Eddy published a severe stricture on Theosophy in her short book *No and Yes*, in which she wrote that it sprang "from the Oriental philosophy of Brahmanism, and blends with it magic and enchantments." [198]

Actually, Theosophy was thoroughly occult in character, and was closely connected with both spiritualism and Eastern religious thought. In the first place, the background of the movement lay in spiritualism. Madame Blavatsky originally came to America in 1874 to defend spiritualist phenomena, and her apartment in New York became something of a spiritualist center. Though she later diverged from spiritualist theory, she never repudiated the validity of spiritualist phenomena. And the Theosophical movement garnered most of its adherents in the United States from the ranks of spiritualists — not just in its early stages, as did Christian Science, but throughout its whole development. Further, Theosophical doctrine is heavily dependent upon Eastern religious thought. It was only after Madame Blavatsky's return from a journey to India in 1879 that the Theosophical teaching fully emerged. And it was sufficiently in consonance with Hindu thought that a brief alliance developed in India between Theosophy and a reformist Hindu sect. Interestingly, Madame

197. Helen Blavatsky and William Q. Judge, "Some of the Errors of Christian Science," (Point Loma, California, n.d.), p. 3.
198. *No.*, p. 14.

Blavatsky's primary objection to Christian Science lay in her belief that the practice of healing only delayed the action of Karma, or the law of compensation, which required that one suffer for one's bad deeds.[199]

Given Mrs. Eddy's opposition to the occult spirit in general, her antipathy toward Theosophy is understandable. But the deeper reason for her strong feelings on the subject is found in the fact that she saw it as a particularly aggressive form of animal magnetism. In *No and Yes* she wrote, "Theosophy is no more allied to Christian Science than the odor of the upas-tree is to the sweet breath of springtide."[200] The reference to the upas-tree is significant, for it is an Asiatic shrub which yields a poison that can be used in arrows. In this light one can understand the meaning of the fact that in Mrs. Eddy's private instructions for the handling of animal magnetism there are more references to Theosophy than to any other religious group. For Mrs. Eddy felt that many of the adverse mental influences that impeded the demonstration of Christian Science emanated from Theosophists. From her perspective, the rise of Theosophy at about the same time as Christian Science represented the growth of the tares among the wheat and so epitomized the experience of the movement in the decade of the 1880s.

199. Blavatsky and Judge, "Errors," p. 6.
200. *No.*, p. 14.

4

Into the Mainstream

In the 1880s, Mrs. Eddy and her loyal followers struggled to maintain the integrity of her teachings and the coherence, even the survival, of the movement. Though the movement did advance during this period, it was predominantly on the defensive. The decade of the 1890s, however, saw the Christian Science movement shift to the offensive to become a real force in American religious life. During this period, Mrs. Eddy, having established her authority beyond question in the movement and withdrawn from Boston, created the basic institutions of the Christian Science movement. The Mother Church, which she founded in 1892, functioned so as to protect the Christian Science movement from the heterodoxy and schism that had almost caused its dissolution in the 1880s, and to provide channels for the perpetuation of her teaching in the years ahead. And as Christian Science emerged into the mainstream of American religious life in the decade in which The Mother Church was formed, it came into conflict with the religious orthodoxies which it challenged. In the years immediately following her discovery of Christian Science, Mrs. Eddy had expected that the orthodox churches would speedily embrace her teaching. But bitter experience soon blasted this sanguine hope, and conflict with the orthodox churches became one of the most persistent and unpleasant aspects of the early history of the movement.

THE LEADER AND THE MOVEMENT

Mary Baker Eddy maintained that in her leadership of the movement she constantly sought to turn her students' attention away from her personality toward the study and practice of her teaching. But at the same time, she insisted that without an appreciation of her mission and role as the discoverer and founder of Christian Science, her teaching could not be grasped. For this reason, gaining an understanding of Mrs. Eddy's place in Christian Science must be part of any effort to assess the character of the movement. Moreover, this subject comes naturally into our discussion at this point. For as the movement grew in the 1890s, Mrs. Eddy, by then in retirement from the Boston scene, began to assume her permanent place as the remote and revered leader of thousands of Christian Scientists. At the same time, the spread of her teaching made Mrs. Eddy a national figure, so that her character and relation to the movement that she led became intimately associated in the public mind with Christian Science.

Coming to grips with these issues is no easy matter. For by the mid-1890s Mrs. Eddy had become the focal point of bitter controversy that continues until this day. Non-Christian Scientists found Mrs. Eddy an interesting and somewhat enigmatic figure. She was an undoubted success in an age that admired success. And what is more, she was a woman who had made a name for herself in what was still very much a man's world. It is worth remarking that she was in her mid-forties when she discovered Christian Science, in her sixties during her tremendously active years in Boston, in her late eighties when she founded the *Monitor,* and in her ninetieth year when she died. Mark Twain, who certainly had no love for Mrs. Eddy, called her "probably the most daring and masterful woman who has appeared on the earth for centuries."[1] The generalship and executive capacities that she displayed in the founding of the movement elicited much amazed comment from her critics as well as her followers. By any calculation her life was an extraordinary one.

Mrs. Eddy by no means welcomed the increasing public interest in her personality that inevitably accompanied the growing prosperity of Christian Science. Yearning for seclusion, she granted relatively few interviews and tried to stay out of the public gaze as much as possible. Ironically, however, Mrs. Eddy's very remoteness only intensified public curiosity about her. And by the turn of the century if not before, she was very good copy in the press.

Some newspaper commentary was favorable to Mrs. Eddy — the Hearst chain, for one, was generally approving — but with other segments of the press she did not fare so well. In 1906 and 1907, *McClure's Magazine,* the most prominent of the muckraking journals, published a series of articles

1. Twain, *Christian Science,* p. 102.

on Mrs. Eddy by Georgine Milmine, which were reissued in revised form as a book in 1909.[2] Copiously documented but radically biased against its subject, Miss Milmine's series was the first in a line of debunking biographies of the founder of Christian Science. Shortly before the articles were published, Joseph Pulitzer's *New York World* sent two reporters to Concord in an effort to anticipate *McClure's* revelations. Their story, published on the front page of the *World* on October 28, 1906, was that Mrs. Eddy was a virtual prisoner of Calvin Frye and others who were in control of her large fortune. In a wildly distorted account of a brief interview with her, they pictured Mrs. Eddy as a living skeleton, cancer-ridden, senile, unsteady on her feet, and doped for the occasion. Soon after, the *Concord Evening Monitor* vigorously refuted the *World's* charges. A number of other newspapers, furthermore, were highly critical of the sensationalism and distortion of its attack on Mrs. Eddy. In the summer of 1907, for example, the well-known journalist Arthur Brisbane drew a completely different picture of her in his report of an interview published in the *New York Evening Journal.*[3]

By that time, however, the *World* had gone even further. Enlisting the aid of her son and foster son, they prompted an eventually unsuccessful suit designed to wrest from Mrs. Eddy all control of her own affairs. This "Next Friends Suit" was one of the most difficult experiences that Mrs. Eddy had ever undergone. Blighting the peace of her later years, it brought her name to the attention of the American public as never before. It is safe to say that by the time she died, Mrs. Eddy's name was a household word.

Opinions of her character and achievement varied greatly. On the one hand, numerous medical men, ministers, and other of her critics vied for epithets to denounce her—"Mother Eddy," wrote Charles Eliot Norton, "is the most striking and ugliest figure in New England today." [4] On the other hand, tens of thousands of her followers revered her as their spiritual leader, while many sympathetic non-Scientists saw her as a high-minded and unjustly maligned benefactor of mankind. This divergence of opinion is especially conspicuous in the biographical literature on her life — a literature which in itself provides a fascinating study of the nature of image-making. Of few historical figures have such totally

2. Georgine Milmine, *Life of Mary Baker G. Eddy* (New York, 1909).
3. Arthur Brisbane, *What Mrs. Eddy Said to Arthur Brisbane* (New York, 1905).
4. Quoted in Peel, *Christian Science,* p. 153.

divergent accounts been written. This literature on Mrs. Eddy's life, to say the least, has not on the whole been notable for its scholarly dispassion.[5]

To some degree, the sensationalism of debunking accounts of Mrs. Eddy's life was encouraged by the excessively roseate view of her that Christian Scientists sometimes promulgated. Plaster saints are easily broken, and Mrs. Eddy's image in the minds of not a few of her followers was that of a plaster saint. To take a somewhat extreme example, consider this description of Mrs. Eddy written by a Christian Scientist in 1896: "Youth, radiant with sunshine and flowers of June and crowned with light and love of God could not have appeared sweeter or more lovely. Like an angel of beauty, she appeared among us. She tripped along over the balcony as would a child." [6]

The virtues which Christian Scientists often attributed to Mrs. Eddy are hardly relevant to the appraisal of a religious leader. For instance, one can scarcely predicate spiritual profundity on good education. Yet some Christian Scientists lionized their leader as among the best educated women of her day. It is true that her education was fairly good for a New England woman raised in the early nineteenth century. But it was spotty and had obvious deficiencies; and many of her followers might have been shocked by her reference in a letter to "Irving's *Pickwick Papers.*" [7] Similarly, a number of Christian Scientists pictured Mrs. Eddy even when she was in her eighties as miraculously youthful in appearance. She did show remarkable vitality in her later years, despite intermittent illness; and certainly Mrs. Eddy never failed mentally. But the relatively few pictures taken in the last decade of her life show her face, though remarkable in its lively and determined expression, as decidedly that of an elderly woman.

Actually, it would have been quite impossible for anyone to measure up to the ideal embodied in the portrait of Mrs. Eddy cherished by many Christian Scientists. She had her obvious human failings — for example, a somewhat awed respect for titles and social status that reflected her provincial New England background. A newspaper interviewer in 1901,

5. Peel's volumes *Mary Baker Eddy: The Years of Discovery* and *Mary Baker Eddy: The Years of Trial* are unquestionably the most authoritative and complete treatments of her life to date.

6. Unsigned, "Impressions of a First Visit to Mother," *CSJ*, XIV (Dec. 1896), 443.

7. Quoted in Milmine, *Life of Mary Baker G. Eddy*, p. 397.

seeing Mrs. Eddy's pleasure at the conversion to Christian Science of Lord Dunmore, noted that "like Moore, she 'dearly loves a lord.'" [8] Still the author of *Science and Health* could write that "wealth, fame, and social organization . . . weigh not one jot in the balance of God." [9] Mrs. Eddy also found it necessary on a limited number of occasions in the last decade of her life to take hypodermic injections for the relief of extreme pain. In *Science and Health* she provided for this eventuality, though many of her followers would have been hard put to understand why their leader needed to make this compromise.[10]

Still, one cannot hope to understand Mrs. Eddy's character simply by modifying and combining what has been said about her by critics and by partisans. Her picture cannot be painted in gray. She was too definite, too complex, and altogether too interesting for such colorless treatment. Her life had a central dynamic that must be grasped if it is to make any sense at all. For Mrs. Eddy was, in the final analysis, a woman of religious vision. In evaluating her character and life-work, one must take seriously her belief that she had discovered basic religious truth and had a divinely-appointed mission to expound it. Her own zeal, the demands that she made upon herself and others, the vigor with which she defended her teaching from perversion and attack, her apparent arbitrariness in decision-making, even the excesses and irregularities of her highly-charged temperament — all these phenomena come into perspective when seen from this standpoint. Much of the material that friendly biographers have soft-pedaled or eliminated from their accounts becomes relevant to an understanding of her character, while many elements in her life that hostile commentators have dwelt upon become of less importance or begin to make a different kind of sense.

A most revealing depiction of Mrs. Eddy's character in her later years as a woman of religion was written by one of the foremost figures of the early movement, Judge Septimus B. Hanna.

During a single conversation Mrs. Eddy would change her manner and countenance many times. Sometimes she would appear youthful and sprightly, almost to girlishness. This is what I would call her normal appearance, and she would present this appearance when talking about ordinary social or current events and affairs; the instant, however, she would begin talking about Christian Science or spiritual matters, her whole look and manner

---

8. *New York Herald*, May 5, 1901.   9. *S&H.*, p. 239.

10. See *Ibid.*, p. 464. See also "A Statement by The Directors," *CSJ*, XLVI (March, 1929), p. 669.

would change. Her features would seem to enlarge from their normal, delicate look to an almost masculine and decided way, and at such times words and sentences would be uttered in the stately and majestic way she expressed her thoughts in writing; her eyes would become larger than normal and would seem dark — almost black — she would seem to be oblivious to the presence of others, and looking away into space or into the future. Her whole demeanor would be that of one enraptured or illuminated. At such times I could only describe her as being on the Mount of Vision.[11]

The religious impulsion that is reflected in this passage was central to Mrs. Eddy's mature character. It was apparent in many ways in her life — in the hours she consistently devoted to study and prayer, for instance, in the spiritual struggles she went through in making important decisions, and in the rigor of the self-discipline which she imposed on herself. But this impulse was perhaps most conspicuously manifested in the sense of mission that took possession of Mrs. Eddy's experience in the years following her discovery of Christian Science. One may quarrel over what happened in her life at this point, but that *something* happened which radically changed her experience at that point is beyond doubt. For one sees in the record of her life at this point the germination of a new sense of life-purpose — the development and promulgation of her teaching. True, in the record of Mrs. Eddy's experience before the mid-1860s there are suggestions of traits that later emerged — a latent fire and evidence of as yet unfulfilled energies. But nothing in her biography until the beginning of her work in Christian Science makes the Mrs. Eddy of later years comprehensible. The conclusion is inescapable that the sense of life-purpose that took possession of her beginning in 1866 was the determining factor in her experience. This conviction, moreover, deepened with the years. One can see its intensification particularly in her writings during the 1880s, when Christian Science was challenged by mind-cure and came under sustained attack on the part of the clergy. Even the photographs taken of Mrs. Eddy during this troubled decade reveal her deepening sense of command at a glance.

One could, of course, take the position that Mrs. Eddy's claim to spiritual authority as the discoverer of religious truth was only the manifestation of a distorted psyche. If this approach is taken, as in some instances it has been, then Mrs. Eddy's sense of mission is treated as the objectification of psychological factors presumed to be more basic. But here as in any case, the intellectual historian has the obligation of letting the evidence

11. Hanna Reminiscences, Archives.

speak for itself as best he can without imposing a theoretical construct upon it. And the biographical evidence in Mrs. Eddy's case attests overwhelmingly to the genuineness of her religious motivation. Whether one grants the validity of what she claimed to have discovered or not, there is no more reason to subject her life and motivation to psychological reductionism than that of any other religious figure.

In *The Varieties of Religious Experience*, William James points out, "There can be no doubt that as a matter of fact a religious life, exclusively pursued, does tend to make the person exceptional and eccentric." [12] With this in mind, it can be said that the great failure of many of Mrs. Eddy's critics lies in the fact that they let their hostility to her becloud their comprehension of the central religious impulsion that determined her conduct. So doing, they put primary emphasis upon the exceptional and eccentric aspects of Mrs. Eddy's conduct, without seeing them in Jamesian terms as the consequences of her religious orientation. It may also be said that Mrs. Eddy's admirers projected a distorted image of her in many instances for much the same reason: their failure to comprehend the full dimensions of her character as a woman of religion. Certainly the character of extraordinary people generally, and religious visionaries particularly, is rarely comprehensible to those of more prosaic natures. It is not surprising that some of Mrs. Eddy's greatest admirers and most devoted followers should have written accounts of her which were one-dimensional and in some cases positively distorted.

In most cases, their devotion to her and the cause of Christian Science was beyond question. Yet one cannot escape the impression that some Christian Scientists who wrote about their association with Mrs. Eddy — even the intimates of her household — did not know her very well. No one could have given her more faithful service than her devoted secretary and right-hand man of twenty-eight years, Calvin Frye. Yet Frye, though dogged in his devotion, was a singularly unimaginative man; and it is not surprising that Mrs. Eddy, who on the whole deeply appreciated his services, should have grown very short with him on some occasions. There is a certain sense in which Mrs. Eddy, despite the love that her followers showed toward her, was in her later years a somewhat lonely woman. True, she could be very warm and tender with members of her household and sometimes even cried when they had to leave her for a time. But she found relatively few Christian Scientists with whom she

12. James, *Varieties*, p. 24.

could communicate about anything at her own level. And sometimes she seems to have tried to watch her step with them. Not many of her followers, for example, could appreciate her brand of humor, which tended toward irony and even sarcasm on occasion. In a larger sense, few of them could really understand or respond in kind to a woman who lived at Mrs. Eddy's level of spiritual and nervous intensity. In the final analysis, it is the difference between the sensibility of Mrs. Eddy and of her followers that explains the limited understanding of her in the Christian Science movement itself.

This study is not primarily concerned with Mrs. Eddy's character; and Christian Science can, of course, be discussed on its own merits as a religious teaching apart from any consideration of its discoverer. But Mrs. Eddy, like other religious teachers, so identified her life with her mission and message that they cannot wholly be separated. As she declared in *Science and Health,* "without a correct sense of its highest visible idea, we can never understand the divine Principle." [13] The continuous attack on her personality by enemies of Christian Science, as Mrs. Eddy saw it, really constituted an attempt to destroy her teaching by discrediting her. Therefore she insisted that Christian Scientists understand her mission and character, and charged the spokesmen of the movement with the responsibility of bearing true witness to the facts of her life. As she wrote to one of them in 1902, "The united plan of the evil-doers is to cause the beginners either in lecturing or teaching or in our periodicals to keep Mrs. Eddy as she *is* out of sight, and to keep her as she is *not* constantly before the public. . . . Keeping the truth of her real character before the public will help the students and do more than all else can for our Cause." [14]

This point was frequently emphasized in her class teaching and correspondence with Christian Scientists. In her last class in 1898 Judge Hanna rose and accorded her full recognition. He told her that every argument "the ingenuity of evil can suggest whispers trying to hide your mission, and the light returns only when we see you as you are — the revelator of this Truth." Others in the class echoed what Hanna had said, and Mrs. Eddy in grateful reply told them that had they not seen her place she would have had to teach them of it. "I could not have avoided telling

13. *S&H.,* p. 560.
14. Mrs. Eddy to Septimus B. Hanna, Oct. 13, 1902. Hanna Reminiscences.

you," as one of the class members recollected her words, "that when my students become blinded to me as the one through whom Truth has come to this age, they miss the path." [15]

Mrs. Eddy felt that her womanhood was essential to the very nature of her mission; for she and her followers believed that it had been given to her to reveal the Motherhood of God. Indeed, Mrs. Eddy conceived of her relationship to the movement as that of a mother to her child, as her articles and letters to students over the years plainly reveal. One of her poems, written in a period when the movement was undergoing great difficulties, well illustrates this attitude. Entitled, "The Mother's Evening Prayer," its first and last verses read:

> O gentle presence, peace and joy and power;
>   O Life divine, that owns each waiting hour,
> Thou Love that guards the nestling's faltering flight!
>   Keep Thou my child on upward wing to-night.
>
> No snare, no fowler, pestilence or pain;
>   No night drops down upon the troubled breast,
> When heaven's aftersmile earth's tear-drops gain,
>   And mother finds her home and heavenly rest.[16]

Mrs. Eddy's students during the 1880s and 1890s were in the habit of referring to her as "Mother," both in direct address and in writing about her. This appellation, which had been bestowed by Civil War soldiers upon their nurses, was first used as a term of endearment for Mrs. Eddy by a student in the 1870s. In 1902, however, Mark Twain made its use a subject of ridicule. And Mrs. Eddy found it regretfully necessary in that year to forbid her followers to refer to her publicly as "Mother," though many of them continued privately to do so.

To some Christian Scientists, Mrs. Eddy's womanhood took on even more portentous significance in the light of the following passage from the book of Revelation:

And there appeared a great wonder in heaven; a woman clothed with the sun, and the moon under her feet, and upon her head a crown of twelve stars.

And she being with child cried, travailing in birth, and pained to be delivered. . . .

And she brought forth a man child, who was to rule all nations with a rod of iron; and her child was caught up unto God, and to His throne.[17]

---

15. Emma Shipman, "Mrs. Eddy and the class of 1898," in *We Knew Mary Baker Eddy* (Boston, 1943), p. 73.

16. *Mis.*, p. 389.   17. Rev., 12: 1–5.

The Shakers believed that their leader, Mother Ann Lee, represented this "Woman of the Apocalypse." And a number of Mrs. Eddy's followers came to hold the same conviction about her.

Mrs. Eddy did feel that John's prophecy had a "special suggestiveness in connection with the nineteenth century." [18] But she never publicly advocated the literal identification of herself with the woman of the Apocalypse. This woman, she wrote in an unpublished book in 1898, "prefigures no special person or individuality; and to identify her with some particular person would be as chimerical as fancying that the Statue of Liberty represented some individual woman." [19] In *Science and Health* her definitive statement on the subject reads: "The woman in the Apocalypse symbolizes generic man, the spiritual idea of God; she illustrates the coincidence of God and man as the divine Principle and divine idea." [20] Christian Scientists sometimes spoke of Mrs. Eddy as a "type" of what she discovered; and this typological mode of thought, which can be traced back to Puritanism, probably best explains Mrs. Eddy's own concept of her relation to John's prophecy. For she seems to have accounted herself as the individual who had most advanced consciousness of "the coincidence of God and man as the divine Principle and divine idea," [21] illustrated by the "Woman of the Apocalypse." And in this limited respect Mrs. Eddy identified herself as having fulfilled the prophecy of this woman's appearance.

Actually, on the basis of her own thought there is just as much warrant for likening her role to that of the Virgin Mary. If Mary gave birth to Jesus, who was the embodiment to human perception of the Christ, and if Mrs. Eddy gave birth (or statement) to Christian Science, which is the reduction to human comprehension of Divine Science, the parallel is clear. The whole Quimby contention, in essence, involved the question of whether or not Christian Science had had a "virgin birth" — whether it had been generated through a process of intellectual development or whether it had been conceived through spiritual revelation. [22] It must be emphasized, however, that Mrs. Eddy strongly rejected any comparison of herself with Mary. "I believe in but one incarnation," she wrote in 1902 in reply to Mark Twain's charge that she had assumed the position of the Virgin Mary. "I have not the inspiration nor the aspiration to be first or second Virgin-mother — her duplicate, antecedent, or subse-

18. *S&H.*, p. 560. 19. Eddy, *Repaid Pages.*
20. *S&H.*, p. 561. 21. *S&H.*, p. 561.
22. See the discussion of this point and its implications in Peel, *Discovery*, pp. 243–292.

quent." [23] What Mrs. Eddy *did* claim was the world's acknowledgment of her as the discoverer and founder of Christian Science and her followers' recognition of her as leader of the movement — no more, but certainly no less.

Everything in Mrs. Eddy's conduct in relation to the Christian Science movement supports the contention that she was a leader determined to lead. Indeed, by the time she died, Christian Scientists generally referred to her as "our Leader," or sometimes "our revered Leader." After she requested her students to cease calling her "Mother," Mrs. Eddy stipulated that they should refer to her by the term "Leader" instead. After it became her established designation, Mrs. Eddy wrote into the *Manual* the requirement that it be employed in the movement for no other individual.[24]

As the leader of the movement Mrs. Eddy was utterly convinced that she spoke as one directed of God. "No greater mistake can be made than to fail to obey or delay in obeying a single command of mine," she wrote to a student in 1896. "*God* does speak through me to this age. This I discern more clearly every year of my sojourn with you." [25] The fact that Mrs. Eddy often changed her mind and reversed her course did not in the least affect her conviction that her steps were divinely directed. Adam Dickey, a prominent Christian Scientist who was very close to Mrs. Eddy in her later years, recalled that "the changing of her mind was a privilege that our Leader reserved for herself, and she exercised it without any regard to what had gone before." Her approach in working out a problem, as she explained to him, was to take a step as nearly as she could in the right direction. Perhaps she might shortly find it had been wrong, but the step gave her a new point of view that she would not have had if she had not taken it. "I would not condemn myself, therefore, for what seemed to be a mistake," she told Dickey, "but would include it as part of the working out of the problem." [26]

In some instances those close to Mrs. Eddy would question the wisdom of some important decision she had made but their counsel was seldom heeded. In 1898, for example, she drew up a list of twenty-six topics for the Bible lessons which Christian Scientists were to study during the week and hear read in church on Sunday. Some members of the Bible Lesson Committee of The Mother Church, feeling that the number of topics she

23. *My.*, p. 136.   24. *Man.*, p. 65.
25. Quoted in Knapp, *Ira Oscar Knapp*, pp. 132–133.
26. Adam H. Dickey, *Memoirs of Mary Baker Eddy* (Boston, 1927), pp. 35–36.

selected was too small, drew up an additional list of as many more subjects and presented them to her. One of the members of the Committee was called to her home some time later with others on another matter. His account of what transpired when these other affairs had been discussed is worth reprinting:

. . . Mrs. Eddy called me to a seat beside her and turning to me, she said, so energetically that I almost jumped from the sofa, "That will never do — that will never do!" What she meant I did not know, but not leaving me long in ignorance, she continued: "The additional list of topics sent me for the Lessons are needless. They can all be used under the present list of subjects, which include every one of those you gave me. Tell the committee the original subjects were given of God — they are sufficient, and they will remain forever.[27]

And the lessons on the twenty-six original topics are studied by Christian Scientists today.

In the *Manual of the Mother Church*, Mrs. Eddy codified the duties which she felt Christian Scientists owed to her as their leader. In one provision entitled "Alertness to Duty" she wrote that a member of The Mother Church shall "not be made to forget nor to neglect his duty to God, to his Leader, and to mankind."[28] Article XXII of the *Manual*, comprising eighteen sections and occupying seven pages, is devoted to spelling out more specifically the "Relations and Duties of Members to Pastor Emeritus" — Pastor Emeritus being Mrs. Eddy's official title in The Mother Church. Easily the most controversial and extreme of these stipulations is the one that requires a Christian Scientist to begin service in Mrs. Eddy's home for three years within ten days of being requested by her to do so, on pain of excommunication from The Mother Church.[29] Mrs. Eddy felt that Christian Scientists could gain in her service "the Science which otherwise would cost them half a century;"[30] and that if they did not heed her call, their love for Christian Science and for her must be slight.

This particular demand that Mrs. Eddy made upon her followers was severe indeed, for it often required that Christian Scientists leave home and family to serve her and the Cause. Most of those who were summoned came willingly, however, regarding the opportunity as a great blessing.

27. Irving Tomlinson, *Twelve Years with Mary Baker Eddy* (Boston, 1945), p. 103.
28. *Man.,* p. 42.   29. *Ibid.,* p. 67.
30. Quoted in Milmine, *Life of Mary Baker G. Eddy,* p. 179.

Though their reminiscences testify to the value of their experience in Mrs. Eddy's home, the life of a Christian Scientist with her was far from easy. She seems to have intended many of those who served her to assume positions of leadership in the movement, and with this in mind to have prepared them as she saw fit for future responsibilities. One day Dickey commented to her on the quality of the members of her household, "Mother, this is the cream of the country." Replied Mrs. Eddy, "The cream, — I want them to be the butter."[31] Her discipline was strict and her requirements formidable. It was a dedicated Christian Scientist indeed who could hold up in her service.

Each member of her household had his particular practical duties to perform and was expected to perform them to the letter. In addition, most of the members of the household were required to do mental work for Mrs. Eddy and for the movement as she stipulated; and if she did not feel that their work was being done well, she brought them up sharply. A reprimand from Mrs. Eddy was evidently not a very pleasant thing to endure. Martha Wilcox, one of her helpers at Pleasant View and later an important teacher of Christian Science, recalled that Mrs. Eddy once instructed her to do some mental work on a particular problem. Retiring to her room, Mrs. Wilcox tried to do so for some hours. Called to Mrs. Eddy's study she was asked, "Martha, why did you not do your work?" In Mrs. Wilcox's account the conversation continued:

I replied, "Mother, I did." She said: "No you didn't, you just had a nice talk with the devil. Why did you not know God's allness?" I said, "Mother, I tried." And her reply was: "Well, if Jesus had just tried and failed, we would have no Science today." Then she had a card hung on the inside of the door of my room on which was printed in large letters, "Faith without works is dead." I looked at that for two weeks.[32]

In church affairs and in the movement generally, Mrs. Eddy's word was law just as it was in her household. The *Manual* spelled out clearly her extensive prerogatives concerning the government of The Mother Church.[33] And though Mrs. Eddy's letters to church officials over the years were sometimes couched as requests, they were almost invariably in substance commands. After she had decided upon the founding of the *Monitor,* for instance, she wrote to the Board of Trustees of The Mother

31. Dickey, *Memoirs,* p. 77.
32. Martha Wilcox Reminiscences, Archives.
33. See particularly *Man.,* Art. XXII, "Relation and Duties of Members to Pastor Emeritus," 64–70.

Church on August 8, 1908: "It is my request that you start a daily newspaper at once, and call it the *Christian Science Monitor*. Let there be no delay. The cause demands that it be issued now." [34] By Thanksgiving of that year, the first issue was on the stands.

When Mrs. Eddy felt that her commands were God-impelled and for the benefit of the movement, she did not hesitate to make any demand upon her students that she felt they were capable of fulfilling. In March 1897, for example, after the publication of her volume of *Miscellaneous Writings, 1883–1896*, Mrs. Eddy enjoined teachers of Christian Science to cease their teaching activities for one year. She explained that the book is "calculated to prepare the minds of all true thinkers to understand the Christian Science textbook more correctly than a student can." [35] For many teachers this request meant a considerable financial sacrifice, but there was no question as to their compliance with it.

Mrs. Eddy was deeply appreciative of this "coming and going at the word," as she once referred to a student's loyalty in a warmly thankful letter.[36] Her students for their part felt that obedience to her was utterly natural. One of them wrote that he would no more think of taking issue with Mrs. Eddy than with a teacher who had mastered a language unknown to him.[37] Another, a veteran of the Civil War, observed that his three years in the army had taught him that a soldier's first duty to his country was loyalty and next obedience; and that now, as a soldier of Christian Science, he saw the necessity of loyalty to the Leader and obedience to her rules.[38] This attitude might be described as normative for a Christian Scientist according to Mrs. Eddy's own requirements. But any acquaintance with the movement during this period or since shows that something more was involved in the attitude of a number of Christian Scientists toward Mrs. Eddy than loyalty and obedience based upon a conviction of the demonstrated merit of her leadership. For it is clear that in the minds of some Christian Scientists — though a minority — respect and reverence for Mrs. Eddy shades off into slavish adulation.

In May of 1900 the *Journal* printed "A Letter from a Recent Convert to His Father" in which a young Ohioan hastened to defend his fellow

---

34. Quoted in Lyman P. Powell, *Mary Baker Eddy: A Life Size Portrait* (Boston, 1930), p. 233.

35. Mary Baker Eddy, "Class Teaching," *CSJ*, XIV (March 1897), 454.

36. Shipman, in *We Knew Mary Baker Eddy*, p. 62.

37. Unsigned, "Obedience," *CSJ*, XVII (Sept. 1899), 28.

38. Unsigned, "Our Leader," *CSJ*, XXVII (Jan. 1910), 622.

Christian Scientists against the charge that they worshiped Mrs. Eddy. "To Scientists," he explained, "the idea is ridiculous; nothing could be farther from us. Our gratitude, reverence, and love are very great. We believe that Mrs. Eddy was especially fitted for the reception and revelation of this Truth, and her life before and since has attested this." But worship her? — Never! [39] On many other occasions, Christian Scientists have echoed this statement in defending themselves against the oft-repeated charge that they adulated their leader; but their demurrers have convinced very few.

Indeed, if the father of the young man quoted above had carefully examined the issue of the *Journal* in which his son's reply to him was printed, he would have found enough to justify his suspicions. In an article on "A Trip to the Rockies," a Christian Scientist told of his and his friends' rescue from grave dangers in Yellowstone Park through the practice of Christian Science. He uttered "a prayer of gratitude," so he wrote, "to God and to our dear Leader and Mother for our deliverance." [40] Similar sentiments are not difficult to find in the literature of the movement in the two decades before Mrs. Eddy's death, though they did grow progressively rarer.

In part, it was Mrs. Eddy's seclusion that made her so fascinating to some Christian Scientists. After she left Boston in 1889, concentration on her personality among Christian Scientists began to be conspicuous in several ways. At first, it was most apparent in expressions of disappointment by Christian Scientists who had aspired to study with Mrs. Eddy personally. As she grew more inaccessible, items of information concerning her life and habits came to have enormous interest for a number of her followers. By the early 1890s Mrs. Eddy's letters to various students were being copied and passed around in the movement to such an extent that the *Journal* had to condemn the activity. [41] After her death, cultish fascination with anything to do with Mrs. Eddy was conspicuous among some Christian Scientists. Those of this disposition delighted in circulating writings purported to have originated with her and in relating stories of her healing prowess, many of them obviously apocryphal.

The highest aim of many Christian Scientists when Mrs. Eddy was alive was to see her in person. To this end some of them would go to almost any lengths, even to virtually camping on her doorstep. Eventually

39. Unsigned, "Letter from a Recent Convert to His Father," *CSJ*, XVIII (May 1900), 94.
40. James A. Logwood, "A Trip to the Rockies," *CSJ*, XVIII (May 1900), 81.
41. *CSJ*, XI (May 1893), p. 90.

she felt obliged to give notice through the *Journal* that she saw visitors only by appointment, and added that "to tease the attendant is not only vulgar but useless." [42] One woman lingered by her gate so long that Mrs. Eddy stopped her carriage and rebuked her sharply: "Have you no God? . . . Then never come here again to see me." [43] In 1902 she introduced a new by-law into the *Manual* prohibiting Christian Scientists from "Haunting Mrs. Eddy's Drive" [44] — an injunction that may have been of symbolic as well as practical significance.

Years before, Mrs. Eddy had had occasion to explicitly stricture adulation of herself on the part of her followers. The occasion that called forth her comment on this subject was the controversy aroused by the publication of her small book, "Christ and Christmas," in 1894. "Christ and Christmas" was a poem of fifteen stanzas each accompanied by an illustration made under her supervision by a local New England artist.[45] The illustrations were not very good, but one of them had a significance which Mrs. Eddy's critics were quick to point out. For it showed the figure of Jesus hand-in-hand with a woman holding a scroll marked CHRISTIAN SCIENCE. Both figures had halos of identical size and the woman bore a suspicious resemblance to Mrs. Eddy. Clergymen and mind-curers united in asserting that Mrs. Eddy was arrogantly exalting her own personality by putting herself on a par with Jesus,[46] and for certain Christian Scientists the book became something of an icon. Mrs. Eddy hastened to explain through the *Journal* in language similar to her discussion of the "Woman of the Apocalypse" that "the illustration in 'Christ and Christmas' refers not to my personality, but rather foretells the typical appearing of the womanhood, as well as the manhood of God, our divine Father and Mother." Still she thought it best to stop the printing of the little book. It "retired with honor," she wrote, "and mayhap taught me more than it has others." [47] In compiling *Miscellaneous Writings* in 1897, Mrs. Eddy modified this earlier article, changing its title from "Hear, O Israel" to "Deification of Personality." It gives permanent place in her writings to her clearest statement on the subject of her personality:

42. Mary Baker Eddy, "Take Notice," *CSJ*, XIII (July 1895), 164.
43. Interview in *Boston Journal*, June 21, 1899.
44. *Man.*, p. 48.
45. Reprinted in Mary Baker Eddy, *Poetical Works* (Boston, 1897).
46. This contention is often found in the critical Protestant literature on Christian Science written after the poem was published.
47. Mary Baker Eddy, "Hear O Israel," *CSJ*, XI (Feb. 1894), 472.

Whosoever looks to me personally for his health or holiness, mistakes. He that by reason of human love or hatred or any other cause clings to my material personality, greatly errs, stops his own progress, and loses the path to health, happiness, and heaven. The Scriptures and Christian Science reveal "the way," and personal revelators will take their proper place in history, but will not be deified.[48]

Never did Mrs. Eddy retract any of her claims to leadership or revise her own high estimate of her mission. And she continued to accept gratefully tributes that honored what she conceived to be her divinely-appointed work. Yet she was also quick to rebuke her followers' tendency toward personal adulation. Inculcating in them what she felt was a right view of herself was for Mrs. Eddy a difficult, long-term problem. She had to strike a precarious balance between ensuring that her revelation and authority were acknowledged on the one hand, and avoiding personal dependence and adulation on the other. Her guideline to Christian Scientists was the often-quoted statement: "Follow your Leader only so far as she follows Christ." [49] But Mrs. Eddy had no doubt that she did follow him, and that she had made plain to her followers through her writings how they could follow him also.

THE NECESSITY AND PERIL OF ORGANIZATION

Late in the evening of June 27, 1888, William B. Johnson, one of Mrs. Eddy's most trusted lieutenants, returned home from a meeting of the Christian Scientist Association and announced despairingly to his family: "We may lose Mrs. Eddy." No, she was not ill, he hastened to explain. But at the meeting it had become painfully apparent that a cabal of discontented students, representing about one third of the Association, had decided to abandon the movement. And Mrs. Eddy, fearing that she could never rebuild the church at Boston, had seriously discussed the possibility of going to Chicago.[50] This plan, however, was short-lived, born of desperation. Instead, she moved in October of 1889 to Concord, New Hampshire, which was to remain her home until she returned to the Boston area three years before her death. In the *Journal* for November 1889, Mrs. Eddy announced that she had definitely retired from the Boston scene and did not wish to be consulted about the lesser affairs of

48. *Mis.,* 308.   49. *Mess. '01,* p. 34.
50. Johnson, *History,* I., p. 156.

the movement — which she proceeded to enumerate just so there could be no mistaking her meaning.[51]

If Mrs. Eddy did not wish to be consulted about lesser affairs, it was because she was preeminently concerned with larger affairs. The main object of her retirement, she said, was to have the opportunity to work on an extensive revision of *Science and Health,* a task which she completed by late 1890. But this was only part of her purpose: for in the broadest sense, she left Boston in order to establish the movement on new foundations altogether. The fruit of her efforts during this period was the foundation of the institutional structure of the Christian Science movement.

The founding of the Christian Science church in its final form was, like the working out of Mrs. Eddy's basic teaching, a matter of *discovery*. This process began with Mrs. Eddy's realization at about the time she left Boston that the institutional structure of the movement as it then existed was inadequate for its present and future needs. Bit by bit she dismantled the old structure. In September 1889, she disbanded the Christian Scientist Association, an organization composed of those who had studied with her. The next month she closed the flourishing Massachusetts Metaphysical College, the primary vehicle for formal instruction in Christian Science. In December, the Church of Christ, Scientist, which had been founded in 1879, was formally disorganized. And in May of the following year, the National Christian Scientist Association, the only truly national organization in the movement, adjourned at her request for three years. Then, in the 1890s, all the functions of the old church and more were established on a new basis altogether. A major reorganization of the church was accomplished by the founding of The Mother Church in September 1892; its governing law, the *Manual of The Mother Church,* was published in 1895; and in 1898 Mrs. Eddy established the major administrative agencies through which her teaching was to be promulgated. When she died in 1910, The Mother Church continued to conduct the affairs of the movement under the seal of her authority.

Indeed, perhaps the most amazing thing about Mrs. Eddy's death was the fact that it had so little apparent effect on the movement. True, some of her followers had not expected her to die at all. And when she did, a few of them confidently anticipated her return from the grave — a

51. Mary Baker Eddy, "Seven Fixed Rules," *CSJ,* VII (May 1889), 69.

hope that prompted Billy Sunday to expostulate, "If old Mother Eddy rises from the dead I'll eat polecat for breakfast and wash it down with booze!" [52] But the general reaction in the movement to Mrs. Eddy's passing was calm. The next issues of the *Journal* and the *Sentinel* printed a brief tribute entitled simply "Mary Baker Eddy," [53] and the affairs of the church carried on much as usual. Seven years later an intensive struggle for control between the Board of Directors of The Mother Church and the Trustees of the Publishing Society nearly split the church apart, but in 1910 the proof that its well-being did not depend upon Mrs. Eddy's personal presence seemed complete. Hence, the smooth functioning of the church after Mrs. Eddy's death was the fulfillment of the organizational efforts that began after she left Boston in 1889.

In sociological terms, Mrs. Eddy presided over the transformation of her church from a charismatic into a bureaucratic institution. In so doing, she ensured the perpetuity of the church as a functioning organization that could operate without her personal superintendence. Indeed, a good deal of the history of the church between its founding in 1891 and Mrs. Eddy's death in 1910 centers upon her efforts to get the officials of The Mother Church to accept the increasing share of responsibility with which she wanted to entrust them.[54] Mrs. Eddy, of course, never relinquished leadership of the movement and made numerous key decisions concerning church affairs as long as she lived. But after 1895, many, even most, of these decisions were promulgated in the form of church by-laws registered in the *Manual*. Hence the *Manual* came to serve as a kind of impersonal intermediary between Mrs. Eddy and her church for fifteen years prior to her death; thus her authority, while unquestioned, had not generally been exercised directly. In relatively few religious movements has so complete a transition from charismatic to bureaucratic authority been accomplished in such a deliberate manner by the movement's founder.

To characterize The Mother Church as a bureaucratic institution, however, is technically accurate but historically incomplete. For to Mrs. Eddy and her followers, The Mother Church represented far more than a

---

52. Quoted in A. Sheldrick, "What Is a Real Revival?" (East Northfield, Conn., n.d.), pamphlet, p. 2.

53. "Mary Baker Eddy," *CSJ*, XXVIII (Jan. 1911) 283; *CSS*, VIII (Dec. 10, 1910), 53.

54. This point is evident in the letters that Mrs. Eddy wrote over the years to the Board. Archives.

bureaucratic institution, though it certainly fulfilled the functions of one. In *Science and Health* Mrs. Eddy defined *Church* in these terms:

The structure of Truth and Love; whatever rests upon and proceeds from divine Principle.

The Church is that institution, which affords proof of its utility and is found elevating the race, rousing the dormant understanding from material beliefs to the apprehension of spiritual ideas and the demonstration of divine Science, thereby casting out devils, or error, and healing the sick.[55]

It is important to bear in mind that this definition contains two distinct parts. The first brief paragraph defines Church as a spiritual conception, inseparable from the character of reality itself; the second defines Church as a human institution with a definite mission to fulfill. In Mrs. Eddy's usage, however, the two are not polar opposites, for the first embraces the second. As she wrote in the church *Manual,* "The First Church of Christ, Scientist, in Boston, Mass., is designed to be built on the Rock, Christ; even the understanding and demonstration of divine Truth, Life, and Love, healing and saving the world from sin and death; thus to reflect in some degree the Church Universal and Triumphant." [56] Even though the church as an institution is less than the spiritual idea of church, it must reflect that idea. Church as an instrument for the furthering of the spiritual understanding of mankind, that is, must in itself reflect in some measure the spiritual ideals which it exists to further. Hence its formation and structure, the purposes which animate it, and the relations of those within it must approximate the spiritual ideal of church. It must be, to as high degree as possible, the "structure of Truth and Love," and its operations must "rest upon and proceed from divine Principle."

This characterization of church as "that which rests upon and proceeds from divine Principle" is coordinate with the whole tenor of Mrs. Eddy's teaching. For she claimed to have discovered a demonstrable science based upon absolute Principle. An institution designed to implement and to embody this claim, she came to feel, must reflect the stability of this Principle and not admit of contrary claims and varying views. Yet the Church of Christ, Scientist, founded in 1879, which was and remains the basic institution of the Christian Science movement, had not been organized in such a way as to accomplish this end. For the church had been established by a voluntary compact of the members of Mrs. Eddy's association. Though she did remain its only official pastor, final authority in it rested not with her but in the membership. Indeed, they had overruled

55. *S&H.,* p. 583. 56. *Man.,* p. 19.

some of the provisions she had written into its constitution. Though Mrs. Eddy's counsel was on the whole heeded by the church, in principle and sometimes in practice effective government lay in the hands of the majority. Hence the church was prey to and reflected the factionalism that was so much a part of the movement's history through the late 1880s.

This tendency, which kept the movement almost perpetually on the brink of dissolution, helped make Mrs. Eddy acutely aware of the long range necessity of protecting her teaching in the process of its perpetuation. Since the Church of Christ, Scientist, as first organized obviously could not provide a stable structuring for the movement when it was to a large degree confined to Boston, how could it be expected to function as Christian Science attained national, even international proportions? By the early 1890s it had become clear to Mrs. Eddy that some more adequately unified organization was needed if the movement was to progress smoothly.

Though Mrs. Eddy did become convinced of the necessity of church organization, she never placed value on religious organizations as such. The institutionalizing of Christian Science was justifiable to her only by what it could accomplish practically. The church as an institution must provide, in the words of the second part of her definition of "Church" already quoted, "proof of its utility." The institution itself had spiritual significance for her only in the sense that it shadowed forth the reality of church which was not institutional. Just a few months before The Mother Church was formed Mrs. Eddy wrote in the *Journal:*

> It is not essential to materially organize Christ's Church. It is not absolutely necessary to ordain Pastors and to dedicate Churches; but if this be done, let it be in concession to the period, and not as a perpetual or indispensable ceremonial of the Church. If our church is organized, it is to meet the demand "suffer it to be so now." The real Christian compact is Love for one another. This bond is wholly spiritual and invisible.[57]

Similarly, a month before founding The Mother Church she wrote in a letter that the true church was "in the hearts of men." [58] And in a message at the laying of the cornerstone for The Mother Church, Mrs. Eddy acknowledged the present utility of church institutions; but she went on to say that "the time cometh when the religious element, or

57. *Mis.,* p. 91.
58. Quoted in Hugh A. Studdert Kennedy, *Christian Science and Organized Religion* (San Francisco, 1930), p. 76.

Church of Christ, shall exist alone in the affections, and need no organization to express it." [59] If for her The Mother Church was as close an approximation as possible to the spiritual ideal of church, it was still a human institution; and as such it was beset with the perils that attend all efforts to institutionalize religious truth.

Perhaps the most obvious of these perils of institutionalization was the spirit that many Christian Scientists displayed during the 1890s in the building and dedication of churches. The construction of The Mother Church edifice in 1894 proved a great stimulus to the construction of other branch churches. Within three years of the completion of The Mother Church, some twenty of them had been dedicated. In 1899, the *Journal* began running a regular column on "Churches and Societies," a good portion of which was taken up with descriptions of newly dedicated branch churches. Some of these buildings were quite modest, the fruits of great sacrifice. Others were more lavish, the most opulent of them all being Mrs. Stetson's church in New York, completed in 1903. Occasionally a Christian Science church attained real architectural distinction. Bernard Maybeck's First Church in Berkeley, California, constructed in 1913, was probably the most notable of any of them. Other Christian Science churches, however, were a good deal more prosaic. And as the critics of the movement sometimes noted, many of them looked disconcertingly like banks.

In the first edition of *Science and Health* Mrs. Eddy had said that "a magnificent edifice was not the sign of Christ's Church." [60] Whatever her opinion on the necessity of organization, she never modified this position. In her letters concerning the building and dedication of churches, Mrs. Eddy often tried to offset a love of symbolism and display that was taking root in the minds of many of her followers. For example, she wrote in November 1894 to the Board of Directors urging them to hasten the completion of The Mother Church: "Finish this church in 1894, even if you have to give up some of your gods, such as mosaic floor in the auditorium, or other decorations." [61] The branch church in which Mrs. Eddy showed the keenest personal interest was the one erected in her own city of Concord, New Hampshire. In a letter to the editors of the periodicals after they had printed an open invitation for Christian Scientists to attend the laying of the cornerstone in 1898, Mrs. Eddy wrote:

59. *Mis.*, p. 145. 60. *S&H.*, first ed., p. 167.
61. Johnson, *History*, II, 439.

Are you so asleep on so important a subject as to make the laying of our church cornerstone in Concord a desecration instead of a quiet, solemn, brief ceremony? You who profess to know there is *no matter* to elevate the usual material ceremony above *all precedent*.

Not over fifty persons shall be present on this occasion with my consent.

With love and all the patience God will give me for such sin and folly, such a waste of time and money, only to obey mammon and make sport for our enemies.[62]

Her consistent position, in the words of a letter she wrote to a branch church in Lawrence, Massachusetts, was that "the pride of circumstance and power is the prince of this world, that has nothing in Christ." [63] It may or may not be significant in this connection that though Mrs. Eddy lived for three years within ten miles of the enormous Mother Church extension, constructed in 1907, she never visited it and may never have even seen it.

Mrs. Eddy's attitude in this matter is just one indication of her consistent opposition to any manifestation of ecclesiastical formalism, in the movement or outside of it. Repeatedly she attacked conventional Christianity for having reduced the vitality of true religion to a mere matter of ceremony, doctrine, and creed. "Surely it is not enough," Mrs. Eddy declared, "to cleave to barren and desultory dogmas, derived from the traditions of the elders who thereunto have set their seals." [64] When she refers to religious dogmas or creed, it is almost always in a disparaging manner. Mrs. Eddy denied that Christian Scientists had any creed or doctrinal beliefs, and set forth her brief statement of the important points of Christian Science as its "religious tenets." And as we shall see, Christian Science church services are notable for their simplicity and almost total lack of ritual and ceremony. Mrs. Eddy's implicit criteria in the construction of all aspects of the institutional church was that it must implement and not obstruct the voicing and hearing of the Word.

UTILITY AND STRUCTURE:

THE CHARACTER OF THE CHRISTIAN SCIENCE CHURCH

To summarize what has been said about the institutional character of the Christian Science movement so far: Mrs. Eddy desired to articulate an institutional structure for the movement which was simple yet effective;

---

62. Mary Baker Eddy to Archibald McClellan, no date, Longyear Foundation.
63. *Mis.,* p. 155.   64. *S&H.,* p. 354.

which would do the needful work of bringing order to the movement without calling undue attention to itself; and which should fulfill the necessity and at the same time avoid the perils of organization. All her efforts in the reorganization of the church that began after she left Boston in 1889 were pervaded by the uniform purpose of fulfilling these requirements. Just how she went about doing so can be seen by examining the character of the institutions which she founded in the 1890s, beginning with The Mother Church itself.

The most obvious fact about the structure of The Mother Church was that it marked a departure from the pattern of Congregational church polity, to which the church as originally organized had conformed. The church founded in 1879 had been established by a voluntary compact of members of Mrs. Eddy's association. But Mrs. Eddy alone directed every phase of the reorganization of the church that began in August 1892. First she selected twelve trusted students to organize the church formally as a corporation. These twelve then named twenty others who with Mrs. Eddy's approval became its "First Members." Only *after* the organization was formed and the First Members notified of their election was the reorganization of the church made known to the movement and a general invitation issued for Christian Scientists to join it. The applications of those who wished to do so were passed upon by the First Members. In order to ensure that the members of The Mother Church would be loyal Christian Scientists, Mrs. Eddy stipulated that their applications must be countersigned by an authorized teacher of Christian Science and that applicants could not be members of other denominations.

During the first years of the existence of The Mother Church, the First Members held primary power in the organization, though they were obedient to Mrs. Eddy's wishes. But the Board of Directors, which had been created by a deed of trust about three weeks before the church was formed, eventually had a far more important role in the movement. At the time of their appointment, the office of Director was not looked upon as a major position of authority; the Directors simply looked after the affairs of the church. But in 1901 Mrs. Eddy vested in it all the powers which it had formerly shared with the First Members, a body which she formally dissolved in 1908. The Directors, it must be emphasized, were never elected by either the original twelve who had formed the church or the First Members; and their appointment was never ratified by the church membership as a whole. They derived their authority solely through Mrs. Eddy's delegation of power to them through a deed of trust. As a self-perpetuating body, the Board has continued to fill vacancies in its own ranks through the present. By this arrangement, power in The Mother Church was centralized in a single governing body — initially the First Members, finally the Board of Directors. By constructing her church in this way, Mrs. Eddy made sure that it would be as firm a bulwark as she could erect against the heterodoxy and schism that had threatened the earlier church.

Most of Mrs. Eddy's followers welcomed her plan for the government of The Mother Church. But approval was not unanimous. Disapproval centered mainly among those who accepted the necessity of the church organization, but were still wedded to the congregational idea of church polity. Their spokesman was a man in high position: the Reverend Lanson P. Norcross, pastor of the church in Boston at the time the new organization was formed. Norcross, formerly a Congregational minister, had been pleased when in March 1889, Mrs. Eddy encouraged the founding of local Christian Science churches and declared that they should have an independent form of government. Next to following her, he told the National Association, the most important principle they could observe was "the autonomy and freedom of theological churches to follow the great Congregational principle of managing their own affairs." [65] The appointment by Mrs. Eddy of a Board of Directors and the election of First Members by twelve students designated by her dismayed him. "Do we want a Bishop or Board of Bishops," he asked; "are we becoming simply a denomination, with all the evils of denominationalism as seen in a strictly centralized government, lodged in a body that will hamper and oppress us?" [66]

Actually, the plan which Mrs. Eddy devised for church government, taken *in toto,* presents a more mixed picture than one would gather from Norcross's comments. For the element of theological autocracy in the government of The Mother Church was counterpoised by a continuing congregational and democratic element in the government of the branch churches. Power in these branch churches is vested in the congregations, which elect all primary officers from among their own number. Thus the church with no established hierarchy or professional clergy to superintend it is free to conduct its own affairs within the general framework of the *Manual of The Mother Church.*

The political analogy becomes inescapable here, and has often been used to characterize the structure of the Christian Science church as a whole. Like the Federal Government, this structure, embracing both The

65. Johnson, *History,* II, 335.   66. *Ibid.,* p. 341.

Mother Church and its branches, is a mixed system. Just as citizens of states are citizens of the United States, so members of branch churches are at least in most cases, members of The Mother Church, hence under dual authority. The delimitation of spheres of authority, however, is quite distinct. The Mother Church does control the policy of the movement as a whole; but it does not interfere with nor dictate to its branch churches in matters of local government. Each branch church has its own set of by-laws, distinct from and in many particulars quite different from the *Manual* that governs The Mother Church. But just as the Constitution delimits the powers of the states, so the *Manual* puts certain restrictions on the branch churches. Each church must have its own form of government; no conferences of churches are to be held except within states on problems concerned with state legislation; and no church can try to assume the position of The Mother Church in relation to other branch churches.[67]

The Manual of The Mother Church, which defines the one relation of The Mother Church to its branches, is the basic law governing the church. It stands in the same relation to the Christian Science church as does *Science and Health* to the theology of Christian Science. Yet there is nothing of the spirit of canon law about the *Manual.* A small volume of some ninety pages, it provides only the most skeletal framework for church organization and discipline.

When Mrs. Eddy founded The Mother Church, she had no intention of drawing up the set of by-laws that constitute the *Manual,* on the basis of which the Board exercises its authority. At first the procedures by which the church was governed consisted of a brief set of six rules dealing with church services, business meetings, and admission requirements. But this set of rules contained no provisions for discipline, for the teaching of Christian Science, or for many other church activities. Many such rules had been promulgated by Mrs. Eddy and duly voted upon and accepted by the members of The Mother Church for several years after The Mother Church was founded. It was not until 1895 that she came to feel that these rules should be codified and published in a unified form. A committee of Christian Scientists helped her to compose the *Manual* for this purpose. And thus was born a volume which, though slight in size, stands as part of the basic literature of Christian Science.

67. See *Man.,* pp. 70–74, on the relationship of The Mother Church to its branches.

Mrs. Eddy's authority lay behind every by-law in the *Manual*; and though the church nominally had to approve her rules, there was no question but that it would do so. The by-laws that constitute the *Manual,* other than the basic provisions in effect when it was compiled, were developed to meet specific situations as they arose. Mrs. Eddy continually revised the *Manual* in all eighty-nine editions that were published before it assumed its final shape at the time of her death. During the period of nearly fifteen years in which it underwent revision, the movement passed through such varied experiences that Mrs. Eddy could provide guidelines for virtually any future problem the church would undergo.

When the *Manual* was first published, Christian Scientists almost universally accorded Mrs. Eddy praise for the work. In an article written late in 1895, she indicated how her own attitude toward it had changed. "Heaps upon heaps of praise confront me, and for what?" she wrote. "That which I said in my heart would never be needed, — namely laws of limitation for a Christian Scientist." This passage, taken by itself, has sometimes been cited as proof that for Mrs. Eddy the *Manual* was a mere concession to necessity. Reading further puts the matter in a different light: "Thy ways are not ours. . . . Thou knowest best what we need most, — hence my disappointed hope and grateful joy . . . eternity awaits our Church Manual." [68] After the *Manual* was compiled, then, Mrs. Eddy came to regard it as the divinely inspired detailing of the highest possible human sense of church government. To her, the formation of its rules was not a matter of personal dictation to the church, but of divine wisdom marking the way by which the cause of Christian Science could be protected. The *Manual,* she said, was "a monitor more than a master." [69] In a letter republished as part of the book itself she wrote:

The Rules and By-Laws in the Manual . . . originated not in solemn conclave as in ancient Sanhedrim. They were not arbitrary opinions nor dictatorial demands, such as one person might impose upon another. They were impelled by a power not one's own, were written at different dates, and as the occasion required. They sprang from necessity, the logic of events, — from the immediate demand for them as a help that must be supplied to maintain the dignity and defense of our Cause: hence their simple, scientific basis, and detail so requisite to demonstrate Christian Science, and which will do for the race what absolute doctrines destined for future generations might not accomplish. [70]

68. *Mis.*, p. 130.   69. *New York Herald,* May 5, 1901.
70. *Man.*, p. 3.

"This Church Manual is God's law, as much as the Ten Commandments and the Sermon on the Mount," Mrs. Eddy once told a student. "It is God's law and will be acknowledged as law by law." [71] This last statement turned out to be prophetic; for in the years following Mrs. Eddy's death a struggle developed between the Board of Directors of The Mother Church and the Trustees of the Publishing Society for the control of the church. The dispute was lengthy and complicated, and several accounts of it from different points of view are available.[72] Its details need not concern us here, but a major issue involved in the dispute is very much to our point. During the course of the conflict, the vital question arose as to whether or not the *Manual* should have become inoperative after Mrs. Eddy's death. The Board, which occupies the position of Mrs. Eddy's designated executor of the *Manual*, argued that she had intended it to be permanent; and it had an explicit declaration by Mrs. Eddy to back up this view. In February 1903, she had written them a letter with the request that it be placed on the church records. In it she emphatically instructed the Board:

. . . Never abandon the By-Laws nor the denominational government of The Mother Church. If I am not personally with you, the Word of God, and my instructions in the By-Laws have led you hitherto and will remain to guide you safely on. . . . The present and future prosperity of Christian Science is largely due to the By-Laws and government of "The First Church of Christ, Scientist," in Boston. None but myself can know, as I know, the importance of the combined sentiment of this Church remaining steadfast in supporting its present By-Laws. Each of these many By-Laws has met and mastered or forestalled some contingency, some imminent peril, and will continue to do so.[73]

In a decision handed down in November 1921, the Massachusetts Supreme Court sustained the Directors' position, thus insuring the continuity of the structure of the Christian Science church as Mrs. Eddy had conceived it.

As a useful organizational structure, The Mother Church had functions that could be described as both negative and positive. In its more negative

71. Shannon Reminiscences, Archives.
72. See Charles Braden, *Christian Science Today: Power, Policy, Practice* (Dallas, 1958), for an account unfavorable to the Board; see also Norman Beasley, *The Continuing Spirit* (New York, 1958), for a favorable account.
73. Quoted in *Permanency of The Mother Church and Its Manual* (Boston, 1954), p. 18.

aspect, the Church was charged with maintaining standards in the teaching and practice of Christian Science. In its more positive aspect, the Church had the task of providing channels for the propagation of correct Christian Science. These twin missions of discipline and education were not, of course, altogether separable and in practice tended to overlap. But they can be distinguished from each other for purposes of discussion.

The establishment of a mechanism for maintaining standards in Christian Science teaching and practice was one of the reasons for the reorganization of the Church in 1892. It was in part to this end that Mrs. Eddy devised the scheme, described earlier, for admission of members to the new church on a very select basis. It was also in part to this end that she clothed the Board of Directors with extensive disciplinary powers in the church *Manual,* writing in a section entitled "Authority" that "The Christian Science Board of Directors has the power to discipline, place on probation, remove from membership, or to excommunicate members of The Mother Church." [74]

The earliest celebrated case in which it did so was that of Mrs. Josephine Curtis Woodbury, one of the more flamboyant females in the early years of the movement. Converted to Christian Science in 1879, Mrs. Woodbury assumed a position of importance in the movement, but also showed herself to be a troublemaker whose teaching of Christian Science was at the very least distorted. Her distinct personal flair attracted a large group of devoted students who like their teacher, and unlike the rank and file of the movement, were imaginative, sentimental, with pronounced leanings toward the mystical and occult. Mrs. Woodbury evidently had leanings in other directions as well. For though she advocated sexual abstinence, and had long since ceased having marital relations with her husband, Mrs. Woodbury in June 1890 gave birth to a child. Her explanation of the event was characteristically bizarre: the babe had been immaculately conceived. Until her child's "sharp birth-cry saluted my ears," Mrs. Woodbury maintained, she had not been aware that she was pregnant. Her abdominal swelling she attributed to "some fungoid formation." Before a large crowd at Ocean Point, Maine, she baptized her child "The Prince of Peace" in a pool of crystal water which she called "Bethesda." Mrs. Woodbury had finally gone too far; and Mrs. Eddy, who already had abundant reason to be suspicious of her, was thoroughly disgusted. "The Prince of Peace," she was reported as saying, was more likely the "imp of Satan" than a child of light.[75]

74. *Man.,* pp. 51–52.
75. An account of this episode is given in Peel, *Trial,* pp. 268–271.

Mrs. Woodbury's antics represented just the sort of extravagant yet sinister inversion of Christian Science that Mrs. Eddy wanted to keep out of the movement. And when The Mother Church was reorganized in 1892, Mrs. Woodbury was admitted by the First Members only on probationary status. Eventually she became embroiled in several sensational lawsuits involving the paternity of the "Prince of Peace" that further damaged her already fragile reputation; and in April 1896 she was forever excommunicated from The Mother Church. In the final disposition of the Woodbury case, the recently-constituted Board of Directors acted largely upon Mrs. Eddy's promptings. But the significant point here is that it was the Board which acted — that the disciplining of Mrs. Woodbury was accomplished through the established channels of the church organization and in accordance with its by-laws.

While the Board has exercised the disciplinary powers it invoked in Mrs. Woodbury's case less frequently than one might suppose, and even then reluctantly, it has exercised them. In 1909 Mrs. Stetson, whose alleged efforts to injure her enemies by mental means were discussed in an earlier chapter, was excommunicated from The Mother Church. Ambitious and power-loving, Mrs. Stetson sought to build her own church in New York City into a rival to The Mother Church, and thus in effect to violate the relation between The Mother Church and its branches that Mrs. Eddy had established.[70] The Board's exercise of authority in these and other cases has often been criticized by those outside the movement and to some extent within it as unnecessarily restrictive. Yet without some strong central authority the Christian Science movement would probably have long since lost all coherence. For the chaotic conditions that prevailed in the movement in the years before The Mother Church was formed would in all likelihood have continued to prevail if the Woodburys and Stetsons had flourished unchecked. To some extent, it was the contusion of "the tares and the wheat" in the 1880s that had impelled Mrs. Eddy to found The Mother Church in 1892. Since that date, there have been enough instances of heterodoxy and potential schism in the movement to confirm her judgment that the establishment of a central authority was a practical necessity for the progress of "the Cause."

Still, it would be a mistake here to place undue emphasis upon the mechanism for discipline given in the *Manual* and its implementation. For the practical channels which Mrs. Eddy established in the *Manual* for the

76. A detailed and somewhat biting discussion of the Stetson episode can be found in Swihart, *Since Mrs. Eddy.*

propagation of correct Christian Science are in the final analysis of much greater historical significance than her provision for correcting, in occasional instances, its unsound teaching and practice. In this respect, the year 1898 was an extremely important one in Mrs. Eddy's work with The Mother Church. In it she created the agencies through which The Mother Church fulfilled its more positive function of providing channels for the propagation of her teaching: the Christian Science Publishing Society, the Committee on Publication, the Board of Lectureship, and the Board of Education. In addition, Mrs. Eddy taught a class of about seventy students in November 1898 in order to put the teaching of Christian Science on a sounder basis and reinvigorate the field.

Mrs. Eddy's regulation of the teaching of Christian Science was perhaps the most important of her undertakings in 1898. No aspect of the movement's activities except the actual work of healing was so fraught with opportunity and danger for the perpetuation of Christian Science. In the 1880s the wildcat teaching of the mind-cure movement had made Mrs. Eddy especially mindful of the need for the correct teaching of Christian Science. Again and again she reiterated that only those holding certificates from the Normal Course of the Massachusetts Metaphysical College should be considered legitimate Christian Science teachers. Between the closing of the College and the creation of the Board of Education, the teaching of Christian Science was carried on with relatively little regulation by those so certified. After the creation of the Board of Education in 1898, teaching was systematized on a well-defined basis.

The major function of class instruction was to perpetuate sound Christian Science within the movement, but the church had a number of missionary functions which helped to extend Christian Science to the world. Before the church was formed, missionary activities were carried on informally by Mrs. Eddy's students. With the founding of The Mother Church, a Board of Missionaries was created to "supply sections that had no healers or teachers in Christian Science." [77] The creation of the Board simply provided an institutional channel for the carrying on of an activity which Christian Scientists had been pursuing for many years. In 1906 the Board was dissolved. Christian Science was advancing so rapidly in the United States that most sections of the country were being supplied with teachers and practitioners, and the functions of the Board of Missionaries were in part being fulfilled by the Board of Lectureship which Mrs. Eddy had created in 1898.

77. Clifford Smith, *Historical Sketches* (Boston, 1941), p. 190.

The Board of Lectureship more than any other permanent body in The Mother Church fulfilled and continues to fulfill a missionary function. Its general purpose was to spread the message of Christian Science. In outlining its functions in the *Manual*, Mrs. Eddy also charged the Board with the responsibility of replying to current condemnations of Christian Science and bearing true testimony as to the facts of her own life. In general, the lectures seem to have accomplished their intended purpose to a large extent. Though in later years most lecture audiences would be made up of already convinced Christian Scientists, the early lectures spoke mainly to prospective converts. Often lecturers were introduced by prestigious members of a community — judges, city officials, and sometimes clergymen — who generally expressed polite interest in Christian Science if not approval of its doctrine. On many occasions, however, lecturers reported that they ran into difficulties of various sorts. One of them noted that in Maine he had received a card before going on the platform. On it was written: "I read the Bible and know its power unto salvation. If what I hear is true, you and all your Board are going to Hell, and when you get there please remember that at Belfast, May 5, 1904, you were duly warned." [78]

One of the major ways in which Mrs. Eddy's teaching was disseminated was through the circulation of Christian Science literature, published by the Christian Science Publishing Society. *Science and Health*, of course, was the preeminent item; and Christian Scientists spared no effort to see that it was widely circulated. The literature of the movement also included the Christian Science periodicals; the *Journal*, founded in 1883; the *Sentinel*, founded in 1898; and the *Christian Science Quarterly*, containing the weekly Bible Lessons, which began publication in 1899. In 1903 with interest in Christian Science spreading in Germany among other foreign countries, the Publishing Society began distribution of a German-language periodical called *Der Herold der Christian Science*. As Christian Science took root in different countries, *Heralds* appeared in a number of foreign languages, though with the English text of articles always included. All these items, together with biographies of Mrs. Eddy and historical accounts of the movement, constituted "authorized" Christian Science literature. Christian Scientists are generally wary of literature hostile to Mrs. Eddy and her teachings. Yet The Mother Church maintains no index, and Christian Scientists generally feel free to read items about their faith not published under its auspices.

78. *CSS*, VII (Oct. 29, 1904), 137.

The Mother Church not only tried to provide a reliable official literature for its members; it also attempted to correct misstatements about Christian Science in the public press. Before establishing the Committee on Publication in 1898, Mrs. Eddy had written a by-law in the *Manual* providing for a committee of three to deal with the press under her supervision. She had had a good deal of experience in this area already. In her own writings — notably *No and Yes,* in the chapter "Some Objections Answered" in *Science and Health,* and the "Message for 1901" — Mrs. Eddy provided models for the "corrective work" undertaken by the Committee she appointed. This Committee on Publication was not confined to Boston, but had representatives in every state and in foreign countries as well. Though the Committee made use of the press to disseminate items of information about Christian Science, its primary function, as outlined by the *Manual,* is to correct public misrepresentations of Christian Science. Christian Scientists gained a not undeserved reputation for being extremely sensitive to criticism. But in all fairness it must be added that their responses were far more temperate than those of their enemies and generally tried more to correct what they felt were false attitudes than to strike back at their opponents. In 1899 a Christian Scientist observed that when the history of the movement was written, inoffensiveness would be among the conspicuous virtues of Mrs. Eddy's followers.[79] The tenor of Christian Scientists' "corrective letters," many of which were published in the *Sentinel,* confirms this judgment.

In the article from the *Journal* quoted earlier in which Mrs. Eddy expressed reservations about church organization, she also dwelt on the need for simplicity in worship. "It is imperative," she wrote,

at all times and under every circumstance, to perpetuate no ceremonies except as types of these mental conditions: remembrance and love, — a real affection for Jesus' character and example. Be it remembered that all types employed in the service of Christian Science should represent the most spiritual forms of thought and worship that can be made visible.[80]

In her ideal of what a church service should be, Mrs. Eddy showed strong

79. "Put Up Thy Sword," *CSS,* V (Jan. 29, 1903), 344. The operations of the Committee on Publication have of necessity been given only cursory treatment here. An extensive and informative exploration of the subject is Lee Zeunert Johnson. *The Christian Science Committee on Publication: A Study of Group and Press Interaction.* Ph.D. Dissertation. Syracuse University, 1963.
80. *Mis.,* p. 91.

distrust of religious formalism, together with a greater emphasis upon private prayer than public worship. The first chapter of *Science and Health* was entitled simply "Prayer." Therein she made it plain that for her, public profession, audible worship, ceremony, and creed had nothing really to do with prayer. "Whatever materializes worship," she wrote, "hinders man's spiritual growth and keeps him from demonstrating his power over error." [81]

Material symbols for Mrs. Eddy had no place in the highest form of worship; for the practicing Christian Scientist, she maintained, could realize in his own life the spiritual realities that they symbolized. Of the Eucharist, she wrote, "If Christ, Truth, has come to us in demonstration, no other commemoration is requisite . . . and if a friend be with us, why need we memorials of that friend?" In a similar spirit, she defined the meaning of baptism as "a purification from all error." [82] To her the ceremony of baptism had little meaning if men are not thus purified. And though the rite of baptism is not practiced in Christian Science churches, Mrs. Eddy deals with the subject often as a necessary element of regeneration. Christian Science branch churches do hold Communion services twice yearly. On these occasions — and on these occasions alone — the congregation is invited to kneel for a few moments of silent prayer, followed by the audible repetition of the Lord's Prayer. This practice is the only tangible observance of a sacrament to be found in Christian Science churches.

In her desire to simplify and purify public worship as much as possible, Mrs. Eddy had to move as cautiously as she did in the founding of The Mother Church. Most of her followers came out of the main Protestant denominations and were often reluctant to give up their old forms of worship. Mrs. Eddy realized that if she made too radical a break with the traditions they were accustomed to, she might alienate them entirely. Hence she felt that she had no choice in certain instances but to make compromises. One such instance of her concession to students in these matters was a christening service held in 1887. Twenty-nine children of members of the congregation had never been christened, having been born after their parents adopted Christian Science. The parents importuned Mrs. Eddy to make it possible for their infants to partake of this benefit, and she reluctantly consented. So during a Sunday Service in February she moved slowly from child to child, repeated each one's name,

---

81. *S&H.*, pp. 4–5.   82. *Ibid.*, pp. 34–35.

and pronounced the blessing "May the baptism of Christ, with the Holy Spirit, cleanse you from sin, sickness, and death." [83] This was the first and last such rite performed in the church.

But in the massive reconstruction of the church that began in 1892 there were to be no more concessions. Mrs. Eddy's designation of the order of Christian Science church services was to be an essential phase of the founding of the church. Her most crucial break with conventional practice along these lines lay in the institution of the Bible and *Science and Health* as "impersonal pastor" for all Christian Science services. The movement had had a good deal of experience with personal pastors before Mrs. Eddy took this large step, but she had never been fully satisfied with the system of preaching in the movement. Several local churches had adopted the practice of reading from the Bible and *Science and Health* before the sermon, and in a few cases in place of the sermon. The success of these experiments encouraged Mrs. Eddy to "ordain" the "impersonal pastor" for The Mother Church and five months later, as the only pastors for all branch churches. After April 1895, readers and not preachers officiated at all Christian Science church services. The most obvious objection to this method of conducting services was that the personal element would be left out entirely. This, of course, was just its benefit as far as Mrs. Eddy was concerned.

When the system of using "impersonal pastor" was first employed, the lessons that were read consisted of Bible citations from the "International Series" generally used in Protestant churches, with correlative passages from *Science and Health*. In 1898, Mrs. Eddy instructed the Bible Lesson Committee of The Mother Church to prepare lessons based on twenty-six topics which she designated. Thereafter these lessons were read daily by Christian Scientists and became the main feature of the Sunday Service. On them, she said, "the prosperity of the cause of Christian Science largely depends." Before the reading of the Lesson Sermon, the first reader quotes a brief statement by Mrs. Eddy explaining the authority with which the sermon is invested for Christian Scientists.

The canonical writings, together with the word of our textbook, corroborating and explaining the Bible texts in their spiritual import and application to all ages, past, present, and future, constitute a sermon undivorced from truth, uncontaminated and unfettered by human hypotheses, and divinely authorized.[84]

83. Johnson, *History*, I, 362.
84. See *The Christian Science Quarterly*, all editions.

The relative formality of the Sunday Service, which centers upon the reading of the Lesson Sermon, is counterbalanced by the Wednesday evening meetings, which include testimonials of Christian Science healing. When these meetings were initiated in the early 1880s, Mrs. Eddy felt it necessary to hold them on Friday night; for in this way they would not conflict with the regular Wednesday meetings of the orthodox churches, which many of those interested in Christian Science still wanted to attend. It was only in 1898 that she gave notice to the field that all testimony meetings should be held on Wednesday. In these meetings, after a hymn, a reading from the Bible and from *Science and Health,* repetition of the Lord's Prayer, and another hymn, the congregation is invited to share testimonies and remarks on Christian Science. The element of congregational participation in these meetings is distinctly reminiscent both of Quaker services and of revival meetings. Both services share a quality of simplicity that was most important to Mrs. Eddy. A correspondent for the *Chicago Inter-Ocean,* after attending services in The Mother Church, reported that he found them "simple, unique, devotional, and suggestive." Mrs. Eddy could have asked for no more.[85]

THE CHURCH MILITANT

Christian Scientists in the early 1890s had cause to be pleased with the progress of the movement. For in that decade it had become apparent that the movement was picking up momentum and becoming a true "church militant." Gaining steadily in numbers and repute, it moved with decisive thrust into the mainstream of American denominational life. The Mother Church, founded in 1892, was rapidly gaining acceptance throughout the movement as the universal Church of Christ, Scientist; and plans were being developed for the construction of a fine church edifice in Boston. Moreover, the relations of the Christian Science movement with other denominations, always a troublesome problem, seemed to be improving. Most conspicuously, the Christian Scientists had been invited to present Mrs. Eddy's teachings at the World's Parliament of Religions held in conjunction with the Columbian Exposition at Chicago. Mrs. Eddy, though most gratified by the invitation, was not at first unqualifiedly enthusiastic about the Parliament; and she urged those responsible for the presentations on Christian Science to exercise the greatest caution in preparing for it. Most of her followers, however, looked

85. Quoted in *CSJ,* XIII (Dec. 1895), 382.

upon the occasion as a God-appointed opportunity for dispelling public confusion about Christian Science and proclaiming its message. Having experienced years of scorn on the part of the orthodox clergy, they viewed participation in the Parliament as a great triumph for the Cause.

The reception accorded the Christian Scientists at the Parliament more than fulfilled their expectations. None of the many religious groups represented there attracted greater public attention. On Wednesday, September 20, a large audience gathered at the Christian Scientists' denominational congress to hear papers on various aspects of Mrs. Eddy's teaching read by well-known figures in the movement. Two days later Judge Hanna addressed a full assembly of the Parliament in a packed auditorium. His address was composed of a series of excerpts from Mrs. Eddy's writings prepared by a committee and gone over by her. She wanted to be sure that on this most important occasion the teachings of Christian Science were as authoritatively represented as possible.

The last occasion at which her teaching had been presented before as large a gathering of distinguished men of religion was eight years before in Tremont Temple. By a curious irony, one of the dignitaries sharing the platform with Hanna at the Parliament was Joseph Cook, who sat red-faced and agitated during Hanna's reading of Mrs. Eddy's address and afterward exploded in wrath to his colleagues. It is clear, though, that the situation at the Parliament presented an almost perfect contrast to that of Mrs. Eddy eight years before. Her audience at Tremont Temple had been mostly cold and hostile; only a small clique of her followers gave her support. In 1893, Hanna's audience included hundreds of enthusiastic co-believers; and the large crowd of non-Christian Scientists were, if not altogether approving, at least cordial and interested. In 1885, Cook had introduced Mrs. Eddy with cold disdain. But eight years later, Charles Bonney, the guiding spirit and president of the Parliament, presented Hanna in glowing terms. "When science becomes Christian," he declared, "then the world indeed advances towards the millennial dawn." The rise of Christian Science, Bonney continued, represented a "striking manifestation of the interposition of divine providence in human affairs." For the Christian Scientists had been "called to declare and emphasize the real harmony between religion and science." [86]

Bonney's purpose in promoting the Parliament had been to harmonize as much as possible religious faiths of great diversity, welding them into a phalanx of opposition to atheistic materialism. Superficially, Christian

86. Quoted in Johnson, *History*, II, p. 189.

Science seemed to reconcile science and religion in such a way as to accomplish this end. But in actuality, it by no means reconciled science with Christianity as anybody but the Christian Scientists conceived of either. Yet there were many points which Christian Scientists shared with other Christians — a common ground which the growing enmity of the orthodox churches to Christian Science in future years would largely obscure. The Parliament was an important forerunner of the ecumenical activity that has characterized twentieth century American religious life. Given the Scientists' radical religious claims, there is and has been little room for full ecumenical fellowship between the Christian Science movement and other Christian churches. Yet to a discerning eye, the Parliament might have shown that there was a good deal more room for dialogue and fellowship than the orthodox Churches and many Christian Scientists were disposed to admit.

Whatever storms future years might bring in the relations of Christian Science to the mainline Christian churches, Mrs. Eddy's followers looked upon their experience at the Parliament as a triumph for the cause. Of course, they had shared the limelight with two other groups which had become public curiosities and of which Mrs. Eddy by no means approved: Vedantists and Theosophists. Yet they felt great satisfaction in finally being accorded some degree of respectful recognition by other religious bodies. Not long after the events in Chicago, Hanna commented in an editorial for the *Journal* that the Parliament had disproved the "notion that Christian Scientists belong to the army of cranks." [87]

For their part, the Scientists grew very cautious in their remarks about other religious bodies. The watchword on this subject came from Mrs. Eddy in an article called "Take Heed!" in the *Journal* for November 1893. Therein she enjoined her followers "not to speak or write critically of any church denomination, but to promulgate Christian Science through correct statement and healing." "This alone," she concluded, "is consistent with our attitude and the brotherly place accorded us in the Congress and Parliament of Religion in A.D., 1893." [88] The day was far distant in which the *Journal* had regularly printed jokes about clergymen. In the 1880s, it is true, Mrs. Eddy and her followers had proven in response to clerical attacks that they could give as well as they got, but in later years Mrs. Eddy and her followers were to refrain from severe

---

87. Septimus B. Hanna, "Christian Science at the Parliament," *CSJ*, XI (March 1894), 553.
88. Mary Baker Eddy, "Take Heed," *CSJ*, XI (Nov. 1893), 357.

assaults on their clerical opponents.[89] *Science and Health* does contain a number of statements condemning ecclesiasticism and religious formalism in general. Mrs. Eddy wrote, for example, that "Truth should emanate from the pulpit, but never be strangled there."[90] But she said nothing critical of any Protestant denomination, though her views, of course, differed from the doctrines of Protestants. Her harshest references to other religious groups were contained in several explicit strictures on Judaism. Yet even if she could write of Jews that "Creeds and rituals have not cleansed their hands of rabbinical lore,"[91] she could also try in a long passage to establish a basis on which Jew and Christian could unite in a pure monotheism.[92] Certainly no religion was regarded more unfavorably by Christian Scientists than Roman Catholicism. In 1895 Mrs. Eddy told a group of Christian Scientists that there was no greater difference between the pagan Plato's doctrines and those of Jesus than between "the Catholic and Protestant sects."[93] Yet her several derogatory references to Catholicism in *Science and Health* are indirect and relatively mild. She advised the editors of the periodicals not to publish any statements unnecessarily offensive to "priestcraft."[94] And when Pope Leo XIII died in 1903, she wrote a warm tribute to him.[95]

"A genuine Christian Scientist," Mrs. Eddy wrote three years later in a message to her followers, "loves Protestant and Catholic, D.D. and M.D., — loves all who love God, good; and he loves his enemies."[96] This statement was typical of many she made cautioning Christian Scientists to entertain the spirit of love and forebearance to other religious groups. To some extent, her encouragement of such an attitude was simply good policy, a way of conserving whatever gains her church was making in its relations with other churches. But it also reflected her belief that the spirit of denominational rivalry was inimical to the practice of Christian Science. "Christianity," Mrs. Eddy wrote in 1899, is not "the opinions of a sect struggling to gain power over contending sects and scourging the sect in advance of it."[97]

Seldom if ever, then, does one find really hostile references to other religious bodies in the literature of the Christian Science movement from

---

89. For an example of a vigorous rejoinder by Mrs. Eddy to her theological critics, see *Mis.*, p. 246.

90. *S&H.*, p. 236.   91. *Ibid.*, p. 134.   92. *Ibid.*, p. 361.

93. *Mis.*, p. 111.

94. Bates and Dittimore, *Mary Baker Eddy*, p. 262.

95. *My.*, pp. 294–295.   96. *Ibid.*, p. 4.   97. *Ibid.*, p. 148.

the early 1890s on. Often, however, one does find Christian Scientists displaying a superior and slighting attitude toward other denominations. Though still a minority group, they were growing rapidly enough in the 1890s to move to the offensive. Frequently Christian Scientists crowed over the large number of members being added to the fold. As early as 1892, the *Journal* ran a series of articles by converts from many faiths tracing their pathways, for example, "From Unitarianism to Christian Science." [98] Moreover, Christian Scientists often commented with obvious self-satisfaction on the difficulties other denominations were experiencing. One of them wrote, for example, that he was "astonished at the attitude of the Christian churches. They seem like a steamer in a dark night in the ocean. They have no light enough to pierce the darkness . . . and keep blowing their whistles and ringing their bells for fear something will bump into them. They are thus unfit for commercial purposes." [99] The *Sentinel* delighted in quoting remarks by noted ministers — among them Washington Gladden — on the weakness of orthodoxy.[100] Further, it took careful note of the heresy trials of religious liberals, generally siding with the ministers under attack. And it also commented on several occasions on the difficulty the denominations were experiencing in re cruiting enough ministers to fill their pulpits.

By the last years of the nineteenth century, with the membership of The Mother Church approaching fifteen thousand and growing rapidly, the Christian Scientists came to feel that they represented the wave of the future. In an interview with the *New York Herald* in 1898, Mrs. Eddy predicted that "at the present rate of increase, I believe that in fifty years, aye less, that Christian Science will be the dominant religious belief of the world, that it will have more adherents than any other denomination." [101]

Her best known critic, Mark Twain, came to share this opinion, but was not so pleased at the prospect. Twain's hostility to Christian Science was not motivated by doctrinal considerations as such. Indeed, he was not altogether opposed to Mrs. Eddy's teaching. But he was seriously distressed that her highly organized church would come to represent the Standard Oil Company of American religion. And he viewed Mrs. Eddy, whom he intensely disliked for a number of reasons, as a would-be monarch or Pope. His book *Christian Science,* published in 1907 but

98. Vol. X of the *CSJ* contains a number of such articles, which are valuable sources for an understanding of conversions to Christian Science.

99. John Linscott, "Scientific Worship," *CSJ*, XI (Sept. 1893), 247.

100. *CSS,* II (Sept. 21, 1899).   101. *New York Herald,* April 17, 1898.

composed mainly of materials written four years before, gives a comic gloss to an essentially serious attitude. In an even more stinging unpublished manuscript called "The History of Holy Eddypus," Twain wrote an account of a world empire dominated by Christian Science. In it Christianity is replaced by "Eddymania," religion is known as "Eddygush," heaven is renamed "Eddyville," and the dollar is called "Eddyplunk." [102]

The development of the Christian Science movement in the twentieth century has hardly confirmed Mrs. Eddy's hopes nor Twain's fears. And most of the Protestant clergy would probably not have gone as far as either in their assessment of the movement's future strength. Yet clergymen more than any other group were mindful of and distressed by the rapid growth of Christian Science. Though some Protestant liberals, as we shall see, saw something to praise in Christian Science, most clergymen looked upon it as an heretical teaching, dangerous to religion and to public health as well. Indeed, the increasing severity and frequency of their denunciations of it provide one fairly reliable index of its spread. As the movement began to grow to really significant proportions in the 1890s, the clerical attack on Christian Science, foreshadowed in the period before The Mother Church was formed, intensified as well.

One obvious source of clerical hostility to Christian Science lay in the fact that the movement garnered most of its members from the Protestant denominations. The Reverend Ray Clarkson Harker of Cincinnatti, complained that the Christian Scientists' raids on other denominations were unfair:

It is said that the Methodists pick up folks, that the Baptists wash them, that the Congregationalists starch them, and that the Episcopalians take them. This was said in merriment, we suppose; but it may be said in all solemnity that, if all that Christian Science can do is take folks after they have been picked up, washed, and starched, its mission is poor indeed.[103]

Many clergymen were well aware that the attractiveness of Christian Science pointed to the failures of orthodoxy, and more specifically, to their failure as spiritual leaders. Mournfully, some of them noted that the adherents of the new faith often showed a spirit of religious commitment that the members of their own churches lacked. Theodore Seward, an Episcopalian layman sympathetic to Mrs. Eddy's teaching, wrote that

102. Mark Twain, "The History of Holy Eddypus," Mark Twain Papers, University of California at Berkeley.
103. Ray Clarkson Harker, *Christian Science* (Cincinnati, 1908), p. 47.

in attending Christian Science services he often said to himself: "What would not the ministers give for such congregations as these, such unfailing attendance, such enthusiasm, such zeal for the Truth, such affection for their pastors and for one another." [104] And speaking of those who had left their old church homes for Christian Science, James M. Gray, Dean of the Moody Bible Institute, exclaimed in 1907, "The pathos of their departure, alas! has reached the proportions of a tragedy." Gray further acknowledged that many who had taken up Christian Science were among the most spiritually-minded people in the churches — a point which other ministers noted with sadness. A universalist clergyman, for example, introducing a Christian Science lecturer in 1900, observed, "One of the most serious objections I would find with Christian Science is that it has claimed as its own too many of the most liberal and helpful members of my own church." [105] Possibly one of those to whom he had reference was the lecturer on the occasion, Irving Tomlinson, himself a former Universalist minister.

Clergymen were naturally disturbed at the inroads that the Christian Science movement was making in the mainline Protestant denominations. And it was natural that they should have taken what measures they could to prevent its growth. Of course, the religious situation in the late nineteenth and early twentieth centuries was sufficiently turbulent that the clergy had many more things to worry about than Christian Science. Certainly many more ministers were concerned with the effects of scientific materialism on Christian faith than with the growth of the Christian Science movement. Even so, the movement was advancing rapidly enough and gaining sufficient notoriety to attract substantial clerical attention whatever other spiritual dangers the clergy had to contend with. And besides, the generally anxious state of mind caused by the religious situation as a whole may have inflamed their sensitiveness to the specific threat posed by Christian Science.

Sometimes forbearing clergymen would gently try to persuade those of their congregation interested in Christian Science to relinquish their heterodox views. Others used more drastic methods. In some cases, ministers would single out those who had taken up the study of Christian Science in their congregations during the course of a sermon attacking the new teaching. In a few instances they went so far as to read them

104. Theodore F. Seward, *How to Get Acquainted with God* (New York, 1910), p. 94.
105. *CSS*, III (Sept. 6, 1900), 10.

out of the church as an object lesson to others. Some Christian Scientists reported, too, that they were spared no denunciation after they had definitely committed themselves to Mrs. Eddy's teaching. A former Lutheran from Ohio, for example, wrote that her minister told her that she was "a fanatic, a disgrace to the church and my family, a deluded person and a sinner." This woman recalled also that the same minister was once asked if Christian Science treatment might be sought for a woman dying of consumption. He declared, she said, that "he would rather have her die than healed by what he called witchcraft, and she did." [106]

Such forms of hostility sometimes intimidated prospective converts to Christian Science from openly professing their new faith. Others, however, found in opposition from their families or clergymen the needed spur to sever their old denominational connections completely. Ira Knapp, one of Mrs. Eddy's most devoted early followers, made his break in just this way. In his home town of Lyman, New Hampshire, in 1884, he suffered through a long sermon against Christian Science by a Methodist minister with whom he had discussed the subject. At the end of the sermon Knapp rose in his pew, disputed the minister's points one by one, continued his arguments after the services ended, then stalked out of the church never to return.[107] One of the more sudden and startling breaks made by a convert to Christian Science from an orthodox church was, no doubt, that of Mrs. Jessie Hughes Roberts of Denver. Once an ardent Episcopalian, Mrs. Roberts continued to attend Episcopal services even after having had class instruction from Mrs. Eddy. She describes what happened at the last such service she attended in these words: "At the Communion service . . . as the words from the Litany 'From Thy wrath and eternal damnation, O Lord, deliver us' were being repeated, I could stand it no longer, and jumped to my feet, exclaiming aloud, 'Good Lord, deliver us!' " [108]

A church could not prevent one of its members from becoming a Christian Scientist. But it could and often did cast a shadow over his leave-taking by refusing to grant the convert a letter of recommendation to the Church of Christ, Scientist. In many cases, churches not only refused to grant letters of recommendation requested by converts to Christian Science, but also made a great issue of the request in church meetings and along other channels, thereby embroiling fledgling Christian Scientists in painful controversies. It was easy enough for a convert to avoid

106. *CSJ*, IX (Sept. 1891), 262.   107. Knapp, *Ira Oscar Knapp,* p. 14.
108. Autobiography of Mrs. Jessie Hughes Roberts, Longyear.

such unpleasantness by simply requesting a letter of dismissal, rather than recommendation; for such a letter was for the most part promptly granted. Though the Christian Science Church accepted such letters, Mrs. Eddy encouraged her followers to ask for letters of recommendation. Not only did she feel it was their due; she also believed that Christian Scientists witnessing to the effects of their new faith on their lives were good missionaries to the clergy and laity of the church from which they were departing. As time went on, the Protestant churches became increasingly willing to grant letters of recommendation to Christian Scientists. It is doubtful that the change was brought about by any growing sympathy among them to Mrs. Eddy's teaching. Rather, it was probably caused by their growing recognition that the Church of Christ, Scientist, was a stable and growing institution, and that conversions to it were inevitable.

Perhaps the most perplexing situations faced by converts to Christian Science were those of clergymen of other denominations who took up its study and practice. Given the turbulent religious situation of the late nineteenth century, it is not surprising that many ministers should have been attracted to Christian Science. Sometimes they sought new truths to take hold of, sometimes physical healing, sometimes merely a living. Many of them had had amazingly checkered religious careers. The Reverend Joseph Adams, who studied with Mrs. Eddy in 1886, was an Englishman by birth. Converted by Charles G. Finney, he joined the Congregational Church, became an evangelist, rejected Congregationalism for Methodism, rejected Methodism for Congregationalism, then rejected Congregationalism for Christian Science. Not surprisingly, Adams ended up by rejecting Christian Science for mind-cure. Up until the early 1890s, most clergymen who drifted into Christian Science drifted right out again. Thereafter, a small but significant number of clergymen became firm adherents of Christian Science and in some cases well respected leaders of the movement.

Often they had gone through years of mental struggle before deciding to leave the pulpit for Christian Science. One Congregational minister who began its study in the early 1890s stayed in the ministry four years before making a decisive break. Mrs. Eddy's ideas began filtering into his sermons; and one of his parishioners told him disgustedly that everything he said "goes in one ear and out the other, for all I can think of is that horrid Christian Science." [109] Another minister, a revivalist, became interested in Christian Science and preached it at revival meetings. "To

109. *CSJ,* XIV (Oct. 1896), 47.

my great surprise," he wrote, "my converts and brethren and sisters concluded that I was beside myself." [110] Other ministers found it necessary to go on preaching orthodox doctrine even after having embraced Christian Science. The Reverend Severin E. Simonson, a Methodist, investigated and sporadically practiced it over a period of thirteen years before deciding in 1899 "that there was only one thing for me to do as an honest man, and that was to take my stand for Christian Science." Only in the last service which he conducted as a Methodist minister did he permit himself to preach Christian Science.[111]

As Simonson soon found, taking his stand for Christian Science was very difficult indeed. One incident in particular was most painful. When he resigned from the ministry, the Methodist Episcopal Conference of New York passed a resolution acknowledging his years of service and regretting his departure. Later that day, the Reverend James Monroe Buckley arrived at the Conference to protest the motion. Buckley was a powerful figure in American Methodism during the last decades of the century. Besides being editor of the influential *Christian Advocate,* he was the leader of the General Conference of the Methodist Episcopal Church. A powerful speaker and able writer, Buckley was a formidable and implacable foe of Christian Science. He had entered the lists against it early with an article in 1885 for the *Century* and a book published in 1892 on *Christian Science, Faith Healing, and Kindred Phenomena.* Addressing the Conference, Buckley said that he had traveled all night to prevent the passage of a resolution in any way favorable to Simonson. No one "infected with the bacilli of Christian Science," he declared, "should receive any resolution of regret from the Conference." "Atheists," he went on, "cannot do as much harm, in my opinion, as can Christian Scientists. They are a mischievous abomination. We should count ourselves well rid of this man." On Buckley's recommendation, the resolution was rescinded.[112]

Not all clergymen displayed Buckley's naked hostility to Christian Science and anyone who adopted it. In their reactions to the conversion to Christian Science of members of their churches or clerical colleagues, ministers were often moved more by sorrow than anger. And few converts to Christian Science who had once served with dedication in Prot-

110. *CSJ,* XVI (Sept. 1898), 430.

111. Severin E. Simonson, *From the Methodist Pulpit into Christian Science and How I Demonstrated the Abundance of Substance and Supply* (Sherman Oaks, Calif., 1928), p. 80.

112. *Ibid.,* p. 131.

estant denominations could sever their ties with them without a pang. One exchange of letters preserved in the autobiography of Andrew Graham illumines the depth of feeling in both parties which such conversions could arouse. Graham had been for thirty-four years a priest in the Episcopal church before adopting Christian Science in 1912. To his Bishop he wrote that it had become

impossible for me to remain in the Episcopalian Church, either as a layman or a Priest, without being disloyal to my confirmation and particularly to my ordination vow. . . . The only sorrow I have in connection with the matter is the thought that it may perhaps wound the faith of some of my friends, who, misinterpreting Christian Science, will feel that I have renounced the Lord who redeemed me. It is not my intention to present reasons or enter into argument. I will only say that the essence of my faith has not been touched.

In reply, the Bishop of New York notified Graham "with sickness of heart" of his suspension from the priesthood. "It is a beautiful and holy tie that you have broken," wrote the Bishop. "I wish from the depth of my soul you had found, in the old path, your life and peace. I must add God bless and guide you lifelong." [113]

Shortly before renouncing the Episcopalian priesthood for Christian Science, Graham had assembled a packet of about thirty pamphlets and books attacking the religion he was soon to adopt. He intended to send this collection of anti-Christian Science material to a young clergyman of his acquaintance, so that he might be "protected from the poison of Christian Science teaching." [114] Later, as a Christian Scientist, Graham was glad that by an oversight the packet had not been sent. Yet his young colleague probably did not remain unarmed against Christian Science for long. For the extensive Protestant literature on the subject, which had been accumulating since the early 1890s, was well circulated among the ministry. Articles on Christian Science appeared frequently in the denominational periodicals; several sizeable books on the subject were published; and anti-Christian Science sermons were often reprinted in pamphlet form and distributed by denominational authorities to clergymen under their charge. By the time of Mrs. Eddy's death, this literature constituted a formidable arsenal from which a minister who wanted to attack her teaching could draw his weapons.

113. Andrew Graham, *Autobiographical Notes*, p. 124.
114. *Ibid.*, p. 111.

Given the ready availability of this literature, it was easy enough for a minister to compose a sermon on Christian Science without even looking at *Science and Health*. Not surprisingly, anti-Christian Science sermons often bear an even greater resemblance to one another than one could explain on the basis of the common orientation of their authors. Again and again one finds that the arguments and phrases of such staple items as Buckley's *Christian Science, Faith Healing, and Kindred Phenomena*,[115] or H. F. Haldeman's *Christian Science in the Light of Holy Scripture*,[116] or William P. McCorkle's *Christian Science Examined* [117] are repeated in many sermons. Actually, many ministers were not attacking Christian Science so much as what they had come to believe it was through second-hand accounts.

Some clergymen, though, went to considerable lengths in gaining a first-hand knowledge of the new teaching before judging it. Not that they generally approached the subject in an impartial frame of mind, though some did to the best of their abilities. But they did make the effort to study Mrs. Eddy's writings and sometimes to take a class from her or, after she retired to Concord, from an authorized Christian Science teacher. In the 1880s she had offered free instruction to clergymen in order to have fair play at their hands. A number of ministers took up her offer. Sometimes they plied her with questions and came near to disrupting the class with arguments. Others listened respectfully; and a few, though a very few, were converted.

The specific criticisms that Protestant clergymen leveled at Christian Science have been dealt with in some detail earlier. Our concern here is with the situation in which these attitudes were expressed. And nothing, perhaps, is more revealing of that situation than the fact that the most acute assessment of the theology of Christian Science in this period was made by a Jew, Rabbi Morris Lefkovitz, whose comments on the role of Jesus in Mrs. Eddy's teaching were discussed earlier.[118] Attacking Christian Science as an essentially un-Jewish faith which no Jew could conscientiously practice, Lefkovitz noted entirely without approbation those basic Christian elements in Mrs. Eddy's teaching which her orthodox

115. James M. Buckley, *Christian Science, Faith-Healing, and Kindred Phenomena* (New York, 1892).

116. H. F. Haldeman, *Christian Science in the Light of Holy Scripture* (New York, 1902).

117. William P. McCorkle, *Christian Science Examined* (Richmond, Va., 1899).
118. See p. 184.

Protestant critics could not discern. Far more conscious than he of the differences between Christian Science and orthodoxy, they often denied that it even included the very doctrines that Lefkovitz had found so objectionable. Tirelessly (and Christian Scientists felt, tiresomely) they proclaimed that Mrs. Eddy's teaching was "neither Christian nor scientific." And many sermons on Christian Science enumerated various essential Christian doctrines which clergymen insisted that Mrs. Eddy utterly denied, but which Lefkovitz correctly maintained were essential to its teaching.

Lefkovitz was far more accurate theologically in his assessment of the essential Christianity of Mrs. Eddy's teachings than were many of her Protestant critics. But they were at least half right in sensing that the meaning of Christian doctrines in the context of her teaching as a whole was far different from their significance within the framework of orthodox theology. These doctrines were transmuted by Mrs. Eddy's basic metaphysics into teachings which the orthodox quite understandably could not accept. In Protestant criticism of Christian Science, honest disagreement is often compounded with confusion as to Mrs. Eddy's real intent, so that the real similarities and differences between her teaching and orthodoxy are often obscured. Repeatedly, Christian Scientists functioning under the Committee on Publication of The Mother Church sought to set the record straight by pointing out misunderstandings in clerical attacks on Mrs. Eddy's teaching and emphasizing often neglected continuities between Christian Science and orthodoxy.[119] But the attacks continued.

Some clergymen, convinced that Christian Science was utterly irreconcilable with Biblical Christianity, attacked it with all the vehemence they could muster. Indeed, the tone of the assaults on it is sometimes almost rabid. Fundamentalist denunciations of Christian Science often went to extremes. A tract published by the Bible Students' Library of Oakland in 1892 declared that the rise of Christian Science proved that the last days were at hand. "Christian Science," it went on, "is a sort of witch's cauldron in which every conceivably heathen and Christian heresy is found seething and simmering to produce the subtle essence called mental medicine."[120] Of well-known clergymen, Buckley was the most fervent in his anti-Christian Science rhetoric. "I profess to understand Christian Science to the bottom of it," he told a Chautauqua audience in 1896. "I tell you

119. See p. 190.
120. Unsigned, "Christian Science: What Is It? Is It Science? Is It Christian?" pamphlet (Oakland, Calif., 1892), p. 58.

that in fact it is evil, only evil, and that continually." [121] Buckley was a Methodist; but in general, of the major denominations, Baptists were often harshest in their strictures on Mrs. Eddy's teaching. None exceeded in scorn the Reverend A. Lincoln Moore of the Riverside Baptist Church in New York. "Christian Science," he told his congregation in 1906, "is unchristian, anti-Christian, anti-biblical, Christless, Godless, — in brief, Pagan. . . . The attitude of the Christian Church must be one of un-compromising hostility, and every battery of righteousness must be turned upon this system which would destroy the intellectual, moral, and spir-itual welfare of society." [122]

A good deal of Protestant invective against Christian Science was aimed directly at Mrs. Eddy. Moore referred to her as "this modern witch of Concord" and said that she was "a decrepit old woman" showing "unmis-takable proofs of senility and decay." [123] Two years later an Episcopalian priest, Harmon Van Allen of Boston, wrote in a tract called "The Falsity of Christian Science, So-called" that the

fair minded observer sees in Mrs. Eddy: an uncultivated woman, married three times, and once divorced, passing through various forms of religious belief and finally settling down in one of her own invention; manifestly covetous, inconceivably puffed up with vanity, blasphemously claiming divine honors for herself, and unable to write a page of clear, rational English prose.[124]

Some ministers presented Mrs. Eddy as sincere but dangerously deluded, others as merely corrupt. "I believe that most Christian Scientists are sincere and honest," wrote the Reverend A. D. Sector of St. Louis in 1900. "I also believe that Mrs. Eddy is a conscious fraud of the first magnitude and a conscienceless charlatan and imposter." [125]

Some ministers, while not approving Christian Science doctrine, were disturbed by the animosity that their colleagues displayed in attacking it. The Reverend H. Heber Newton declared, "The Christian Scientist is justified in complaining that the very terms in which some critics de-nounce his belief belies (sic) their profession as followers of Jesus Christ,

---

121. Quoted in George Preston Mains, *James Monroe Buckley* (New York, 1917), p. 216).
122. Moore, *Christian Science,* pp. 80–81.
123. *Ibid.,* p. 3.
124. Van Allen, "The Falsity of Christian Science, So-called," p. 3.
125. A. D. Sector, "Christian Science Dissected," pamphlet (St. Louis, 1900), p. 9.

who never denounced anybody but hypocrites." [126] The Reverend De Witt T. Van Doren of New York declared that though he was not in sympathy with Christian Science, he felt that Protestant "theological archers" were in "danger of falling into the spirit of Pharisaism" by reason of their intolerance of it.[127] Furthermore, some liberals, as we shall see, spoke with guarded approval of Christian Science (though they often ended up damning it with faint praise). But these were minority voices; and Protestant opinion on Christian Science remained overwhelmingly hostile and often strident in its expression of this hostility.

THE LIBERAL PROTESTANT RESPONSE

The liberal Protestant response to the emergence of Christian Science need not occupy us long, for it represented only a minority report of Protestant clergymen. Yet it is significant for what it reveals about Protestant liberalism — indeed about the character of liberalism in general. The liberal temper in many of its manifestations can be understood as having an essentially conservative purpose: that of maintaining existing structures by modifying them sufficiently to quell dissidence. Much of twentieth century political and economic reform, for example, can be seen as an effort to preserve the capitalist system through piecemeal accommodation of varying interest groups in the economy. Similarly, the Protestant liberalism that flourished in the latter part of the nineteenth century can be understood as an effort to preserve traditional Christianity by accommodating it to the modern temper. It is understandable, then, that some clergymen found what they thought was a better way of combating Christian Science than damning it outright. Instead, they sought to understand the source of its appeal and absorb into their theologies whatever truths it might contain.

The liberal approach to Christian Science, though never predominant among the Protestant clergy, was in evidence in the earliest days of the development of the movement in Boston. By 1885, three distinguished Boston ministers, each representative of a different phase of New England religious liberalism, had shown marked if guarded interest in the new teaching. And the respective reasons for their interest in Christian Science

126. H. Heber Newton, *Christian Science: The Truths of Spiritual Healing and Their Contribution to the Growth of Orthodoxy* (New York, 1900), p. v.

127. DeWitt T. Van Doren, "A Minister's Defense of Christian Science," *Literary Digest*, XXIII.

furnished one good indication of the character of the liberalism they espoused. The eldest of these, and the first to indicate his support, was Reverend Andrew Preston Peabody, for many years a Professor at Harvard University. Peabody was an orthodox Unitarian, and his theology was conservative enough for him to deem Joseph Cook on the whole a salutary influence in New England religious life. But he was still firmly enough wedded to the Unitarian tradition of rational inquiry to insist that Christian Science be given a fair hearing. By preaching before the Christian Scientists several times during 1883 and 1884, he effectively served notice on his less charitable colleagues that this tradition was not dead.[128]

A Unitarian in name also, but a product of a quite different tradition, was Reverend Cyrus Bartol. Optimistic and imaginative, Bartol had preached for over half a century at Boston's South West Church, long a fountainhead of liberal religious influences. During his heydey, he had consorted with the Emersonian circle; and though he managed, just managed, to stay within the Unitarian fold, his liberalism partook not of the rationalism of Peabody's orthodoxy, but of the warmth of Transcendental faith. His interest in Christian Science, expressed in several sermons which he preached on that subject in 1884, stemmed from his feeling that the new movement represented a recrudescence of the Transcendentalist revolt against materialism, specifically against the medical materialism which affirmed, as he put it, that "the body is the man." [129]

Phillips Brooks, rector of Trinity Episcopal Church and in the 1880s Boston's most popular pastor, spoke of Christian Science from the standpoint of the liberalism just coming to flower. A genial apostle of the humanistic, undogmatic New Theology, Brooks believed that a meaningful Christianity was not to be found in doctrinal platforms, but in the ways in which faith could have a real bearing in the everyday lives of Christians and enrich the quality of the culture as a whole. He commented on Christian Science only in passing; but what he did say is clear indication of his emphasis upon the necessity of relating religion to human needs. In a St. Luke's Day Sermon in 1884, he dwelt on the new interest in healing that Christian Science had aroused. What legitimized this interest for Christians, he maintained, was that man being both body and soul,

128. See *CSJ*, II (April 1884), *CSJ*, II (Dec. 1884), 2; *CSJ*, II (Jan. 1885), 2; *CSJ*, II (April 1885), 13, for references to Peabody.

129. For Bartol's opinion of Christian Science, see "The Pantheistic Panacea," *Unitarian Review and Religious Magazine* XXIV (Dec. 1885), 509.

"the ministry that would redeem and relieve him must have a word to speak to, and a hand to lay upon, both soul and body." [130]

Even in the hostile Protestant literature on Christian Science, there is one frequently sounded note of guarded approval. Ministers of varying orientations who found themselves in almost complete disagreement with Mrs. Eddy's teaching sometimes saw limited value in it as a protest against materialism. It is debatable whether Christian Science can be said to have been a reaction against materialism, as some commentators maintained; but that it constituted a protest against it is undeniable. In *Science and Health* Mrs. Eddy wrote, "Contentment with the past and the cold conventionality of materialism are crumbling away";[131] and one can find many similar statements scattered throughout her writings. The term *materialism,* however, is not very precise; and when clergymen spoke of Christian Science as a protest against it, they did not always have the same thing in mind.

Professor H. F. Cushman of Tufts University, who discussed Mrs. Eddy's teaching as a protest against materialism in his book *The Truth in Christian Science* in 1902, defined materialism as any non-idealistic sort of activity, "from ordinary forms of commercial life to the achievement in practical science." Men become materialists, he said, when their lives are "given over to pleasure, self-aggrandizement, money-making, or any end that does not rise above what the senses may perceive." [132] Some of the critics of Christian Science said that it was in itself only a form of commercial materialism, a means of money-getting through the practice of healing. But Cushman felt that Christian Science was in part a protest against the excessively commercial spirit and hurried tempo of American life. Some clergymen agreed with him, and in testimonies and articles by Christian Scientists there is evidence to confirm this view.

Clergymen also spoke of Christian Science as a protest against scientific materialism. The very conception of true science as Christian, so fundamental to Christian Science, supports this contention. Moreover, there are many statements in Mrs. Eddy's writings which confirm it. Perhaps the clearest of them is this passage from *Science and Health*:

Belief in a material basis, from which may be deduced all rationality, is slowly yielding to the idea of a metaphysical basis, looking away from matter

130. Alexander V. G. Allen, *Life and Letters of Phillips Brooks,* 2 vols., (New York, 1900) II, 578.

131. *S&H.,* VII.

132. H. F. Cushman, *The Truth in Christian Science* (Boston, 1902), pp. 22–23.

to Mind as the cause of every effect. Materialistic hypotheses challenge meta-physics to meet in final combat. In this revolutionary period, like the shepherd boy with his sling, woman goes forth to battle with Goliath.[133]

The "Goliath" of scientific materialism was a real terror to Protestants at the time that *Science and Health* was first published. And some reviews of the first edition of the book in 1875 commended it as a thrust against Darwinism. But even those more liberal clergymen who had managed to reconcile the theory of evolution with Christian theism found scientific materialism a real challenge. Washington Gladden, who was extremely critical of Mrs. Eddy's theology, spoke for many of his colleagues when he wrote in an article on "The Truths and Untruths of Christian Science" in 1903:

> The fundamental truth to which Christian Science has drawn attention is the reality and the supremacy of spiritual forces. The materialists have attacked their reality, and most of us have been sufficiently tinctured with materialism to have little faith in their supremacy. Against this deadly unbelief the Chris-tian Scientist lifts up his battle cry.[134]

Perhaps the most revealing aspect of the interpretation of Christian Science as a protest against materialism was the view that it constituted a protest against ecclesiastical materialism.[135] Persuaded by events that the time for self-criticism had come, some clergymen attributed the growth of Christian Science to the failure of the churches. As the Reverend Gray, quoted earlier, exclaimed about the converts Christian Science was win-ning from the orthodox denominations: ". . . God alone knows upon whom lies the heavier guilt, those who left or those whose indifference and worldliness forced them to go." [136] A fuller analysis of the appeal of Christian Science as a protest against ecclesiasticism was offered by Epis-copalian Reverend Lyman P. Powell:

> To an age grown weary and impatient of ecclesiasticism and machinery, Chris-tian Scientists have brought something of the warmth and glow, the freshness and the spontaneity, the poise and the sincerity, and the gladness and the

---

133. *S&H.*, p. 268.

134. Washington Gladden, "The Truths and Untruths of Christian Science," *The Independent,* CV (March 19, 1903), 777. Woodbridge Riley voices essentially the same view in *American Thought: from Puritanism to Pragmatism* (New York, 1915), p. 50.

135. There is a good deal of evidence to support this contention in Mrs. Eddy's conception of the nature of church. See pp. 289–293.

136. Gray, *The Antidote to Christian Science,* p. 6.

other worldliness which suffused the Apostolic age and made it all alive with spiritual power. . . . They are protests in the flesh against the worldliness and ecclesiasticism which afflict the church.[137]

Others who took up the same line of thought often suggested that the strength of Christian Science lay in the fact that it made religion real in the lives of men. The Reverend George F. Greene said in 1902 that though he thought its theology "eclectic, fragmentary, and now and then, flagrantly absurd," Christian Science did give its followers a sense of the immediacy of divine power.[138]

In this passage, Greene was referring to the practice of healing for which the Scientists were so well known. And it is not surprising that many clergymen, recognizing with Greene the "immediacy of divine power" that Christian Science practice brought to individual lives, should have begun to reconsider the whole subject of spiritual healing.[139] Protestant interest in healing, of course, was not wholly the product of the influence of Christian Science. Though in the face of disaster Protestants generally resigned themselves to the will of God, they did often pray for the recovery of the sick. Yet few ministers devoted systematic thought to the nature of spiritual healing or attempted to practice it as a conspicuous phase of their ministry until the advent of Christian Science. One who did was a man whom we have met before: the Reverend A. J. Gordon. In a book on *The Ministry of Healing* he stated cogently why in his view revivification of apostolic healing was a necessity in the late nineteenth century. That period, he said, "can never be made to harmonize with a religion that is entirely heavenly in its origin, in its course, and in its consummation." [140] In effect, Christian Scientists were to say the same thing. Moreover, Gordon spoke out against the view that Christian healing was no longer a requirement for Jesus' followers in very much the same terms as did Mrs. Eddy, and challenged Christians to revivify its practice.

137. Lyman Pierson Powell, *Christian Science: The Faith and Its Founder* (New York, 1908), p. 8. This book is generally hostile to Christian Science, though it is worth noting that Powell later became a defender of Christian Science and wrote an admiring biography of Mrs. Eddy, *Mary Baker Eddy: A Life-Size Portrait* (New York, 1930).

138. George Francis Greene, "Christian Science and the Gospel of Jesus Christ," (Cranford, New Jersey, 1902).

139. The background and recent history of the spiritual healing movement in the Protestant churches is discussed in the dissertation by B. Crandell Epps, *Religious Healing in the United States, 1940–1960.* Boston University, 1961.

140. A. J. Gordon, *The Ministry of Healing,* p. 2.

In responding to this challenge, some ministers merely reiterated the view that early Christian healing was a thing of the past and had no contemporary relevance. Others claimed that medical science was the only legitimate present mode of healing. Referring to Jesus' prophecy that those who came after him would perform greater works than he, Episcopalian Bishop William Lawrence of Massachusetts declared that these greater works were being wrought "through advance in medical and surgical skills." [141] But a significant minority of clergymen felt compelled to acknowledge that the Christian Scientists had a point. A Baptist minister in Brooklyn, for example, wrote in 1897, "They tell me that the same Master who commanded us to baptize, also commanded us to heal. I do not know how to answer them." [142] Similarly, a Presbyterian in Denver told his congregation in 1907, "The atonement covers the whole nature of man, and the failure of the church to see it has been a very serious mistake." [143]

Though Bishop Lawrence, as noted above, along with many other Episcopalians, strongly opposed the practice of spiritual healing, interest in it tended to center in the Episcopalian church. One of the earliest expressions of this interest was the St. Luke's Day sermon preached in 1884 by Phillips Brooks. In later years, as Christian Science grew in popularity, some Episcopalians spoke of the need for a revivification of Christian healing with more urgency. Two of those who did so, the Reverend H. Heber Newton and Bishop Frederick Dan Huntington, were important figures in the Social Gospel movement. It is not surprising that they should have looked with some sympathy upon a practice, which, like social action, made religion meaningful in terms of the affairs of men. In 1900, Huntington told an Episcopal Congress that "if anything is certain this is certain: That if the Church of Christ, Catholic, had done its duty, the Church of Christ, Scientist, had not been." [144] In the same year, Newton wrote on Christian Science and other heterodox movements, claiming that the truths on which they were founded could be incorporated into a progressive orthodoxy. In an article called "Christian Science: The Truths of Spiritual Healing and Their Contribution to the Growth of Orthodoxy," he asserted that orthodoxy has been "found faithless to the example

141. Quoted in *CSS*, IV (Jan. 30, 1902), 348.
142. Quoted in *CSJ*, XV (May 1897), 81.
143. Coyle (no first name cited), "Christian Science Eliminated from Mrs. Eddyism" (Denver, 1907).
144. Quoted in *CSS*, III (Nov. 22, 1900), 184.

and words of its Master"; for, Newton said, it had ignored Jesus' command to heal which the Christian Scientists have taken up.[145]

Clearly Newton was following the classic liberal tactic of blunting the appeal of a dissident group by modifying existing practices. So too, the Emmanuel Movement which grew up in the Episcopalian Church as a response to Christian Science seems to have been initiated in order to steal its thunder. The movement had its origins in the Emmanuel Episcopal Church at Boston in 1906 and centered there for over two decades thereafter. Its growth was rapid. A half dozen years after it was founded, the Emmanuel Movement was national, even international in scope. And its healing techniques had a strong influence on other spiritual healing movements in various Protestant denominations. Of the relation between Christian Science and the Emmanuel Movement, its founder the Reverend Elwood Worcester wrote:

The doctrines of Christian Science . . . have been denounced, ridiculed, exploited times without number, apparently with as much effect as throwing pebbles at the sea checks the rising of the tide. . . . The more absurd the Christian Science dogma is made to appear, the more difficult it becomes to account for men's faith in it. Unless we are prepared to confess ourselves utterly at a loss to explain this infatuation, we must be able to pass beneath the vulgar and repulsive exterior of Christian Science and to find truth in it, a gift for men, a spiritual power answering to men's needs which the churches at present do not possess. . . . With all its obscurity we find in the Sacred Book of Christian Science great truths — freedom from the fetters of sense and passion, the power of the soul over the body, victory of the mind over its tyrants fear and anger, the presence of God manifested with power; above all, the promise of an immense immediate good as a result of faith.

Later Worcester went on to say that the Emmanuel Movement "bears no relation to Christian Science, either by way of protest or imitation, but it would be what it is had the latter never existed."[146] His own words, quoted above, tend to contradict this assertion. And though Worcester was undoubtedly sincere in his work, the Emmanuel Movement has been widely and rightly understood as in the main a reaction against Christian Science.

Though the practice of non-medical healing united the Emmanuel Movement with Christian Science, little else did. Indeed, the differences

145. H. Heber Newton, *Christian Science,* p. 14.
146. Elwood Worcester, Samuel McComb, Isador H. Coriat, *Religion and Medicine: The Moral Control of Nervous Disorders* (Boston, 1909), pp. 10–11, 12–13.

between the two are irreconcilable. Where Christian Science taught that healing was the result of divine power, the leaders of the Emmanuel Movement held that it came about through psychological suggestion united with faith. They were much more apt to speak of subconscious mind as the source of healing than of what Christian Science called the divine Mind. Often they spoke of their work as a form of psychotherapy. And it was in large part out of the Emmanuel Movement that modern psychological pastoral counseling grew.

Worcester and his colleagues made nowhere near the claims for their healing practice that Christian Scientists made for theirs. In the first place, they consistently held that a change in mental attitudes could affect functional but not organic disease. Organic diseases are those in which bodily tissue or bone is affected; functional diseases are those in which a bodily organ is not doing its work. The distinction between the two has never been precise, and has grown less so since the early years of the Emmanuel Movement. Even some critics of the movement during these early years felt that its distinction between organic and functional disease was too neat. For Mrs. Eddy, this distinction could have little ultimate meaning; for she held that *all* bodily conditions objectify mental states. She did imply, however, that treatment of organic disease was more difficult than treatment of functional disease, for she wrote, "Christian Science heals organic disease as surely as it heals what is called functional, for it requires only a fuller understanding of the divine Principle of Christian Science to demonstrate the higher rule." [147]

Further, the leaders of the Emmanuel Movement, consciously trying to reconcile religion with science, advocated that clergymen work along with physicians in diagnosing and curing disease. Dr. Samuel McComb, Worcester's closest associate, maintained that if Jesus were alive, he would be willing to work hand in hand with doctors. If through their diagnosis he learned that a patient was afflicted with an organic disease, McComb surmised, he might decline to treat him; but if he found out that he was suffering from a functional ailment, he would take his case.[148] Some medical men were strongly critical of the Emmanuel Movement, though their opposition to it was not so implacable as was their hostility to Christian Science. A few of them, however, became much interested in the work of the Emmanuel Movement. The most conspicuous medical doctor to take an active interest in the Emmanuel Movement was Doctor Richard

147. *S&H.,* p. 162.
148. Quoted in Alfred Farlow, "Christian Science and the Emmanuel Movement," Archives.

Cabot of the Harvard Medical School. Cabot maintained that the Christian Scientists gravely erred by refusing to cooperate with physicians, especially in the diagnosis of disease.[149] (It should be noted, though, that Mrs. Eddy permitted Christian Science practitioners to consult with a medical doctor on the anatomy involved in cases which they had failed to cure.)[150]

Though sometimes they acknowledged their debt to Christian Science, the leaders of the Emmanuel Movement were generally critical of it for what seemed to them its extremism. The Christian Scientists, on the other hand, were just as critical of the Emmanuel Movement. Often they did express their satisfaction that Mrs. Eddy's teaching had had so great an influence as to spark a movement of this kind. Yet from their own standpoint they could claim that the workers in the Emmanuel Movement lacked real trust in God, for they limited His healing power. Further, they argued that healing in the Emmanuel Movement was wrought through the action of mortal mind, which in Christian Science is seen to be capable of all error and the cause of all disease. Christian Science maintained that divine power will cure any disease in proportion as one discerns the spiritual fact in place of the distorted material appearance. But the leaders of the Emmanuel Movement, in the words of the Reverend Lyman Powell, claimed only that when "faith is added to suggestion and the two are exercised within the bounds designated by scientific medicine, many functional disorders can be completely cured, and ameliorating conditions brought about even in some other ailments." [151]

More than a decade before the Emmanuel Movement got started, Mrs. Eddy wrote, "If the lives of Christian Scientists attest their fidelity to Truth, I predict that in the twentieth century every Christian church in our land, and a few in far-off lands, will approximate the understanding of Christian Science sufficiently to heal the sick in his name." [152] But she also consistently maintained that the healing power of Christian Science is inseparable from its theology. In effect, the Emmanuel Movement represented an effort to duplicate the Christian Scientists' healing works, but leave their theology behind. Therefore to Mrs. Eddy's followers, its rise in response to Christian Science seemed a limited triumph at best.

149. Farlow, "Christian Science."
150. *Man.,* p. 47.
151. Lyman P. Powell, *The Emmanuel Movement in a New England Town* (New York, 1909), pp. 33–34.
152. Eddy, "Pulpit and Press," p. 22.

Promise and Fulfillment

Probably the most important but least accessible aspect of any religious movement is its impact on the individuals who embrace its teaching. This point is especially significant in the case of a religious teaching which claimed to make a real difference in men's lives and which was so often extolled by its adherents as a practical form of Christianity. The most tangible manifestation of the practicality of Christian Science lay, of course, in the healings which it effected. But the real meaning of healing must be understood in terms of its impact upon religious belief. For Christian Science claimed to offer men a new and vital religious alternative wherein Christian promises were to be fulfilled through the revivification of spiritual power. In practice, as we shall see, Mrs. Eddy's teaching was subject to the process of secularization. But in intent and to a significant degree in actuality, it marked a definite and distinctive alternative to other forms of religious thought and practice — especially the Social Gospel, which was the major innovation within American Protestantism during the late nineteenth century.

"THE POWER OF THE WORD"

In the preface to *Science and Health,* Mrs. Eddy gave clear statement to the basis of Christian Science healing practice. "The physical healing of Christian Science," she explained, "results now, as in Jesus' time, from the operation of divine Principle, before which sin and disease lose their reality in human consciousness and disappear as naturally and as necessarily as darkness gives place to light and sin to reformation." [1] Taken on its own terms, there is nothing mystical about this passage; for it asserts that there is an understandable principle on the basis of which sin, disease, and death can be effaced in human consciousness. Note too Mrs. Eddy's assertion that this process takes place in *human consciousness* — just where the claims of suffering and pain seem to obtain. This healing, Mrs. Eddy maintains, is an integral part of the salvation of mankind from the claims of the flesh. Salvation in this sense is not a remote eventuality but an immediate possibility to be achieved step by step. From a human standpoint, of course, healing appears as an improvement of the human condition. But in terms of its ultimate spiritual purpose, healing is a step on the way to the proof of man's spiritual perfection in Science. If man's spiritual selfhood is not that of a material creature subject to disease, pain, and eventual death, then the overcoming of physical disorders on a spiritual basis constitutes a partial advance in the demonstration of his true being. Mrs. Eddy always insists that one must begin right where he is to demonstrate his true spiritual status. Commenting on the text from John, "The Word was made flesh," she wrote, "Divine Truth must be known by its effects on the body as well as on the mind before the Science of being can be demonstrated." [2]

There is a certain strain of no-nonsense practicality in Mrs. Eddy's writing on this point—an insistence that the practical requirement for the demonstration of spiritual healing power not be avoided, an abhorrence of evasions, and a distrust of abstractions. "The proof of what you apprehend, in the simplest definite and absolute form of healing," she once admonished her followers, "can alone answer this question of how much you understand of Christian Science Mind-healing." [3] Metaphysics, Mrs. Eddy insisted, could be meaningful only when put into practice. Mere belief in metaphysical abstractions seemed to her quite meaningless. "Who ever heard of trying to believe in the Mozart *Requiem* or in a Strauss waltz?" she asked in an early defense of her teaching.[4] And in *Science and Health* she made a consistent distinction between *belief,* the mere acceptance of Christian Science, *faith,* the disposition to trust in God and rely on His power for healing, and *understanding,* the spiritual perception which enables one to practically demonstrate divine power. Mrs. Eddy's followers echoed her continued emphasis upon the practical demonstration of divine power in articles they wrote for the Christian

---

1. *S&H.,* p. xi.   2. *S&H.,* p. 350.   3. *Rud.,* pp. 6–7.
4. Mary Baker Eddy, Letter to the *Lynn Transcript,* June 5, 1878.

Science periodicals, with such titles as, "Theory Becomes Practice," "Prayer in Daily Life," "Christian Science is Practical Christianity," "Dynamic Christianity," and "Demonstrating Christian Science."

There was, it is true, a certain abstraction in the demeanor of some of Mrs. Eddy's followers — a remoteness from experience which belies the whole tenor of her teaching. In 1854, Thoreau recorded in his journal that he had met "with several people who cannot afford to be simple and true men, but personate, so to speak, their own ideal of themselves, trying to make the manner supply the place of the man." [5] Such types were not uncommon in the Christian Science movement, though they were far from a majority. People of this kind were often obsessed with "high thoughts" and seemed to be wholly occupied with them. They affected a weird metaphysical pietism, and seemed to float somewhere over the surface of life. Elbert Hubbard, who was not without sympathy for Mrs. Eddy's teaching, noted that some Christian Scientists had a "plaster-Paris smile . . . that refused to vacate its premises." [6] Some of the more ethereal of Mrs. Eddy's followers also affected a high-pitched, super-ficially sweet tone of voice — so that Ezra Pound, for example, could readily identify a woman he referred to in a letter as having "a Christian Science voice." [7]

This tendency toward abstraction in some of Mrs. Eddy's followers was reflected in their rather odd and evasive patterns of speech. Mrs. Eddy did teach that things were not what they appeared and that sense impressions were deceptive. In this sense, one could speak of disease as a "belief," or of some accident or disaster as not having taken place at the level of basic reality. To many people, Mrs. Eddy's denial of common sense perception even when correctly explained seemed hard to take. But when her followers casually referred to apparent realities as unrealities, they made Christian Science look ridiculous. A young man recalled in a testimony that when he first became interested in Mrs. Eddy's teaching, he asked a Christian Scientist at his boarding house about it. At the conclusion of her high flown remarks he asked her if she meant that according to Christian Science, all physical objects have existence only in the imagination. Yes, she said, everything about them is only a "delusion of the senses." "Well," the young man replied, "I guess if I were to bump

5. Quoted in Joel Porte, *Emerson and Thoreau: Transcendentalists in Conflict* (Middletown, Conn., 1965).

6. Quoted in Freedman Little Champhey, *Art and Glory: The Story of Elbert Hubbard* (New York, 1968), p. 147.

7. D. D. Paige, ed., *The Letters of Ezra Pound, 1907–1941* (New York, 1950), 17.

your head against the table you would think it was something more than imagination." [8] Concluding his remarks, he said that later he came to understand Christian Science in quite a different sense than the woman had presented it to him.

Yet the attitude she typified was often expressed in the movement, and the response it evoked from her inquirer was characteristic of the amazement with which many people greeted such pronouncements. Some Scientists prefaced almost any reference with *seem* or *seeming,* saying that they "seemed to have a cold" or had a "seeming headache." One woman was even reported to have referred in a testimony to her "seeming husband." Stories went the rounds of Christian Scientists in the last stages of some horrible infirmity stoutly reiterating that there was nothing really wrong with them. One old tale relates that a member of a Christian Science family asked to have carved on his tombstone the words "Told you I was sick." In a more serious vein, Christian Scientists were sometimes charged with cruelty for failing to acknowledge and minister to human suffering.

Whatever some Christian Scientists' language, however, it was probably quite rare for their human sympathies to be dampened by their conviction that evil was ultimately unreal. But Mrs. Eddy apparently felt that such instances were not rare enough. For in *Science and Health* she condemned as "superficial and cold" telling cripples "Nothing ails you." She wrote that "Sickness is neither imaginary nor unreal, — that is, to the frightened, false sense of the patient. Sickness is more than fancy; it is solid conviction." [9] In Christian Science, the assertion of the ultimate unreality of evil and the allness of God is no warrant for ignoring human suffering. Rather, it establishes a basis upon which disease and suffering can be destroyed. And the healing work of the practitioner, Mrs. Eddy insisted, can be effective only if it is impelled by a true affection which recognizes and responds to human need.

By conviction and temperament, Mrs. Eddy was actually quite far removed from the more ethereal of her followers. In William James' terms, she was in some ways more tough-minded than tender-minded. Her speech was sometimes frighteningly direct, and her impatience with high-minded affectations scarcely concealed. "Scientific growth," Mrs. Eddy once wrote, "manifests no weakness, no emasculation, no illusive vision, no dreamy absentness." [10] And when her followers did manifest these

8. Gottleib A. Wizner, "How I Came Into Christian Science and What It Has Done for Me," *CSS,* II (Sept. 21, 1899), p. 42.
9. *S&H.,* p. 460.   10. *Mis.,* p. 206.

traits, she called them down. In one of her classes in the 1880s, for example, a student made a statement which Mrs. Eddy regarded as too absolute. "Come down," she told the student. "Your head is way up there in the stars, while the enemy is filling your body with bullets." [11] With the indirect language which some of her followers used Mrs. Eddy had little patience. She told one student not to say that someone has a belief of sickness, but to say simply that he is sick. And when a follower to whom she gave a glass of lemonade said, "This seems very good," Mrs. Eddy countered, "It *is* good. Enjoy it." [12]

If carried sufficiently far, the abstraction manifested in these mannerisms that Mrs. Eddy opposed had very serious consequences for the practice of Christian Science. For some of her nominal followers, dwelling in the cloudland of the absolute was an excuse for failing to confront evil in their immediate experience — or, worse, a rationalization for committing it. For an example of this tendency, we can turn again to Mrs. Stetson, who is generally reliable as a source for illustrations of the distorted practice of Christian Science. In examining Mrs. Stetson's students as to her conduct and teaching, the Board of Directors of The Mother Church had great difficulty in getting direct replies to their questions. For the testifiers could avoid unpleasant issues by speaking from the standpoint of "the absolute." On this basis, they could claim that Mrs. Stetson had never made certain damaging statements, since such statements were made "in the relative." When one of them was asked if she were testifying in the absolute on a certain point, she said, "certainly — I try to stay where Mrs. Eddy tries to take us. There is no human place. I recognize only one." The Board discovered that in *civil suits* Mrs. Stetson's students at her instruction had testified "in the absolute." In this way, they could deny things that they did not wish the court to believe were true, but which in fact were true. The First Reader of Mrs. Stetson's church reported that when he saw what sort of legerdemain she was counseling her students to practice, "It began to dawn on me that by this sort of reasoning I might commit murder or arson, and if by any mischance I should be caught, I could say I had never done it, and would go scot-free simply because it was the human that did it, and that was not me." [13]

This, of course, was sheer Gnosticism, thoroughly opposed to the spirit of Christian Science, as the disciplining of Mrs. Stetson well shows. Mrs. Eddy's theological critics, of course, often spoke of the Gnostic indul-

11. Knapp, *Ira Oscar Knapp*, p. 15.
12. Edward Norwood Reminiscences, Archives.
13. Swihart, *Since Mrs. Eddy.*

gence of evil as the inescapable consequence of her teaching. But she saw it as the worst possible distortion of that teaching. Both privately and publicly, Christian Scientists spoke out against it frequently and forcefully. Referring to Mrs. Eddy's insistence that sin be uncovered and repented of, Judge Hanna wrote,

The contrast between this doctrine — which is consistent with Mrs. Eddy's teaching throughout — and the notions of those within our ranks who believe that they have overcome the claims of evil to such an extent that they can live and are living, in what they are pleased to call the "absolute," is so great that one cannot but wish that this class would come down from their high altitude and go wrestling with evil to its overthrow in their consciousness, for sooner or later this must be done.[14]

This "wrestling with evil to its overthrow" — the practical destruction of evil in consciousness and experience — is central to the intent of Mrs. Eddy's teaching. Indeed, she was convinced that the redeeming power of true Christianity extended past the eradication of sin to the healing of disease and eventually death. It is at this point that the topic of physical healing, as the most tangible manifestation of the practical thrust of Mrs. Eddy's teaching, requires more sustained attention.

As the foregoing discussion suggests, it was entirely characteristic of Mrs. Eddy to stake her claims for Christian Science in its ability to prove itself in practice. As she well knew, the future of the movement would be decided neither in Boston nor in Concord, but "in the field." Not that she believed that the healing efficacy of Christian Science as such gave it authority; for that authority, she maintained, lay in revelation. But Mrs. Eddy did maintain that people would be individually convinced of the truth of her teaching as it bore fruit in experience. On the basis of demonstration, of actual provability, Christian Science would have, as she put it, "a fair fight."

"Testimony in regard to healing of the sick is highly important," Mrs. Eddy wrote in the *Manual*: "More than a mere rehearsal of blessings, it scales the pinnacles of praise and illustrates the demonstration of Christ." [15] Certainly testimony of Christian Science healing was the most powerful single advertiser for Mrs. Eddy's teaching. It was circulated by word of mouth, in the Wednesday evening meetings, and in the regular sections devoted to accounts of healing in the *Journal* and *Sentinel*. The publication of written testimonies in the periodicals began with the print-

14. Hanna Reminiscences.   15. *Man.*, p. 47.

ing of "Letters from the Field" in the early *Journals.* These letters touched upon many other matters besides physical healings, and it was only in 1889 that a section of each issue was devoted specifically to testimonies of healing. Just how important Mrs. Eddy considered these testimonies can be seen in a letter she wrote to the editor of the periodicals in 1903, when she felt that an insufficient number of healing accounts were being printed: "I started this great work and *woke the people* by demonstration. Our periodicals must have more testimonials in them. The *Sentinel* is of late a Shakespeare without a Hamlet. . . . Healing is the best sermon, healing is the best lecture, and the entire demonstration of C.S." [16]

Of course, Mrs. Eddy's followers felt that Christian Science healing embraced far more than the cure of bodily disorders. As we shall see, they believed that divine power extended to "the healing of the nations"; and they also spoke of it as operative in the more personal areas of business activity and financial supply. They told, further, of demonstrating Christian Science in the working out of personal relationships, in the making of a decision, or the finding of lost articles. Christian Scientists believed, too, that unfavorable weather conditions could be dispelled through demonstration. Indeed, a practicing Christian Scientist was likely to resort to prayer in almost every sort of problematic situation. One of them told in 1891, for example, of having frustrated an attempt by a band of robbers to steal the money from a train on which he was riding in Utah: the robbers detached the wrong box car.[17] It should be recalled, also, that Mrs. Eddy subordinated the healing of sickness to the healing of sin; and many Christian Scientists spoke of having been healed of the desire for alcohol or tobacco, or in some instances regenerated from lives of sensual indulgence and crime. Yet unquestionably, physical healing was and remains the most conspicuous single aspect of Christian Science healing. Most first generation Christian Scientists were converted through the healing of a physical disorder, and Mrs. Eddy's teaching aroused as much opposition among those who considered it a menace to public health as it did among the clergy. The character of Christian Science healing practice, therefore, deserves to be discussed in greater detail.

The significance of Christian Science healing lies not in the mere fact of its occurrence, but in how it is effected and what it means in religious terms. Mind-curers, Mrs. Eddy acknowledged, did produce what appeared to be physical healings; but they did so through the exercise of that very

16. Mary Baker Eddy to Archibald McClellan, June 19, 1903. Longyear.
17. *CSJ*, XIV (May 1896), 84–85.

same material mentality which produced disease in the first place. From Mrs. Eddy's standpoint, therefore, their practice was spiritually regressive and of no positive religious significance. Regular medical practitioners, she acknowledged, were often noble in their aims and more honest in their methods than mind-curers; but they too worked through the modes of mortal mind, and the consequence of whatever cures they effected was not, as in Christian Science, the spiritual growth as well as the physical healing of the patient.

What, then, is the character of Christian Science healing as a religious experience? One of Mrs. Eddy's poems, which has been set to music as a hymn, begins with words that suggest an answer to this question:

> Saw ye my Saviour? Heard ye the glad sound?
> Felt ye the power of the Word? [18]

The whole dynamic behind the growth of the Christian Science movement lies in the fact that Mrs. Eddy's followers overwhelmingly believed that they had felt the power of the Word through an experience of healing.

The healing experiences to which they testified vary quite widely, both with respect to the ills treated and the character of the treatment. And it is difficult to make meaningful generalizations which can illuminate the character of a Christian Science healing experience. But despite this variety, there are certain key elements common to every healing experience. These are 1) the willingness of the patient or those responsible for him to turn to Christian Science and rely upon spiritual power for healing; 2) the act of prayer itself through which the healing is effected; 3) the objectification of the healing in a changed physical condition, and the consequent validation of the reality of spiritual healing power. The exact character of each of these elements in the healing experience differs from case to case, yet their presence in some form in every case identifies them as what one might call the structural elements in the healing experience. And through an analysis of each in turn, we can better grasp the character of Christian Science healing as a religious experience.

A Christian Scientist wrote that a friend once said to her of Mrs. Eddy's teaching: "My dear, it is too radical." "Take away the radicalism," the Christian Scientist replied, "and there is nothing left of it." [19] Not the

18. "Communion Hymn," *Mis.,* pp. 398–399.
19. *CSJ*, II (Feb. 1885), 5.

least aspect of the radicalism of Christian Science was Mrs. Eddy's demand on her followers for "radical reliance upon Truth" in the treatment of disease. The paragraph from *Science and Health* which contains this phrase is an important one, and it would be well to have it before us:

> The "flesh lusteth against the Spirit." The flesh and Spirit can no more unite in action, than good can coincide with evil. It is not wise to take a halting and half-way position or to expect to work equally with Spirit and matter, Truth and error. There is but one way — namely, God and His idea — which leads to spiritual being. The scientific government of the body must be obtained through the divine Mind. It is impossible to gain control over the body in any other way. On this fundamental point, timid conservatism is absolutely inadmissible. Only through radical reliance on Truth can scientific healing power be realized.[20]

Some Christian Scientists, it is true, suffering from diseases they could not cure or under the influence of solicitous relatives or friends, did go back to the use of medicine. It was conceivable that if this sort of retreat was infrequent, one could remain a member of a Christian Science church. But no one could be a conscientious Christian Scientist who relied generally upon the use of medicine.

Mrs. Eddy's insistence upon "radical reliance on Truth," however, was somewhat tempered by compromise. It was noted in an earlier chapter that she sanctioned the use of hypodermic injections for the relief of Christian Scientists from extreme pain, so that they might later handle their own case mentally. Also, Christian Scientists generally, including Mrs. Eddy, availed themselves of the services of dentists and oculists. Indeed, for a time in the 1880s advertisements for dentists could be found in the *Journal* immediately following those of Christian Science practitioners. There could be no ultimate justification for these concessions; and Christian Scientists were more conscious in this early period than at present that the use of glasses and the resort to dentists were unfortunate, but practically necessary, compromises. They especially rejoiced, therefore, when they were able to testify that through the practice of Christian Science poor eyesight or dental troubles had been overcome.

In the first years of the twentieth century the practice of Christian Science was threatened by a wave of legal actions, which will be discussed at a later point. In these new circumstances Mrs. Eddy felt it necessary to caution her followers on several counts. In the *Journal* for March 1901, she announced that Christian Scientists must submit to vaccination when

20. *S&H.*, p. 167.

compulsory and report cases of contagion as required by law. In December of the following year she advised them temporarily to "decline to doctor infectious or contagious diseases." She also wrote that Christian Scientists should

be influenced by their own judgment in taking a case of malignant disease. They should consider well their ability to cope with the claim, and they should not overlook the fact that there are those lying in wait to catch them in their sayings; neither should they forget that in their practice, whether successful or not, *they are not specially protected by law*.[21]

Three years later, in view of the continuing legal threat to Christian Science practice, Mrs. Eddy called her followers' attention to counsel which had in substance been a part of *Science and Health* from the beginning:

Until the advancing age admits the efficacy and supremacy of Mind, it is better for Christian Scientists to leave surgery and the adjustment of broken bones and dislocations to the fingers of a surgeon, while the mental healer confines himself chiefly to mental reconstruction and to the prevention of inflammation. Christian Science is always the most skillful surgeon, but surgery is the branch of healing which will be last acknowledged.

In the final edition of *Science and Health,* it should be noted, Mrs. Eddy qualified this statement with the testimony that through "mental surgery" alone, she and her students had cured "broken bones, dislocated joints, and spinal vertebrae." [22]

Even were a Christian Scientist to make concessions in all the areas in which Mrs. Eddy said it was permissible to do so, however, he would still be under the obligation to rely upon spiritual healing in the vast majority of possible disorders. The areas in which she was willing to compromise were limited. She did advise that Christian Scientists not take surgical cases. But it should be remembered that in her day surgery was employed in far fewer types of diseases than at present, and that she regarded it largely as a mechanical aid in cases of torn flesh and broken bones. As the art of surgery expanded its domain in the years after her death, some Christian Scientists resorted to surgery for the cure of disorders which could not have been treated in that way when she was alive. Though they could justify so doing on the basis of Mrs. Eddy's own words, changing conditions made their actions a clear violation of her

21. "Wherefore," *My.,* p. 227.
22. "Christian Science and the Episcopal Congress," *Boston Herald,* Dec. 2, 1900. The reference is to *S&H.,* p. 401.

intent. For that intent plainly was that except in certain limited areas Christian Scientists should rely upon prayer for healing.

This demand was often extremely taxing on the faith of Mrs. Eddy's followers. Many of them reported that at some point, usually in the early stages of their practice of Christian Science, they were tempted to go back to reliance upon medicine. One man wrote that when he was new in Christian Science, some friends prevailed upon him to take medicine for an ailment. But this surrender gave him no peace, and a Christian Scientist advised him that he could not improve until he threw his medicines away. "I could see nothing but the demand of Truth to destroy them. For long hours I argued the case, and then got up, opened my traveling bag, and commenced the work of destruction." [23] Radical as this commitment might seem to those outside the movement, convinced Christian Scientists saw it as an expression in Mrs. Eddy's terms, of "a reasonable faith in the omnipotence of good." [24] And this faith, they felt, was justified in other instances as in this by the accomplishment of the work of healing.

Christian Science claimed to heal all manner of diseases through spiritual power alone. What was the nature of this power and how did it operate? These questions seemed quite mysterious to many observers. Indeed, the mere fact that Christian Science treatment involved no visible action of any sort was often a source of puzzlement to those outside the movement. In 1884 the *Boston Morning Journal* noted that the method of Christian Science healing "is a simple one and likely to try the faith of the patient to the utmost. It consists in sitting quiet and doing nothing." [25] The Christian Scientist, however, would have claimed that in giving a treatment he was doing real work, mental work as it was often called in the movement, though Mrs. Eddy never used the term in this sense. To her Christian Science treatment was truly prayer, as she indicated in the opening sentence of the first chapter of *Science and Health*: "The prayer that reforms the sinner and heals the sick is an absolute faith that all things are possible to God, — a spiritual understanding of Him, an unselfed love." [26] The prayer that is involved in this treatment is far more than the thinking of pleasant thoughts. It is a sustained and sometimes lengthy process whereby the practitioner works at the problem of healing conscientiously, systematically, and specifically.

23. *CSJ*, IX (Oct. 1891), 281.　　　24. *Mis.*, p. 200.
25. *Boston Morning Journal*, May 10, 1884.
26. *S&H.*, p. 1.

Aside from the fact that it involved no apparent activity, the oddest thing about Christian Science treatment to outsiders was that it could be carried on across long distances. In Boston during the 1880s, "absent treatment" was a frequent target of ridicule; and ministers sometimes declared that it savored of witchcraft. But to Mrs. Eddy and her followers, "absent treatment" was no mystery and hardly witchcraft — though wrong use of mental powers certainly was. As she explained it, "Science can heal the sick, who are absent from their healers, as well as those present, since space is no obstacle to Mind." [27] Elsewhere she wrote that "Christian Science, recognizing the capabilities of Mind to act of itself, and independent of matter, enables one to heal cases without even having seen the individual, — or simply after having been made acquainted with the mental condition of the patient." [28] As precedent for their claims, Christian Scientists often point to Scriptural examples of healing from a distance, such as Jesus' cure of the centurion's servant, recorded in the Gospel of Matthew.

In many instances those outside the movement receiving Christian Science treatment had little or no idea of what was being done for them. Mrs. Eddy had said that an atheist could be healed in Christian Science; and a number of testifiers in the periodicals reported that at the time of their healing, they had no faith whatever. In some cases, too, those needing aid might be unconscious or in a coma when Christian Science treatment was begun. Many people who had played a completely passive role in their own healing later testified that only after their recovery had convinced them of the truth of Christian Science did they take up its study. Usually, though, a practitioner would recommend that a new patient study *Science and Health,* other items of Christian Science literature, or certain passages from the Bible while the work was being done. Perhaps, too, he might suggest that the patient hold some simple spiritual truth clearly in thought to aid his receptivity. According to Christian Scientists' accounts, a number of cases were often treated in one or more visits of practitioner and patient. Often in such instances the practitioner would treat the case audibly, trying to rouse the patient's thought into the spiritual perception needed for healing. Indeed, Mrs. Eddy once wrote that she had healed "more disease by the spoken than the unspoken word." [29]

A large proportion of those willing to try Christian Science healing did not resort to a practitioner at all, but simply studied *Science and Health*

27. *Ibid.,* p. 179.　　28. *Mis.,* p. 43.　　29. *No.,* p. 2.

on their own. The last chapter of the book, called "Fruitage," is composed of a hundred pages of testimonies by those who had been healed in this manner. Often in their desperation, so they often testified, the sick would study the book by the hour; and as they did so, the light would break in on them and they would realize that they had been healed. For many such people, *Science and Health* took the place of the medicine which they had forsaken as useless. As one Christian Scientist wrote of his brother's protracted recovery from a serious illness, "For months during his struggle *Science and Health* by Mrs. Eddy, or passages from this inspired book, were kept within immediate reach and were eagerly absorbed by him mentally as the tonic or pellet would be taken by one who had faith in the medicine prescribed by a physician." [30] A number of Christian Scientists, whose healing had been protracted, like the one referred to above, counted the long period of preliminary study and struggle a blessing. Had their recoveries been rapid, they often said, there would have been no incentive for them to get to know Christian Science; rather, they would merely have rejoiced in improved health and gone about their business spiritually unchanged. Often it was this study of Mrs. Eddy's writings during the period of recovery that caused future Christian Scientists to think of her teaching not just as a therapeutic agent, but as a religion.

Yet the instantaneous healing of disease remained the ideal in Christian Science treatment. Mrs. Eddy pointed to Jesus' instantaneous healing of the worst forms of disease as the highest ideal to which a Christian Scientist could aspire in the healing work. "If Spirit or the power of divine Love bear witness to the truth," she wrote, "this is the ultimatum, the scientific way, and the healing is instantaneous." [31] Mrs. Eddy herself claimed that at one point when she most clearly discerned that God knew no disease she felt so bound to Him that she was able "instantaneously to heal a cancer which had eaten its way to the jugular vein." [32] She by no means expected this sort of work from all Christian Scientists, however; and most of the healing work was carried on through a process known as argument, specific affirmations of truth and denials of error relative to the problem at hand. In the chapter "Christian Science Practice" in *Science and Health* she gives the general sorts of arguments to be used in handling specific diseases. These arguments, she wrote, may be varied "to meet the peculiar or general symptoms of the case you treat." [33] But the point of the whole process lies in the practitioner's thought being

30. *CSJ*, XXVII (May 1909), 107.   31. *S&H.*, p. 411.
32. *Un.*, p. 7.   33. *S&H.*, p. 412.

lifted to inwardly discerning, in Mrs. Eddy's words, "the spiritual fact of whatever the material senses behold." [34] She cautions her readers to "Remember that the letter and mental argument are only human auxiliaries to aid in bringing thought into accord with the spirit of Truth and Love, which heals the sick and the sinner." [35]

Mrs. Eddy insisted, therefore, that whatever the arguments employed, the healing work must never be reduced to a mere repetition of formulas, and in the *Manual* she includes an article forbidding the use of formulas in Christian Science practice.[36] Her insistence on this point marks one clear difference between Christian Science and mind-cure, in which the use of formulas was quite common — "Dr." Hazzard's earlier-quoted "Prayer for a Dyspeptic" is a clear, if somewhat outlandish example. In Christian Science each treatment must be unique, a matter of inspiration. It cannot be reduced to a routine procedure, however much technical competence in healing a practitioner must gain. Important in this connection is the fact that Mrs. Eddy devoted the first six pages of her chapter on "Christian Science Practice" in *Science and Health* to a discussion of the motives for mental practice rather than its methods. In these pages she points to the necessity for the practitioner to approach his work compassionately, with a true affection for humanity. "If the Scientist reaches his patient through divine Love," she wrote, "the healing work will be accomplished at one visit, and the disease will vanish into its native nothingness like dew before the morning sunshine." [37]

It was, however, this "divine Love," and not the practitioner as such that Mrs. Eddy felt actually accomplished the healing work. As we have seen, her controversy with the mind-curers hinged upon her repudiation of the belief that genuine healing can result from the action of mind on mind. Strictly speaking, it is not proper for a Christian Scientist to speak of himself as having healed anything (though at times, as in the quotation cited earlier about the healing of cancer, Mrs. Eddy herself does so). In Christian Science, healing is understood to proceed from "the operation of divine Principle," as Mrs. Eddy puts it, and not from the power of human thought. Indeed, Mrs. Eddy wrote that the human mind is not "a spiritual factor in the healing work." [38] The natural question that arises here is: How is the practitioner involved in the healing? One article for the *Sentinel* dealt with this problem in these terms: "The Christian Scientist does not pretend to do the healing. He only serves as a means

34. *Ibid.*, p. 585. 35. *Ibid.*, pp. 454–455. 36. *Man.*, 43.
37. *S&H.*, p. 365. 38. *Ibid.*, p. 185.

through which the Truth which heals is brought to the consciousness of the patient."[39] A formulation of the Christian Scientists' general position on the subject might read: the practitioner deals with the false beliefs which the patient is entertaining within his own thought, dispelling them as he discerns the spiritual fact in place of the material appearance, and the patient responds, not to the practitioner's thought as such, but to the power of Truth which he has understood relative to the false beliefs the patient has held.

Let us say that the practitioner is called upon to treat a case of blindness. He might consider Mrs. Eddy's statement: "Sight, hearing, all the spiritual senses of man, are eternal. They cannot be lost. Their reality and immortality are in Spirit and understanding, not in matter, — hence their permanence."[40] This statement would indicate to the practitioner the spiritual fact "in Science" — man's perfect capacity to see. The material sense testimony, however, would indicate that man sees through a visual organism, and that some material condition has impaired the individual's capacity to see. The practitioner would dwell upon the spiritual fact of the situation, trying to discern that man's capacity to see is perfect and indestructible. He would also mentally refute the material evidence, realizing that what appears as the eye simply manifests the sense of sight that his patient is entertaining. As the practitioner inwardly beholds the spiritual fact of perfect sight, the power of Truth dispels the false sense of sight and the patient is healed.

As this brief discussion suggests, the real healing is conceived of in Christian Science as a spiritual breakthrough that takes place in the patient's consciousness, as he yields to the spiritual truth that the practitioner has discerned through the act of prayer. The physical healing, which according to Christian Science inevitably follows, is only the outward manifestation of this change in consciousness. The discernment of the spiritual fact will *appear* as the normalization of the physical condition, even though the actual healing is not in the first instance physical at all. This explanation, of course, states the case from the Scientists' perspective. For the non-Scientist or even the potential convert, healing meant an objective change in the physical condition. And Mrs. Eddy's followers maintained that through the practice of Christian Science these changes definitely did occur.

39. Alfred Farlow, "God's Creation Real," *CSS*, III (Oct. 25, 1900), 117.
40. *S&H.*, p. 486.

Not all testimonies of Christian Science healing report the cure of definite diseases of a serious nature. As noted earlier, some of them do not deal with the healing of physical disorders at all. Moreover, some of the physical healings that Christian Scientists reported involved purely nervous disorders or illnesses that may well have been nervous in origin. A number of testimonies referred, sometimes in quite vague terms, to such complaints as dyspepsia, back pains, and general nervous debility. Sometimes a testifier would relate that he — or in most instances, she — had been for years an invalid, but would give no specific cause for the condition. Such accounts have sometimes been cited as evidence for the claim that Christian Science is effective only for the cure of nervous disorders, but has no efficacy in cases of actual physical disease. Bronson Alcott voiced this view in 1879 when he wrote of Mrs. Eddy that she may have the "skill to remove, perhaps cure, some of the nervous maladies incident to improper modes of diet and regimen, both of body and mind." [41] Later, many members of the medical profession were to use a similar argument in challenging the Scientists' claims. Even so, some commentators on Christian Science noted that the cure of a nervous ailment was no mean achievement. "Whence comes the idea that an 'imaginary' disease is a small matter?" asked a writer for *The Monist* in 1902. "If one were to choose between being hit by an express train and having his legs broken, and being missed and having his legs paralyzed by nervous shock, he would far better take the hit." [42]

Yet the Scientists claimed to heal far more than nervous or imaginary diseases. They often pointed to the large mass of testimonies in which the disorders healed were definitely not nervous in origin; chronic headaches or dyspepsia could be a nervous condition; cancer or a broken bone could not. And in almost every issue of the *Journal* and *Sentinel* one can find one or more accounts of the healing of such severe disorders as cancer, broken bones, third-degree burns, blindness, deafness, leprosy, epilepsy, Bright's disease, heart disease, pneumonia, appendicitis, scarlet fever, and a wide variety of other diseases. Further, Christian Scientists often testified to the cure of diseases in the severest forms. For in many instances the cases that fell to Christian Science were those which medicine had failed to reach; and when a practitioner was brought in as a last resort, the disease had often reached a critical or sometimes terminal stage. The ranks of the movement, it was said, had been "recruited from the graveyard."

41. Alcott, *Journals,* p. 489.
42. Edward T. Brewster, "The Evolution of Christian Science," *The Monist,* XVII (April 1907), 186.

As an example of what might be called a "hard-core" testimony of recovery from extreme physical illness, we can cite the following account published in the *Christian Science Sentinel* in 1908. The testimony was provided by Dr. Edmund F. Burton, who had been a member of the surgical staff at Cook County Hospital in Chicago and an instructor at Rush Medical College. The rapid development of tuberculosis of the lungs forced him to leave both posts. Burton went to Arizona, then to California, in an effort to overcome the disease. But his condition rapidly deteriorated. In addition, he became dependent on the use of heavy drugs, having used morphine to dull pain and then resorted to cocaine to compensate for the dulling effects of the morphine. Finally, he suffered a complete breakdown, his stomach refused to digest food, and he lapsed into a period of unconsciousness lasting over forty-eight hours. Burton's account continues:

A number of physicians who had known me for several months, in consultation pronounced me incurable, and told my friends that I had from a few days to a few weeks to live. A private sanitarium to which my wife applied refused to admit me on account of the hopelessness of the case. . . .

During the evening following this verdict a lady suggested with much trepidation the advisability of calling a Christian Science practitioner, and my wife consented that this be done, not with a feeling that anything could be accomplished, but in the same spirit of desperation in which any other harmless although probably useless thing would have been allowed. A practitioner came and remained with me three hours. At the end of the first hour I was sleeping quietly, and when I awoke about eight o'clock in the morning it was with a clear mind and the absolute conviction, which has not changed since, that I was free and well. I asked what had been done for me, insisting that a radical change had taken place in my physical and mental condition. Naturally the conviction that I had been healed came very slowly to those about me, and it was months before it was fully acknowledged, but to me there was such a mental change from the first there was no room for doubt. There is no need here to give figures, although I shall be glad to do so privately to any one, physician or layman, but I will say that so far as I know there is no instance in medical literature of the recovery of any one taking the amount of these drugs which I was taking up to the time referred to. And to one who knows the state of the nervous system and of the digestive organs which exists in such cases, it is stating it mildly to say that the most remarkable feature of the cure was that there was no period of convalescence. From the time of my waking on the morning following the treatment there was no nervousness or twitching, sleep was natural and quiet, appetite healthy, digestive functions all in good working order, and mind clear and composed. The same afternoon

I drove my automobile for two hours without weariness or excitement of any kind. During the following thirty days I gained thirty pounds in weight.
. . . I was forced by my own healing to the conclusion that there was a power in Christian Science of which I had never taken account.[43]

One could, of course, simply maintain that Burton and others whose testimony seemed equally conclusive were mistaken or lying in their reports of such impressive cures. Skepticism in this matter is natural. It is true that thoroughgoing medical examination of individual cases of Christian Science healing would have been helpful in establishing their validity. But it should be kept in mind that Christian Scientists did not treat their patients under controlled experimental conditions, and that therefore in the very nature of the situation conclusive documentary evidence is generally lacking. Indeed, the testimony concerning Christian Science healing is so massive, the criteria for evaluating it so debatable, and the medical questions involved so complex, that a full study of the subject would require a work at least as long as the present one. And even if one admits that a substantial number of testimonies reporting recoveries from severe or terminal illnesses are true, he still may not be led to embrace Christian Science. Many who admitted the phenomenal evidence of impressive cures claimed that these were not effected through Christian Science, but came about through unexplained spontaneous recovery, mental suggestion, or according to some ministers, through the work of the devil. Much work undoubtedly remains to be done in assessing the records of Christian Science healing, yet it is clear in literally hundreds of cases that something happened of so radical a nature as to decisively convince the testifiers of the reality of spiritual healing power.

ROOTS OF THE CONVERSION EXPERIENCE

It would be easy enough to say that the Christian Science movement attracted converts because it held out the promise of physical healing, and it is indisputable that most of those who embraced the new faith were initially attracted to it for this reason. As we shall see, some nominal Christian Scientists maintained their interest in the religion only because they wanted to keep well. But serious Christian Scientists continued their study of Mrs. Eddy's teaching after an initial healing experience because they felt it contained religious truth. To this group, which probably in-

43. Quoted in Benjamin O. Flower, *Christian Science as a Religious Belief and a Therapeutic Agent* (New York, 1909), pp. 79–84.

cluded most of Mrs. Eddy's followers during our period, a healing was important more as the occasion of a conversion experience than as a physical recovery. Indeed, Christian Science made its deepest appeal not so much to sick bodies as to troubled souls. And the ranks of the movement were recruited from those who had come to despair quite as much of orthodox religion as of *materia medica*.

Though many Christian Scientists had been working members in Protestant churches before their conversions, a significant minority were what can be called religious dropouts. In some cases their religious convictions had been shaken by scientific materialism; more often they had come to doubt orthodoxy through the influence of the higher criticism. Rarely did Christian Scientists testify that before their conversion they had embraced agnosticism or outright atheism. Those who did usually gave evidence of being people who had a strong interest in religious questions, despite their apostasy. A Christian Scientist from Connecticut, for example, wrote in 1903:

. . . I had been taught to read the Bible and attend church. I went to different churches, talked with ministers and other good people, investigated every religion I could hear of, but was always disappointed. . . . I read the Bible, but it seemed to contradict itself, and to tell of a God who made mistakes and corrected them in anger afterwards. At last I gave up and decided that there was no God or heaven. I was sure only of the hell here on earth. I was never satisfied and was on the verge of suicide when a neighbor asked me to go to a Christian Science meeting with her.[44]

In some cases, Christian Scientists recalled that for years before beginning the study of its teachings they had been utterly indifferent to religion. A few had been living the life of hardened sinners. A Californian wrote that he first studied Mrs. Eddy's writings in his favorite haunt — a saloon;[45] another of her followers testified that before Christian Science found him he was "heading at a rapid rate to eternal smash."[46]

Most converts to Christian Science, however, counted themselves as believing Christians before their conversion, even though they were becoming disenchanted with Protestant orthodoxy. Many who remained active members of churches had long been harboring doctrinal doubts and had pursued their church work with secret misgivings. One woman wrote in 1887 that before coming into Christian Science she had begun to believe that "God knew nothing of church work, especially fairs, tableaux,

44. *CSS*, V (May 2, 1903), 561.   45. *CSJ*, XIV (Feb. 1897), 592–593.
46. *Ibid.*, XII (Dec. 1894), 5

socials, lectures, oyster suppers, and missionary meetings, with ice cream and cake accompaniment, where so much money is raised to help His cause." [47]

Christian Scientists couched their discussions of the failure of Protestant orthodoxy in their lives in different terms. But in essence they had come to feel it inadequate for the same reason that it was losing its hold in the culture generally; for in various ways the implicit spiritual-secular dualism of orthodoxy was vitiating its sustaining meaning in their lives. Just as they spoke of Christian Science healing as physically liberating, so they spoke of its theology as spiritually liberating. It seemed to them to make spiritual power an immediate reality, and to relate the things of religion to the affairs of everyday life. As an acquaintance of Mrs. Eddy's a few years after her discovery noted, she "made a protest against the idea . . . that we should take but little thought as to our bodies and our earthly lives, and consider only the life to come." [48]

To a considerable extent, Mrs. Eddy's experience before 1866 presaged that of converts to Christian Science later. Most basically, the factor that impelled her footsteps leading to Christian Science was her effort to move past the aforementioned Protestant duality. Mrs. Eddy had been raised in a form of Christianity which more than any other exalted God and abased man. What disturbed her most as a young woman about her father's "relentless theology," as she put it, was the same thing that disturbed many another sensitive individual in the early nineteenth century: a view of God which held Him capable of demanding the eternal punishment of all but a handful whom he had selected for salvation. When as a girl she stood out vigorously against the Calvinist doctrine of predestination, she was really protesting the idea that there must be an infinite distance between the divine and the human moral order — that God could be in Himself benign, and yet malign according to human moral perception. As she naïvely put it during her examination for church membership, she was unwilling to be saved if her brothers and sisters were to be damned.

In her later experience, Mrs. Eddy was to find the duality against which she had protested ramified from theology into life. For until her early forties, she endured long years of repeated personal sorrows and chronic ill-health, amounting at last to virtual invalidism. In her responses to the personal calamities that befell her, she tried again and again, but unsuccessfully, to tread the orthodox Christian path of resignation. But

47. *Ibid.*, XV (April 1897), 16.   48. Quoted in Peel, *Discovery*, p. 209.

her interest in life was too strong for these efforts to be successful. In particular, she was influenced by her elder brother Albert Baker, who, as a young apostle of secular Enlightenment, had opened her thinking to education and the possibilities of an improvable present. With her efforts at Christian resignation failing, Mrs. Eddy turned to experimentation with homeopathy and thus set foot on the road that led to Christian Science. Her efforts to find a positive principle of healing — first in homeopathy, then through her relationship with Quimby, finally in the discovery of Christian Science — marked her departure from this path.

In later years, Mrs. Eddy's followers were often to relate how disenchanted they had become with the orthodox idea of resignation to suffering as the will of God in this life, with a promised recompense of bliss in the beyond. One Christian Scientist wrote in 1907 that he had been "embittered by ministerial platitudes, that the ways of Providence are inscrutable, we must not pry into mysteries beyond our understanding, must resign ourselves to inevitable death." [49] Others told of poignant instances in which they had found the idea of resignation emotionally impossible to entertain. One woman whose husband had recently died told in 1891 of her minister's and family's admonishment that "God chastened whom he loved. Oh, how bitter it made me," she commented.[50] Articles in the periodicals often dwelt on the untenability of the idea of resignation. As one of them pointed out, to resign oneself to suffering contradicted man's basic impulse; for people were resigned only "in relation to what they can't prevent. . . . But if they are in any way able to remedy discord, heal disease, or prevent death, they at once proceed to do so, never stopping to think that possibly these threatening evils may be the dispensations of Providence." [51] With obvious point, the *Journal* once reprinted a story about a hardshell Southern Baptist tried in court for resisting the will of God: he had placed a lightning rod on a new house, thus vainly trying to ward off such electric bolts as the Almighty might be pleased to send his way! [52]

That God could visit destruction upon His people or even sanction the existence of evil was another aspect of orthodox teaching which deeply distressed those who were converted to Christian Science. Like many others in the eighteenth and nineteenth centuries, they could not worship a God who seemed morally inferior to his worshippers. Of course, Calvinism had lost its hold in American religious life well before Christian

49. *CSJ*, XXV (June 1907), 234.   50. *Ibid.*, IX (August 1891), 202.
51. *Ibid.*, "Resigned to the Will of God," XVII (April 1899), 69.
52. *Ibid.*, IX (July 1891), 146.

Science began to win converts. Therefore predestination had not presented the problem to those who adopted Mrs. Eddy's teachings that it had to her and others of her generation. But the essential issue involved — the problem of a supposedly good and omnipotent God who could nevertheless cause or sanction evil and suffering — remained real as long as evil was regarded as intrinsic to nature and man. The idea that God could sanction sickness and death seemed to many Christians to detract from the perfection of His nature as much as the belief that He could eternally damn the majority of mankind. One Christian Scientist who said that he had struggled with the problem of evil for thirty years before finding an answer to it in Mrs. Eddy's works declared,

it is impossible to reconcile the existence of evil — sin, disease, and death — with the existence of a benevolent, all-wise, and all-powerful deity. . . . It is stated that suffering is necessary as a discipline to enable man to attain to a higher and better manhood. Why was man so constituted as to make it necessary for him to suffer in order to reach this higher condition? [53]

Another writer for the *Journal* neatly illustrated horror at attributing evil to God by citing the story of a boy looking out of his window and telling his mother what he saw: "It's a funeral, mamma, God has been killing someone else." [54]

As we have seen, Mrs. Eddy maintained that "perfect God and perfect man" was the reality of creation, and that since evil had no legitimate existence one could challenge its claim to power. Her way of treating the problem of evil was thought the Achilles' heel of Christian Science by its critics. But her followers found it far more logical than the conventional Christian explanations which took refuge in the inscrutability of God's purposes to explain the existence of evil. To them it seemed to absolve God of responsibility for or even knowledge of evil, thereby vindicating His total goodness. Moreover, Mrs. Eddy's view of God as wholly good, incapable of causing or countenancing suffering, impelled the conviction that no form of sin, disease, or death should be accounted as spiritually legitimate. Hence Christian Scientists believed that the good life should be established here and now insofar as they were capable of demonstrating it.

For those converted from some form of orthodoxy to Christian Science, healing had religious significance as proof that Christian promises were to be fulfilled in the present. A former Presbyterian wrote in 1909 that he was "dissatisfied with the mystery and contradictions of orthodoxy"

53. *CSS*, III (Nov. 1, 1900), 141.   54. *CSJ*, XV (June 1897), 241.

and with "promises that could not be taken literally." [55] Mrs. Eddy, of course, did take these promises quite literally. In *Science and Health* she quoted Jesus' statement "These signs shall follow them that believe. . . . they shall take up serpents, and if they drink any deadly thing, it shall not hurt them. They shall lay hands on the sick, and they shall recover." Then she commented that "It were well had Christendom believed and obeyed this sacred saying. . . . Jesus' promise is perpetual." [56] To those who had believed that this promise was confined to Jesus' disciples or was for some other reason unrealizable in the present, her claim that spiritual healing power was present and available came as good news indeed. As one of Mrs. Eddy's followers recalled in 1909, "Although a close Bible student, teacher of a Bible class, and the wife of a minister, I gradually awoke to the realization that so far as our children were concerned I was without the least practical trust in the presence and power of God." [57]

For many like-minded Protestants, the lack of healing in orthodoxy was a serious and inexplicable omission in the light of the Gospels. The testimony of one Christian Scientist about his disillusionment with orthodoxy on this score is typical:

I was taken very ill: the minister came. I asked him to pray for me and heal me. He kindly informed me that the day of miracles was past, but that of course he would pray for me. I looked no more to that source for help, for it shook my faith, and I wondered if Christ's saving power were out of date also.[58]

By restoring the faith of her followers in the present reality of spiritual power, Mrs. Eddy made the Bible live again for them. For they saw in the Biblical narratives interpreted in the light of Christian Science the workings of that same spiritual power which she claimed to explain. Dozens of testimonies emphasized, as one of them put it, that "the Bible was a new book after this truth dawned upon me." [59] No words, it is safe to say, could have pleased Mrs. Eddy more.

"TRIALS AND SELF-DENIALS"

In the first flush of a healing experience, grateful for physical recovery and with their old religious doubts resolved, fledgling Christian Scientists were sometimes possessed of an untempered zeal for their new faith.

55. *Ibid.*, XXVII (April 1909), 52.   56. *S&H.*, p. 328.
57. *CSJ*, XXVII (May 1909), 115.   58. *Ibid.*, XII (Aug. 1894), 208–209.
59. *Ibid.*, XXVII (Nov. 1909), 491.

Their inclination often was to talk it from the housetops, and the message they preached was in many cases very far from clear Christian Science. The claims of Christian Science, even when correctly presented, are extraordinary enough; but when incorrectly explained or baldly stated without any explanation at all they seemed strange indeed. The early literature of the movement contains many accounts like that of one young student who tried assiduously to convince a friend that the horse they were looking at was not there.[60] Similarly, some young converts would rush precipitately into the healing work, trying to prove the wonderful value of their new faith by curing anything in sight, and in many instances it seemed to them that their enthusiasm was justified by success. One young Christian Scientist said that through her work, diseases "fled away as clouds sail along the horizon before a still breeze."[61] Often, however, students who had this sort of experience later testified that the healing work grew less easy once they came to grasp the dimensions of what it involved. And every young student who wished to practice seriously faced the eventual necessity of settling down to learn what Christian Science was all about through long, hard study.

This was and remains no mean task; for while Christian Science is not complex intellectually, a real grasp of its teaching requires a great deal of work. Hence it was not unusual for converts to spend many hours a day poring over Mrs. Eddy's writings and other Christian Science literature just trying to assimilate the rudiments of her teaching. But any serious student, no matter how seasoned, found it necessary to devote considerable time to study and prayer. Working Christian Scientists sometimes spent several hours a day in this effort, while public practitioners of Christian Science generally spent a great many more. To begin with, conscientious students of Christian Science would daily spend upwards of half an hour in studying the Lesson Sermons composed of citations from the Bible and *Science and Health* given in the *Christian Science Quarterly* and read aloud in the Sunday church services. Students of Mrs. Eddy's writings might also work with concordances to *Science and Health* and her other works to find everything she had to say on a given subject or even her various uses of a particular word. They might also spend considerable time in the study of the Bible, in keeping up with or contributing to the periodicals of the movement, or in reading other items of Christian Science literature.

The central activity in the life of a working Christian Scientist, how-

60. *Ibid.,* XII (Sept. 1894), 245.   61. *Ibid.,* XVIII (Sept. 1900), 6.

ever, was prayer. Mrs. Eddy considered the subject of such great importance that she devoted the first chapter of *Science and Health* to its consideration. Therein she writes:

To enter into the heart of prayer, the door of the erring senses must be closed.
Lips must be mute and materialism silent, that man may have audience with
Spirit, the divine Principle, Love, which destroys all error.

   In order to pray aright, we must enter into the closet and shut the door.
We must close the lips and silence the material senses. In the quiet sanctuary
of earnest longings, we must deny sin and plead God's allness. We must resolve to take up the cross, and go forth with honest hearts to work and watch
for wisdom, Truth, and Love. We must "pray without ceasing." [62]

As this passage suggests, prayer in Christian Science involves not so much
petitions to God as affirmations of His presence. Prayer might be intended
simply to spiritualize one's thought, to protect oneself from harm, to seek
spiritual guidance, or to effect the healing of disease or sin. It might
require from a few moments of quiet thought to hours of mental effort.
But prayer, as Mrs. Eddy discusses it, is ultimately not so much a specific
act as a frame of mind. In this sense, working Christian Scientists en-
deavored to *live* prayerfully, that is, to approach every situation from the
standpoint of prayer. In the final analysis, this was the most exacting demand involved in the practice of Christian Science; for such prayer
"without ceasing" was an open-end process.

   Prayer in this sense connotes an attitude of thought which subordinates
human will to the requirements of demonstration. This requirement,
which is stressed throughout Mrs. Eddy's writings, is nowhere better set
forth than in the following prayer in the *Manual* which she enjoins Christian Scientists to pray each day: " 'Thy kingdom come'; let the reign of
divine Truth, Life, and Love be established in me, and rule out of me all
sin; and may Thy Word enrich the affections of all mankind, and govern
them." [63] In this prayer, Mrs. Eddy affirms as a present possibility that
man can now literally be actuated and governed by God. As she elsewhere
explained, "Through the accession of spirituality, God, the divine Principle
of Christian Science, literally governs the aims, ambitions, and acts of the
Scientist." [64]

   Balancing Mrs. Eddy's assertion of this possibility in the "Daily Prayer"
is the phrase, "and rule out of me all sin." Sin in Christian Science means
living in terms of material selfhood. Men face the choice, Mrs. Eddy
teaches, of living in terms of a personal self, with its limited material aims

62. *S&H.,* p. 15.   63. *Man.,* p. 41.   64. *Mis.,* p. 204.

and ambitions, or seeking the demonstration of their spiritual identity. So doing requires them, she maintains, to challenge personal sense and all that proceeds from it, including self-love, willfulness, and hate, at every point. To accept this challenge is to take up the cross and is absolutely necessary in order to work out one's salvation from sin. And the healing of sin, Mrs. Eddy maintained, is the "emphatic purpose of Christian Science." [65] This purpose transcends the healing of disease. For the belief of a private material body subject to sickness and death proceeds, as does sin, from the erroneous belief in material selfhood.

While Mrs. Eddy did not dwell at length on moral questions as such, she did maintain that certain moral requirements are intrinsic to the working out of one's full demonstration over sin. A comparatively slight requirement, though one which many new Scientists found difficult to meet, was the stipulation that members of The Mother Church totally abstain from the use of alcohol and tobacco. The use of these items was frowned upon by many Protestants in this period, but Christian Scientists had special reasons for eschewing them. Mrs. Eddy's teaching stressed the necessity of remaining free from all false material appetites; furthermore, since both alcohol and tobacco were drugs operating through chemical action on the system, their use was obviously not in harmony with Christian Science. For this reason, too, some of Mrs. Eddy's followers went to the point of refusing to drink tea and coffee, though she herself laid down no such explicit requirement in her writings. In a larger sense, Mrs. Eddy maintained that all sensual indulgence and slavery to the passions must be overcome if men would demonstrate their full freedom from materiality.

Yet at the same time, Mrs. Eddy explicitly rejected asceticism and warned Christian Scientists against trying to live beyond the level of their actual spiritual growth. "Emerge gently from matter into Spirit," she advised the readers of *Science and Health*. "Think not to thwart the spiritual ultimate of all things, but come naturally into Spirit through better health and morals and as the result of spiritual growth." [66] Mrs. Eddy's comments on marriage, to which she devoted a short chapter in *Science and Health,* are especially illuminating in reference to this point. She referred to marriage as "the legal and moral provision for generation among human kind." [67] But marriage, as she spoke of it, was a human and not a spiritual institution; and Mrs. Eddy makes no provision for marriages within the Christian Science church (though she does require

65. *Rud.,* p. 2. 66. *S&H.,* p. 485. 67. *Ibid.,* p. 56.

in the *Manual* that Christian Scientists be married by an authorized clergyman).[68] Marriage, she taught, is not necessary for man *in Science* — in his perfect spiritual estate; but until men grow into a greater understanding of their spiritual being, marriage must continue, must be purified and elevated, and made to serve the improvement of the race. Nor need marriage be entered into on a purely "suffer it to be so now" basis, for Mrs. Eddy indicated that it hints the union of the masculine and feminine qualities that constitute spiritual completeness, and, further, that it offers real opportunities for joy, communion, and spiritual enrichment. And though Mrs. Eddy had a low estimate of sexual activity even in marriage, she insisted that if the marriage compact is entered into all its demands should be fulfilled unless by mutual consent they are abrogated.

The guiding principle that informs Mrs. Eddy's approach to this subject, as to others, is that man's perfection must be demonstrated step by step and human patterns can be dissolved only as they are superseded by actual demonstration. To the extent that this demand is taken seriously, it places a responsibility on all Christian Scientists to work to their utmost to achieve the highest spiritual good in every area of their experience.

Many of Mrs. Eddy's followers were only too glad to fulfill the requirements of Christian Science practice as just sketched. For they felt that they were pioneering in a work as fraught with significance for all mankind as that of the early Christians. As Mrs. Eddy expressed it in her poem "Christ and Christmas":

> As in blest Palestina's hour
>   So in our age,
> 'T is the same hand unfolds His power
> And writes the page.[69]

Mrs. Eddy's own single-minded dedication to the fulfillment of her mission was often cited by her followers as exemplifying a dedication to which they aspired. From the first her work in Christian Science had been beset with difficulties — poverty and neglect in the years of discovery, dissension and schism in the infant movement, continued opposition from the clergy, and various forms of personal abuse. Fired by a sense of mission, Mrs. Eddy developed an extraordinary capacity to nerve endeavor in her followers, and Christian Scientists often found themselves undertaking tasks of incredible difficulty at her request. To many of them she

68. *Man.,* p. 49.   69. Eddy, *Poetical Works,* p. 36.

opened unlimited vistas of action. In 1899 she told a class of sixty-five: "We, to-day, in this classroom, are enough to convert the world if we are of one Mind." [70] Her sermons in Boston during the 1880s appear to have been unusually effective. In the record of one of them, delivered on the Fourth of July, 1887, the fire is still apparent:

Never was there a more solemn and imperious call than God makes to us all, right here, for fervent devotion and an absolute consecration to the greatest and holiest of all causes. . . .

Will you doff your lavender-kid zeal, and become real and consecrated warriors? Will you give yourselves wholly and irrevocably to the great work of establishing the truth, the gospel, and the Science which are necessary to the salvation of the world from error, sin, disease, and death? Answer at once and practically, and answer aright! [71]

Had Mrs. Eddy not had a solid core of devoted followers who were willing to "answer aright," Christian Science could never have become a significant religious force in American life. These early workers were for the most part middle-aged, of modest means, and conspicuous for nothing but their religious beliefs and the ardor with which they embraced them. It was among these workers that one finds the first practitioners and teachers of Christian Science, the officials of The Mother Church in its early years and of its branches, the members of Mrs. Eddy's staff at Pleasant View and Chestnut Hill, and the missionaries who brought Christian Science to new communities and sometimes distant lands.

A special bond seems to have united those Christian Scientists who worked closely with Mrs. Eddy during those troubled years in the 1880s when she was still in the midst of things in Boston. William Lyman Johnson, the son of one of these workers, later wrote,

With these people Christian Science was their all in all, for there were few that had not been "brought out of great tribulation" by it. They had made sacrifices, had been maligned, scorned and laughed at; attempts had been made to undermine not only their individual work, but that of the whole Cause.

And at the evening meals which some of these workers often shared, Johnson recalled, "there was a free and generous exchange of thought, a simple association which bore the fruits of faithfulness and unity." [72]

The difficulties to which Johnson referred above were a very real part

70. *Mis.*, p. 279. 71. *Ibid.*, p. 177.
72. Johnson, *History*, I, p. 80.

of the experience of many of Mrs. Eddy's followers in these early years —
and to some extent throughout the history of the movement. The trials
which they encountered often began very early in their experience with
Christian Science. In many cases, young students were pressured by
ministers, friends, and family members to forsake their new faith;
indeed, conversions to Christian Science in some instances came near to
breaking up families. Mrs. Eddy's own sister, Abigail Tilton, a wealthy
matron in a New England town, was so thoroughly scandalized by her
sister's work in Christian Science that she would have nothing more to
do with her.

Some of the heaviest burdens in the early movement were borne by
those who entered into the professional practice of Christian Science. By
1910, those who had done so numbered over four thousand. Many of
them had not begun their healing work with any intention of so doing,
but found themselves called upon for help so often that they decided to
make it their full time occupation. In 1892, for example, Captain Joseph
Eastaman wrote that after having healed his wife, he discussed Christian
Science with his friends and acquaintances. Some merely laughed at him,
but others asked him to relieve their sufferings. After treating a wealthy
ship owner successfully, Eastaman was engaged to treat his wife and
daughter, who, he said, "on recovery, freely introduced me to their suffering friends. Here virtually, though I knew it not, began my practice." [73]

Actually building up a practice, however, was as Eastaman and others
found often very difficult. As Christian Science became well-known, practitioners in urban centers were sometimes swamped with patients. But before the mid 1890s, and in small communities thereafter, they might wait
in their offices day after day without a single call for help. Since female
practitioners outnumbered males about five to one and most of the women
were married, only a minority of practitioners were dependent upon
their healing work for a livelihood. But for those males who had families
to support, earning an adequate income from the practice alone presented
a formidable problem. The son of William B. Johnson recalled that not
until three years after his father entered the practice in 1884 did the family
cease to feel the pinch of poverty. The sign which his father hung in the
window of their home, the young Johnson recalled, while it was a "nine
days' wonder and attracted many queer glances, sarcastic remarks, and
gibes," drew no patients. Even after Johnson had built up a practice, the

73. Captain Joseph S. Eastaman, "The Travail of My Soul," *CSJ*, X (July 1892),
155.

family fortunes were none too good, for much of his work was done without payment.[74]

Far more serious than the financial problems faced by practitioners of Christian Science was the opposition that they encountered to the very conduct of their healing work. Most Christian Scientists in other respects were ordinary enough people. But their commitment to healing through spiritual power alone struck probably the majority of Americans as ridiculous and even downright dangerous. Since supernatural Protestantism was so much more vital a force when Mrs. Eddy was alive than it is now, probably more Americans then than now were disposed to admit such healing as a possibility. But unless convinced by cases of which they had personal knowledge or by their own experience, they frequently tended to deprecate its practice.

Sometimes opposition to Christian Science took the form of ridicule. At the popular level a number of cartoons in newspapers and magazines lampooned what their originators conceived to be the more extravagant tendencies of the Scientists. One of them, captioned "Christian Scientist," pictured a naked gentleman sitting contentedly on a burning stove musing to himself, "I wonder what's burning." [75] Christian Science could become the object of really stinging satire at the hands of those who knew how to wield a pen. One of the most effective satires on Mrs. Eddy's teaching was contained in Mark Twain's *Christian Science*. The extravagant parody of Christian Science healing which occupies its opening pages is probably the best piece in an otherwise unfortunate book. As Twain's highly imaginative account begins, he has fallen over an Alpine cliff and is being treated by a visiting Christian Scientist. When he learns through a messenger that she is giving him "absent treatment" and says that there is nothing the matter with him, he asks,

"Did you tell her I walked off a cliff seventy-five feet high?"
"Yes."
"And struck a boulder at the bottom and bounced?"
"Yes."
"And struck another one and bounced again?"
"Yes."
"And struck another one and bounced yet again?"
"Yes."
"And broke the boulders?"
"Yes."

74. Johnson, *History* I, 11.   75. *Miniature Life,* n.d.

"That accounts for it; she is thinking of the boulders. Why didn't you tell her I got hurt, too?"

"I did. I told her what you told me to tell her: that you were now but an incoherent series of compound fractures extending from your scalplock to your heels, and that the comminuted projections caused you to look like a hat-rack."

"And it was after this that she wished me to remember that there was nothing the matter with me?"

"Those were her words. . . ."

"Does she seem to be in full and functionable possession of her intellectual plant, such as it is?"

"*Bitte?*"

"Do they let her run at large, or do they tie her up?" [76]

Twain's satire, however humorous, is not without a serious point. For it mocks the radical claims of the Scientists for the actuality of divine healing power. And this same attitude was expressed — if with considerably less skill — in innumerable ways in the public response to the practice of Christian Science. [77]

As an abstract idea, Christian Science healing could often be a target for humor. But actual situations were often less than amusing. The pioneers of the movement told some really harrowing tales of the early trials through which they passed. Miss Phoebe Haines, for instance, wrote that in the winter of 1893, at five in the afternoon she was telegraphed to see a little boy in a neighborhood town. To get to him she had to ride seven hours in thirty below weather over roads almost drifted full with snow. Arriving around midnight she set to work, and by the next morning the child was vastly improved. At the noon meal the boy's grandfather burst in carrying a gun. Told that the boy had recovered, he put it down and said that "if he had died, I should have shot that old woman on sight." [78]

Threatening as this experience was, its outcome was happy enough. But failures in Christian Science practice, particularly in children's cases, sometimes drove communities to a pitch of fury. In 1889 a Christian Scientist in Pierre, South Dakota, described an extreme situation of this sort. The eleven-month-old child of a close friend died, after both women had tried to help him through Christian Science treatment. The next morn-

---

76. Twain, *Christian Science,* pp. 4–7.

77. A less stinging, but humorous comment on Christian Science is by Peter Finley Dunne, *Mr. Dooley's Opinions* (London, 1902), pp. 3–4.

78. Phoebe Haines Reminiscences, Longyear.

ing, she wrote, a Methodist minister gathered a crowd around him on the street and denounced this pernicious doctrine, "till the people were infuriated and threatened mob law." After a town meeting at which the same sentiment prevailed, the two women were informed by a committee that the community wished them to leave town.[79]

But the worst suffering which a Christian Scientist in such a case as this had to endure was not the hostility of the populace, but grief and the sense of having failed. "Why this termination?" asked the anguished woman whose friend's child had died. What she was asking for, however, was an explanation of *her* failure in treating the case; she was not questioning the truth of Christian Science itself. But for a large segment of public opinion, and for the medical profession especially, failures in Christian Science practice constituted clear proof that its principle was erroneous and its practice dangerous. Though Christian Science owed its growth largely to the successful healings its adherents accomplished, public opinion tended to center upon those cases where the "demonstration" had not been made. The Scientists often complained that these failures attracted a disproportionate amount of attention in relation to healings which were accomplished. Where a success in Christian Science practice caused a ripple, a failure caused a wave.

The *Journal of The American Medical Association* represented a growing body of opinion when it urged in 1899 that steps be taken "to restrain the rabid utterances and irrational practices of such ignorant and irresponsible persons" as the Christian Scientists.[80] Largely at the instigation of the medical profession, such steps were already being taken. They consisted both of attempts to pass or fortify state laws regulating the practice of medicine so as to proscribe Christian Science healing, and of prosecutions for manslaughter of individual Christian Scientists in whose care a patient died or for having violated state medical laws. Such efforts to impede Christian Science practice by law were nothing new: as far back as 1887, a Christian Scientist in McGregor, Iowa, was finally acquitted after three trials for practicing medicine without a license; similar prosecutions in Boston in 1888 and in California in 1893 rocked the movement. Further, the Massachusetts state legislature in 1896 had debated the passage of a bill to restrict healing. But these incidents, difficult as they were for the Scientists, were sporadic. It was only in the last few years of the century, as the Christian Science movement gained increasing

79. Maurine Campbell Reminiscences, Longyear.
80. *Journal of The American Medical Association*, Nov. 18, 1899.

momentum and claimed new converts by the thousands, that the movement to restrain irregular healing through legal action went into high gear.

This whole effort to restrict Christian Science healing practice by law forms both a crucial chapter in the life of the movement during this period and a significant episode in American legal history, and it deserves more extensive treatment than we can give it here. To the Scientists, of course, the issue seemed perfectly clear: the legal effort to restrain their healing practice was really a subversion of their religious liberties under the Constitution. As Mrs. Eddy wrote, "The Constitution of the United States does not provide that *materia medica* shall make laws to regulate man's religion; rather does it imply that religion shall permeate our laws." No state power, she argued, "can quench the vital heritage of freedom — man's right to adopt a religion, to employ a physician, to live or to die according to the dictates of his own rational conscience and enlightened understanding." [81] On the whole, state legislatures and the courts seemed to have agreed with her. For in no state was a law permanently enforced or left on the statute books prohibiting the public practice of Christian Science.

Still, individual Christian Scientists were tried for violating state medical laws before these laws were struck down by the courts or repealed by the state legislatures; and they sometimes faced manslaughter charges on other grounds. Yet it was not just failures in their practice which entangled Christian Scientists in legal embroilments. For the Scientists were sometimes prosecuted after startling successes in healing had brought their work to public notice and aroused the antagonism of the ministry and medical profession. Of course it was really Christian Science rather than the individuals accused that was on trial in these proceedings. As one judge said in summarizing the case to the jury, "the case is not so important to the person at the bar as to the community as a whole." [82] And the case for the defense, as one might expect, often included a parade of witnesses testifying to the healing power of Christian Science. But for the person at the bar, the trial could be devastating. Not a few defendants felt, as a practitioner in San Bernardino, California, put it, that they were "passing through the valley of persecution." [83]

Such incidents, while not characteristic of the experience of Christian Scientists generally, do reveal something of the general climate of hostility

81. *My.,* p. 222.
82. The Christian Science periodicals in the early years of the century often contain extended accounts of these trials.
83. *CSJ,* XVI (July 1898), 289.

in which many of the pioneers of the movement carried on their work. In a larger sense, they point to a permanent aspect of the practice of Christian Science as Mrs. Eddy described it. A working Christian Scientist at any period, she made clear, could expect opposition to his spiritual labors — opposition which, whatever its form, stemmed from mortal mind's resistance to spiritual Truth. The way of the genuine Christian Scientist, Mrs. Eddy emphasized on many occasions, was never strewn with flowers; for it requires taking up the cross. "We need 'Christ and him crucified,' " she wrote in *Science and Health*. "We must have trials and self-denials, as well as joys and victories, until all error is destroyed." [84]

SECULARISM AND THE PROBLEM OF CLASS

Without a solid core of devoted workers who were willing to bear the burdens of the movement in its early days, Christian Science could never have become a significant religious force in American life at all. But their spirit was by no means characteristic of the movement as a whole, and any acquaintance with its literature shows that some Christian Scientists reflected very little of their pioneering dedication. For some Christian Scientists, Mrs. Eddy's teaching was very far from a revealed truth, the establishment of which demanded and deserved unstinted sacrifice. It was, rather, a convenient method for attaining the purely human ends of health, wealth, comfort, status, and success. The motives which impelled the practice of Christian Science cannot, of course, be precisely labeled, classified or quantified. These motives were sometimes various and mixed in the minds of individual Christian Scientists, not to speak of the movement as a whole. But the early literature of the movement reveals a distinct strain of secularism which, though far from the spirit of Mrs. Eddy's writings, was to some extent a part of the practice of Christian Science in this period and since.

Christian Scientists often rejoiced that their religion was, as Mrs. Eddy so often said, "demonstrable." As she explained it, the meaning of Biblical revelation once grasped becomes a basis for demonstration. But that which is demonstrated is always the allness of God and the spiritual perfection of man. The full demonstration of these realities constitutes salvation as defined in Christian Science. And salvation in this sense is the only thing that Mrs. Eddy ultimately claimed to offer. Healing is considered indispensable in Christian Science, for in no other way can spiritual fact be

84. *S&H.*, p. 39.

demonstrated. Indeed, if one assumes the truth of Christian Science, he can see that healing is altogether rational and an absolute requirement for man. But he can also see that its purpose is entirely incidental to salvation. Hence Christian Science as Mrs. Eddy taught it is definitely not a mere instrument for the realization of humanly defined ends. To apply it in this utilitarian sense at the every day level of experience is to misunderstand the purpose of demonstration in Mrs. Eddy's teaching. For demonstration in this sense requires seeking to realize in experience the divine ideal of manhood — defined in Christian Science as the Christ — and not a humanly outlined end or value.

In most cases, of course, those who became Mrs. Eddy's followers came to Christian Science for healing. This was entirely in accord with her expectation and intent. But those who *continued* to practice Christian Science on a long-term basis solely or even mainly for the purpose of staying well or otherwise improving their human situation were clearly secularizing Mrs. Eddy's teaching. To the extent that her followers did so, they lost the ontological consciousness and Christian commitment that was central to Christian Science as she taught it. "Mortal mind," she wrote, "must waken to spiritual life before it cares to solve the problem of being. . . ."[85] It is clear that a significant minority of Christian Scientists had not awakened to "spiritual life" sufficiently to care to "solve the problem of being," but that they were interested in solving human problems as such. Often in this form of Christian Science practice God becomes a dependable impersonal principle upon which (not Whom) one can rely in times of distress, little is said of sin or the conflict of Spirit and flesh, bearing the cross is scarcely referred to, and "bleeding footsteps" are regarded as quite unnecessary.

In this way, the practice of Christian Science was channeled into a narrow utilitarianism. The injunction "use your Christian Science" became something of a shibboleth in the movement. Unless its meaning was carefully understood as a reminder that Christian Science must be practiced, this injunction could easily be taken as a warrant for treating Mrs. Eddy's teaching as a practical problem solver to be used as a human convenience. Sometimes Christian Scientists talked about their demonstrations as if they had been produced by clever reliance upon some ever-ready principle happily tailored to human use. Certainly there is a profound difference between saying that any idea that seems to work is good, and

85. *Ibid.*, p. 556.

saying that if an idea is good, it has to work. An essential phase of the emergence of Christian Science can be written in terms of this distinction.

It could not be truly said that all or even most of Mrs. Eddy's followers practiced Christian Science in this utilitarian sense. As we have seen, many of them made enormous personal and financial sacrifices in order to carry on their work in the movement. And though most Christian Scientists first became interested in Mrs. Eddy's teaching as a means toward healing, an important minority investigated and adopted it solely in their search for truth. One Christian Scientist in 1902 spoke for many others when he wrote, "I was not brought into Christian Science for any special physical healing, but came, as an humble investigator, searching for the Truth — reaching out and feeling after God." [86] Once Mrs. Eddy expressed great satisfaction upon learning that a follower who was to work in her home had become a Christian Scientist for the same reason.[87] And sometimes her followers who had first turned to Christian Science for physical healing testified that they had done so almost as if making a confession. "What was my surprise," wrote a Christian Scientist in the *Journal* in 1897, "on finding that it was not only a curative for the body . . . but that it was a religion. I found that the healing was but a sign of the absolute truth of Divine Principle understood and correctly applied." [88]

It is clear, however, that this attitude was not characteristic of all Christian Scientists. Often enough one reads testimonies of healing by people who seemed to have treated Mrs. Eddy's teaching only as a therapeutic agent. Christian Scientists whose practice was differently motivated were sometimes critical of this sort of utilitarianism. Of her brother, one of Mrs. Eddy's followers wrote in 1897 that he wants Christian Science "only to heal the ills of the flesh. He wants to enjoy the pleasures of the flesh, and has no idea of nor hunger for the great spiritual uplifting that would come with Science." [89] Those who adopted Christian Science solely or largely as a means for continuing in good health often drifted into passivity in its practice. When they had no physical need to meet, they showed no inclination to apply themselves to the study of its teachings. And if they did have physical problems, they were more apt to call a practitioner for aid than to treat themselves. If they found Christian Science of no

86. *CSS*, V (Nov. 27, 1902), p. 206.
87. Dickey, *Memoirs of Mary Baker Eddy*, p. 91.
88. *CSJ*, XV (April 1897), 26–27.   89. *Ibid.*

immediate help, they often returned to the use of medicine without a qualm.

The utilitarian practice of Christian Science can perhaps best be seen in the area of business and financial affairs. To some degree, one can discern in the movement a version of that latter-day generation of the Protestant Ethic, the Gospel of Wealth. Actually, Mrs. Eddy had very little to say about business affairs. Yet she always insisted that followers demonstrate Christian Science in all areas of their experience, without exception. And Christian Scientists who were businessmen often called attention to this point. One can see an increasing concern with business affairs in the *Journal* beginning in the early 1890s; for the financial crisis of 1893 and the five year depression that followed it impelled many Christian Scientists to think about the relation of their religion to economic life. In 1904, for example, an article on "Christian Science and the Business Life" declared that "religion must be applicable to every phase of living" and that it must not "disregard any condition which needs a saviour." [90]

Certainly business life in that period did need "a saviour." In view of the great industrial progress of the time, it is easy to forget just how precarious business life was and how many businessmen simply went under. Christian Science appealed to many harried businessmen because it seemed to offer them a different way of life than the constant struggle for profits or even economic survival. As one Christian Scientist wrote, "Business life engrosses the attention of a large majority of the inhabitants of the earth. What is it but a series of fears, problems, doubts, perplexities, losses, gains, frauds, successes and failures?" [91] Many articles, most of them written by businessmen, spoke of the effect of Christian Science in economic affairs. One businessman declared that it put commercial relations on a plane of "conscious fraternity, rather than competition," since one could know that "There is no conflict of interest and discord in the one Mind." [92] Another declared that through Christian Science one could be freed from "the delusion that mortal man plans, erects, builds, and brings to pass anything." [93] An increasing number of testimonies in the periodi-

90. "Christian Science and the Business Life," *CSJ*, XXII, (Sept. 1904), 345.

91. Emma Estes, "Life," *CSJ*, XIII (Feb. 1896), p. 461.

92. H.P.T., "Thoughts for Businessmen," *CSS*, VII (Feb. 18, 1905), 387.

93. Willard S. Mattox, "Christian Science and Social Science," *CSJ*, XXI (Dec. 1903), 533.

cals about the effect of Christian Science in business affairs vouched for the validity of such statements.

Certainly this was a legitimate extension of Christian Science as Mrs. Eddy taught it. Yet one finds too that some of her followers went far past practicing Christian Science in the area of business affairs and spoke of it as a method for the solution of business problems. "In this busy age, when the lines of competition are so clearly drawn," read an article for the *Sentinel* in 1903, "men of affairs are compelled to seek and hold fast to practical things. They are not looking for theories. They want facts." [94] The emphasis upon Christian Science as a practical means for controlling business affairs at some points resembled the rhetoric of success cults. Occasionally the *Journal* or the *Sentinel* quoted from the widely-circulated magazine *Success,* the Horatio Alger ethic of which was appealing to some Christian Scientists. One Scientist echoed Russell Conwell's famous lecture "Acres of Diamonds" when he wrote that after talking about Christian Science with his business acquaintances he was often asked: "Have you discovered a field of diamonds? . . . If so, others will look where your discovery was made." [95]

Never did Christian Scientists state flatly that the accumulation of wealth as such was desirable. Indeed, most of them said that it was utterly foreign to the spirit of Christian Science. Yet other Christian Scientists struck a different note. Though they did not speak of wealth as an end in itself, they often justified the acquirement of material riches as an expression of spiritual riches. Even while scorning the almighty dollar, a Christian Scientist wrote that "thought must have its expression, and this expression seems material as did the loaves and the fishes to the hungry multitude; but make it not real, give it not of itself power." [96] Yet many, though not most, Christian Scientists undoubtedly sought "the loaves and the fishes" for their own sake. And when they repeated, as they often did, Jesus' words, "Seek ye first the kingdom of God and his righteousness; and all these things shall be added unto you," it was the last part of the statement rather than the first that they somewhat breathlessly emphasized. Mrs. Stetson epitomized the attitude of many other Christian Scientists in her attitude toward the things of the world. "We need health and strength and peace," she wrote to one of her students:

94. J. E. Fellers, "A Businessman's Point of View," *CSS*, IV (Oct. 3, 1903), p. 68.
95. *CSJ*, X (June 1892), 120.
96. George W. Delano, "Christian Science in Business," *CSJ*, XII (Sept. 1894), 224.

But let us not forget that we also need *things,* things which are but the type and shadow of the real objects of God's creating, but which we can use and enjoy until we wake to see the real. We surely need clothes. Then why not manifest a beautiful concept? Clothes should, indeed, be as nearly perfect as possible, in texture, line, and color. It is certain, too, that we need homes. Then why not have beautiful homes? Our homes should express the highest sense of harmony and happiness. . . . We have a right to everything that is convenient, most comfortable, most harmonious.[97]

The emphasis in some quarters of the movement upon wealth was strongly reminiscent of some aspects of New Thought. Though Mrs. Hopkins together with some other New Thought leaders tended toward mysticism, other elements in the movement emphasized the attainment of success and riches through positive thinking. These groups paved the way for the success psychologies of Dale Carnegie and Norman Vincent Peale. The most conspicuous of them was the Unity School of Christianity. And some of the pronouncements of its founder, Charles Fillmore, though they go beyond anything to be found in the literature of Christian Science, do seem akin to some statements one can find in it. In his pamphlet "Prosperity Thoughts," for example, we read:

Get into the right thought, and you will demonstrate prosperity. . . . When Jesus was shown the piece of money with the image of Caesar upon it, and said, "Render therefore unto Caesar the things that are Caesar's; and unto God the things that are God's," he did not mean to make a great separation between the two, as if they were at enmity. The lesson was one of right relationship — know where the material belongs, and put it there; know where the spiritual belongs, and render upon it its own.

Then you advocate the accumulation of riches? we are asked. No; we advocate the accumulation of *rich ideas.* . . . The rich ideas will keep one in constant touch with abundance.[98]

Some Christian Scientists were quite aware of the snare of secularism that had entrapped many of their fellows and spoke out against the use of Christian Science for human ends. One of them testified that a business transaction which he had concluded successfully had been of particular satisfaction to him, for he had not made a cent from it. "A demonstration of the allness of God in business," he wrote, "does not always result in the attainment of some particular end or object." [99] In 1908, Alfred Farlow,

97. Quoted in Swihart, *Since Mrs. Eddy,* p. 47.
98. Charles Fillmore, *Prosperity Thoughts* (Kansas City, n.d.).
99. *CSS,* III (Sept. 20, 1900), 6.

the able head of the Committee on Publication, explored the proper relation between Christian Science and business in the journal *The American Business Man*. His comments read in part:

> . . . When the Christian places himself under the dominion of God, Spirit,
> his present material wants are provided for, his 'needs' are to be supplied. . . .
> and it is evident that such needs depend largely upon the situation and con-
> dition of the individual. . . . To some an increase of earthly substance would
> be an advantage. It would enable them to accomplish more good and do it with
> greater ease and comfort, while in other instances an abundance of supply
> would beget carelessness and indolence, afford undeserved and ill-used power.
> . . . There are many people in the world who need to be richer, others who
> need to be poorer.
> . . . It seems to us that a Christian Scientist can judge better as to his real
> advancement by noting how many of his pet sins he is escaping, rather than
> by counting the amount of money he is gaining. A Christian Scientist might
> believe that in disposing of a block of stock at a goodly price he has demon-
> strated Christian Science, but what shall we say of the individual who bought
> the block of stock and paid more for it than it was worth? What sort of
> demonstration has he made? [100]

The type of Christian Science practice that Farlow criticized by implication in the preceding quotation was made possible by the subservience
of religion to class values. The pursuit of these values — wealth, comfort,
status, and success — was certainly not warranted by Christian Science
teaching. But they were among the predominant values of the American
middle class. The conclusion is warranted, therefore, that the class orientation of some Christian Scientists did noticeably affect their practice of
its teaching. For through it, they seemed to be trying to perpetuate and
protect the level of contentment to which their class aspired. The foregoing suggests only that a process of secularization was to some degree
evident in the *practice* of Christian Science. It says nothing whatever about
the character of Christian Science as a religious teaching — except, perhaps, that it could be distorted in this manner. It is easy enough, of course,
to say that no religious teaching is practiced entirely according to its
founder's intent. Yet Mrs. Eddy did establish clear guidelines for the
practice of Christian Science — guidelines which in their rigorous demands for selflessness and dedication are not coordinate with a secular
quest for a fulfilled bourgeois existence.

100. Alfred Farlow, "Christian Science in Business Life," *American Business Man,*
XI (May 1908), 155–157.

Yet the assertion that Christian Science is in its very character a form of bourgeois Protestantism geared to the realization of middle class values has often been made. This contention, in fact, is almost a commonplace in sociologically-oriented discussions of Christian Science. A good example is the following reference to Christian Science in H. Richard Niebuhr's *The Social Sources of Denominationalism*. Writing from the perspective of Neo-orthodoxy, Niebuhr assailed Christian Science as a preeminent form of the American "accommodation of the faith to bourgeois psychology." Speaking of the general movement in America toward a bourgeois religion, he writes:

In its final phase the development of this religious movement exhibits the complete enervation of the once virile faith through the influence of the middle class which had grown soft in the luxury the earlier heroic discipline made possible by its vigorous and manly asceticism. Here the gospel of self-help has excluded all remnants of that belief in fatality which formed the foundation of Puritan heroism. Here the comfortable circumstances of an established class have simplified out of existence the problem of evil and have made possible the substitution for the mysterious will of the Sovereign of life and death and sin and salvation, the sweet benevolence of a Father-Mother God or the vague goodness of the All. Here the concern for self has been secularized to its last degree; the conflicts of sick souls have been replaced by the struggles of sick minds and bodies; the Puritan passion for perfection has become a seeking after the kingdom of health and mental peace and its comforts.[101]

It should be clear that Niebuhr's remarks, though they do reflect an aspect of Christian Science practice, represent a complete misconstruction of its teaching. Indeed, to the degree that Christian Science was practiced in the secularized sense that Niebuhr describes, its teachings were not fulfilled but violated.

Yet this observation does not take the matter far enough. For it does not sufficiently take account of the often repeated contention that the Christian Science movement is and since the 1880s has been predominantly middle class in social composition. This point, while defensible on the whole, is less easy to prove than one might suppose. Impressionistic approaches to the problem of identifying the class composition of the movement can be most misleading. The conspicuous wealth of some of Mrs. Eddy's followers together with the elaborateness of a minority of

101. H. Richard Niebuhr, *The Social Sources of Denominationalism* (New York, 1929), pp. 104–105.

Christian Science churches have occasionally prompted the identification of the movement as an upper-class phenomenon — a view for which there is no hard evidence whatever. Yet it is difficult to establish with the same certitude that the Christian Science movement is middle class in social composition. To call a movement "middle class" in a country so pervaded by middle classness as the United States may amount to saying very little at all. In fact, sociologists have often found it necessary to apply the categories of lower middle class, middle middle class, and upper middle class to the American situation in order to make meaningful distinctions possible.

In the United States, occupation level is probably the most reliable index to class stratification. And there are enough indications of the levels of Christian Scientists to support the conclusion that the movement was and is predominantly middle class in composition. One study concludes that in 1910, approximately 51 percent could be identified as professionals; 31 percent as proprietors, managers, officials, clerks, and kindred workers; and 16 percent skilled, semi-skilled, and unskilled workers. This last group could be designated lower class and lower middle class, leaving the conclusion that the preponderance of the movement is located in the middle and upper range of the middle class. These figures, while open to some challenge, are on the whole consistent for the period 1900–1950; and the conclusions they suggest are supported by other indices as well.[102]

Is there not, then, a contradiction in saying that Christian Science as a religious teaching is not oriented to the realization of middle class values but has been practiced predominantly by members of the middle class? Any apparent contradiction is resolved when we look at the issue from another perspective. Rather than looking for some explanation of the middle class character of the movement in terms of the teaching of Christian Science, we can ask: are the characteristics of the middle class mentality and life style which conduce to the practice of Christian Science *other* than the commonly identified middle class values of comfort, status, and success? In thinking through this question we can begin to make

102. This point is explored in Neal DeNood, *The Diffusion of a System of Belief.* Ph.D. Dissertation, Harvard University, 1937. For other sociologically oriented discussions of Christian Science, see Harold W. Pfautz, *Christian Science: The Sociology of a Social Movement and a Religious Group.* Ph.D. Dissertation. University of Chicago, 1954; Isidor Thorner, *Christian Science and Ascetic Protestantism: A Study in the Sociology of Religion, Personality Type, and Social Structure.* Ph.D. Dissertation. Harvard University, 1951; and Bryan R. Wilson, *Sects and Society: A Sociological Study of the Elim Tabernacle, Christian Science, and Christadelphians* (Berkeley, 1961).

better sense out of the whole question of the class orientation of the Christian Science movement. For there are at least three identifiable characteristics that go far in explaining the middle class character of the movement.

Perhaps the most obvious characteristic is the relatively high educational level of the middle class. While Christian Science is not intellectually complex, it does require a capacity to read intelligently, to take ideas seriously, and to relate them to practice understandingly. Obviously, this capacity is more apt to be found among the highly literate middle class which has far more access to educational opportunities than the lower class. And it is found in greater degree among the middle and upper sections of the middle class than in the lower middle class.

A less specific but equally important factor involves the ethos of the middle class mentality. To a high degree, the middle class in general and the American middle class in particular tends to activism, to the belief that progress is possible and that man can master his own destiny. This activist ethos, which wholly negates submission to undesirable conditions as iron necessities, is clearly reflected in the Protestant ethic, with its emphasis on achievement, success, and upward mobility. But it is far more than an economic ethic, and breeds a life-attitude conducive to the practice of a religion which bids man banish all forms of evil from his experience.

An even more basic point is that the American middle class is to a higher degree Protestant than is the lower class, in which, due to the patterns of immigration and industrial employment, Roman Catholicism is more predominant. Though Christian Science, as we have discussed, is not essentially Protestant in the character of its theology, it is far closer to Protestantism than Roman Catholicism. And it largely attracted, for reasons which we have examined, Protestants who had become disenchanted with their orthodox faiths. Hence the very Protestant character of the middle class was in itself a major factor conducive to the practice of Christian Science. It is also worth noting that the influence of Christian Science outside the United States has been greatest in countries with a strong Protestant tradition.

These points establish only that certain tendencies of the middle class mentality — its educational level, activist character, and Protestant orientation — can be conducive to the practice of Christian Science. But this statement must be balanced against the assertion, developed in the foregoing pages, that another tendency of the middle class mentality — its secular orientation to the attainment of comfort, status, and success — can definitely be inimical to the practice of Christian Science. Both these points deal with the conditions and motives that underlie Christian Science practice, and neither can tell us anything about the essential character of Mrs. Eddy's teaching itself. Otherwise, how would it even be possible to identify the secularized practice of Christian Science as a distortion of its basic character? For given Mrs. Eddy's insistent demand for radical redemption of mortals from all phases of the flesh, the character of her teaching, whatever elements entered into its practice, can in no way be defined as secular.

THE SOCIAL QUESTION

The greatest accomplishment of Christian Science, in terms of the religious situation into which it was projected, was the restoration of vitality to the individual spiritual experience of those who practiced it. Mrs. Eddy's teachings were clearly addressed to the redemption and healing of individual men. And one is struck, in reading the testimonies of Christian Scientists, at how complete was their conviction that divine power was at work in their own particular life-situations. Obviously, then, the social and political questions that were becoming of increasing concern to many Protestants around the turn of the century had less significance for the Christian Scientists. Articles on these problems appeared only rarely in the *Journal* and *Sentinel,* and Mrs. Eddy devotes little attention to them in her writings in proportion to her treatment of other subjects.

At the same time, the greatest danger to the correct practice of Christian Science was the spirit of secularism which is to some degree in evidence in the early literature of the movement. For this reason, the increasing social concern evident in the development of the movement in the first decade of the twentieth century is of real importance. For it reflects a significant reorientation of the thought of the movement away from the personal and private to the social and universal, a genuine broadening of the Scientists' concerns. The central event in this reorientation was, of course, the founding of the *Christian Science Monitor* by Mrs. Eddy in 1908. The importance that Mrs. Eddy attached to the *Monitor* can be gauged from the fact that she considered its establishment her greatest single achievement apart from the writing of *Science and Health*.

By founding the *Monitor,* Mrs. Eddy committed the Christian Science movement in a limited way to the ideal of social concern then assuming so important a place in Protestantism. It is a curious and significant fact that the first issue of the *Monitor* came on the stands on November 25, 1908, within three weeks of the date that the Federal Council of Churches convened in Philadelphia. Just as the publication of the *Monitor* marks the high point of social concern in the Christian Science movement, so the formation of the Federal Council of Churches marks the greatest triumph scored up to that time by the Social Gospel.

When Mrs. Eddy fixed the date for the first publication of the *Monitor*, she did not have the impending meeting of the Federal Council of Churches in mind. Yet the closeness of the two events is more than fortuitous; for, in a very rough way, the career of Social Gospel had paralleled that of the Christian Science movement over the preceding four decades. Christian Science was first fully articulated in the first edition of *Science and Health,* published in 1875. So too, the Social Gospel, though related to earlier developments within American Protestantism, may be said to date from the response of some ministers to the labor crisis of 1877. For both movements, the 1880s was a period of foundation, of trial and testing. And while the Social Gospel was not, like Christian Science, institutionalized in a specific church, both penetrated into the church life of America in the 1890s. Moreover, the first decade of the new century saw both movements steadily increasing in influence and prestige.

To some extent as well, one can draw valid parallels between Christian Science and the Social Gospel in terms of their spirit and substance. Both emerged in the soil of American culture and have been often identified as specifically American contributions to Christianity. Both claimed to cut back behind centuries of barren theology, Protestant as well as Catholic, to restore the vital meaning of the Gospel. Both proclaimed that men can be liberated from iron-bound determinism — in the Social Gospel, from the laws of laissez-faire economics, in Christian Science from physical laws that bind men to sickness and death. And both represented in different ways statements of the Christian message in terms relevant to man's present life-situation.

It is understandable, therefore, that some ministers of the Social Gospel spoke approvingly of the practice of spiritual healing as yet another way in which Christianity could be made humanly relevant.[103] Nor is it surprising that the *Sentinel* should have quoted approvingly from one of the major Social Gospel leaders, Washington Gladden, on the inadequacies of orthodoxy.[104] Yet the major prophet of the Social Gospel, Walter Rauschenbush, had nothing good to say of Christian Science. For he spoke of it as part of a mystical tendency within Protestantism, a form

103. See p. 341.
104. Gladden is cited to this effect in *CSS,* XII (Sept. 21, 1909), 3.

of selfish spirituality which turned its back on the world.[105] Christian Scientists would certainly not have agreed that Mrs. Eddy's teaching encouraged either mysticism or selfishness. Yet Rauschenbush was surely right in pointing out that Christian Science and the Social Gospel have fundamentally different concerns. For the Social Gospel, as Rauschenbush and others described it, concentrates religious interest on the ethical problems of social life. Christian Science, however, focuses upon the ontological conditions that underly all social problems.

In her teaching, Mrs. Eddy raised basic ontological questions about the nature of man's being which the leaders of the Social Gospel, along with most other Protestants, had regarded as settled. From her standpoint, they accepted the very errors that made social problems possible, indeed inevitable. Regarding man's finiteness as self-evident, they accepted as given the plurality of human wills, minds and interests. Their primary concerns were ethical, not ontological, and they looked upon the root of evil of human life in ethical terms. Rauschenbush, for example, said, "Sin is essentially selfishness. . . . That definition is more in harmony with the Social Gospel than with any individualistic type of religion. The sinful mind, then, is the unsocial or antisocial mind." [106] But for Mrs. Eddy, this sin of selfishness was predicated upon a more primary error: the belief in a mind apart from God. "When we realize that there is one Mind," she wrote, "the divine law of loving our neighbor as ourselves is unfolded; whereas a belief in many ruling minds hinders man's normal drift towards the one Mind, one God, and leads human thought into opposite channels where selfishness reigns." [107]

Through ethical persuasion and moral uplift, the ministers of the Social Gospel felt that it was possible to change the disposition of the heart from selfishness to concern with the universal welfare. But if Mrs. Eddy is right, then as long as men accept their nature as finite, selfishness and conflict remain unavoidable. In several passages, she indicated that the conflict of interests in society depends upon the belief in a plurality of minds.[108] In 1904 at the height of the Progressive era, one of Mrs. Eddy's followers elucidated her conception of the root cause of social conflict by writing in an article called "Christian Science and Economic Reform" that:

No harmony is possible under the old conditions of thought. To effect perma-

105. Walter Rauschenbush, *A Theology for the Social Gospel* (New York, 1917), p. 103.

106. *Ibid.*, p. 15. 107. *S&H.*, p. 205.

108. See, for example, *S&H.*, p. 571; *Mis.*, p. 18.

nent social reform, the study of spiritual causation is necessary. The Socialist considers the cause of all discord to be material inequality and individualism. The co-operator considers the cause to be competitive and private unchecked capitalism, and many others would give yet different explanations, but Christian Science shows plainly that these causes are not causes, but the effect of a false sense of substance as matter, a false sense of existence as temporal.[109]

Perhaps the best way of contrasting Christian Science with the Social Gospel in this matter is with reference to the idea of the Kingdom of God. In the Social Gospel the Kingdom is defined in social terms. Rauschenbush called it the "Christian transfiguration of the social order." [110] But as Mrs. Eddy discussed the Kingdom, it meant in the first instance the submission of individuals to the government of God, their demonstration in their own situation of the oneness of Mind. Her "Daily Prayer" begins with the quotation from the Lord's Prayer, "Thy kingdom come." Next she goes on to deal with this idea in terms of the individual: "let the reign of divine Truth, Life, and Love be established in me, and rule out of me all sin." Finally, she extends the prayer to all mankind: "and may Thy Word enrich the affections of all mankind, and govern them!" [111] In Christian Science, this enrichment of "the affections of all mankind" will ameliorate social evils, curing the sickness of society as well as of the body; but the establishment of the Kingdom of God cannot be effected in terms of the amelioration of social conditions as such.

The two aspects of Mrs. Eddy's approach to social affairs as just discussed — her insistence that salvation is primarily individual and that meaningful reform must be predicated upon spiritual awakening — could have predisposed Christian Scientists to be unconcerned with social problems. Yet the element in Mrs. Eddy's teaching which prevented it from being practiced, except by a minority of her followers, as a metaphysical system abstracted from human affairs, was her continual emphasis upon demonstration. For her, the power of Spirit must be demonstrated in all phases of experience. Politics, economic life, and social relations must be brought under the divine government. And "human law is right," she wrote, "only as it patterns the divine." [112] Further, Mrs. Eddy did not feel that the achievement of human good was to be directly and exclusively the work of Christian Scientists. The advent of divine Science, she believed, had exerted a "leavening" effect upon the affairs of the world. The coming

109. Reuben Pogson, "Christian Science and Economic Reform," *CSJ*, XXII (Aug. 1904), 290.

110. Rauschenbush, *Theology*, 3.   111. *Man.*, p. 41.

112. *Mis.*, p. 283.

of Truth had affected human activities in a way of which men were not consciously aware, giving rise to reform and progress in many areas.[113] And since the divine government had to be established in every phase of life, Christian Scientists could not ignore any evidence of progress which tended toward this end, nor any evidence of evil which obstructed its realization.

Christian Scientists generally felt that they should be "in the world but not of the world." They should not remove themselves from practical social and political affairs, yet they should not identify themselves with any particular political party. In this matter they were following Mrs. Eddy's lead. Her own political course before the "discovery" of Christian Science is fairly clear. She had been raised a Jacksonian Democrat (her brother was a Locofoco and was very active in politics) but by the late 1850s was firmly committed to anti-slavery and the Republican party. Though it is probable that her sympathies, like those of most Christian Scientists, remained Republican, Mrs. Eddy refused to identify herself as a Republican or a Democrat. In 1901 an interviewer for the *New York Herald* asked her about the attitude of Christian Science on broad political questions. He recorded that she "thought this over before replying and said cautiously: — 'We are not indifferent to the forms of government, but we support the best in earth. A church to be universal must in many things be neutral about forms of government and at the same time support what is right to support.'" [114] Again, when asked in 1908 about her political views, Mrs. Eddy declared in the *Boston Post* that she had "none in reality, other than to help support a righteous government; to love God supremely, and my neighbor as myself." [115]

Mrs. Eddy's statement that her politics included helping to "support a righteous government" was far from rhetorical: she meant it completely. The same brief article in the *Boston Post* in which the statement was made included also the reminder that she had always believed "that those who are entitled to vote should do so." Periodically, articles in the *Sentinel* and the *Journal* would remind Christian Scientists of their obligations in this matter. An editorial in 1902 on "Christian Citizenship" for example, declared that it "is the plain duty of every citizen to participate in the government of his country, and he is the best citizen who most carefully, and

113. This idea is expressed at many points in Mrs. Eddy's works. See, for example, *S&H.*, p. 224; *My.*, p. 181.

114. *New York Herald*, May 5, 1901.

115. *Boston Post*, Nov. 1908.

prayerfully, and punctually exercises the right of suffrage." [116] Underlying this injunction was the belief that it was the Christian Scientist's duty to support whatever candidate, programs, or policies seemed to offer the highest human good, even while he worked in his own way for the betterment of mankind.

It would be extremely difficult to make any but the most tentative assertions about the political and social attitudes of Christian Scientists in this period. Judging from their comments on social questions in the Christian Science periodicals, and especially from the editorial policy of the *Christian Science Monitor,* they seem to have been on the whole socially concerned if not socially active people, conspicuously civic-minded, and moderately progressive in their politics.[117] Mrs. Eddy's two most often-quoted political pronouncements during her later years identify her with a fairly liberal political position. In a message to her followers in 1899 she said that she foresaw "great danger threatening our nation — imperialism, monopoly, and a lax system of religion." [118] The next year she returned to this theme in a statement for the public press, including among her enumeration of "the most imminent dangers confronting the coming century" the evils of "industrial slavery and insufficient freedom of honest competition." [119]

Actually, there was a certain radicalism in Mrs. Eddy's comments on society. For her claim as to the unreality of matter — certainly a radical doctrine metaphysically — is reflected in a number of passages which express her contempt for worldliness, material conservatism, human honors, place and power. In *Science and Health* Mrs. Eddy wrote, for example: "Take away wealth, fame, and social organizations, which weigh not one jot in the balance of God, and we get clearer views of Principle. Break up cliques, level wealth with honesty, let worth be judged according to wisdom, and we get better views of humanity." [120] If her teaching was not in harmony with the ideals and methods of social Christianity, it certainly did not stand for the preservation of the status quo. The confidence that Christian Science marked an overturning in the field of religion disposed some of her followers to be sympathetic to overturnings in other areas. In the first edition of *Science and Health,* she had said, "The

116. "Christian Citizenship," *CSS,* X (Oct. 23, 1907), 120.

117. The political orientation of the *Monitor* is discussed by Erwin Canham in *Commitment to Freedom: The Story of the Christian Science Monitor* (Boston, 1958).

118. *My.,* p. 129.   119. *New York World,* Dec. 1900.
120. *S&H.,* p. 239.

time for thinkers has come; and the time for revolutions, ecclesiastical and social, must come." [121]

In an extended passage in *Science and Health,* Mrs. Eddy spoke of the liberation that Christian Science brought to mankind in the accents of American revolutionary rhetoric. She spoke of the rights of man as in the highest sense his rightful claim to divine sonship, and of his bondage to material sense as enslavement to the tyranny of error, and of the work of Christian Science as that of leading men into their heritage of full spiritual freedom. And she saw the abolition of Negro slavery as the prelude to the abolition of man's slavery to the bondage of material sense.[122]

Mrs. Eddy's use of this revolutionary language describing the impact of Christian Science on mankind was far from meaningless rhetoric. For it underscores her claims for the drastic importance to the race of her discovery. Hence her belief that those who were making a contribution to the movement were working for humanity's benefit in a far more important way than they could through the ordinary channels of political activity. In 1907, for example, she urged a student to "avoid being identified *pro* or *con* in politics. . . . Keep out of the reach of such subjects. Give all your attention to the moral and spiritual status of the race." [123] There was nothing, of course, to prevent a Christian Scientist from going into the field of politics if he so chose, and some of them in Mrs. Eddy's day and since have found themselves at the center of political life or deeply involved in reform crusades.[124] Yet Christian Scientists sincerely believed that their work for the movement placed them at the center of mankind's spiritual life. Indeed, they often spoke of Christian Science as the preeminent reform of a reforming period. To them it seemed to strike deeper than any other reform, cutting the root of social evils while others were busy snipping its weeds. Edward Kimball, one of the leading lights of the early movement, voiced a general attitude of Mrs. Eddy's followers when he spoke once in a lecture of "this great crusade of reform which is now progressing in the name of Christian Science." [125] He and his fellow Christian Scientists felt that they had every reason to consider themselves the most genuine progressives of the day and the teaching they advocated the greatest possible benefaction to humanity.

121. *S&H.,* first edition, p. 3.   122. *S&H.,* 225–228.
123. Stetson, *Sermons,* 51
124. One Christian Scientist who was deeply involved in political life was John Works, Senator from California, 1912–1918. Works' papers are at the Bancroft Library, University of California at Berkeley.
125. *CSJ,* XVII (May 1899), p. 2.

We can summarize the ideas developed so far in this chapter by saying that Christian Scientists tended to see social problems in eschatological perspective. They saw their work as the establishment of a new level of spiritual consciousness at which social problems, like any other manifestations of error, could not occur. Yet Mrs. Eddy did not teach that men must wait for an apocalypse before social problems are ameliorated. For her teaching includes some indication of how they can be approached on a new basis and, within certain limits, solved. Mrs. Eddy made few pronouncements on social affairs, and even those are given as her opinion rather than doctrine; and further, there is no party line on social and political issues in the Christian Science church, however alike its members might think on certain issues. Yet social problems, like any other, can be conceived of in Mrs. Eddy's terms as determined by mental causation and as subject to healing through prayer.

One can perhaps best see the meaning of this point through a discussion of Mrs. Eddy's comments on foreign affairs. In a dozen communiques, mostly to the public press, she dealt with the interrelated subjects of the Spanish-American War, the Japanese-Russian War of 1904–1905, the peace movement, and the question of naval armament. Her interest in these issues was deep and she seems to have been well informed concerning them. Mrs. Eddy subscribed to and read a number of periodicals dealing with political subjects, and paid particularly close attention to the *Literary Digest,* many issues of which she marked and annotated.

In part, her comments on foreign affairs simply expressed her own personal judgment of what seemed most nearly right under the circumstances. Mrs. Eddy implied that the intervention of the United States in Cuba in 1898 was a necessity;[126] she expressed approval of President Roosevelt's efforts in promoting the Treaty of Portsmouth (noting, too, that he had not acted under his Constitutional powers in arranging it);[127] she supported the peace movement as a force for good;[128] and she declared in 1908 that though she believed in the arbitration of international disputes, naval armament was in that period necessary "for the purpose of preventing war and preserving peace among nations." [129]

But another strain in this set of statements shows Mrs. Eddy speaking

126. "Other Ways than By War," *Boston Herald,* March, 1898. Reprinted in *My.,* pp. 277–278.

127. "Practice the Golden Rule," *Boston Globe,* Aug. 1905.

128. "Mrs. Eddy's Acknowledgment of Appointment as Fondateur of the Association for International Conciliation," *My.,* p. 283.

129. "War," *CSJ,* XXVI (May 1908); reprinted in *My.,* p. 283.

distinctly from the standpoint of Christian Science. In this sense, she could not but say that "War is in itself an evil, barbarous, devilish," and that she was "absolutely and religiously opposed to war." [130] Writing in 1904 on "How Strife May Be Stilled," she declared that from a spiritual standpoint war was not unavoidable: "Whatever brings into human thought or action an element opposed to Love, is never requisite, never a necessity, and is not sanctioned by the law of God, the law of Love." [131] Hence in her article on the Spanish-American War titled "Other Ways Than By War," she wrote:

The government of divine Love is supreme. Love rules the universe, and its edict hath gone forth: "Thou shalt have no other gods before me," and "Love thy neighbor as thyself." Let us have the molecule of faith that removes mountains, — faith armed with the understanding of Love, as in divine Science, where right reigneth.

Six years later, at the time of the Russian-Japanese War, she declared in a similar vein that "God is Father, infinite, and this great truth, when understood in its divine metaphysics, will establish the brotherhood of man, end wars, and demonstrate 'on earth, peace, good will toward men!' " [132]

A half year after writing these words, Mrs. Eddy requested that every member of The Mother Church pray "each day for the amicable settlement of the war between Russia and Japan." [133] Convinced Christian Scientists had no doubt but that such prayer could decisively shape the course of events. Indeed, this was not the first occasion on which Mrs. Eddy had requested her followers to pray on such a matter. In 1900, during the Boxer Rebellion, she had asked them to "Pray for our imperiled countrymen in China for the peace, prosperity, and brotherhood of all mankind." [134] Interestingly enough, one of these "imperiled countrymen" was a Christian Scientist: Mrs. William Conger, the wife of the American minister in Peking. "How largely her understanding of Truth entered into the determination of events," an editorial in the *Journal* commented later, "the world may never surmise." [135] Whatever the world's opinion, Mrs. Eddy and her followers did believe that prayer was the greatest con-

---

130. "How Strife May Be Stilled," *Boston Globe*, Dec. 1904. Reprinted in *My.*, p. 278.
131. "How Strife May Be Stilled," *My.*, p. 279.
132. "How Strife May Be Stilled."
133. "The Prayer for Peace," *CSS* VII (June 17, 1905). Reprinted in *My.*, 279.
134. *My.*, 274.
135. "A Recruit for China," *CSS*, IV (July 10, 1902), 120.

tribution they could make toward the peace of mankind — even if at a lesser level they had to make the best judgments they could about the practical disposition of affairs.

The attitudes of Christian Scientists in the domestic field as well reflected their conviction that only through a basic change in human consciousness could meaningful reform be accomplished. Believing that the amelioration of social and economic evils required basic spiritual regeneration, they were extremely distrustful of any sort of social panacea. During the turbulent 1890s, they found occasion to express this distrust often. In the early months of the depression which began in 1893, an article in the *Journal* on "Christian Science in Its Relation to the Present Crisis" declared, "We need but glance along the record of events of the past quarter of a century, to ascertain how worldly and human devices have in every instance failed to bring about any permanent sense of relief or contentment." [136] Three years later during the Presidential campaign of 1896, when the agitation over the currency issue was at its height, Mrs. Eddy reiterated forcefully the inadequacy of material measures to solve basic problems. In October she replied to a newspaper request, also made of many Protestant ministers, to name the Biblical passage she found most meaningful, by naming the First Commandment as her "favorite text." Some of her further remarks, which she later included in *Science and Health,* take on particular significance in view of the heated political context in which they were made. "One infinite God, good," Mrs. Eddy wrote,

unifies men and nations; constitutes the brotherhood of man, ends wars; fulfills the Scripture, "Love thy neighbor as thyself;" annihilates pagan and Christian idolatry, — whatever is wrong in social, civil, criminal, political, and religious codes; equalizes the sexes; annuls the curse on man, and leaves nothing that can sin, suffer, be punished or destroyed.[137]

Mrs. Eddy's contention in this passage that "One infinite God, good . . . equalizes the sexes" points to an aspect of her teaching which has significant social bearing. The advent of Christian Science, she maintained, brought into human consciousness a higher and more spiritual sense of womanhood. It will be remembered that Mrs. Eddy spoke of God as Mother as well as Father, and saw true manhood as including in its completeness the qualities of tenderness and love usually associated with the feminine. Man and woman are distinct spiritual ideas; but the feminine element in creation, Mrs. Eddy maintains, is no less high than the male.

136. C. Henry Clark, "Christian Science in Its Relation to the Present Crisis," *CSJ,* XI (Oct. 1893), 307.
137. *CSJ,* XIV (Dec. 1896); the paragraph is from *S&H.,* p. 340.

For her followers, the fact that Christian Science was discovered by a woman was of no small significance in this regard. And it should not be surprising that they saw in the movement for women's rights some reflection at a human level of the higher concept of divine womanhood to which Christian Science was giving expression. Nor should it be surprising that Mrs. Eddy spoke out on the subject of women's rights more explicitly than on any other single issue. She stood for the equality of the sexes before law, including the right of women to vote and to an improved legal status in the holding and disposition of property.[138] While it would not be quite correct to call Mrs. Eddy a feminist, she did find reason on the basis of the implication of her own teaching to ally herself with the feminist movement, at least to some degree.

The same point can be made with reference to the temperance movement. The Scientists' sympathy with this movement is understandable in view of their rejection of the use of strong drink as an enslaving drug. Yet this was only part of the rationale offered by most temperance advocates, who saw in liquor a device for the subjugation of the working class. Moreover, the Scientists differed with most advocates of the temperance crusade over the best means of promoting temperance. Mrs. Eddy's own view was that Christian Science had achieved far more in promoting it, as she wrote, "than has been accomplished by legally coercive measures, — and because this Science bases its work on ethical conditions and mentally destroys the appetite for alcoholic drinks." [139] The many testimonies in the periodicals on the healing of alcoholism and the use of tobacco as well always claim that through prayer the *appetite* for both had been overcome and thus a spiritual victory won.

The late nineteenth century was a period of increasing social concern in the Protestant churches in general. This concern reached its fullest expression in the Social Gospel movement but was apparent in other ways in the charitable activities of the orthodox denominations. Christian Scientists as individuals may have been much concerned with social problems and taken practical steps for their amelioration. But it was difficult for Mrs. Eddy to find any appropriate expression for this social concern at an institutional level in a way that would be consonant with the spirit of her teaching and the purpose of The Mother Church. Quite naturally, the Scientists were open to the charge that they were unconcerned about the

---

138. For Mrs. Eddy's comments on women's rights, see *S&H.*, p. 63. *Mis.*, p. 245.
139. *Ibid.*, p. 297.

problems of poverty which so occupied the attention of the other denominations. Mark Twain voiced a criticism echoed by many other critics of the movement when he observed that The Mother Church gave no evidence that "it spends a penny on orphans, widows, discharged prisoners, hospitals, schools, night missions, city missions, libraries, old peoples' homes, or any other object that appeals to a human being's purse through his heart." [140] With its increasing social awareness, the Protestant clergy as well often commented sharply on the limited interest the Christian Scientists displayed in projects for social amelioration. After the dedication of the magnificent Mother Church Extension in 1906, the *Methodist Review* noted that though the Christian Science Church could spend huge sums to build its temple, it maintained "no hospitals, no free dispensaries, no missions in the slums, no orphanages . . . it is utterly lacking in sympathy. It cannot succeed long in a suffering world." [141]

Mrs. Eddy's followers were acutely aware of such criticisms, but felt that they were most unfair. Even aside from the basic regeneration that Christian Science promised for all mankind, they claimed, it had done much to alleviate human suffering through healing. Mrs. Eddy dwelt on the humane motivation of her work frequently. She spoke of her efforts to "relieve the sufferings of humanity" and said that her teaching was Christian because it was "compassionate, helpful, and spiritual." [142] In *Science and Health* she wrote further:

> I saw before me the sick, wearing out years of servitude to an unreal master in the belief that the body governed them, rather than Mind.
> The lame, the deaf, the dumb, the blind, the sick, the sensual, the sinner, I wished to save from the slavery of their own beliefs and from the educational systems of the Pharaohs, who to-day, as of yore, hold the child of Israel in bondage.[143]

Regarding the alleviation of poverty specifically, Christian Scientists often claimed that poor people who took up the study of Mrs. Eddy's teaching quickly improved their economic standing. Such demonstrations, they felt, were of more than personal significance; for the fact that poverty could be overcome through prayer was thereby shown as possible for all men. In 1905 one of Mrs. Eddy's followers replied directly to critics who claimed that Christian Scientists did nothing for the poor in an article called "Christian Science: The Gospel to the Poor." This charge, he said,

140. Twain, *Christian Science*, p. 231.
141. "Christian Science," *Methodist Review*, LXXXVII (Sept.–Oct. 1906), 826.
142. *Ret.*, pp. 30, 25.   143. *S&H.*, p. 226.

could well be borne by Scientists until the world learns the power of silent mental work and appreciates the meaning of that work for all mankind. A single demonstration over poverty, he maintained, "does a thousandfold more towards lifting the burden of poverty from off the shoulders of the masses than do all the stereotyped wordy sermons of which the poor man knows there are too many already." [144]

Moreover, while the practical efforts of Christian Scientists on behalf of the poor came nowhere near that of most Protestant denominations, Scientists were not as amiss in this respect as many believed. In the early days at Lynn, Mrs. Eddy had maintained to the best of her ability a home for indigent Christian Scientists. Later, the effort to extend the benefits of Christian Science to the poor had been a major phase of the movement's activities. At Easter Services in 1889, Mrs. Eddy announced the opening of a "Christian Science Mission and Free Dispensary . . . for work among those unable to pay for healing and prevented from hearing the Glad Tidings unless taken to them by messengers of Truth." The purpose of the dispensaries, she said, was in part to help "raise the vocation of Science from being looked on by the world as primarily a means to a livelihood. . . . Mission work will draw the world's attention more distinctly to the humane character of Science than any degree of generosity and self-sacrifice in the routine of a private practice could do." [145]

The Christian Science dispensaries which were set up at Mrs. Eddy's direction in Boston and several other cities, including Cleveland and New York, were only a qualified success. Practitioners accustomed to having patients come to them found it difficult to go out as missionaries into rough slum districts. Further, since they dispensed free Christian Science treatment and literature rather than pellets, their aid was not always welcomed. Nevertheless, some of them scored real successes. Their reports tell of remarkable healings they had performed and of converts to Christian Science they had made. But the dispensary work put too great a burden on the still relatively small movement, and it was discontinued in 1894. The dispensary rooms in the downtown sections of various cities became instead Christian Science reading rooms, where the literature of the movement could be read or purchased.

In 1907 Mrs. Eddy made one further effort in the direction of aiding the poor. Late that year she announced through the *Sentinel* that she wanted to found a Christian Science institution "for the special benefit of the poor

144. Rueben Pogson, "Christian Science: The Gospel to the Poor," *CSJ*, XXII (Nov. 1905), 485.
145. Johnson, *History*, I, 89.

and the general good of mankind." [146] But as she thought the matter through and discussed it with others, she decided that it would be better to provide funds for the poor to study Christian Science rather than to aid them directly. But this plan too was put aside. Eventually, her desire to found a humanitarian institution found expression in the construction of a sanatorium where Christian Scientists could be cared for while being treated for or recuperating from an illness.

Actually, the only significant humanitarian work the Christian Science church undertakes for those outside the movement is not referred to in Mrs. Eddy's published writings, though she authorized it. For The Mother Church does contribute substantial funds for direct relief in emergency disasters such as floods and fires. Also, in both World Wars the Christian Science Church, including The Mother Church and its branches, has expended enormous effort in carrying on widespread relief efforts of various kinds. That the Scientists threw themselves into this work so vigorously suggests that they could have put great energy into humanitarian activities like those conducted by other denominations had it been consistent with their beliefs to do so. [147] But Christian Scientists did not look upon such activities as appropriate to the work for humanity which they felt it was theirs to accomplish. It was not until the founding of the *Monitor* that they found a practical form for involvement in social affairs.

A newspaper was an ideal vehicle for the expression of Christian Scientists' social concern. For it committed them to consciousness of human affairs but not to any particular involvement with them. In this sense, the term "monitor," though it may have been suggested to Mrs. Eddy by the name of a friendly newspaper in her own city, the *Concord Evening Monitor,* was a particularly apt name for her newspaper. For a monitor is a receiving and tracking instrument. By founding *The Christian Science Monitor,* Mrs. Eddy was calling upon her followers to expand their thinking beyond their own personal lives, indeed, beyond the confines of the movement. As an article in the *Sentinel* put it a month after the first issue of the *Monitor* appeared, the effect of the newspaper

has been to lift one's eyes to an horizon far beyond one's own doorstep. The call to help in the world's thinking is no longer something that can pass unheeded, it is an imperative duty. Things we did not like to look at nor think of, problems we did not feel able to cope with, must now be faced

---

146. *CSS,* IX (Dec. 1907), 310.
147. See *Christian Science War Time Activities* (Boston, 1922) and *The Story of Christian Science Activities, 1939–1946* (Boston, 1947).

manfully, and correct thinking concerning the world's doings cultivated and maintained.[148]

The *Monitor,* then, had great significance in terms of the orientation of Christian Scientists toward social affairs. But from another standpoint, it can be seen as an instrument of progressive reform in the field of journalism. In the years before she founded the *Monitor* Mrs. Eddy had had much experience with the press, most of it bad. The whole experience of the "Next Friends Suit" together with the muckraking attacks on her that had preceded it was one of the most difficult that Mrs. Eddy had ever undergone. But it did have one constructive effect; for it was in part responsible for her decision in the early summer of 1908 to found a newspaper. During this period she said to a student referring to the role of the *New York World* in launching the "Next Friends Suit," "Now we will show them what a good newspaper can do." And in the editorial she wrote for the first issue of the *Monitor* Mrs. Eddy said that its purpose was "to injure no man, but to bless all mankind." [149] Though she made no direct reference to the *World,* the contrast between her intentions for the *Monitor* and the journalism represented by the *World* was clear enough. And it was made even clearer when in 1910, the *Monitor* sponsored a series of clean journalism meetings to attack the "yellow" press, as well as to advertise itself. Yet certainly the *Monitor* had not been founded solely in response to the *World*'s attack. In a comment on a letter from a follower written in March, 1908, suggesting that she found a newspaper, Mrs. Eddy said that she had had "this newspaper scheme" in mind for some time. Six years earlier she had referred in a letter to her intention to start a "widespread press." [150] And the *Sentinel,* which had been founded four years before that, included several pages of news items in each issue. One can discern a growing consciousness of public affairs in Mrs. Eddy's thought from her earliest work in Christian Science through the founding of the *Monitor.*

The actual launching of the *Monitor* was a formidable task. Not until August 8, 1908, did Mrs. Eddy instruct the Board of Trustees of The Mother Church to begin the project, though she had informed the Board of Directors of her intentions already. Since she wanted the first issue on the stands before Thanksgiving of that year, the two Boards had just a

148. Quoted in Peel, *Christian Science,* p. 158.
149. *Christian Science Monitor,* Nov. 25, 1908.
150. Quoted in Erwin Canham, *Commitment to Freedom,* pp. 16, 20.

little over a hundred days to finance the undertaking, hire a staff, purchase and install a press, and put the whole thing into operation. As in the building of The Mother Church in 1894, she had set her followers a difficult goal; but in this case as before, they reached it. Other newspapers regarded the founding of the *Monitor* with great interest. Some were sympathetic to the effort, others scornful; but few expected it to succeed. Yet though the *Monitor* did pass through some difficult days, it survived to become one of the most prestigious newspapers in the United States.

The editorial policy of the paper is generally consistent with the social views congruent with Christian Science teaching, as sketched earlier. Mrs. Eddy's scattered comments on various issues furnished specific guidelines for many of the *Monitor*'s editorial policies. Further, she showed deep concern with the paper's editorial policy, just as she had taken an active interest in the practical operations connected with its founding. Daily from the date the first issue of the *Monitor* appeared on the stands until her death, Mrs. Eddy carefully read over the editorials, occasionally commenting on them to the chief editor. After her death, control of the editorial policy of the *Monitor* passed to the Board of Directors. The Board by no means lays down editorial policy on every issue, though on most important questions it does. Generally, it exercises a supervisional authority and allows considerable interpretive leeway among writers for the *Monitor* — though within certain well-defined limits.

The character of the *Monitor* — its freedom from sensationalism, its broad international scope, and its high standard of reporting — has been the subject of much comment and has earned a measure of respect for the Christian Science movement that it might not otherwise have enjoyed. Yet the major significance of the *Monitor* for the movement lies in the fact that it commits Christian Scientists who wish to be faithful to Mrs. Eddy's intentions to look past their own personal destinies. And for many of them, this was indeed a crucial test.

Conclusion:
Christian Science and the American Pragmatic Orientation

It has been the overall purpose of this study to explain the meaning of the Christian Science movement in the context of American religious life. Since we have emphasized the religious character of the Christian Science movement, its emergence has been considered in terms of stages which have analogies in the development of most other religious movements. Christian Science, like other religions, claimed to offer new and vital truths to a spiritually unsettled age; had a central core of teachings related to but in essential aspects different from the alternative religious viewpoints of its time; met and survived the challenge of competition of rival movements, in part its own offshoots; emerged with its own distinct institutional form into the mainstream of the religious life of its time; and attracted converts who were disenchanted with older religious systems. Through our examination of the details of these phases in the emergence of Christian Science, the viability of approaching it in terms appropriate to the analysis of a religious movement should be established.

At this point it becomes necessary to trace the pattern in this process so as to better identify the distinguishing characteristic of Christian Science as a religious movement and understand its meaning in American religious life. So doing requires the use of a term which has not for good reason heretofore been used in this study. For the point of these concluding pages is that Christian Science can be best understood as a *pragmatic interpretation of Christian revelation*. It is the pragmatic character of Christian Science which most adequately conveys its distinctiveness as a religious teaching, most clearly illumines its relations with the patterns of American culture, and most fully explains the source of its appeal. To have used the term *pragmatic* in connection with Christian Science before this point would have been ahistorical, since the term never occurs in Mrs. Eddy's writings and, to my knowledge, was not used by Christian Scientists nor by others in reference to her teaching during the period with which we are concerned. Despite William James' passing interest in Christian Science, there were no direct links between Christian Science and the pragmatic movement in American philosophy.

Yet the emergence of both within roughly the same period is far from fortuitous. Certainly it was not just a coincidence that the development of an indigenous American philosophy should have taken place in the decades following the Civil War when the United States was emerging into modern industrial nationhood and world power. Nor should it be surprising that the pragmatic direction of American culture and thought should have been given expression in the only major religious movement to have originated in the United States after the Civil War — Christian Science. Indeed, since Christian Science was formulated a decade or more before the emergence of pragmatism, Mrs. Eddy's teaching may be said in a limited sense to have anticipated its development.

Pragmatism is a term susceptible to many definitions, and it is important at this point to indicate the range of meanings with which it will be employed here. It can, of course, be used as a term for expediency and uncritical adaptability to conditions; but pragmatism in this sense is a distortion and vulgarization of its genuine philosophic content. In its basic philosophical sense, pragmatism is an attitude which insists that coherent theory must be related to practice, that the meaning of a concept is to be found in its bearing upon experience, and that the truth of an idea is to be tested by the actual consequences of believing in it. Whatever their differences in other respects, the major American pragmatic philosophers Charles Sanders Peirce, William James, and John Dewey, were united in their emphasis upon these points. In its larger aspects, pragmatism can be understood as the philosophic expression of a much broader orientation toward experience than is embraced in traditional philosophic categories. John Dewey pointed out that philosophy is "the conversion of such culture as exists into consciousness";[1] and it is no original observation to say that pragmatism converted the open, fluid patterns of the American experience into philosophic consciousness.[2]

1. John Dewey, *Philosophy and Civilization* (New York, 1931), p. 3.
2. For a good expression of this point of view, see George Herbert Mead, "The Philosophies of Royce, James, and Dewey in their American Setting," in Walter G. Muelder and Laurence Sears, *The Development of American Philosophy* (Boston, 1940), pp. 319–329.

Yet to understand pragmatism in its ultimate meaning, we must relate it to a tradition in American thought that can only be defined in religious terms. This tradition centers in New England, reaches back to American Puritanism, through Jonathan Edwards to Transcendentalism, and from Transcendentalism to pragmatism. It is unified by the tendency to define the content of religion in terms of the immediate possibilities of experience rather than with reference to a future realm of experience. In the broadest sense, this tradition can be called a religious naturalism, if that term is carefully understood. In this context, it refers to the disposition to think in terms of one order of experience, rather than in terms of two opposing orders of experience. In this sense it constitutes a rejection of the dualism of the secular and the sacred, earthly and heavenly, natural and super-natural and approaches the understanding of that which is ultimate in terms of that which is immediate — experienceable in man's present life-situation.

This naturalistic tendency becomes more and more conspicuous with each phase of the development of this tradition. Its first manifestation is in the eschatology of New England Puritanism, which was dominated by the concept of the Kingdom of God. Puritanism held as man's central duty, not the vision or contemplation of God, which is the basic ideal of Medieval Catholicism, but the actual living under the sovereignty or King-dom of God, in obedience to Him in this present experience.[3] Whatever the supernatural elements in Puritanism, the dominance of this tendency gave a distinctly ethical, this-worldly caste to American religious thought. Jonathan Edwards' powerful restatement of Calvinism in the American context in the mid-eighteenth century, though rejecting the Puritan scheme of the covenant, intensified the naturalistic tendency implicit in Puritanism. For Edwards saw the process of regeneration in radically ex-periential and non-legalistic terms as involving the new sense of God and nature entertained by the newly born. It remained for Transcendentalism to entirely discard the theological framework of both Puritanism and Edwardsian theology, and to identify the religious experience with the illumined perception of nature.[4] John Dewey made this line of develop-ment explicit when he rejected the concept of religious experience as such,

3. This distinction, which was first given major statement by Max Weber, is elaborated in H. Richard Niebuhr's seminal study, *The Kingdom of God in America* (New York, 1937).

4. For an appraisal of the continuity between Edwards and the Transcendental-ists, see Perry Miller, "From Edwards to Emerson," in *Errand into the Wilder-ness* (Cambridge, Mass., 1956).

and understood the term *religious* to apply to the ideal potentials of experience itself.[5]

Christian Science is congruent with this tradition as briefly sketched, and is to a certain extent explicable in terms of it. Mrs. Eddy's background lay in New England Puritanism. She was schooled in the New England Theology that stemmed from Edwards, and adopted the term *spiritual sense*, so fundamental to Edwardsian theology, as one of the rubrics of her teaching. The immediate religious background of Christian Science, moreover, lay in New England Transcendentalism, and the development of American pragmatism was contemporaneous with the emergence of Christian Science. It is not difficult, of course, to see profound differences between Mrs. Eddy's teaching and all these other forms of thought. But the continuities are real and are essential to an understanding of the meaning of Christian Science in American religious life. For Christian Science reflects — indeed, in a radically intensified form — this disposition to see religious experience in terms of immediate possibilities.

Relating Christian Science to the pragmatic strain in American culture generally and to the pragmatic movement in philosophy specifically may run counter to the convictions of both scholars and Christian Scientists, though for very different reasons. In general, academic scholars have not taken Christian Science seriously enough to warrant relating it to so prestigious an intellectual movement as pragmatism, while Christian Scientists, holding that their faith is not culture-derived but issues from revelation, often dismiss any effort to relate Christian Science to its cultural context on religious grounds. Still, the relationship developed here is not imposed upon the materials of this study but emerges naturally from them, and tracing it can scarcely be avoided by the intellectual historian who wants to assess the meaning of the emergence of Christian Science when and where it emerged.

My conclusions, then, are as follows: (1) that Christian Science as a religious teaching is best understood as a pragmatic interpretation of Christian revelation; (2) that as such it is Christian, but definitely not Protestant; (3) and that in the pragmatic character of Christian Science one can most clearly see the source of its appeal as well as the greatest potential danger to its correct practice.

In characterizing Christian Science as pragmatic, it is necessary to emphasize at the outset that it is a pragmatic grasp of *Christian revelation*.

5. Dewey's religious attitudes are developed in *A Common Faith* (New Haven, 1934).

Mrs. Eddy never claimed to have discovered a truth that had not been objectified before her time. She claimed, rather, that through her discovery the full practical implications of Biblical revelation, most particularly the Gospel narratives, had been made clear. Underlying everything Mrs. Eddy said was the fact that she *accepted Biblical revelation as given.* Her interpretation of its meaning, of course, is widely at variance with that of traditional Christianity; but she never claimed to have set forth any truth that had not been experimentally lived by Biblical figures, most particularly Christ Jesus.

Moreover, Mrs. Eddy held that the discovery through which she understood the full meaning of the Scriptures was in itself a spiritually empowered revelatory event. Perhaps her most succinct statement of the spiritual fact which she claimed to have envisioned in the discovery of Christian Science was her declaration that she then gained the sense of "Life in and of Spirit, this Life being the sole reality of existence." [6] Mrs. Eddy did say that the healing work she pursued in the years prior to her discovery confirmed the truth of what she envisioned. But her conviction of the reality of this spiritual fact was not, for her, just a warranted conclusion drawn from experimental inquiry, and it obviously could not be substantiated on the basis of human rationality resting on material sense testimony. However great the emphasis upon the practical demonstration of Christian Science in her teaching, demonstration does not make truth true. Mrs. Eddy taught, rather, that basic truth is apprehended only through spiritual sense receptive to revelation. Demonstration confirms only that revealed truth has been understood.

To say that Mrs. Eddy predicates her teaching upon revelation, however, is not to say that she takes the revelation in its ordinary theological sense. She does so only in the sense that spiritual truth must come to human thought from a source absolutely outside itself. But the character and significance of revelation is for her a wholly practical affair. She interprets the revelatory event of the life of Jesus as a demonstration of divine manhood which when correctly understood discloses man's *present* possibilities. And she sees Christian Science as providing the understanding through which these possibilities can be realized in practice. There is, then, no split in Mrs. Eddy's teaching between that which is revealed to be true and that which can be demonstrated as truth. And if demonstration must be based on revelation, it remains true that for her revelation without demonstration is incomplete. Indeed, in *Science and Health* she

6. *Mis.*, p. 24.

cites the proof by demonstration of the truth of her discovery as one aspect of the revelation of Christian Science itself.[7]

Christian Science is, therefore, understood by its adherents as a revelation, not of a dogma, but of demonstrable religious truth. In this sense it may be said to be a spiritually scientific discovery, and Mrs. Eddy's role as a revelator may be defined as essentially that of a discoverer. She claimed to have discovered a truth objective to herself, and sought to focus her followers' attention on her discovery and not on her person. Her active role as the founder of the movement made her its leader, a position which is permanently hers in the Christian Science church. But even in the extensive prerogatives which Mrs. Eddy claimed as leader of the movement, her main interest was in the promulgation in pure form of teachings which she held to be objectively and demonstrably true. Mrs. Eddy did claim that she could not ultimately be separated from her discovery, and that a correct understanding of her mission was crucial to an understanding of her teaching. But ultimately her personality, complex and controversial as it was, cannot be the main issue in any assessment of Christian Science. For granting the radical character of what Mrs. Eddy claimed to have discovered, her claims were in one respect similar to those of any scientific discoverer: to have set forth objective truths the validity of which is entirely independent of the personality of the discoverer, and which are demonstrable by anyone who understands them.

The scientific character that Mrs. Eddy claimed for her teaching might easily be dismissed as rhetoric used with the intent to gain prestige for a religious teaching in an age that to a large extent took material science as its standard for knowledge. But considered as a manifestation of an insistence upon rigor of method, the claim that Christian Science is scientific takes on real and illuminating meaning. Pragmatic thought is, after all, an expression of a scientific world view in the sense that though it upholds the view that experience is an open-ended affair, it is committed to rigorous subjection of claims of experience to the test of provability. Much of Mrs. Eddy's much vaunted rigidity in insisting that Christian Science be practiced without admixture just as she taught it can be understood as an expression of a devotion to scientific rigor rather than religious dogmatism. It is this insistence in part that accounts for her disdain for the free-roving mysticism and eclectic spirituality of the mind-cure movement. Mrs. Eddy's writings are permeated by an insistence upon the right use of method in healing and practice generally. For in the largest sense,

7. *S&H.*, p. 123.

the scientific character of Christian Science is its claim to *be* method — the method for the demonstration of the spiritual fact in practice. It is this pragmatic-scientific aspect of Christian Science which — whatever one thinks of the truth or untruth of the possibilities it claims are present to man — most decisively separates it from the mystical mood and temper.

Christian Science, therefore, is best understood, not as an abstract metaphysical or theological system, but with reference to *what it claims to make possible.* Mrs. Eddy's most metaphysical statements are intended to be understood as pointing to demonstrable conditions of experience. Actually, she never intended to construct a metaphysical system as such. Rather, metaphysics for her was a mode of communication by which the practical significance of Christian revelation could be pointed out. In her own way, Mrs. Eddy voiced a very pragmatic concept of meaning when she spoke of her metaphysics as meaningful only when put into practice. And in one of her most frequently quoted characterizations of Christian Science she speaks of it in pragmatic terms as making something possible, for she refers to it as that through which can be discerned "the spiritual fact of whatever the material senses behold." [8]

At the heart of Christian Science, therefore, is the claim that it is possible for man now to inwardly and subjectively know the spiritual fact of being even before it is objectified in the human situation. For Mrs. Eddy, this process of inner knowing is not just "taking thought" but is truly prayer. And throughout her writings she uses such terms as *know, realize, apprehend, discern, behold, affirm, become conscious, understand, etc.,* to indicate the *active* nature of this process through which alone spiritual healing can be wrought. Prayer in this sense, is, for her, communion with God, in that it is spiritual receptivity to divine Truth. But it is a comprehensible process which, though not humanly visible, makes a difference in actual experience. Mrs. Eddy speaks of it as an *act* which is spiritually substantive, and to which rules and laws (though not formulas) do apply. To be sure, this act is in the first instance inward and subjective. But Mrs. Eddy claims that through the discernment of the spiritual fact the energies of Truth are released into the individual consciousness of the one being treated and act as healing power in the specific situation at hand. The healing power in Christian Science, it should be emphasized, is the power of Truth itself, not of the individual thought that beholds it. But the act of discerning the spiritual fact in Science is central as far as the practitioner of Christian Science is concerned.

8. *Ibid.,* p. 585.

Spiritual reality in Christian Science, of course, wholly transcends common sense testimony. But Mrs. Eddy does not conceive of the term *reality* as appertaining to a transcendental realm wholly uncognizable by human consciousness. For the implicit claim of Christian Science is that men can achieve some grasp of basic reality in their present situation, and that the understanding of true being releases spiritual power into their present experience. In this sense, the meaning of reality in Christian Science is far different from its ordinary meaning in traditional metaphysics in the Platonic tradition. It is to this more traditional concept that John Dewey refers when he writes of reality as "the most obnoxious of all metaphysical words in the most obnoxious sense of metaphysics; for it purports to speak of that which underlies all but which is incapable of being known in fact and as fact." [9] Mrs. Eddy, of course, claims that reality *is* capable of being known and demonstrated "in fact and as fact;" that what the human mind calls reality is not the fact of being, but merely a limited percept treated as fact; and that the percept will change as more of the fact is understood.

Christian Science stands, therefore, for the idea of an experienceable absolute. The Godhead — Life, Truth, and Love — is to the degree of one's spiritual apprehension knowable as the actual condition of being. Since Mrs. Eddy understands God ontologically as the "source and condition of all existence," [10] her assertions about His nature are in the final analysis claims about the nature of experience. And since she understands man as the expression of God's being, these theistic assertions are likewise claims for what is divinely and demonstrably true about man. Thus when Mrs. Eddy states that God is Life, she is asserting as the spiritual fact that man is in no sense dependent upon material organization for life. In the same sense, when she declares that God is Mind, she is proclaiming the possibility that one can demonstrate the infinite intelligence of which truly understood he is the expression. And when she claims that God is All, she is affirming that the true understanding of Him dispels belief in an opposite power and demonstrates His supremacy.

Correlatively, her assertion of the nothingness of evil amounts pragmatically to the claim that the conditions of experience make it possible to actually reduce evil to nothingness in specific situations. Mrs. Eddy's definition of matter is also wholly pragmatic in character, for she treats it, not as an actual substance which is in some metaphysical sense unreal,

9. John Dewey and Arthur F. Bently, *Knowing and the Known* (Boston, 1949), p. 300.
10. *S&H.,* p. 181.

but as a name for limitation. When Mrs. Eddy declares that there is no matter, she is claiming that limitation is not in any sense inherent in being and in man. The problem of the origin of evil or of the belief in matter is not a question which Mrs. Eddy even tries to answer satisfactorily at an intellectual level. Her basic concern is with what can be experienced, not with answering questions which contain, from her viewpoint, false premises to begin with; and her ontological claims regarding the non-existence of evil and matter must be understood entirely in this light.

Since Mrs. Eddy's claims concern the actual conditions of experience and therefore are oriented to what can be experienced, she is obviously not offering a philosophical interpretation of the nature of reality. The only real continuity between Christian Science and philosophic idealism lies in the fact that Mrs. Eddy at points found it helpful to use an idealistic vocabulary to communicate her concept of the potentials of experience. Her denial of the reality of matter is in abstract terms reminiscent of philosophic idealism. But in Mrs. Eddy's teaching this claim is made on a theological rather than a philosophical basis. And Mrs. Eddy holds, moreover, that it is a claim which can be progressively validated in practice. The so-called idealistic element in Christian Science, therefore, is actually the engine of its pragmatic thrust. And the locus of Mrs. Eddy's efforts lay not in offering a philosophic conception of the nature of existence, but a practical understanding of regeneration and its requirements.

The process of regeneration in Christian Science is the demonstration, or pragmatic living out, of what Mrs. Eddy declares as the spiritual fact of being. For her, it is not something to be sought and accomplished in another realm of being, since there is but one actual realm of experience. The basic reference point in her thinking is not a future life for which this is a preparation but one order of experience correctly or incorrectly discerned. Nor is Mrs. Eddy's teaching really oriented to any antecedent order of experience or realm of being in which all spiritual facts are presumed to be wholly demonstrated in final form. Mrs. Eddy does not posit some other-worldly Platonic realm in which man's perfection is already wrought out, but claims that perfection as the *basis* for demonstrating in practice. She always insists that the reality of Life obtains now and that man's perfection is structurally and essentially his. Were this not the case demonstration would be impossible. But without demonstration, the assertion of the reality of perfect God and perfect man points only to what can and must be tangibly manifest in life-practice, not to a condition which is already objectified in experience. Mrs. Eddy's eschatology, therefore, does not point so much to the disruption of a material order (though to mortals that will appear to occur), as the consummate demonstration of the divine order, already established as the reality of being.

Christian Science, it has been claimed, can be best seen as a pragmatic grasp of Christianity. But in view of its radical departure from orthodoxy, its connection with traditional Christianity becomes problematic. Mrs. Eddy claimed to have cut behind historical Christianity to grasp the full significance of Biblical revelation. And the elements which define Christian Science as a distinctive religious teaching definitely do mark a departure from the theology of historical Christianity. But at the same time, Mrs. Eddy always claimed that her teaching was thoroughly Christian. And most of the elements of traditional Christian teaching are present in Christian Science, even though the radicalism of Mrs. Eddy's vision drastically alters their customary meaning.

Perhaps the clearest way of establishing this point is through a contrast between Christian Science and New Thought with respect to the basic Christianity of each. For it is in Mrs. Eddy's differences with New Thought and the variant forms of mind-cure which antedated it that one sees most clearly the essentially Christian nature of her teaching. The New Thought and mind-cure movements (with the exception of Unity) did not claim to be specifically Christian and drew inspiration from a variety of religious sources, among which the Bible was far from the most important. Mrs. Eddy, on the other hand, claimed most emphatically that her teaching was Christian, that it was founded squarely upon the Scriptures, and that it was in fact continuous with Biblical revelation. It was not because of personal rivalry that she so vehemently opposed these movements, which were so often confused with hers in the public mind and which recruited much of their membership from the Christian Science movement. It was, rather, because they negated those very elements in her teaching which most clearly identify it as Christian.

More specifically, the contrast between Christian Science and New Thought highlights those elements in Mrs. Eddy's teaching which link it with her Calvinist background. Unlike New Thought, Christian Science claims to be a redemptive religion. It holds that men need to be radically saved from the flesh, that "mortal mind" has within itself no resources on the basis of which to work out this salvation, and that men are thus wholly reliant upon divine revelation for an understanding of the way that leads to salvation. Mrs. Eddy speaks of mortal mind in very much the same way as did Paul when he referred to the carnal mind. To her mortal mind was not the subject of the healing wrought by Christian Science, but rather the object of this healing. Mind-cure, on the other hand, sought, as its name suggests, not the regeneration of mortals but the amelioration of human ills through the exercise of the benevolent powers of thought. In almost all of its forms, it rejected the radical distinction made by Mrs. Eddy between mortal mind and the divine Mind, and elevated the human mentality to virtually deific status. Thus it held that revelation is unnecessary, since the mind is capable of discerning religious truth through its own enlightened intuitions, and that man requires, therefore, not radical regeneration, but moral and physical improvement through the beneficent exercise of his latent powers.

A more pointed contrast lies in the fact that mind-cure, unlike Christian Science, has no doctrine of radical evil. Mrs. Eddy, of course, did maintain that evil was unreal to God and has no foundation in true being. But she insisted also that evil was completely real to mortals and had to be recognized and dealt with as a mortal belief. Indeed, she claimed that Christian Science revealed as had no other religious teaching the nature and operations of evil. The term *animal magnetism* in her teaching indicates the operation of the radical evil of the belief in a mind apart from God. The most conspicuous manifestation of animal magnetism Mrs. Eddy termed *mental malpractice,* the injurious effect of one human mind upon another. It is important that where mind-curers had no room for this concept in their teachings and for the most part dismissed it as nonsense, Mrs. Eddy identified their very practice as in large part a form of malpractice and the rise of the mind-cure movement itself as the effect of animal magnetism.

Similarly, it is the Christian character of Christian Science which most decisively differentiates it from Oriental religion. The limited congruence between Christian Science on the one hand and Buddhism and Hinduism on the other, lies in their rejection of the belief in the objective reality of a physical universe. But the differences between the two are of much greater ultimate consequence than the similarities, and even the limited area of congruence that they share leads to different attitudes in practice. For if the material picture of man and the universe in Christian Science is false, it is a false sense of a spiritual reality which Mrs. Eddy insists must be demonstrated as the fact of being. Christian Science, therefore, can be said to be a redemptive religion in a way that is uncharacteristic of either Buddhism or Hinduism, for it insists upon the thorough-going practical regeneration of mortals from all phases of the flesh through the demonstration of the spiritual fact. It insists, moreover, that this regeneration is wrought through the Christ, the objective healing power of divine Truth acting on mortal thought. Mrs. Eddy, then, rejects the strongly subjective, mystical quality characteristic of Indian religious thought. For her, God in no sense indwells mortal consciousness, but rather, His power acts upon it to dissolve human error and elevate men to the demonstration of divine manhood. Where Buddhism and Hinduism, particularly as popularized in America, tend to negate man's individuality through absorption into the divine, Mrs. Eddy always maintains that God and man are distinct as Principle and idea.

These defining features, then, constitute the Christian core of Mrs. Eddy's teaching: reliance upon Biblical revelation, specifically the life and work of Christ Jesus; belief in a God absolutely transcendent to mortal thought and wholly distinct from man; and the insistence upon the requirement of the radical regeneration of mortals from the flesh. Certainly some of the critics of Christian Science both in the period of our study and since would have been loath to identify Christian Science as Christian. And whether one chooses to so designate it remains, of course, a matter of individual definition. But the presence of these distinctively Christian elements as essential aspects of Mrs. Eddy's teaching is good warrant theologically for so doing.

The crucial point here, however, is that *Christian Science, while Christian, is definitely not Protestant*. It is possible to speak of Christian Science as Protestant, in the sense that the religious and social background of Mrs. Eddy and most of her followers was Protestant. Further, in a sermon Mrs. Eddy once counseled them to display a Protestant spirit in these words, "Intrepid, self-oblivious Protestants in a higher sense than ever before, let us meet and defeat the claims of sense and sin, regardless of the bans or clans pouring in their fire upon us . . ." [11] Yet she also wrote that Christian Scientists "have no quarrel with Protestants, Catholics, or any other sect," [12] implying a clear distinction between her teaching and other religious positions. There are, of course, some important continuities between Christian Science and various forms of Protestantism, particularly the New England Puritanism in which Mrs. Eddy was raised. Yet when one identifies the *distinguishing* elements of Christian Science as a religious teaching, it is difficult to see how it can be classed as Protestant. For Mrs. Eddy asserted that man and creation understood in Science are the expression of God, hence that the belief in a God-created material universe

11. *Mis.*, p. 172.   12. *My.*, p. 303.

and man are the products of a radical misconception of true being. Salvation in Christian Science, therefore, means the full demonstration of the spiritual fact and is predicated upon the understanding of the truth of being in Science as differentiated from the mortal picture of being as presented to the physical senses. Protestantism, however, accepts as true that very picture of man and the universe which Mrs. Eddy declares is a misconception of being, understands man's materiality as natural to him in his creaturely estate, and conceives of salvation as the moral transformation of a fallen man rather than the demonstration of man's inherent perfection as the son of God. Underlying the specific attacks of Mrs. Eddy's theological opponents upon Christian Science was this basic area of radical disagreement; and whatever the shades of theological difference among them, they agreed with each other in these basic points in which they all disagreed with her. The continuities that do exist between Christian Science and Protestantism are real and important. But they indicate only that both partake of a Christian base. The teaching of Christian Science, however, cannot be located on the spectrum of Protestant theology and should not really be referred to as Protestant at all.

Of course, Protestantism in the late nineteenth century was not untouched by the pragmatic, anti-formalist strain of thought that was also objectified in Christian Science. Though the liberalism of the New Theology and the Social Gospel have analogues in European movements, their character as they emerged in America was decisively influenced by indigenous cultural tendencies. These movements, however, are best understood as *pragmatic reinterpretations of Protestantism* rather than radically new appraisals of Christian revelation. They were in essentials modifications of orthodox Protestantism intended to reconcile it with modernity in an age where the traditional symbols of orthodoxy were undergoing collapse.

The difference between liberal Protestantism and Christian Science can be seen particularly in their Christology. The Christology of liberal Protestantism is in some respect on the surface at least quite similar to that of Christian Science. Jesus is regarded more as an exemplar than as a super natural mediator, the older Protestant concept of the vicarious atonement is rejected, and the Christly nature of Jesus is understood as embodying an ideal manhood to which all men should aspire and which they are capable of achieving. But here the resemblance ends. For Christian Science emphasizes the works of Jesus over his ethical example, which is generally stressed in Protestant liberalism to the detriment of concern for the miracles and the resurrection. In Christian Science, the miracle is understood as a natural demonstration of divine power, this view being predicated on the fact that the true condition of being is spiritual—wholly unfettered by material limitation. The significance of Jesus' life-work lies in the fact that he demonstrated that the ideal man is not subject to material limitation in any form. He is, therefore, an exemplar of a far more radical truth in Christian Science than in liberal Protestantism, though he is an exemplar in both. Liberalism, then, modified the Protestant tradition by emphasizing the moral aspects of Jesus' teaching, but maintained its continuity with the Protestant tradition. Mrs. Eddy claimed to offer an understanding of Jesus' life and works on a basis which departed radically from the Protestant ontology.

An even more telling contrast can be drawn between Christian Science and the Social Gospel. The two movements, the developments of which ran almost parallel, have certain pragmatic elements in common but point in completely different directions. Both did express a certain anti-formalism and offered alternatives to orthodoxy. But the Social Gospel, theologically reliant upon liberalism, stressed the ethical component of Protestantism in conjunction with a rejection of laissez-faire, thus giving rise to the idea that the Christian's ultimate commitment is to the amelioration of the social order. In this sense, traditional Protestant beliefs were radically immanentized and the supernaturalistic elements of orthodoxy were slighted or rejected outright. But the Social Gospel operated well within the world view or cosmology of Protestantism generally. It challenged traditional social ethics and doctrinal interpretations, but it did not in any sense challenge the basic ontology of Protestantism, as did Christian Science. Indeed, on the basis of the belief that social problems like all others flowed from a radical misconception of the nature of being, Mrs. Eddy developed a wholly different approach to the resolution of social problems than that of the Social Gospel. And whatever congruence there might be in the anti-formalism that both represent, they are wholly irreconcilable as religious orientations.

A final point here is that the institutional character of the Christian Science movement puts it well outside the framework of American denominational life. For The Mother Church cannot be understood along the lines of the ordinary sacramental or liturgical idea of church as an institution. In its ultimate spiritual signification, Mrs. Eddy defined church in such a way that it is inseparable from the structure of reality itself. As a human institution, church for her had an entirely instrumental character: it was designed to carry out certain essential purposes necessary to the growth of the Christian Science movement and the dissemination and protection of its teachings. Overall, the Christian Science church may be said to have an educational function. Its mission, as Mrs. Eddy defined it, is to bless the race through the promulgation of demonstrable truth. The end of the church, therefore, is not to exist as a church—indeed, Mrs. Eddy in the first years after her discovery of Christian Science did not want to found a church, and when she did so it was only as a concession to necessity. Thus the character of The Mother Church, as it took shape in the 1890s was as streamlined as possible to fulfill its intended function. Similarly, its services are designed to inspire through the communication of truth rather than through participation in symbolic rites. And its governing law, the *Manual,* is a skeletal system of providing the bare necessities of church government while allowing a good deal of flexibility in the day-to-day administration of church affairs.

How then are we to account for the emergence of Christian Science in American religious life? What made it a religious movement of significant proportions rather than just a minor sect? We have to account for this phenomenon in the first instance in terms of the religious situation into which Christian Science was projected. For the emergence of Christian Science coincided with a particularly crucial stage in American religious development. All the major mutations in American religious life before the late nineteenth century had transpired within the framework of Protestant supernaturalism. In the late nineteenth century, however, the very structure of Protestant supernaturalism itself began to give way, not just for a few intellectuals but for the laity in general. To a large extent, the dilemmas of present day Christianity can be traced back to the profound religious reorientation that began to assume major proportions in the period in which Christian Science first emerged on the American scene. Of course, Mrs. Eddy's teaching had been formulated just after the Civil War, a decade or more before this reorientation began to become apparent. Yet the significant fact here is that Christian Science gained a following and came to prominence in the midst of a period of profound spiritual turmoil.

The character of this orientation was marked by a rejection of the dualistic supernaturalism of orthodoxy and a longing, expressed in different ways, for religious experience which was vital, immediate, and comprehensible in practical terms. By the late nineteenth century, it was becoming increasingly impossible for the modern mind to accept a religious orientation which divided man's experience into the natural and supernatural, the here and the hereafter, the sacred and the secular. Progress, industrialization, the impact of science — indeed, almost all the elements characteristic of modern life — conspired to render increasingly meaningless the symbols, doctrines, and promises of orthodoxy. If religion were couched in terms of an apposition of the life to come to this life, then men were increasingly willing to let go any concern with the life to come and live in terms of the present alone. Correlatively, their institutionalized professions of faith tended to devolve into a meaningless conventionalism that masked the increasing secularism of the culture. This process had reached such a point in Europe by this period that Friedrich Nietzsche could declare the death of God, not as a theological pronouncement, but as a cultural diagnosis of the decline of the whole scheme of supernatural transcendence in the modern mind. The significant point for our purpose was that this decline in America was just becoming apparent in the period when Christian Science emerged in American religious life, though it was not to become generally characteristic of the culture until nearly a century later.

In the light of these points it should not be surprising that the main direction of religious innovation in this period was toward a more pragmatic conception of what religion includes. Whether we are speaking of the advent of the New Theology, the development of the Social Gospel, or even the popularity of variant forms of mysticism, the tendency was the same: toward a conception of religious experience in more pragmatic — more immediate, experienceable, and vital — terms. The New Theology verbalized this tendency in terms of an identification of God's kingdom with the progress of human culture. The Social Gospel expressed it by urging upon Christians the uplifting work of living the Gospel through aiding in the efforts at social amelioration. The Pentecostal movement reflected this trend through emphasizing speaking in different tongues and other manifestations of religious immediacy. William James spoke for a generalized mood among many of the religiously concerned of his day when he attempted, in his *Varieties of Religious Experience,* to adduce the meaning of religion in terms of concrete experiences rather than abstract formulations of theology. James approached religion through the analysis of mystical experience, but in mysticism he saw a strongly pragmatic element: for it was what seemed to him and to others as well most immediate and vital in religious life. This same concern for immediacy and vitality was voiced in a variety of ways in religious thought at that time and since in a renewed interest in the idea of Holy Spirit, God's operative and sustaining power. And it was, of course, the Holy Spirit that Christian Science claimed to reduce to human understanding and demonstration.

Those who embraced Christian Science as a religious teaching had in almost all cases in some way experienced the devitalization of orthodoxy that was so much a part of the inner history of Protestantism in their age. For in a variety of ways they had come to feel that orthodox doctrines and symbols, together with the institutions which perpetuated them, had lost whatever meaning and comprehensibility and vitality they once might have had. Some could no longer accept belief in a God who, as the Creator of a universe in which suffering and death seemed constant, appeared to be morally inferior to His worshipers. Others had lost faith in the doctrines of orthodoxy through the influence of scientific materialism or the higher criticism. For still others, the experiential immediacy of religion simply seemed to evaporate and its symbols became hollow shells. And many of those who turned to Christian Science found welcome surcease from the prevalent Protestant belief that in the face of suffering one must resign oneself to the will of a God who in some sense decreed it as a necessity. In any case, the doctrines, institutions, and symbols of orthodoxy seemed to converts to Christian Science quite remote from the felt realities of experience. Hence they were receptive to a religion which claimed that Christian promises were to be realized in the present; which offered demonstration instead of doctrine; and which taught that symbols of religious truth could be replaced by the discernment and demonstration of the spiritual fact of being.

To Christian Scientists, Mrs. Eddy's teaching constituted a revelation of spiritual power far beyond what they found in either liberal or orthodox Protestantism. To them, its glory lay in its promise that *now* men could begin the demonstration of eternal life. It lay in the conviction that men could be fully delivered from sickness, sin, and death, and that these forms of evil were neither necessary to being nor spiritually legitimate. Glowingly, Christian Scientists spoke of the release they had found through the study of Mrs. Eddy's teachings from physical suffering, the fear of death, the bondage to sin, and the dreariness of meaningless lives. And often they contrasted the spiritual power which they felt Christian Science had brought into their experience with the ineffectiveness of the orthodoxies they had left behind.

For such people, Christian Science healing was indeed a crucial religious experience, but not because of the material change it effected in their physical well-being. For healing validated the claim that spiritual power was presently effective in experience — that religion, therefore, was a matter of immediate experience and not just of ultimate assurance. The experience of healing was, therefore, not so much a matter of a physical change as a religious awakening. And in Christian Scientists' testimonies of healing, particularly those which involved a conversion experience, the really crucial factor is the religious awakening which accompanied and gave ultimate significance to the healing experience. Mrs. Eddy's claims for the efficacy of spiritual healing power were indeed radical, for they extended to the healing of virtually every disease on record. But the ultimate radicalism of her claims was for the immediacy and *experience-ability* of spiritual power through which these diseases were healed. And to her followers, the practice of Christian Science in individual instances seemed to make good these claims in an overwhelming way.

It was, therefore, the pragmatic quality of Christian Science that accounted for its religious appeal. But it must be carefully understood here that this defining element in the character of Christian Science made it if anything more demanding as a religious teaching than the orthodoxies which it claimed to supersede. Though Mrs. Eddy did define the meaning of salvation in radically experiential terms, salvation is in the final analysis the only thing she claims to offer. And there is no denying the fact that her demands on those who would practice Christian Science according to her standards were rigorous in the extreme. Christian Scientists often testified that the practical requirements of being a follower of Mrs. Eddy were difficult indeed. They found that they were required to put off old ways of thinking, to commit themselves to reliance upon spiritual power for healing, and in many cases to endure the bitter reproaches of those who could only see her teaching as dangerous heresy or quackery. But to devoted Christian Scientists, the effort expended in the study of Mrs. Eddy's teaching and the personal sacrifices entailed in its practice seemed well worthwhile.

To the degree that Christian Science was secularized in practice — and there is some evidence that it was — its character as a pragmatic grasp of Christian revelation was vitiated. The point can be stated in terms of two ways in which the term *pragmatic* may be used. In its larger and more philosophic sense, *pragmatic* signifies a quality of being experientially meaningful. But in its lesser and more popular usage, it connotes convenience and mere expediency. The secularized practice of Christian Science amounts to the reduction of a pragmatic religious teaching in the larger sense to a pragmatic problem-solver in the lesser sense. The teachings that inspire any movement that gains some widespread popularity are, of course, subject to being distorted in practice. But the particular *character* of this distortion in the case of Christian Science can only be understood as an inversion of its basic strength.

The process by which the pragmatic character of Christian Science was inverted into a narrow utilitarianism should be familiar to students of American religion. For it is essentially the same process that was at work in the secularization of Puritanism in the seventeenth and eighteenth centuries. Puritanism was characterized especially by a strongly activist thrust which bade men obey the divine will in all phases of their lives. Through a subtle, long-term process, this activist tendency in Puritanism was channeled into the secularism of the "gospel of wealth" and cult of success. Obedience to the divine Word was subverted into moralism, the establishment of God's Kingdom on earth was identified with the attainment of the good life in purely human terms, and the religious impetus of original Puritanism was cooled into a form of rationalism. Christian Science shares with Puritanism the activist tendency which commits its adherents to seek to extend their religion into all phases of daily activity. Indeed, the pragmatic character of Christian Science, and in part the origins of pragmatism itself, are to some degree traceable to the activist thrust of New England Puritanism. Little wonder, then, that the practice of Christian Science should have been subject to the same distortions which plagued the development of Puritanism and impels the misinterpretation of Pragmatism as a philosophy of mere expediency. The secularized practice of Christian Science bears very much the same relationship to Mrs. Eddy's teaching as does the cult of success to original Puritanism and the ethic of expediency to Jamesian or Deweyan Pragmatism. Christian Science, in its more secularized form, becomes a kind of rationalistic neo-Protestantism which must be distinguished from Mrs. Eddy's basic vision.

This study has traced the emergence of Christian Science in American religious life as a step by step clarification of its basic vision. This vision, as a pragmatic grasp of Christianity, should now stand forth in clarity and distinctness. Originally promulgated in an age of spiritual breakdown, it speaks now to an age which is experiencing the effects of the radical dislocation of the American religious experience which began to be in evidence in the period when Christian Science emerged into national prominence.

Christian Science confronts us now, not as a fledgling sect beset by disruption and defection and struggling for its very life, but as an established

American denomination. Much can be and hopefully has been learned about the movement and its teaching through our analysis of the stages in which it emerged in American religious life. Yet the vital question remains: what does Christian Science claim to offer *now* in the circumstances of a continuing religious crisis nearly a century after its birth?

That there is a crisis in contemporary religious consciousness has been abundantly recognized within almost every major religious tradition. Whether we speak of the end of the Protestant era, the "Death of God," or the post-Christian Age, it is clear that twentieth century Western man has experienced and is experiencing a major change in religious consciousness. However expressed, this change means that religions of mediation and symbols are losing their hold on popular religious consciousness, and that many are longing for a deeper and more vital religious experience, a touching of ultimate realities in the immediate circumstances of experience.

In this context, it can be seen that Christian Science offers a radical and distinct alternative to prevailing contemporary directions of religious thought. Understanding its uniqueness, of course, implies nothing about its truth. Christian Science identifies the real content of Christianity with a radically changed sense of what is now possible to men. The key element wherein it departs from traditional Christianity lies in its challenge to the belief in the material structuring of experience. It claims to open up the possibility of a spiritual rebirth, wherein men can break the circle of the belief in mortality, and begin the concrete step by step demonstration of their spiritual being as revealed in the life and teaching of Christ Jesus. Mrs. Eddy claimed to have cut behind dogma, tradition, and creed to a true sense of the "living God" and an understanding of the reality of man in his likeness. She claims that through spiritual sense, which breaks personal material selfhood, one can actually and progressively demonstrate the presence of the divine order, already established as the spiritual fact of being. Healing, far from a material therapy, is part and parcel of this redemption from the belief in limited material selfhood. Through the practice of healing, she claims, divine power becomes actual in immediate experience, the vital sense of God's presence becomes a reality to men, and the true order of being comes to light.

Christian Science, therefore, maintains that true Christianity implies something far more radical for the actual living of life than other Christian teachings. The question, of course, is whether this claim is valid. Christian Scientists feel that it is a valid claim — valid in the light of their own life-experiences. And as Mrs. Eddy well recognized, the validity of this claim can only be finally judged on the basis of individual experience. Yet the importance of Christian Science as an indigenous American denomination, its continuing appeal to a significant minority of American and other Christians, and the distinctiveness of its unique vision, all indicate that it is a claim which must be taken seriously by students of religious thought.